Statistics for Social and Behavioral Sciences

Advisors:

S.E. Fienberg
W.J. van der Linden

AF700956

For other titles published in this series, go to
http://www.springer.com/3463

Mark D. Reckase

Multidimensional Item Response Theory

Springer

Mark D. Reckase
Michigan State University
Counseling, Educational, Psychology,
and Special Education Department
461 Erickson Hall
East Lansing MI 48824-1034
USA

MATLAB® is the registered trademark of The MathWorks, Inc.

ISBN 978-1-4614-1714-9 e-ISBN 978-0-387-89976-3
DOI 10.1007/978-0-387-89976-3
Springer Dordrecht Heidelberg London New York

© Springer Science+Business Media, LLC 2009
Softcover reprint of the hardcover 1st edition 2009
All rights reserved. This work may not be translated or copied in whole or in part without the written permission of the publisher (Springer Science+Business Media, LLC, 233 Spring Street, New York, NY 10013, USA), except for brief excerpts in connection with reviews or scholarly analysis. Use in connection with any form of information storage and retrieval, electronic adaptation, computer software, or by similar or dissimilar methodology now known or hereafter developed is forbidden.
The use in this publication of trade names, trademarks, service marks, and similar terms, even if they are not identified as such, is not to be taken as an expression of opinion as to whether or not they are subject to proprietary rights.

Springer is part of Springer Science+Business Media (www.springer.com)

Preface

Item response theory (IRT) is a general framework for specifying mathematical functions that describe the interactions of persons and test items. It has a long history, but its popularity is generally attributed to the work of Fredrick Lord and Georg Rasch starting in the 1950s and 1960s. Multidimensional item response theory (MIRT) is a special case of IRT that is built on the premise that the mathematical function includes as parameters a vector of multiple person characteristics that describe the skills and knowledge that the person brings to a test and a vector of item characteristics that describes the difficulty of the test item and the sensitivity of the test item to differences in the characteristics of the persons. MIRT also has a long history, going back to the work of Darrel Bock, Paul Horst, Roderick McDonald, Bengt Muthen, Fumiko Samajima, and others starting in the 1970s.

The goal of this book is to draw together in one place the developments in the area of MIRT that have occurred up until 2008. Of course, it is not possible to be totally comprehensive, but it is believed that most of the major developments have been included.

The book is organized into three major parts. The first three chapters give background information that is useful for the understanding of MIRT. Chapter 1 is a general conceptual overview. Chapter 2 provides a summary of unidimensional IRT. Chapter 3 provides a summary of the historical underpinnings of MIRT. Chapter 2 can be skipped if the reader already has familiarity with IRT. Chapter 3 provides useful background, but it is not required for understanding of the later chapters.

The second part of the book includes Chaps. 4–6. These chapters describe the basic characteristics of MIRT models. Chapter 4 describes the mathematical forms of the models. Chapter 5 summarizes the statistics that are used to describe the way that test items function within an MIRT context. Chapter 6 describes procedures for estimating the parameters for the models.

The third part of the book provides information needed to apply the models and gives some examples of applications. Chapter 7 addresses the number of dimensions needed to describe the interactions between persons and test items. Chapter 8 shows how to define the coordinate system that is used to locate persons in a space relative to the constructs defined by the test items. Chapter 9 describes methods for converting parameter estimates from different MIRT calibrations to the same coordinate system. Finally, Chap. 10 shows how all of these procedures can be applied in the context of computerized adaptive testing.

Chapters 4–9 have been used for a graduate level course in MIRT. In the context of such a course, Chap. 10 can be used as an example of the application of the methodology. The early chapters of the book are a review of basic concepts that advanced graduate students should know, but that need to be refreshed.

Chapters 7–9 should be particularly useful for those who are interested in using MIRT for the analysis and reporting of large-scale assessment results. Those chapters lay out the procedures for specifying a multidimensional coordinate space and for converting results from subsequent calibrations of test forms to that same coordinate system. These are procedures that are needed to maintain a large-scale assessment system over years. The content of these chapters also addresses methods for reporting subscores using MIRT.

There are many individuals that deserve some credit for the existence of this book. First, my wife, Char Reckase, did heroic labors proofing the first drafts of the full manuscript. This is second only to the work she did typing my dissertation back in the days before personal computers. Second, the members of the STAR Department at ACT, Inc. helped with a lot of the early planning of this book. Terry Ackerman, Jim Carlson, Tim Davey, Ric Leucht, Tim Miller, Judy Spray, and Tony Thompson were all part of that group and did work on MIRT. Several of them even agreed to write chapters for an early version of the book – a few even finished first drafts. Although I profited from all of that work, I decided to start over again several years ago because there had been a substantial increase in new research on MIRT.

The third contributors to the book were the graduate students who reacted to first drafts of the chapters as part of my graduate courses in IRT and an advanced seminar in MIRT. Many students contributed and there are too many to list here. However, Young Yee Kim, Adam Wyse, and Raymond Mapuranga provided much more detailed comments than others and need to be honored for that contribution.

East Lansing, MI *M.D. Reckase*

Contents

Chapter 1
Introduction

Test items are complicated things. Even though it is likely that readers of this book will know what test items are from their own experience, it is useful to provide a formal definition.

> "A test item in an examination of mental attributes is a unit of measurement with a stimulus and a prescriptive form for answering; and, it is intended to yield a response from an examinee from which performance in some psychological construct (such as ability, predisposition, or trait) may be inferred."
>
> Osterlind 1990, p. 3

The definition of a test item itself is complex, but it does contain a number of clear parts – stimulus material and a form for answering. Usually, the stimulus material asks a specific question and the form for answering yields a response. For most tests of achievement, aptitude, or other cognitive characteristics, the test item has a correct answer and the response is scored to give an item score.

To show the complexity of a test item and clarify the components of a test item, an example is provided. The following test item is a measure of science achievement and the prescriptive form for answering is the selection of an answer choice from a list. That is, it is a multiple-choice test item.

Which of the following is an example of a chemical reaction?

A. A rainbow
B. Lightning
C. Burning wood
D. Melting snow

Selecting a response alternative for this test item is thought of as the result of the interaction between the capabilities of the person taking the test and the characteristics of the test item. This test item requires different types of knowledge and a number of skills. First, persons interacting with this test item, that is, working to determine the correct answer, must be able to read and comprehend English. They need to understand the question format. They need to know the meaning of "chemical reaction," and the meanings of the words that are response alternatives. They need to understand that they can only make one choice and the means for recording the choice. They need to know that a rainbow is the result of refracting light,

M.D. Reckase, *Multidimensional Item Response Theory*, Statistics for Social and Behavioral Sciences, DOI 10.1007/978-0-387-89976-3_1,
© Springer Science+Business Media, LLC 2009

lightning is an electrical discharge, melting snow is a change of state for water, but burning wood is a combination of the molecular structure of wood with oxygen from air to yield different compounds. Even this compact science test item is very complex. Many different skills and pieces of knowledge are needed to identify the correct response. This type of test item would typically be scored 1 for selecting the correct response, C, and 0 for selecting any other choice. The intended meaning of the score for the test item is that the person interacting with the item either has enough of all of the necessary skills and knowledge to select the correct answer, or that person is deficient in some critical component. That critical component could be reading skill or vocabulary knowledge, or knowledge of the testing process using multiple-choice items. The author of the item likely expects that the critical component has to do with knowledge of chemical reactions.

Test items are complicated devices, while people are even more complex. The complexities of the brain are not well understood, but different people probably have different "wiring." Their neural pathways are probably not organized in the same way. Further, from their birth, or maybe even from before birth, they have different experiences and learn different things from them. On the one hand, people who have lived all of their lives in a hot climate may have never watched snow melt. On the other hand, those from cold climates may recognize many different types of snow. From all of their experiences, people develop complex interrelationships between the pieces of information they have acquired and the methods they have for retrieving and processing that information. No two people likely have the same knowledge base and use the same thought processes when interacting with the test item presented on the previous page.

A test consists of collections of test items. Each of the test items is complex in its own way. The people who take a test also consist of very diverse individuals. Even identical twins will show some differences in their knowledge and skills because their life experiences are not exactly the same after their birth. The interactions of test takers with the test items on a test result in a set of responses that represent very complex processes.

Early procedures for test analysis were based on very simple methods such as counting the number of correct responses in the scored set of items. The assumption was that people with more correct responses (each counting for one point) had more of a particular ability or skill than those who had fewer correct responses. Answering one test item correctly added the same amount to the number of correct responses as answering any other item correctly.

Those who analyze test data have always known that some test items are more difficult than others. To capture the observed differences in test items, more complex ways of describing test item functioning were developed. Measures of item discriminating power, the proportion of persons choosing each alternative, and a selection of other statistical indicators are regularly collected to describe the function of test items. Item response theory methods have also been developed. These methods describe the functioning of test items for people at different levels on a hypothesized continuum of skill or knowledge. All of these methods provide relatively simple summaries of the complex interaction between complicated people and complicated test items. It is the purpose of this book to provide methods that describe these interactions in ways that more realistically depict the complexity of the data resulting from the administration of tests to people.

1.1 A Conceptual Framework for Thinking About People and Test Items

People vary in many different ways. The focus in this book will be on measuring the ways people differ in their cognitive skills and knowledge, although many of the methods also apply to measuring attitudes, interests, and personality characteristics as well. It will be left to others to generalize the methods to those other targets of measurement. Although it might be argued that for some skills and knowledge a person either has that particular skill or knowledge or does not, in this book it is assumed that people vary in the degree to which they have a skill or the degree to which they have knowledge. For the item presented on the first page of this chapter, a person may know a lot about chemical reactions or very little, or have varying degrees of knowledge between those extremes. They may have varying levels of English reading comprehension. It will be assumed that large numbers of people can be ordered along a continuum of skill or knowledge for each one of the many ways that people differ.

From a practical perspective, the number of continua that need to be considered depends on the sample of people that is of interest. No continuum can be defined or detected in item response data if people do not vary on that particular skill or knowledge. For example, a group of second grade students will probably not have any formal knowledge of calculus so it will be difficult to define a continuum of calculus knowledge or skill based on an ordering of second grade students on a calculus test. Even though it might be possible to imagine a particular skill or knowledge, if the sample, or even the population, of people being considered does not vary on that skill or knowledge, it will not be possible to identify that continuum based on the responses to test items from that group. This means that the number of continua that need to be considered in any analysis of item response data is dependent on the sample of people who generated those data. This also implies that the locations of people on some continua may have very high variability while the locations on others will not have much variability at all.

The concept of continuum that is being used here is similar to the concept of "hypothetical construct" used in the psychological literature (MacCorquodale and Meehl 1948). That is, a continuum is a scale along which individuals can be ordered. Distances along this continuum are meaningful once an origin for the scale and units of measurement are specified. The continuum is believed to exist, but it is not directly observable. Its existence is inferred from observed data; in this case the responses to test items. The number of continua needed to describe the differences in people is assumed to be finite, but large. In general, the number of continua on which a group of people differ is very large and much larger than could be measured with any actual test.

The number of continua that can be defined from a set of item response data is not only dependent on the way that the sample of test takers vary, but it is also dependent on the characteristics of the test items. For test items to be useful for determining the locations of people in the multidimensional space, they must be constructed to be sensitive to differences in the people. The science item presented on first page of this chapter was written with the intent that persons with little knowledge of chemical reactions would select a wrong response. Those that understood the meaning of the term "chemical reaction" should have a high probability of selecting response C. In this sense, the item is expected to be sensitive to differences in knowledge of chemical reactions. Persons with different locations on the cognitive dimension related to knowledge of chemical reactions should have different probabilities of selecting the correct response.

The test item might also be sensitive to differences on other cognitive skills. Those who differ in English reading comprehension might also have different probabilities of selecting the correct response. Test items may be sensitive to differences of many different types. Test developers expect, however, that the dimensions of sensitivity of test items are related to the purposes of measurement. Test items for tests that have important consequences, high stakes tests, are carefully screened so that test items that might be sensitive to irrelevant differences, such as knowledge of specialized vocabulary, are not selected. For example, if answer choice C on the test item were changed to "silage," students from farm communities might have an advantage because they know that silage is a product of fermentation, a chemical process. Others might have a difficult time selecting the correct answer, even though they knew the concept "chemical reaction."

Ultimately, the continua that can be identified from the responses to test items depend on both the number of dimensions of variability within the sample of persons taking the test and the number of dimensions of sensitivity of the test items. If the test items are carefully crafted to be sensitive to differences in only one cognitive skill or type of knowledge, the item response data will only reflect differences along that dimension. If the sample of people happens to vary along only one dimension, then the item response data will reflect only differences on that dimension. The number of dimensions of variability that are reflected in test data is the lesser of the dimensions of variability of the people and the dimensions of sensitivity of the test items.

The ultimate goal of the methods discussed in this book is to estimate the locations of individuals on the continua. That is, a numerical value is estimated for each person on each continuum of interest that gives the relative location of persons on the continuum. There is some confusion about the use of the term "dimensions" to refer to continua and how dimensions relate to systems of coordinates for locating a person in a multidimensional space. To provide a conceptual framework for these distinctions, concrete examples are used that set aside the problems of defining hypothetical constructs. In later chapters, a more formal mathematical presentation will be provided.

To use a classic example (Harman 1976, p. 22), suppose that very accurate measures of length of forearm and length of lower leg are obtained for a sample of girls

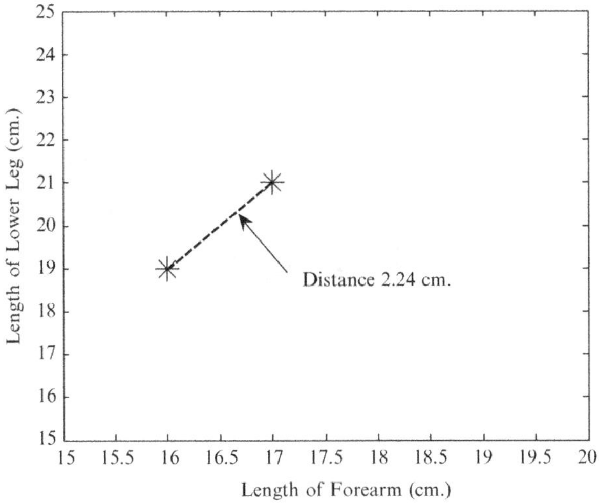

Fig. 1.1 Distance between two girls based on arm and leg lengths

with ages from seven to 17. Certainly, each girl can be placed along a continuum using each of these measures and their ordering along the two continua would not likely be exactly the same. In fact, Harman reports the correlation between these two measures as 0.801. Figure 1.1 shows the locations of two individuals from the sample of 300 girls used for the example. In this case, the lengths of forearm and lower leg can be considered as dimensions of measurement for the girls in this study. The physical measurements are also coordinates for the points in the graph. In general, the term "coordinate" will be considered as numerical values that are used to identify points in a space defined by an orthogonal grid system. The term dimension will be used to refer to the scale along which meaningful measurements are made. Coordinate values might not correspond to measures along a dimension.

For this example, note the obvious fact that the axes of the graph are drawn at right angles (i.e., orthogonal) to each other. The locations of the two girls are represented by plotting the pairs of lengths (16, 19) and (17, 21) as points. Because the lengths of arm and leg are measured in centimeters, the distance between the two girls in this representation is also in centimeters. This distance does not have any intrinsic meaning except that large numbers mean that the girls are quite dissimilar in their measurements and small numbers mean they are more similar on the measures. Height and weight could also be plotted against each other and then the distance measure would have even less intrinsic meaning. The distance measure, D, in this case was computed using the standard distance formula,

$$D = \sqrt{(x_1 - x_2)^2 + (y_1 - y_2)^2}, \tag{1.1}$$

where the x_i and y_i values refer to the first and second values in the order pairs of values, respectively, for $i = 1, 2$.

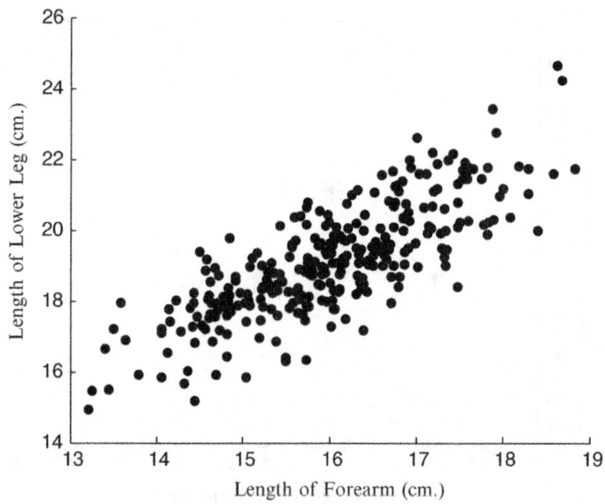

Fig. 1.2 Scatter plot of arm and leg lengths for 300 girls with ages from 7 to 17

The use of the standard distance formula is based on the assumption that the coordinate axes are orthogonal to each other. If that were not the case, the distance formula would need another term under the radical that accounts for the angle between the axes. Although this may seem like a trivial point, it is very important. Coordinate axes are typically made orthogonal to each other so that the standard distance formula applies. However, having orthogonal axes does not mean that the values associated with the coordinate axes (e.g., the coordinates used to plot points) are uncorrelated. In fact, for the data provided by Harman (1976), the correlation between coordinates for the points is 0.801. This correlation is represented in Fig. 1.2.

The correlation between coordinates has nothing to do with the mathematical properties of the frame of reference used to plot them. Using orthogonal coordinate axes means that the standard distance formula can be used to compute the distance between points. The correlations between coordinates in this orthogonal coordinate system can take on any values in the range from -1 to 1. The correlation is a descriptive statistic for the configuration of the points in this Cartesian coordinate space. The correlation does not describe the orientation of the coordinate axes.

The coordinate system does not have to be related to specific continua (e.g., the dimensions) that are being measured. In fact, for the mathematical representations of the continua defined by test results, it will seldom be the case that the constructs being measured exactly line up with the coordinate axes. This is not a problem and using an arbitrary set of coordinate axes is quite common. An example is the system of latitude and longitude that is used to locate points on a map. That system does not have any relationship to the highways or streets that are the ways most people move from place to place or describe the locations of places. The latitude and longitude system is an abstract system that gives a different representation of the observed system of locations based on highways and streets.

Suppose someone is traveling by automobile between two cities in the United States, St. Louis and Chicago. The quickest way to do this is to drive along Interstate Highway 55, a direct route between St. Louis and Chicago. It is now standard that the distances along highways in the United States are marked with signs called mile markers every mile to indicate the distance along that highway. In this case, the mile markers begin at 1 just across the Mississippi River from St. Louis and end at 291 at Chicago. These signs are very useful for specifying exits from the highway or locating automobiles stopped along the highway. In the context here, the mile markers can be thought of as analogous to scores on an achievement test that show the gain in knowledge (the intellectual distance traveled) by a student.

A map of highway Interstate 55 is shown in Fig. 1.3. Note that the highway does not follow a cardinal direction and it is not a straight line. Places along the highway can be specified by mile markers, but they can also be specified by the coordinates of latitude and longitude. These are given as ordered pairs of numbers in parentheses. In Fig. 1.3, the two ways of locating a point along the highway are shown for

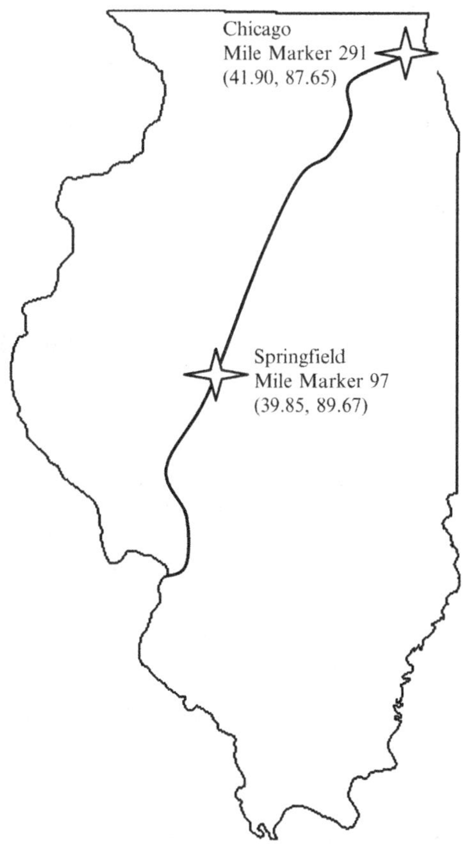

Fig. 1.3 Locations of cities along Interstate Highway 55 from East St. Louis to Chicago

the cities of Springfield, Illinois and Chicago, Illinois, USA. Locations can be specified by a single number, the nearest mile marker, or two numbers, the measures of latitude and longitude.

It is always possible to locate points using more coordinates than is absolutely necessary. We could add a third coordinate giving the distance from the center of the Earth along with the latitude and longitude. In the state of Illinois, this coordinate would have very little variation because the ground is very flat, and it is probably irrelevant to persons traveling from St. Louis to Chicago. But it does not cause any harm either. Using too few coordinates can cause problems, however. The coordinates of my New York City apartment where I am writing this chapter while on sabbatical are 51st Street, 7th Avenue, and the 14th floor, (51, 7, 14). If only (7,14) is listed when packages are to be delivered, they do not uniquely identify me. It is unlikely that they will ever arrive. Actually, there is even a fourth coordinate (51, 7, 14, 21) to identify the specific apartment on the 14th floor. Using too few coordinates results in an ambiguous specification of location.

The purpose of this book is to describe methodology for representing the locations of persons in a hypothetical multidimensional cognitive space. As this methodology is described, it is important to remember that a coordinate system is needed to specify the locations of persons, but it is not necessary to have the minimum number of coordinates to describe the location, and coordinates do not necessarily coincide with meaningful psychological dimensions. The coordinate system will be defined with orthogonal axes, and the Euclidean distance formula will be assumed to hold for determining the distance between points. The coordinates for a sample of persons may have nonzero correlations, even though the axes are orthogonal.

1.2 General Assumptions Behind Model Development

The methodology described in this book defines mathematical functions that are used to relate the location of a person in a multidimensional Cartesian coordinate space to the probability of generating a correct response to a test item. This relationship is mediated by the characteristics of the test item. The characteristics of the test item will be represented by a series of values (parameters) that are estimated from the item response data. The development of the mathematical function is based on a number of assumptions. These assumptions are similar to those presented in most item response theory books, but some additional assumptions have been included that are not typically explicitly stated. This is done to make the context of the mathematical formulation as clear as possible.

The first assumption is that the location of the persons being assessed does not change during the process of taking the test. This assumption may not be totally true in practice – examinees may learn something from interacting with the items that change their locations, or there may be other events that take place in the examination setting (e.g., cheating, information available in the room, etc.) that results in some learning. It may be possible to develop models that can capture changes during the process of the test, but that is beyond the scope of the models presented here. There are models that consider the changes from one test session to the next (Embretson 1991; Fischer 1995b). These will be placed in the larger context of multidimensional item response theory models.

The second assumption is that the characteristics of a test item remain constant over all of the testing situations where it is used. This does not mean that the observed statistics used to summarize item performance will remain constant. Certainly, the proportion correct for an item will change depending on the capabilities of the sample of examinees. The difficulty of the item has not changed, but the difficulty has a different representation because of differences in the examinee sample. Similarly, a test item written in English may not function very well for students who only comprehend text written in Spanish. This suggests that one of the characteristics of the item is that it is sensitive to differences in language skills of the examinee sample, even if that is not the clear focus of the item. This means that in the full multidimensional representation of the item characteristics, there should be an indicator of the sensitivity to differences in language proficiency. When the examinee sample does not differ on language proficiency, the sensitivity of test item to such differences will not be detectable in the test data. However, when variation exists in the examinee population, the sensitivity of the test item to that variation will affect the probability of correct response to the test item.

A third assumption is that the responses by a person to one test item are independent of their responses to other test items. This assumption is related to the first assumption. Test items are not expected to give information that can improve performance on later items. Similarly, the responses generated by one person are assumed to not influence the responses of another person. One way this could occur is if one examinee copies the responses of another. It is expected that the control of the testing environment is such that copying or other types of collaboration do not occur. The third assumption is labeled "local independence" in the item response theory literature. The concept of local independence will be given a formal definition in Chap. 6 when the procedures for estimating parameters are described.

A fourth assumption is that the relationship between locations in the multidimensional space and the probabilities of correct response to a test item can be represented as a continuous mathematical function. This means that for every location there is one and only one value of probability of correct response associated with it and that probabilities are defined for every location in the multidimensional space – there are no discontinuities. This assumption is important for the mathematical forms of models that can be considered for representing the interaction between persons and test items.

A final assumption is that the probability of correct response to the test item increases, or at least does not decrease, as the locations of examinees increase on any of the coordinate dimensions. This is called the "monotonicity" assumption and it seems reasonable for test items designed for the assessment of cognitive skills and knowledge. Within IRT, there are models that do not require this assumption (e.g., Roberts et al. 2000). The generalization of such models to the multidimensional case is beyond the scope of this book.

The next several chapters of this book describe the scientific foundations for the multidimensional item response theory models and several models that are consistent with the listed assumptions. These are not the only models that can be developed, but also they are models that are currently in use. There is some empirical evidence that these models provide reasonable representations of the relationship between the probability of correct response to a test item and the location of a person in a multidimensional space. If that relationship is a reasonable approximation to reality, practical use can be made of the mathematical models. Such applications will be provided in the latter chapters of the book.

1.3 Exercises

1. Carefully read the following test item and select the correct answer. Develop a list of all of the skills and knowledge that you believe are needed to have a high probability of selecting the correct answer.

The steps listed below provide a recipe for converting temperature measured in degrees Fahrenheit (F) into the equivalent in degrees Celsius (C).

1. Subtract 32 from a temperature given in degrees Fahrenheit.
2. Multiply the resulting difference by 5.
3. Divide the resulting product by 9.

Which formula is a correct representation of the above procedure?

A. $C = F - 32 \times 5/9$
B. $C = (F - 32) \times 5/9$
C. $C = F - (32 \times 5)/9$
D. $C = F - 32 \times (5/9)$
E. $C = F - (32 \times 5/9)$

2. In our complex society, it is common to identify individuals in a number of different ways. Sometimes it requires multiple pieces of information to uniquely identify a person. For example, it is possible to uniquely identify students in our graduate program from the following information: year of entry, gender (0,1), advisor, office number – (2004, 1, 3, 461). Think of ways that you can be uniquely identified from strings of numbers and other ways you can be identified with one number.

3. Which of the following mathematical expressions is an example of a function of x and which is not? Give the reasons for your classification.

A. $y = x^3 - 2x^2 + 1$
B. $y^2 = x$
C. $z^2 = x^2 + y^2$

Chapter 2
Unidimensional Item Response Theory Models

In Chap. 3, the point will be made that multidimensional item response theory (MIRT) is an outgrowth of both factor analysis and unidimensional item response theory (UIRT). Although this is clearly true, the way that MIRT analysis results are interpreted is much more akin to UIRT. This chapter provides a brief introduction to UIRT with a special emphasis on the components that will be generalized when MIRT models are presented in Chap. 4. This chapter is not a thorough description of UIRT models and their applications. Other texts such as Lord (1980), Hambleton and Swaminathan (1985), Hulin et al. (1983), Fischer and Molenaar (1995), and van der Linden and Hambleton (1997) should be consulted for a more thorough development of UIRT models.

There are two purposes for describing UIRT models in this chapter. The first is to present basic concepts about the modeling of the interaction between persons and test items using simple models that allow a simpler explication of the concepts. The second purpose is to identify shortcomings of the UIRT models that motivated the development of more complex models. As with all scientific models of observed phenomena, the models are only useful to the extent that they provide reasonable approximations to real world relationships. Furthermore, the use of more complex models is only justified when they provide increased accuracy or new insights. One of the purposes of this book is to show that the use of the more complex MIRT models is justified because they meet these criteria.

2.1 Unidimensional Models of the Interactions of Persons and Test Items

UIRT comprises a set of models (i.e., item response theories) that have as a basic premise that the interactions of a person with test items can be adequately represented by a mathematical expression containing a single parameter describing the characteristics of the person. The basic representation of a UIRT model is given in (2.1). In this equation, θ represents the single parameter that describes the characteristics of the person, η represents a vector of parameters that describe the characteristics of the test item, U represents the score on the test item, and u is

M.D. Reckase, *Multidimensional Item Response Theory*, Statistics for Social and Behavioral Sciences, DOI 10.1007/978-0-387-89976-3_2,
© Springer Science+Business Media, LLC 2009

a possible value for the score, and f is a function that describes the relationship between the parameters and the probability of the response, P($U = u$).

$$P(U = u \mid \theta) = f(\theta, \eta, u). \tag{2.1}$$

The item score, u, appears on both sides of the equation because it is often used in the function to change the form of the function depending on the value of the score. This is done for mathematical convenience. Specific examples of this use will be provided later in this chapter.

The assumption of a single person parameter for an IRT model is a strong assumption. A substantial amount of research has been devoted to determining whether this assumption is reasonable when modeling a particular set of item response data. One type of research focuses on determining whether or not the data can be well modeled using a UIRT model. For example, the DIMTEST procedure developed by Stout et al. (1999) has the purpose of statistically testing the assumption that the data can be modeled using a function like the one given in (2.1) with a single person parameter. Other procedures are available as well (see Tate 2003 for a summary of these procedures). The second type of research seeks to determine the effect of ignoring the complexities of the data when applying a UIRT model. These are generally robustness studies. Reckase (1979) presented one of the first studies of this type, but there have been many others since that time (e.g., Drasgow and Parsons 1983; Miller and Linn 1988; Yen 1984).

Along with the assumption of a single person parameter, θ, most UIRT models assume that the probability of selecting or producing the correct response to a test item scored as either correct or incorrect increases as θ increases. This assumption is usually called the monotonicity assumption. In addition, examinees are assumed to respond to each test item as an independent event. That is, the response by a person to one item does not influence the response to an item produced by another person. Also, the response by a person to one item does not affect that person's tendencies to respond in a particular way to another item. The response of any person to any test item is assumed to depend *solely* on the person's single parameter, θ, and the item's vector of parameters, $\boldsymbol{\eta}$. The practical implications of these assumptions are that examinees do not share information during the process of responding to the test items, and information from one test item does not help or hinder the chances of correctly responding to another test item. Collectively, the assumption of independent responses to all test items by all examinees is called the local independence assumption.

The term "local" in the local independence assumption is used to indicate that responses are assumed independent at the level of individual persons with the same value of θ, but the assumption does not generalize to the case of variation in θ. For groups of individuals with variation in the trait being assessed, responses to different test items typically are correlated because they are all related to levels of the individuals' traits. If the assumptions of the UIRT model hold, the correlation between item scores will be solely due to variation in the single person parameter.

The implication of the local independence assumption is that the probability of a collection of responses (responses of one person to the items on a test, or the responses of many people to one test item) can be determined by multiplying the probabilities of each of the individual responses. That is, the probability of a vector of item responses, **u**, for a single individual with trait level θ is the product of the probabilities of the individual responses, u_i, to the items on a test consisting of I items.

$$P(\mathbf{U}=\mathbf{u}\,|\,\theta)=\prod_{i=1}^{I}P(u_i\,|\,\theta)=P(u_1\,|\,\theta)P(u_2\,|\,\theta)\cdots P(u_I\,|\,\theta), \tag{2.2}$$

where $P(\mathbf{U}=\mathbf{u}|\theta)$ is the probability that the vector of observed item scores for a person with trait level θ has the pattern **u**, and $P(u_i|\theta)$ is the probability that a person with trait level θ obtains a score of u_i on item i.

Similarly, the probability of the responses to a single item, i, by n individuals with abilities in the vector $\boldsymbol{\theta}$ is given by

$$P(\mathbf{U}_i=\mathbf{u}_i\,|\,\boldsymbol{\theta})=\prod_{j=1}^{n}P(u_{ij}\,|\,\theta_j)=P(u_{i1}\,|\,\theta_1)P(u_{i2}\,|\,\theta_2)\cdots P(u_{in}\,|\,\theta_n), \tag{2.3}$$

where $\mathbf{U_i}$ is the vector of responses to Item i for persons with abilities in the $\boldsymbol{\theta}$-vector, u_{ij} is the response on Item i by Person j, and θ_j is the trait level for Person j.

The property of local independence generalizes to the probability of the complete matrix of item responses. The probability of the full matrix of responses of n individuals to I items on a test is given by

$$P(\mathbf{U}=\mathbf{u}\,|\,\boldsymbol{\theta})=\prod_{j=1}^{n}\prod_{i=1}^{I}P(u_{ij}\,|\,\theta_j). \tag{2.4}$$

Although the assumptions of monotonicity and local independence are not necessary components of an item response theory, they do simplify the mathematics required to apply the IRT models. The monotonicity assumption places limits on the mathematical forms considered for the function[1] in (2.1), and the local independence assumption greatly simplifies the procedures used to estimate the parameters of the models.

The three assumptions that have been described above (i.e., one person parameter, monotonicity, and local independence) define a general class of IRT models. This class of models includes those that are commonly used to analyze the item responses from tests composed of dichotomously scored test items such as aptitude

[1] Nonmonotonic IRT models have been proposed (e.g., Thissen and Steinberg 1984, Sympson 1983), but these have not yet been generalized to the multidimensional case so they are not considered here.

and achievement tests. This class of models can be considered as a general psychometric theory that can be accepted or rejected using model checking procedures. The assumption of local independence can be tested for models with a single person parameter using the procedures suggested by Stout (1987) and Rosenbaum (1984). These procedures test whether the responses to items are independent when a surrogate for the person parameter, such as the number-correct score, is held constant. If local independence conditional on a single person parameter is not supported by observed data, then item response theories based on a single person parameter are rejected and more complex models for the data should be considered.

The general form of IRT model given in (2.1) does not include any specification of scales of measurement for the person and item parameters. Only one scale has defined characteristics. That scale is for the probability of the response to the test item that must range from 0 to 1. The specification of the function, f, must also include a specification for the scales of the person parameter, θ, and the item parameters, $\boldsymbol{\eta}$. The relative size and spacing of units along the θ-scale are determined by the selection of the form of the mathematical function used to describe the interaction of persons and items. That mathematical form sets the metric for the scale, but the zero point (origin) and the units of measurement may still not be defined. Linear transformations of a scale retain the same shape for the mathematical function.

For an IRT model to be considered useful, the mathematical form for the model must result in reasonable predictions of probabilities of all item scores for all persons and items in a sample of interest. The IRT model must accurately reflect these probabilities for all items and persons simultaneously. Any functional form for the IRT model will fit item response data perfectly for a one-item test because the locations of the persons on the θ-scale are determined by their responses to the one item. For example, placing all persons with a correct response above a point on the θ-scale and all of those with an incorrect response below that point and specifying a monotonically increasing mathematical function for the IRT model will insure that predicted probabilities are consistent with the responses. The challenge to developers of IRT models is to find functional forms for the interaction of persons and items that apply simultaneously to the set of responses by a number of persons to all of the items on a test.

The next section of this chapter summarizes the characteristics of several IRT models that have been shown to be useful for modeling real test data. The models were chosen for inclusion because they have been generalized to the multidimensional case. No attempt is made to present a full catalogue of UIRT models. The focus is on presenting information about UIRT models that will facilitate the understanding of their multidimensional generalizations.

2.1.1 Models for Items with Two Score Categories

UIRT models that are most frequently applied are those for test items that are scored either correct or incorrect – usually coded as 1 and 0, respectively. A correct response is assumed to indicate a higher level of proficiency than an incorrect response so monotonically increasing mathematical functions are appropriate for modeling the interactions between persons and items. Several models are described in this section, beginning with the simplest. Models for items with two score categories (dichotomous models) are often labeled according to the number of parameters used to summarize the characteristics of the test items. That convention is used here.

2.1.1.1 One-Parameter Logistic Model

The simplest commonly used UIRT model has one parameter for describing the characteristics of the person and one parameter for describing the characteristics of the item. Generalizing the notation used in (2.1), this model can be represented by

$$P(U_{ij} = u_{ij} \mid \theta_j) = f(\theta_j, b_i, u_{ij}), \tag{2.5}$$

where u_{ij} is the score for Person j on Item i (0 or 1), θ_j is the parameter that describes the relevant characteristics of the jth person – usually considered to be an ability or achievement level related to performance on Item i, and b_i is the parameter describing the relative characteristics of Item i – usually considered to be a measure of item difficulty.[2]

Specifying the function in (2.5) is the equivalent of hypothesizing a unique, testable item response theory. For most dichotomously scored cognitive test items, a function is needed that relates the parameters to the probability of correct response in such a way that the monotonicity assumption is met. That is, as θ_j increases, the functional form of the model should specify that the probability of correct response increases. Rasch (1960) proposed the simplest model that he could think of that met the required assumptions. The model is presented below:

$$P(u_{ij} = 1 \mid A_j, B_i) = \frac{A_j B_i}{1 + A_j B_i}, \tag{2.6}$$

where A_j is the single person parameter now generally labeled θ_j, and B_i is the single item parameter now generally labeled b_i.

This model has the desired monotonicity property and the advantage of simplicity. For the function to yield values that are on the 0 to 1 probability metric, the product of $A_j B_i$ can not be negative because negative probabilities are not defined. To limit the result to the required range of probabilities, the parameters are defined on the range from 0 to ∞.

The scale for the parameters for the model in (2.6) makes some intuitive sense. A 0 person parameter indicates that the person has a 0 probability of correct response for any item. A 0 item parameter indicates that the item is so difficult that no matter

---

[2] The symbols used for the presentation of the models follow Lord (1980) with item parameters represented by Roman letters. Other authors have used the statistical convention of representing parameters using Greek letters.

how high the ability of the persons, they still have a 0 probability of correct response. In a sense, this model yields a proficiency scale that has a true 0 point and it allows statements like "Person j has twice the proficiency of Person k." That is, the scales for the model parameters have the characteristics of a ratio scale as defined by Stevens (1951).

Although it would seem that having a model with ratio scale properties would be a great advantage, there are also some disadvantages to using these scales. Suppose that the item parameter $B_i = 1$. Then a person with parameter $A_j = 1$ will have a .5 probability of correctly responding to the item. All persons with less then a .5 probability of correctly responding to the test item will have proficiency estimates that are squeezed into the range from 0 to 1 on the A-parameter scale. All persons with greater than a .5 probability of correct response will be stretched over the range from 1 to ∞ on the proficiency scale. If test items are selected for a test so that about half of the persons respond correctly, the expected proficiency distribution is very skewed. Figure 2.1 provides an example of such a distribution.

The model presented in (2.6) is seldom seen in current psychometric literature. Instead, a model based on a logarithmic transformation of the scales of the parameters (Fischer 1995a) is used. The equation for the transformed model is

$$P(u_{ij} = 1 \mid \theta_j, b_i) = \frac{e^{\theta_j - b_i}}{1 + e^{\theta_j - b_i}} = \Psi(\theta_j - b_i), \tag{2.7}$$

where Ψ is the cumulative logistic density function, e is the base of the natural logarithms, and θ_j and b_i are the person and item parameters, respectively.

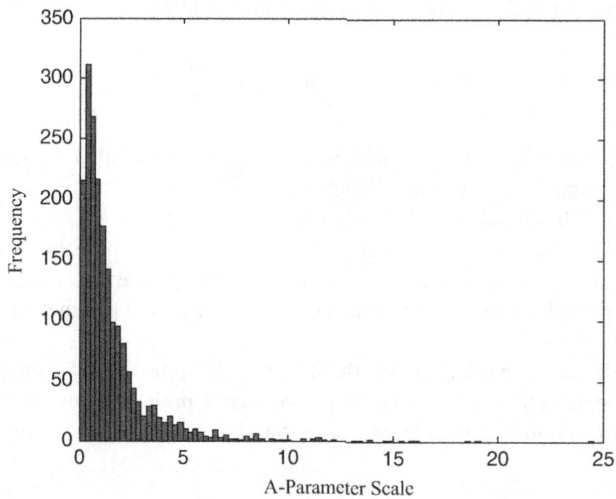

Fig. 2.1 Possible distribution of person parameters for the model in (2.6)

Because this model uses the logistic density function and because it has only a single item parameter, it is often called the one-parameter logistic IRT model. Alternatively, because it was originally suggested by Rasch (1960, 1961), it is called the *Rasch model*. The relationship between the models in (2.7) and (2.6) can easily be determined by substituting the transformations of the parameters into (2.7): $\theta_j = \ln(A_j)$ and $b_i = -\ln(B_i)$.

The scale of the person parameter in (2.7) ranges from $-\infty$ to ∞ rather than from 0 to ∞ for the model in (2.6). The scale for the item parameter is the same for that of the person parameter, but the direction of the scales are reversed from (2.6) to (2.7). Large values of the B_i parameter indicate easy items while small values of b_i indicate easy items. Thus, the b_i parameter is legitimately called a *difficulty parameter* while B_i is an "easiness" parameter.

The models in (2.6) and (2.7) show the flexibility that exists when hypothesizing IRT models. These two models will fit real test data equally well because the model parameters are a monotonic transformation of each other. Yet, the scales for the parameters are quite different in character. Equation (2.6) uses scales with a logical zero point while the parameters in (2.7) do not have that characteristic. It is difficult to say which model is a correct representation of the interactions between persons and an item. Generally, (2.7) seems to be preferred because estimation is more convenient and it has a clear relationship to more complex models.

Some researchers state that the Rasch model provides an interval scale of measurement using the typology defined by Stevens (1946). All IRT models have an interval scale for the person parameter as an unstated assumption because the form of the equation is not defined unless the scale of the person parameter has interval properties. But, in (2.6) and (2.7) we have two interval scales that are nonlinear transformations of each other. This would contradict the permissible transformations allowed by Stevens (1946). The point is that these scales are arbitrary decisions of the model builder. The usefulness of the scales comes from the ease of interpretation and the relationships with other variables, not inherent theoretical properties.

The form of (2.7) is shown graphically in Fig. 2.2. The graph shows the relationship between θ and the probability a person at that trait level will provide a correct response for an item with b-parameter equal to .5. The graph clearly shows the monotonically increasing relationship between trait level and probability of correct response from the model. It also shows that this model has a lower asymptote for the probability of 0 and an upper asymptote of 1. The graph of the probability of a correct response as a function of θ is typically called an *item characteristic curve* or ICC.

Several characteristics of this model can be derived through some relatively simple analysis. A cursory look at the graph in Fig. 2.2 shows that the curve is steeper (i.e., has greater slope) for some values of θ then for others. When the slope is fairly steep, the probability of correct response to the item is quite different for individuals with θ-values that are relatively close to each other. In regions where the ICC is fairly flat – has low slope – the θ-values must be relatively far apart before the probability of correct response results in noticeable change.

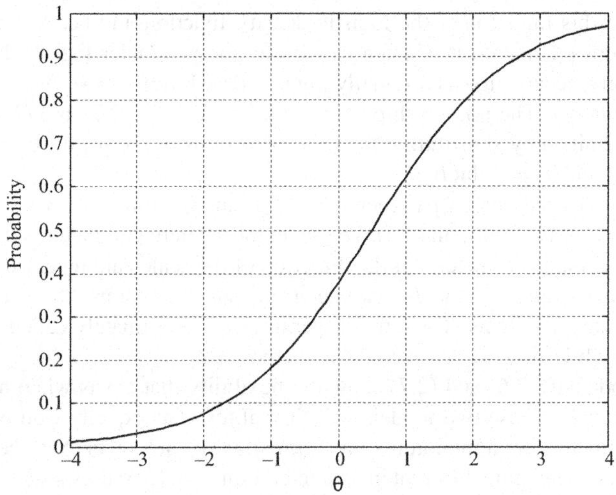

Fig. 2.2 One-parameter logistic model item characteristic curve for $b = .5$

For example, a person with $\theta = .25$ has a probability of correct response to the test item of .44 if the model is correct. A person .5 units higher on the θ-scale (i.e., $\theta = .75$) has a probability of correct response of .56 if the model is correct. The difference in these two probabilities for the .5-unit change on θ is .12. At $\theta = -1.5$, the probability of correct response is .12. At $\theta = -1.0$, a .5 unit change from the original value, the probability of correct response is .18. Over this .5 unit change in the θ-scale, the change in probability is only .06. This analysis indicates that the test item described by the ICC in Fig. 2.2 would be better at differentiating between persons between .25 and .75 on the θ-scale than persons between θ-values of -1.5 and -1.0.

A more analytic way of considering this issue is to determine the slope of the ICC at each point on the θ-scale so that the steepness of the ICC can be determined for any value of θ. The first derivative of the function describing the interaction of the persons and the item provides the slope of the ICC at each value of θ. For the model given in (2.7), the first derivative of $P(u_{ij} = 1 \mid \theta_j, b_i)$ with respect to θ is given by the following expression:

$$\frac{\partial P}{\partial \theta} = P - P^2 = P(1 - P) = PQ, \tag{2.8}$$

where, for simplicity,

$$P = P(u_{ij} = 1 \mid \theta_j, b_i),$$

and $Q = (1 - P)$.

From this expression, it is clear that the slope of the ICC is 0 (i.e., the curve is horizontal) only when the probability of correct response is 0 or 1. This confirms that the asymptotes for the model are 0 and 1. Note that the slope of the ICC is equal to .25 (that is, 1/4, a point that will be important later) when the probability of correct response is .5. A probability of .5 is the result of the model when θ_j is equal to b_i in (2.7) because then the exponent is equal to 0 and $e^0 = 1$ yielding a probability of 1/2.

Note that the difference in probability of correct response for θ values of .25 and .75 (centered around $\theta = .5$) was .12. The slope at $\theta = .5$ can be approximated as the ratio of the difference in probability (.12) over the range of θs to the difference in θ values (.5) $- .12/.5 = .24$. Because this ratio gives the slope for a linear function and the ICC is nearly linear in the θ-range from .25 to .75, it is not surprising that the slope from (2.8) and the approximation have nearly the same value. The similarity merely confirms that the derivative with respect to θ provides the slope.

To determine where along the θ-scale, the test item is best at differentiating people who are close together on the scale, the derivative of the expression for the slope, (2.8), can be used. This is the second derivative of (2.7) with respect to θ. Setting the second derivative to 0 and solving for θ yields the point on the θ-scale where the test item is most discriminating – the point of maximum slope. The derivative of (2.8) with respect to θ is

$$\frac{\partial(P - P^2)}{\partial\theta} = (P - P^2)(1 - 2P). \tag{2.9}$$

Solving this expression for 0 yields values of P of 0, 1, and .5. The values of θ that correspond to the values of 0 and 1 are $-\infty$ and ∞, respectively. The only finite solution for a value of θ corresponds to the value of $P = .5$. That is, the slope of the function is steepest when θ has a value that results in a probability of correct response from the model of .5. As previously noted, a .5 probability results when θ is equal to b_i. Thus, the b-parameter indicates the point on the θ-scale where the item is most discriminating. Items with high b-parameters are most discriminating for individuals with high trait levels – those with high θ-values. Items with low b-parameters are most discriminating for individuals with low trait levels.

The b-parameter also provides information about the ranges of trait levels for persons that are likely to respond correctly or incorrectly to the test item. Those persons with θ-values greater than b_i have a greater than .5 probability of responding correctly to Item i. Those with θ-values below b_i have less than a .5 probability of responding correctly to the item. This interpretation of the b-parameter is dependent on the assumption that the model in (2.7) is an accurate representation of the interaction of the persons and the test item.

Because the b-parameter for the model provides information about the trait level that is best measured by the item and about the likely probability of correct response, it has been labeled the *difficulty parameter* for the item. Although this terminology is somewhat of an oversimplification of the complex information provided by this parameter, the label has been widely embraced by the psychometric community.

It is important to note that for the model given in (2.7), the value of the maximum slope is the same for all items. The only feature of the ICC that changes from test item to test item is the location of the curve on the θ-scale. Figure 2.3 shows ICCs

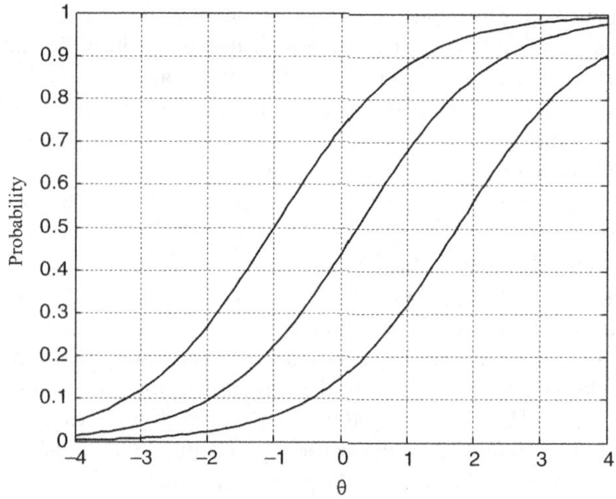

Fig. 2.3 ICCs for the model in (2.7) for $b_i = -1, .25, 1.75$

for three different items. The items have b-parameters with values of 1.75, .25, and -1.0. The graphs in Fig. 2.3 show that the slopes of the three curves are the same where they cross the $P = .5$ line. Because the ICCs for the model have a common value for the maximum slope for the items, the model is said to include an assumption that all test items have the same discriminating power. This is not true in an absolute sense because at different values of θ the slopes of the various items differ. But it is true that a set of items that are consistent with this model will have the same maximum slope, and the magnitude of the maximum slope at $P = .5$ will be $1/4$ for all items.

The one-parameter logistic (Rasch) model has a number of advantages over more complex models including simplicity in form and mathematical properties that make the estimation of the parameters of the model particularly convenient. One convenient mathematical property is that there is a direct relationship between the number-correct scores for a set of test items and the estimates of θ. All persons with the same number-correct score have the same maximum-likelihood estimate of θ.[3] A similar relationship exists between the number of correct responses to a test item and the maximum-likelihood estimate of the b-parameter for the test item. All items with the same proportion of correct responses for a sample of examinees have the same maximum-likelihood b-parameter estimate based on that sample. These relationships allow the θ-parameters for the examinees to be estimated independently of the b-parameters for the test items. A significant contingent of the psychometric

[3] Chapter 6 presents a number of estimation procedures including maximum likelihood. A full discussion of estimation procedures is beyond the scope of this book. The reader should refer to a comprehensive mathematical statistics text for a detailed discussion of maximum-likelihood estimation and other techniques for estimating model parameters.

community maintains that these properties of the one-parameter (Rasch) model are so desirable that models that do not have these properties should not be considered. The perspective of this group is that only when person and item-parameters can be estimated independently of each other do θ-estimates result in numbers that can be called measurements. Andrich (2004) provides a very clear discussion of this perspective and contrasts it with alternative views.

The perspective taken here is that the goal of the use of IRT models is to describe the interaction between each examinee and test item as accurately as possible within the limitations of the data and computer resources available for test analysis. This perspective is counter to the one that proposes that strict mathematical criteria are needed to define measurement and only models that meet the criteria are acceptable. Rather, the value of a model is based on the accuracy of the representation of the interaction between persons and items. The estimates of parameters of such models are used to describe the characteristics of the persons and items. The strict requirements for independent estimation of person and item parameters will not be considered as a requirement for a useful psychometric model.

From this perspective, whether or not the one-parameter logistic model is adequate for describing the interaction of examinees with test items is an empirical question rather than a theoretical question. For example, when test forms are analyzed using traditional item analysis procedures, the usual result is that the point-biserial and biserial correlation indices of the discriminating power of test items vary across items. Lord (1980) provides an example of the variation in discrimination indices for data from a standardized test. Item analysis results of this kind provide strong evidence that test items are not equal in discriminating power. These results imply that a model that has the same value for the maximum slope of the ICCs for all test items does not realistically describe the interaction between persons and items.

2.1.1.2 Two-Parameter Logistic Model

Birnbaum (1968) proposed a slightly more complex model than the one presented in (2.7). The mathematical expression for the model is given by

$$P(U_{ij} = 1 \mid \theta_j, a_i, b_i) = \frac{e^{a_i(\theta_j - b_i)}}{1 + e^{a_i(\theta_j - b_i)}}, \tag{2.10}$$

where a_i is a parameter related to the maximum slope of the ICC and the other symbols have the same definition as were given for (2.7). The first partial derivative of this model with respect to θ_j, which gives the slope of the ICC at each value of θ_j, is given by

$$\frac{\partial P(U_{ij} = 1 \mid \theta_j, a_i, b_i)}{\partial \theta_j} = a_i P_2 Q_2 = a_i (P_2 - P_2^2), \tag{2.11}$$

where P_2 is the probability of a correct response for the model given in (2.10), and $Q_2 = (1 - P_2)$. The subscript "2" is used to distinguish the probability estimates from the model in (2.10) from those for the model in (2.7).

The partial derivative of the slope with respect to θ_j, which is the same as the second partial derivative of the model in (2.10) with respect to θ_j, is given by

$$\frac{\partial(a_i P_2 Q_2)}{\partial \theta_j} = a_i^2(P_2 - P_2^2)(1 - 2P_2). \tag{2.12}$$

Solving this expression for zero to determine the point of maximum slope shows that the only finite solution occurs when $P_2 = .5$, as was the case for the one-parameter logistic model. Substituting .5 into (2.11) gives the value of the maximum slope, $a_i/4$. This result shows that the a_i parameter controls the maximum slope of the ICC for this model. It should also be noted that the point of maximum slope occurs when $\theta_j = b_i$, just as was the case for the one-parameter logistic model. Thus, b_i in this model can be interpreted in the same way as for the one-parameter logistic model – as the difficulty parameter.

Figure 2.4 presents three examples of ICCs with varying a- and b-parameters. These ICCs are not parallel at the point where they cross the .5 probability line. Unlike the ICCs for the one-parameter logistic model, these curves cross each other. This crossing of the curves allows one test item to be harder than another test item for persons at one point on the θ-scale, but easier than that same item for persons at another point on the θ-scale. For example at $\theta = -1$, Item 1 is easier than Item 2 (the probability of correct response is greater), but at $\theta = 1$, Item 1 is more

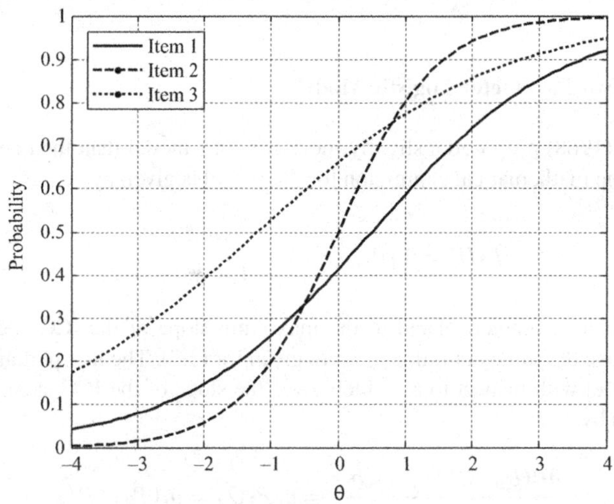

Fig. 2.4 Item characteristic curves for the two-parameter logistic model with a-parameters .7, 1.4, .56 and b-parameters .5, 0, -1.2, respectively

difficult than Item 2 (its probability of correct response is lower). This result is a direct consequence of the difference in the discriminating power (i.e., difference in a-parameters) of the items.

The a-parameter for the two-parameter logistic model also enters into the estimation of the θ-parameter for each examinee. While for the one-parameter logistic model, all examinees with the same number-correct score have the same estimate of θ, for the two-parameter logistic model, the examinees with the same weighted score, S_j given by $S_j = \sum_{i=1}^{I} a_i u_{ij}$, have the same maximum likelihood estimate of θ. Use of the two-parameter logistic model has the effect of weighting highly discriminating items – those with steeper maximum slopes – more heavily when estimating θ than items that are less discriminating. While for the one-parameter logistic model it does not matter which items the examinee answers correctly, the estimate of θ is dependent only on the number of correct responses, for the two-parameter logistic model, the particular test items responded to correctly affect the estimate of θ. Baker and Kim (2004) provide a thorough discussion of person parameter estimation for the different models.

2.1.1.3 Three-Parameter Logistic Model

Another feature of the item and person interaction that is commonly observed in examinee responses to multiple-choice test items is that persons with very low scores on a test will sometimes respond correctly to test items even when they are quite difficult. This empirical observation is often attributed to the possibility that a person can obtain the correct answer to a multiple-choice item by guessing from among the answer choices. Although few would argue that what is called "guessing" is truly a random process, it is also true that few examinees get scores below the number correct that would result from random selection of answer choices. If a person responds to a multiple-choice test item, even with no knowledge of the correct response, it is very unlikely that the probability of a correct response for each test item will be zero. For these reasons, UIRT models have been proposed that have a nonzero lower asymptote for the ICC.

One such model, called the three-parameter logistic model (Lord 1980) because it has three parameters that describe the functioning of the test item, is given by

$$P(U_{ij} = 1 \mid \theta_j, a_i, b_i, c_i) = c_i + (1 - c_i)\frac{e^{a_i(\theta_j - b_i)}}{1 + e^{a_i(\theta_j - b_i)}}, \tag{2.13}$$

where c_i is the lower asymptote parameter for Item i and all of the other symbols have been defined previously. Because it is hypothesized that the nonzero lower asymptote is partially a result of guessing on multiple-choice test items, c_i is sometimes called the pseudo-guessing parameter, or informally as the guessing parameter.

The influence of the c_i-parameter on the ICC can be determined by a straightforward application of limits. As θ approaches negative infinity, the probability of correct response to a test item that is accurately described by this model approaches c_i.

$$\lim_{\theta\to-\infty}\left[c_i + (1-c_i)\frac{e^{a_i(\theta_j-b_i)}}{1+e^{a_i(\theta_j-b_i)}}\right] = c_i + (1-c_i)\lim_{\theta\to-\infty}\left[\frac{e^{a_i(\theta_j-b_i)}}{1+e^{a_i(\theta_j-b_i)}}\right]$$
$$= c_i + (1-c_i)\,0 = c_i. \tag{2.14}$$

The relationship between the lower asymptote of the ICC and the value of c_i can clearly be seen in the ICC for the model in (2.13) with $a_i = 1.8$, $b_i = 1.5$, and $c_i = .16$. The plot of the ICC is given in Fig. 2.5. In the plot, the probability of .16 is indicated by the dashed line. It is clear that no matter how low the trait level of the examinee, the probability of correct response to the test item from the model does not fall below .16.

The slope of the ICC at points along the θ-scale can be determined in the same way as for the previous models. The partial derivative of (2.13) with respect to θ gives the slope at each point. To simplify the expression for the slope and maximum slope, P_3 is used to refer to the left side of (2.13). The right side is represented by $c_i + (1-c_i)P_2$, where P_2 is the expression for the two-parameter logistic model given in (2.10). This notation not only clarifies the mathematics involved in determining the slope and maximum slope of the ICC, but also emphasizes the relationship between the two and three-parameter logistic models.

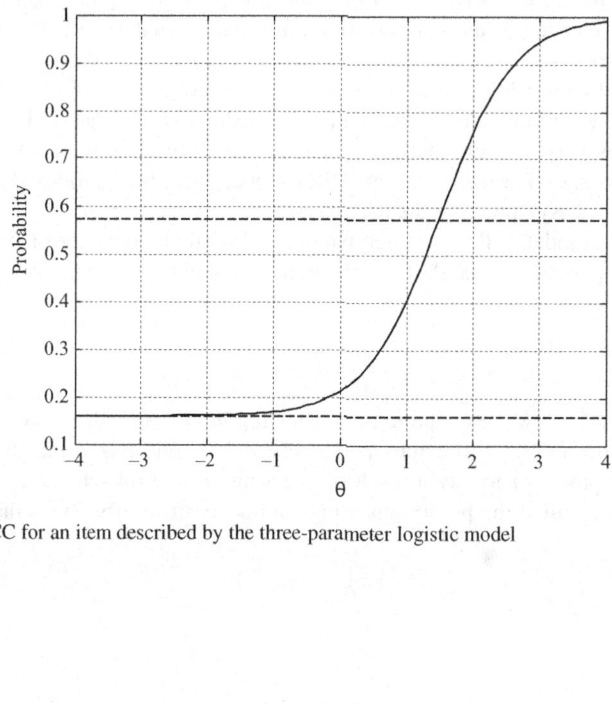

Fig. 2.5 ICC for an item described by the three-parameter logistic model

Given the above substitutions in (2.13), the slope of the three-parameter logistic model is given by

$$\frac{\partial P_3}{\partial \theta} = (1-c_i)a_i P_2 Q_2 = (1-c_i)a_i P_2(1-P_2) = (1-c_i)a_i(P_2 - P_2^2). \qquad (2.15)$$

From this result, it is clear that the slope is a function of all of the item parameters in the model. The point of maximum slope can be determined by taking the derivative of the slope with respect to θ, setting the resulting expression equal to zero and solving the equation for θ. Note that the derivative of the slope is also the second derivative of the model with respect to θ, and therefore it also identifies the point of inflection of the ICC. The maximum slope is given by the solution of

$$\frac{\partial\left[(1-c_i)a_i(P_2 - P_2^2)\right]}{\partial \theta} = (1-c_i)a_i^2(P_2 - P_2^2)(1-2P_2) = 0. \qquad (2.16)$$

The maximum slope is achieved when P_2 (not P_3) is .5. When $P_2 = .5$, $P_3 = c_i + (1-c_i)\cdot.5$. This value is half way between c_i and 1. The point of maximum slope occurs where the ICC crosses the line $P_3 = (c_i + 1)/2$. In Fig. 2.5, this value is shown as the broken line for $P_3 = .58$. Referring back to (2.10), $P_2 = .5$ when $\theta_j = b_i$. Thus, the b-parameter still indicates the point on the θ-scale where the ICC has maximum slope.

Substituting $P_2 = .5$ into (2.15) gives the maximum value of the slope. In general, that value is given by $(1-c_i)a_i/4$. When a nonzero lower asymptote is added to the model, the slope of the ICC at its maximum is less than that for the two-parameter logistic model with the same a_i and b_i parameters.

2.1.1.4 Other UIRT Models

The three models described so far were selected to show the effect of adding item parameters to IRT models and the function and meaning of the item parameters that are most commonly encountered. Although these three models are among the most commonly used of the UIRT models, many other alternative models exist, and even more can be imagined. Any mathematical function that maps a single variable describing examinee capabilities into numbers that range from 0 to 1 can be used as an UIRT model. Linear functions (Lazarsfeld 1966), polynomial functions (McDonald 1967; Samejima and Livingston 1979; Sympson 1983), spline functions (Abrahamowicz and Ramsay 1992), and normal ogive functions (Lord and Novick 1968) have been used. While a full discussion of these different models would unnecessarily distract from the goals of this chapter, UIRT models based on the normal ogive function are presented because of their importance to the development of MIRT models.

The normal ogive equivalent to the three-parameter logistic model is given by

$$P(U_{ij} = 1 \mid \theta_j, a_i, b_i, c_i) = c_i + (1 - c_i) \int_{-\infty}^{z} \frac{1}{\sqrt{2\pi}} \mathrm{e}^{-\frac{z^2}{2}} \mathrm{d}z, \tag{2.17}$$

where $z = a_i(\theta j - b_i)$ and all of the person and item parameters have the same definitions as for the logistic models. The integral specified in the model defines the area under the standard normal distribution from negative infinity to z.

The normal ogive model has slightly steeper ICCs than the logistic model for the same set of item parameter values. To compensate for this difference, Birnbaum (1968) suggested multiplying the exponents in the logistic model by 1.7 to make the two models more similar. When the 1.7 is included in the model, the predicted probabilities differ by less than .01 for all values of θ. That is, if the logistic component of the two and three-parameter logistic models is changed to

$$\frac{\mathrm{e}^{1.7a_i(\theta_j - b_i)}}{1 + \mathrm{e}^{1.7a_i(\theta_j - b_i)}}, \tag{2.18}$$

then the ICCs for the logistic and normal ogive models with the same item parameters will be virtually identical. The constant, 1.7, is sometimes represented by the symbol D in the exponents of the logistic models.

2.1.2 Relationships Between UIRT Parameters and Classical Item Statistics

In the discussion of UIRT models for items with two score categories, three parameters (a, b, and c) have been defined. These parameters determine the form of the ICCs for the test items. These parameters have been given descriptive labels (e.g., difficulty) that have certain intuitive meanings. These same descriptive labels often have definitions in the context of classical test theory. This section provides information about the connections between the IRT-based item parameters and the classical test theory item statistics that use similar terms as labels.

2.1.2.1 Item Difficulty

In classical test theory, item difficulty refers to the proportion of a sample of examinees that give a correct response to a test item. Because the number is a proportion, it ranges from 0 to 1 with numbers near 1 indicating easy test items and those near 0 indicating difficult test items. Because test items are easier as the index increases, some have argued that it is really a descriptor of the easiness of test items rather than their difficulty. However, the term "difficulty" continues in common usage for this statistic. The statistic is often referred to as a p-value, an abbreviation for proportion correct.

The b-parameter that appears in many IRT models indicates the point on the trait scale where the ICC has the steepest slope. For models without a lower asymptote parameter, this occurs at the trait level where the examinee has a .5 probability of getting the item correct. Changing the b-parameter in the model shifts the ICC to the right or left without affecting the shape of the curve. As the b-parameter increases, the curve shifts to the right (toward higher θ-values) and the probability of correct response to the test item at a particular θ-value is lower. Therefore, higher b-values indicate more difficult test items. Lower b-values indicate easier items. Because difficulty increases with increased b-value, it is reasonable to label b-parameters difficulty parameters.

To determine the p-value that corresponds to a b-value, the distribution of θ for a group of examinees must be known. This fact emphasizes the sample specific nature of the classical item difficulty index (p-value) as a measure of the difficulty of the test item. If the distribution of θ is given by $f(\theta)$, the relationship between the p-value and the b-parameter is given by

$$p_i = \int_{-\infty}^{\infty} P(u_i = 1 \mid \boldsymbol{\eta}_i, b_i) f(\theta) \mathrm{d}\theta, \tag{2.19}$$

where p_i is the proportion of examinees in the sample that answer the item correctly (the classical item difficulty for Item i), and $\boldsymbol{\eta}_i$ is the vector of other item parameters for Item i that may be included in the model (e.g., a_i, and c_i). The other symbols were defined previously.

Equation (2.19) provides some insights into the relationship between p and b. If all of the other item parameters in the IRT model are held constant, and the b-parameter is increased in magnitude, the probability of correct response at all θ-values becomes smaller. Accordingly, all values of the product of the probability of correct response and the density of θ will become smaller. Consequently, the value of the integral will be smaller and the p-value will be smaller. This implies that if the values of the other item parameters are held constant, the p-values are functionally related to the b-parameters for a specific sample of examinees. Because the one-parameter logistic model does not have any other item parameters, this functional relationship is always present. The relationship is not a linear one because the p-values are restricted to the range from 0 to 1 while the b-parameters have an infinite range of possible values. Note also that the relationship is an inverse one. As the b-values increase, the p-values decrease. The plot in Fig. 2.6 shows the relationship between the b-parameters for the one-parameter logistic model and the p-values for a sample of 200 examinees sampled from a standard normal distribution. The slight variation in the points from a curve is due to sampling variation in the p-values.

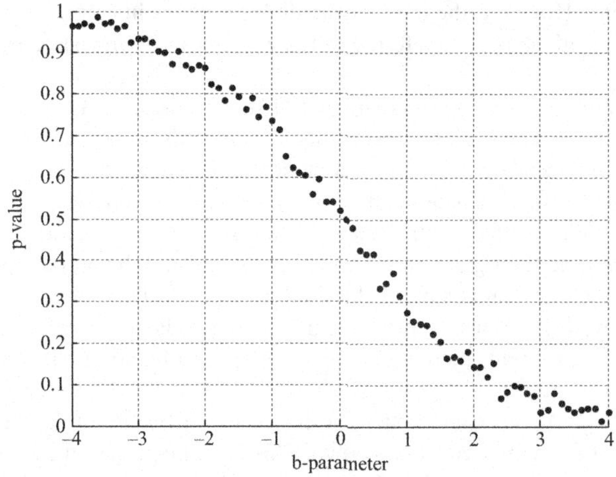

Fig. 2.6 Relationship between the one-parameter logistic model b-parameter and p-value for a sample of 200 from a standard normal distribution

2.1.2.2 Item Discrimination

In classical test theory, item discrimination refers to the capability of a test item to differentiate between those examinees who have a high level of construct assessed by a test from those who have little of that construct. Most commonly, the level of item discrimination is indicated by the correlation between the item score (0 or 1) and the total score on the test. Typically this correlation is computed using either the point-biserial or biserial correlation formulas, depending on the strength of the assumptions the test analyzer is willing to make.

The point-biserial correlation is a Pearson product-moment correlation between a dichotomously scored variable and a continuous variable. This correlation has been used quite frequently because it makes minimal assumptions and it is easy to compute. However, it does have the disadvantage that the range of possible values for the correlation coefficient depends on the difficulty of the test item. When the p-values are high or low, the maximum possible correlation that can be obtained from the point-biserial is less than 1. To avoid this restriction on the possible values of the point-biserial correlation, many classical test theory item analyses are performed using the biserial correlation. The computational formula for the biserial correlation is derived based on the assumption that the test item is measuring a normally distributed, continuous variable. That variable is assumed to be dichotomized at a point on the scale that has p proportion of the normal distribution above the point. The biserial correlation coefficient is an estimate of the population correlation, ρ, between the underlying normally distributed item variable and the total test score.

The conceptual framework used to derive the biserial correlation formula is very similar to that used to develop the two-parameter normal ogive model. In both cases, there is a construct that is measured by the test item and a construct that is measured by the entire test. In both cases, the normal distribution assumption is used to link the performance on the test item to the hypothetical construct measured by the test. The similarity between the conceptual frameworks can be used to show the relationship between the biserial correlation and the a-parameter from the IRT model.

If the item construct and the test construct are both represented using z-scores, and if the relationship between them is assumed to be linear, the relationship can be given by the standard linear regression model:

$$z_i = r_{\mathrm{it}} z_{\mathrm{t}} + \mathrm{e}_{\mathrm{it}}, \tag{2.20}$$

where z_i is the z-score on the item construct, r_{it} is the biserial correlation between the item and test constructs, z_{t} is the z-score on the test construct, and e_{it} is the error of estimation. The error of estimation is assumed to be normally distributed with mean 0 and variance equal to $1 - r_{\mathrm{it}}^2$. Error is also assumed to be independent of item scores and test scores.

Equation (2.20) gives the ICC for Item i when the item score is continuous. That is, it is the regression of the item score on the hypothetical construct for the test. Note that it is a linear function of the score on the total test construct. However, what is of interest here is the equation predicting the dichotomous item score from the test score rather than the continuous item score. To determine the dichotomous item score, a point on the continuous item score can be determined so that 1s are assigned to scores above that point and 0s to scores below that point. Because the item score is assumed to be normally distributed, the point used to dichotomize the score scale can be determined by finding the point that has p-proportion of the normal distribution above it. This value, γ, can be obtained from the inverse normal transformation of p. The inverse normal transformation gives the point with a given proportion of the distribution below it. The desired value is the point with a proportion of the distribution above it. Because the normal distribution is symmetric, the desired point is determined by changing the sign of the z-score determined from the usual inverse normal transformation.

$$\gamma_i = -\Psi^{-1}(p_i). \tag{2.21}$$

For a particular value of the test score z_t, the expected score on the continuous item score is $r_{\mathrm{it}} z_{\mathrm{t}}$. Unless the correlation between the continuous scores on the item and the test is 1, the result of this expression is the prediction of the mean of distribution rather then a specific value. The distribution is assumed to be normal with mean equal to $r_{\mathrm{it}} z_{\mathrm{t}}$ and variance $1 - r_{\mathrm{it}}^2$. To determine the probability of correct response for the item, the area under this normal distribution needs to be computed for the z-score range from γ_i to ∞, the range above the value determined in (2.21). The expression for computing the area under the specified normal distribution is given by

$$P(u_i = 1) = \int_{z_\gamma}^{\infty} \frac{1}{\sqrt{2\pi}} \mathrm{e}^{-\frac{t^2}{2}} \mathrm{d}t, \tag{2.22}$$

where z_γ is the z-score for a given γ_i based on the normal distribution predicted from z_t. That z-score is computed from the following equation using the mean and variance given above.

$$z_{\gamma_i} = \frac{\gamma_i - r_{\mathrm{it}} z_{\mathrm{t}}}{\sqrt{1 - r_{\mathrm{it}}^2}}. \tag{2.23}$$

Because the normal distribution is symmetric, the probability of obtained from integrating from z_γ to ∞ is exactly the same as that obtained from integrating from $-\infty$ to the z-score corresponding to $-\gamma$, $z_{-\gamma}$. The expression that gives the equivalent probability to (2.22) is

$$P(u_i = 1) = \int_{-\infty}^{z_{-\gamma_i}} \frac{1}{\sqrt{2\pi}} \mathrm{e}^{-\frac{t^2}{2}} \mathrm{d}t. \tag{2.24}$$

The important feature to note about this equation is the similarity of the integral to that of the normal ogive model given in (2.17). The integral expressions are identical in the two equations except for the upper limit of integration. If the expressions for the upper limits of integration are set equal, the relationship between the IRT item parameters and the classical item analysis statistics can be determined. That is,

$$z_{-\gamma_i} = -\frac{\gamma_i - r_{\mathrm{it}} z_t}{\sqrt{1 - r_{\mathrm{it}}^2}} = \frac{r_{\mathrm{it}} z_t - \gamma_i}{\sqrt{1 - r_{\mathrm{it}}^2}} = a_i(\theta - b_i). \tag{2.25}$$

In this case, the score on the construct defined by the total test is the same as the IRT scale value so $z_t = \theta$ and the correlation between the item continuous score and the score on the test is given by the biserial correlation, $r_{i\theta}$. Substituting these symbols into (2.25) and rearranging some terms gives

$$\frac{r_{i\theta}}{\sqrt{1 - r_{i\theta}^2}}\theta - \frac{\gamma_i}{\sqrt{1 - r_{i\theta}^2}} = a_i\theta - a_i b_i. \tag{2.26}$$

Both of the expressions for the upper limits of integration are linear equations in θ. Setting the slopes of those equations equal shows that for the normal ogive model the a-parameter is directly related to the biserial correlation between the item score and total test construct,

$$a_i = \frac{r_{i\theta}}{\sqrt{1 - r_{i\theta}^2}}. \tag{2.27}$$

Equation (2.27) is sometimes used with biserial correlations computed using the item scores and number-correct scores from a test. The estimates of the a-parameter obtained using those biserial correlations are, at best, very rough approximations because of the many assumptions made in this derivation. When using (2.27) to estimate a-parameters, the following assumptions need to hold.

1. The regression of the item z-score on the test z-score is linear.
2. Errors of estimation in the prediction of item scores from test scores are normally distributed.
3. The standard deviation of the distributions of errors of prediction of the items scores from the test scores is constant over the range of the θ-values.
4. All persons above the point where the item continuous scale is dichotomized will answer the item correctly.
5. The biserial correlation between the item score and total score is a good estimator of the correlation between the continuous item score and total score.

Although the estimates of the a-parameters given by (2.27) may not be very precise, the derivation does indicate that there is a fairly strong relationship between the biserial correlation and the a-parameter, even if it is not a mathematical function.

Another statistic that is sometimes used as a measure of the discriminating power of a test item is the loading of the test item on the first common factor of the item set. When the test is composed of items that are dichotomously scored, the analysis is often performed on the matrix of inter-item tetrachoric correlations. Because the use of tetrachoric correlations is based on the same assumptions as those underlying the biserial correlation (i.e., the underlying item construct is normally distributed and dichotomized at a point on the construct scale), the argument relating the biserial correlation to the a-parameter for a test item works equally well for item factor loadings. In fact, the argument is even stronger because the factor loading is the correlation between the item construct and the score on the first common factor rather than the number-correct score on the test. The former is a better estimate of θ than is the number-correct score because it is an estimate of the latent variable underlying the item responses and it is on the z-score scale. The relationship between the a-parameter for an item and its factor loading is given by an equation that is the direct analog to (2.27) with all of the same concerns about whether all of the listed assumptions apply. The equation is

$$a_i = \frac{\rho_i}{\sqrt{1-\rho_i^2}}, \tag{2.28}$$

where ρ_i is the loading of Item i on the first common factor from the set of items on the test.

2.1.2.3 Lower Asymptote

The lower asymptote parameter that is represented by c in (2.13) and (2.17) does not have a direct counterpart in traditional item analysis. This parameter indicates the proportion of examinees that will respond correctly to the test item as the ability of the examinee approaches $-\infty$. Some item analysis programs do provide information that can be used to approximate the c-parameter. These programs report the number of examinees choosing each response alternative in the multiple-choice item for groups of examinees at different performance levels defined on the total score for the test as a whole. For example, the analysis sample may be divided into fifths from the top fifth to the bottom fifth based on the number-correct score on the test. Then, the proportion choosing each alternative can be computed for each fifth of the sample. Typically, the proportion choosing the correct answer will decline as the overall performance level of the examinee groups decline. The proportion choosing the correct answer in the lowest group is an estimate of the c-parameter.

Many early descriptions of IRT models labeled the c-parameter as the guessing parameter because it was expected that it would generally be equal to $1/m$, where m is the number of response alternatives for the multiple-choice question. This is the proportion of correct responses that would be expected if the examinees chose responses totally at random. Empirical estimates of the c-parameter (see Lord 1980 for some examples) are often less than $1/m$ suggesting that c is not a random guessing parameter. It is more accurately described as a parameter that describes the performance of examinees with low trait levels. In this book, the latter interpretation is accepted and the c-parameter is referred to as the lower asymptote parameter.

2.1.3 Models for Items with More Than Two Score Categories

Although the majority of the work on IRT models has concentrated on the analysis of data from test items with two scores – 0 and 1, there has been a significant amount of development work on items that have more than two score categories. These models are designed for modeling the interaction of persons with of a variety of types of test items such as writing samples, open ended mathematics items, and rating scale responses to survey questions. Because the actual response activity for these different types of items are different – generating writing samples, solving mathematics problems, rating statements – the IRT models that describe the item/persons interactions with them are different as well. The characteristics of a variety of these models are described in van der Linden and Hambleton (1997) and van der Ark (2001), so they will not be repeated here. Most of the work on the generalizations of these models to the multidimensional case has focused on three of them – the partial credit model (Masters 1982) and the generalized partial credit model (Muraki 1992) and the graded response model (Samejima 1969). The unidimensional versions of these models are described here and the multidimensional versions are presented in Chap. 4.

2.1.3.1 The Partial Credit Model

The partial credit model (Masters 1982; Masters and Wright 1997) is a mathematical form that was designed for test items with two or more ordered categories. The partial credit model is appropriate for test items that are believed to require the successful accomplishment of a number of tasks. To receive the maximum score on the item, all of the tasks need to be correctly completed. The partial credit model is appropriate for open-ended items when scorers consider many different components of the response and score each of them as correct/incorrect or accomplished/not accomplished. The score for the test item as a whole is the number of components that were successfully completed (Verhelst and Verstralen 1997).

The scores on the item represent levels of performance, with each higher score meaning that the examinee accomplished more of the desired task. The boundaries between adjacent scores are labeled thresholds and an examinee's performance is on either side of a threshold with a particular probability. The scoring scale for the item can be dichotomized at each threshold and the model specifies the probability of a response in the categories above or below the selected threshold. This can be done for each threshold.

The mathematical expression for the partial credit model is given by

$$P(u_{ij} = k \mid \theta_j) = \frac{e^{\left[\sum\limits_{u=0}^{k} (\theta_j - \delta_{iu})\right]}}{\sum\limits_{v=0}^{m_i} e^{\left[\sum\limits_{u=0}^{v} (\theta_j - \delta_{iu})\right]}}, \tag{2.29}$$

where k is the score on Item i, m_i is the maximum score on Item i, and δ_{iu} is the threshold parameter for the uth score category for Item i.

For purposes of keeping notation less complex,

$$\sum_{u=0}^{0} (\theta_j - \delta_{iu}) \equiv 0 \quad \text{and} \quad \sum_{u=0}^{k} (\theta_j - \delta_{iu}) \equiv \sum_{u=1}^{k} (\theta_j - \delta_{iu}). \tag{2.30}$$

Note that the simplifying expressions in (2.30) indicate that the value of δ_{i0} has no impact on the model. No matter what value is chosen for this parameter, the term in the summation associated with it will have a value of 0. Often this parameter is set equal to 0 as a convenience, but that does not mean that there is a 0 threshold. The other δ_{iu} parameters specify the thresholds between score categories. This can be seen in (2.7) that shows the probability of each score as a function of θ.

The score characteristic functions shown in Fig. 2.7 are for a test item that has four score categories –0, 1, 2, 3. The curves in the figure show the probability of each score category for a person at a specific θ-level. For example, if θ is equal to -1, the probability of a score of 0 is .07, a score of 1 is .54, a score of 2 is .36, and a score of 3 is .03. A score of 1 is the most likely score at the θ-level, but the other scores are also possible.

The threshold parameters indicate where the adjacent score categories have equal likelihoods. Scores of 0 and 1 have equal likelihoods at -3. Scores of 1 and 2 have equal likelihoods at $-.5$. These threshold points are places where the curves for adjacent score categories cross. For this item, the threshold parameter values are in order from low to high (ignoring the 0 place holder value). This ordering of

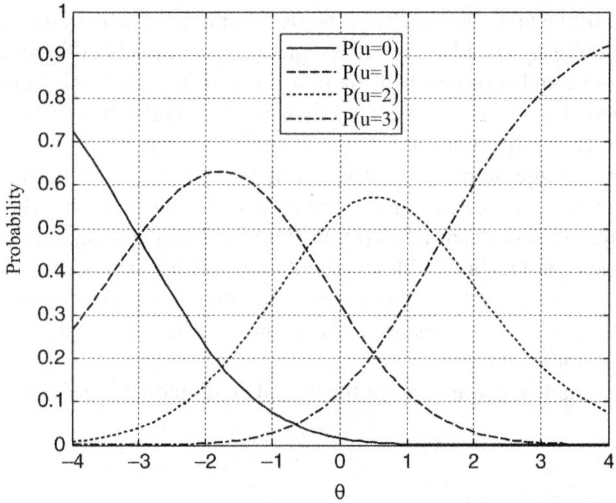

Fig. 2.7 Score category probabilities for an item with δ-parameters 0, −3, −.5, 1.5

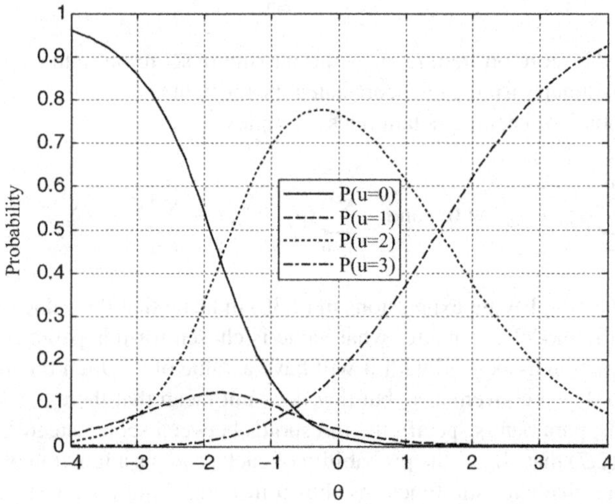

Fig. 2.8 Score category probabilities for an item with δ-parameters 0, −.5, −3, 1.5

threshold parameters is not a requirement of the model. Figure 2.8 shows the score characteristic functions for a test item with threshold parameters that have the same numerical values, but in different order – −.5, −3, 1.5. For this case, the probability of a score 1 for a person at −1 on the θ-scale is much lower than for the previous item – approximately .1. For this item, a score of 1 is never the most likely response. The model is indicating that this is a seldom used score category and it might be more reasonable to consider this a three category item.

The expected score on the item as a function of level on the θ-scale is specified by

$$E(u_{ij} \mid \theta_j) = \sum_{k=0}^{m_i} kP(u_{ij} = k \mid \theta_j). \tag{2.31}$$

The expected score ranges from 0 to m_i as a function of θ. The expected score on the item has an equivalent interpretation to the ICC for dichotomously scored items. The expected score functions for the examples shown in Figs. 2.7 and 2.8 are given in Fig. 2.9. The curves have a different form because of the different ordering of the threshold parameters. Example 2 increases quickly from 0 to 2 because the probability of a score of 1 is very low. As for dichotomously scored items, the curves indicate easy items if they are far to the left and hard items if they are far to the right.

The partial credit model is a member of the Rasch family of item response models. Masters and Wright (1997) indicate that when the item is only considered to consist of two adjacent score categories, the resulting model is the Rasch model for dichotomous items. That is, using the notation defined above,

$$\frac{P(u_{ij} = k \mid \theta_j)}{P(u_{ij} = k - 1 \mid \theta_j) + P(u_{ij} = k \mid \theta_j)} = \frac{e^{(\theta_j - \delta_{ik})}}{1 + e^{(\theta_j - \delta_{ik})}}, \quad k = 1, 2, \ldots, m_i. \tag{2.32}$$

The expression on the right is the Rasch model for dichotomous items with the threshold parameter as the difficulty parameter. This model fits the adjacent score categories using the Rasch model for dichotomous items indicating that all of

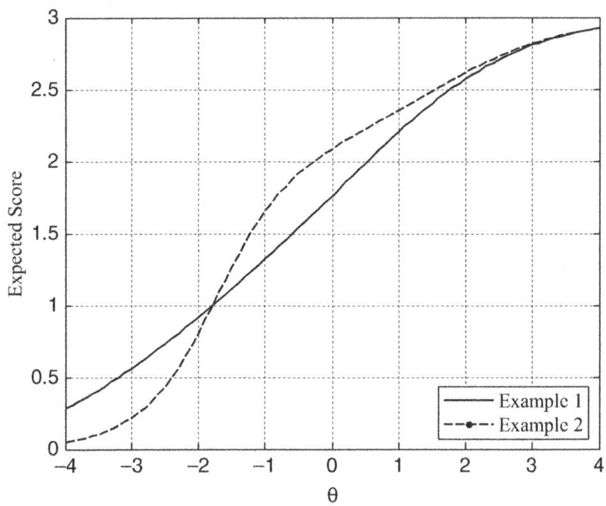

Fig. 2.9 Expected score curves for the two example items

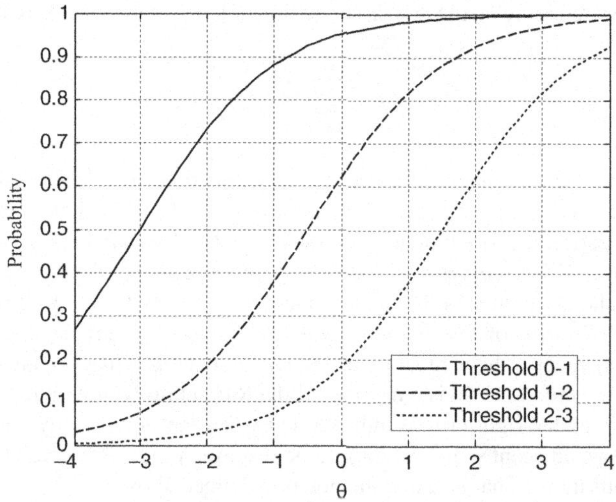

Fig. 2.10 Adjacent score characteristic curves for thresholds −3, −.5, 1.5

the distinctions between score categories have the same slope at the point of inflection and the point of steepest slope for the curves for distinguishing the response functions is at the θ-value corresponding to the threshold value. The curves for adjacent score pairs for the first example item are shown in Fig. 2.10.

It is easily seen in Fig. 2.10 that the .5 probability line intersects the curves at the values on the θ-scale equal to the threshold parameters. Also, the curves do not intersect and have the same slope where they cross the .5 probability line. Further, the slope at the point of inflection is the same as that for the Rasch model for dichotomous items – .25.

2.1.3.2 The Generalized Partial Credit Model

The generalized partial credit model (Muraki 1992) is an extension of the partial credit model proposed by Masters (1982). The extension is the addition of the discrimination parameter, a, to the partial credit model. This is similar conceptually to the relationship between the one-parameter logistic model and the two-parameter logistic model. Although the partial credit model is a member of the family of Rasch models because it has observable sufficient statistics for the item and person parameters, the generalized partial credit model is not. The addition of the discrimination parameter allows variation in the discriminating power of items to be modeled. However, adding a discrimination parameter that is estimated as part of item calibration removes the generalized partial credit model from the family of Rasch models.

Like the partial credit model, the generalized partial credit model is appropriate for test items that are considered to require the successful accomplishment of a number of tasks. To receive the maximum score on the item, all of the tasks need to be correctly completed. The generalized partial credit model is appropriate for open-ended items scored considering many different components of the response. Each component is scored as correct/incorrect or accomplished/non accomplished. The score for the test item as a whole is the number of components that were successfully completed (Verhelst and Verstralen 1997).

The scores on the item represent levels of performance, with each higher score meaning that the examinee accomplished more of the desired task. As with the partial credit model, the boundaries between adjacent scores are labeled thresholds and an examinee's performance is on either side of a threshold with a particular probability. The score scale for the item can be dichotomized at each threshold and the model specifies the probability of being in each of the two resulting categories. This can be done for each threshold.

The mathematical expression for the generalized partial credit model is given below

$$P(u_{ij} = k \mid \theta_j) = \frac{e^{\left[\sum\limits_{u=1}^{k} Da_i(\theta_j - b_i + d_{iu})\right]}}{\sum\limits_{v=1}^{m_i} e^{\left[\sum\limits_{u=1}^{v} Da_i(\theta_j - b_i + d_{iu})\right]}}, \tag{2.33}$$

where k is the score on the item, m_i is the total number of score categories for the item, d_{iu} is the threshold parameter for the threshold between scores u and $u-1$, and all of the other symbols have their previous definitions. Note that d_{i1} is defined as 0. This model has a parameter b_i that indicates the overall difficulty of the test item and a parameter a_i that indicates the overall discrimination power of the item. The discrimination power is assumed to be the same at all thresholds, but a_i may differ across items. The threshold parameters, d_{ik}, indicate where the likelihood of responses changes from being greater for response category $k-1$ to being greater for response category k. For estimation purposes, the sum of the d_{ik}-parameters is usually constrained to sum to 0.

The parameterization used in the PARSCALE program (Muraki and Bock 1991) is used in (2.33). If the a-parameter is set equal to $1/D$ for all items and $\delta_{iu} = b_i - d_{iu}$, the result is the partial credit model in (2.29). Note that the index of summation also starts at 0 instead of 1. If the a-parameter is .588 (i.e., 1/1.7), the b-parameter is 0, and the d-parameters are 3, .5, -1.5, the score category probability curves are the same as those shown in Fig. 2.7.

To show the effects of the discrimination parameter on the form of the functions describing the interactions between persons and an item whose characteristics can be represented by the generalized partial credit model, the score category probability curves are shown for two item – one with $a = .5$ and the other with $a = 1.5$. Both items have $b = -.5$, and d-parameters 0, 3, -1, -2. The curves for each score category, 1, 2, 3, 4, are shown in Fig. 2.11 with the solid lines representing the item with $a = .5$ and the dashed lines representing the item with $a = 1.5$. It is clear that

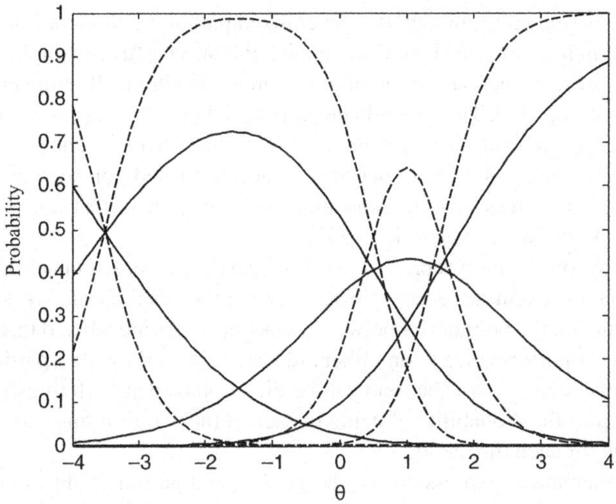

Fig. 2.11 Generalized partial credit model score probability curves for $b = -.5$, $ds = 0, 3, -1, -2$, and $a = .5$ (*solid curves*) and 1.5 (*dashed curves*)

the probabilities for each score category change more quickly when a has a higher value. Also, the curves for adjacent score categories cross at the same value of θ – the value of the corresponding threshold $b_i - d_{iu}$.

The score curves for obtaining the higher of adjacent score categories can be obtained in the same way as for the partial credit model. These curves for $a = .5$ (solid lines) and 1.5 (dashed lines) are shown in Fig. 2.12. The curves for the same score categories cross the .5 probability line at the same points – the values of the thresholds. The slopes of the lines where they cross the .5 probability line are the same as for the two-parameter logistic model – $Da/4$. The slopes are all the same within item, but they differ across the two items.

2.1.3.3 Graded Response Model

The graded response model (Samejima 1969) is designed for test items that have somewhat different requirements than the partial credit models. The partial credit models consider the items to have a number of independent parts and the score indicates how many parts were accomplished successfully. The graded response model considers the test item to require a number of steps but the successful accomplishment of one step requires the successful accomplishment of the previous steps. If step k is accomplished, then previous steps are assumed to be accomplished as well.

The parameterization of the model given here considers the lowest score on Item i to be 0 and the highest score to be m_i. The probability of accomplishing k or more steps is assumed to increase monotonically with an increase in the hypothetical

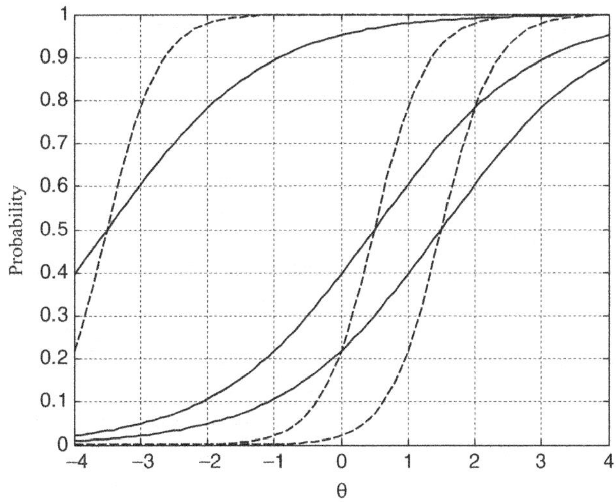

Fig. 2.12 Score characteristic curves for adjacent response categories for $a = .5$ (*solid curves*) and $a = 1.5$ (*dashed curves*)

construct underlying the test, θ. The probability of accomplishing k or more steps is typically represented as a two-parameter normal ogive or logistic model. The probability of receiving a specific score, k, is the difference between the probability of doing the work for k or more steps and doing the work for $k+1$ or more steps. If the probability of performing the work including step k at a particular θ-level is $P^*(u_{ij} = k \mid \theta_j)$, then the probability that an examinee will receive a score of k is

$$P(u_{ij} = k \mid \theta_j) = P^*(u_{ij} = k \mid \theta_j) - P^*(u_{ij} = k + 1 \mid \theta_j), \tag{2.34}$$

where $P^*(u_{ij} = 0|\theta_j) = 1$ because doing the work for step 0 or more is a certainty for all examinees and $P^*(u_{ij} = m_i + 1|\theta_j) = 0$ because it is impossible do work representing more than category m_i. The latter probability is defined so that the probability of each score can be determined from (2.34). Samejima (1969) labels the terms on the right side of the expression as the cumulative category response functions and those on the left side of the expression as the category response function.

The normal ogive form of the graded response model is given by

$$P(u_{ij} = k \mid \theta_j) = \frac{1}{\sqrt{2\pi}} \int_{a_i(\theta_j - b_{i,k+1})}^{a_i(\theta_j - b_{ik})} e^{\frac{-t^2}{2}} \mathrm{d}t, \tag{2.35}$$

where k is the score on the item, $0, 1, \ldots, m_i$, a_i is an item discrimination parameter, and b_{ik} is a difficulty parameter for the kth step of the item.

Using the same symbols, the logistic form of the model is given by

$$P(u_{ij} = k \mid \theta_j) = \frac{e^{Da_i(\theta_j - b_{ik})} - e^{Da_i(\theta_j - b_{i,k+1})}}{(1 + e^{Da_i(\theta_j - b_{ik})})(1 + e^{Da_i(\theta_j - b_{i,k+1})})}. \tag{2.36}$$

Note that this form of the model includes the constant, $D = 1.7$, so that the parameterization of the logistic version of the model will be very similar to that for the normal ogive version of the model.

The cumulative category response functions for the logistic form of the graded response model with step difficulty parameters $b_{ik} = -2, -1, .7$, and 2 and discrimination parameter $a_i = 1$ are presented in Fig. 2.13. The curves are the same as the two-parameter logistic model for dichotomously scored items. They cross the .5-probability line at a point equal to the step difficulty and their slopes are steepest at that point. All of the curves have the same slope at their points of inflection, $a_i/4$.

The probabilities of each of the five response categories, 0, 1, 2, 3, and 4 for this item can be determined from (2.34). The probabilities of each response conditional on level of θ are given by the category response functions in Fig. 2.14. The curve corresponding to the score of 0 is a decreasing function of θ and it crosses the .5-probability line at the value of b_{i1}, -2. The curve corresponding to the highest score category, $m_i = 4$, crosses the .5-probability line at b_{i4}, 2. The other curves do not have an obvious relationship to the item parameters. The intersection points of the curves are not equal to the b-parameters as they are for the partial credit model.

The effect of changes to the a-parameters can be seen in Figs. 2.15a and b. Figure 2.15a shows the probability in each response category for the test item shown

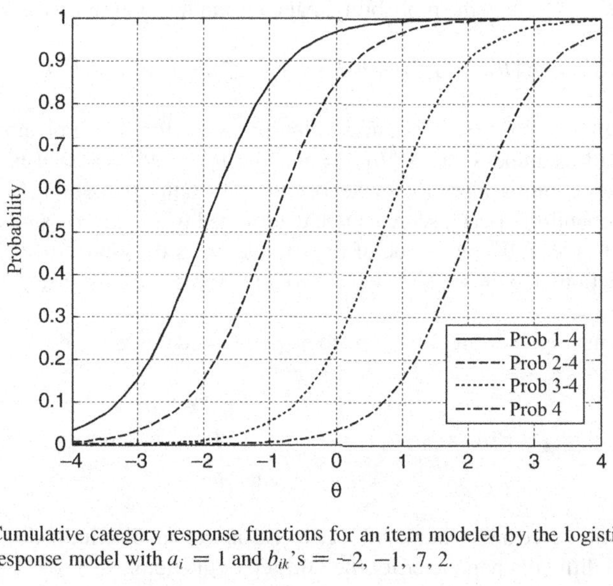

Fig. 2.13 Cumulative category response functions for an item modeled by the logistic version of the graded response model with $a_i = 1$ and b_{ik}'s $= -2, -1, .7, 2$.

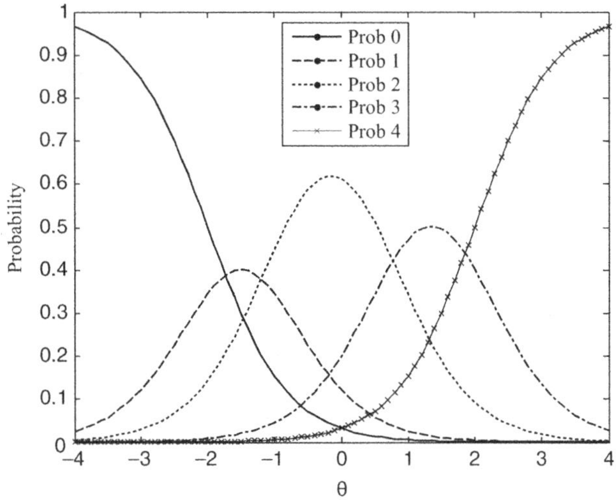

Fig. 2.14 Category response functions for an item modeled by the logistic version of the graded response model with $a_i = 1$ and b_{ik}'s $= -2, -1, .7, 2$

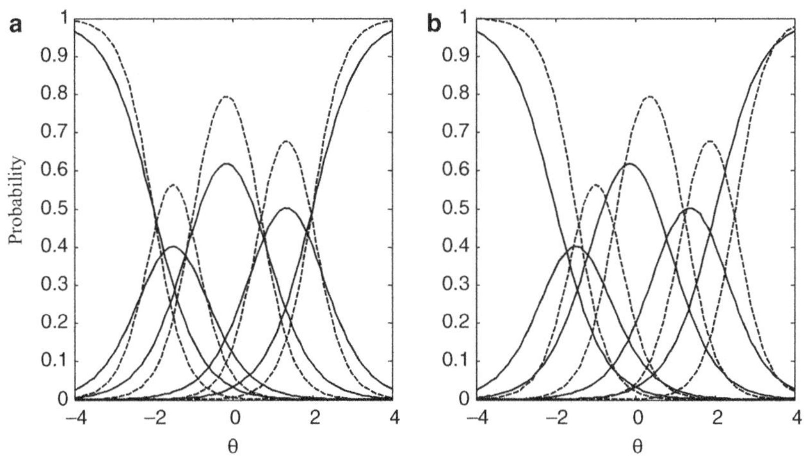

Fig. 2.15 Category response functions for items modeled by the logistic version of the graded response model with (**a**) $a_i = 1$ (*solid lines*) and 1.5 (*dashed lines*), and b_{ik}'s $= -2, -1, .7, 2$ and (**b**) $a_i = 1$ (*solid lines*) and 1.5 (*dashed lines*), and b_{ik}'s $= -2, -1, .7, 2$ (*solid lines*) and -1.5, $-.5$, 1.2, 2.5 (*dashed lines*)

in Fig. 2.14 and an item with the same b-parameters, but with the a_i-parameter equal to 1.5. The graphs show that the increase in a_i-parameter from 1 to 1.5 results in steeper curves for the extreme score categories, and more peaked curves for the categories between the extremes. The curves for the extreme categories still cross the

.5-probability line at the same place, but the curves for the nonextreme score categories do not intersect at the same place. In general, as the a-parameter increases, the probability of obtaining a particular score in the test item changes more quickly with a change in θ-value.

The effect of changes to the b_{ik} parameters for the test item can be seen in Fig. 2.15b. This figure shows the original category response curves from Fig. 2.14 and those for $a_i = 1.5$ and b_{ik} shifted by .5. That is, each b-parameter from the example in Fig. 2.14 was changed by adding .5 to result in $b_{ik} = -1.5, -.5, 1.2$, and 2.5. The shift in b-parameters shifts the category response curves to the right. This means that a person needs a higher level of θ to have a high probability of obtaining a score in a category.

The category response curves for the extreme categories cross the .5-probability line at a value of θ equal to the b_{ik}-parameter for those categories. The peaks of the curves for the other response categories are shifted to the right, but the peaks of the curves do not have any obvious connection to the b_{ik}-parameters. A comparison of Figs. 2.15a and b shows that the maximum probability of a response in a category does not change when the b_{ik}-parameters change but the difference in the parameters remains the same and the a_i-parameter is unchanged.

The expected score on a test item that is accurately modeled with the graded response model can be obtained using the same equation as that for the partial credit models (2.31). That is, the expected score on the test item is the sum of the products of the probability of an item score and the item score. The expected score curves for the three test items represented by the category response curves in Figs. 2.14 and 2.15 are presented in Fig. 2.16.

Example 1 in Fig. 2.16 corresponds to the test item represented in Fig. 2.14. Example 2 is the curve with the a_i-parameter increased to 1.5. That change does

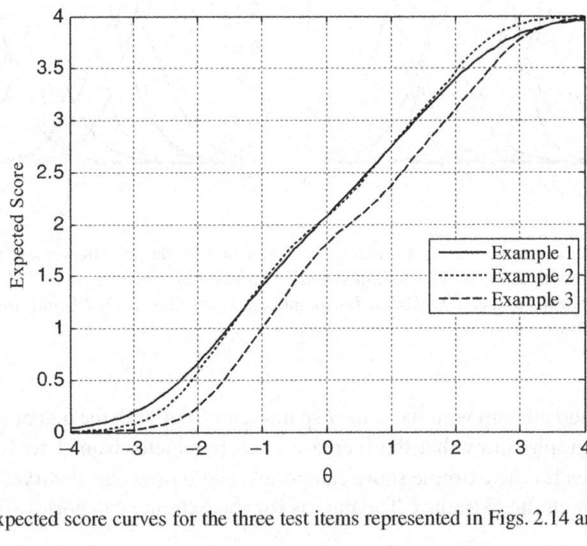

Fig. 2.16 Expected score curves for the three test items represented in Figs. 2.14 and 2.15

not have a dramatic effect on the expected score curve. The curve is somewhat steeper when θ is high or low, but the two curves are almost indistinguishable in the θs in the range from -2 to 2. Example 3 is the curve for the test item with the b_{ik}-parameters shifted up by .5. It is clear that the shift in the b_{ik}-parameters moves the curve to the right. This indicates that a higher θ-value is needed for this test item to have the same expected score as for Example 2. To have that same expected score, the θ-value must be increased by .5. The curves in Fig. 2.16 do not match the normal ogive or logistic forms. They have changes in curvature along the range of θ that results from differences in the distance between the b_{ik}-parameters. The slope of the curve changes along the range of θ depending on the distance between the b_{ik}-parameters.

2.2 Other Descriptive Statistics for Items and Tests

Along with the item parameters for the UIRT models, there are several statistics that describe the function of items and tests that are unique to IRT. These statistics are derived from the IRT models to further describe what the item response data tell about the item/person interactions. The most commonly used of these statistics are the expected summed score on a test composed of a set of items and the amount of information about the location of an examinee provided by the response to a test item or a collection of test items. These statistics can be computed as single descriptive values, but they are usually computed for all levels of θ. When this is done, they are functions of θ rather than single values. The expected summed score function, usually called a test characteristic curve, and the information function are described in this section.

2.2.1 The Test Characteristic Curve

Regression analysis is a methodology that is quite frequently used to predict the value of one variable from the value of another variable. For example, the value of a variable y can be predicted from the value of another variable x. The prediction is made so that error is minimized. Regression procedures were originally developed with error defined as the squared difference between the observed value of y and the predicted value of y. In that case, the expected value of y conditional on the predictor value x is used as the predicted value of y.

In the context of IRT, the variable that is usually predicted is the scored response to the test item. This item score is predicted from the value of θ. A regression predictor of the item score from θ is given by the expected value of the item score conditional on the value of θ, $\mathrm{E}(u|\theta)$. For an item with two score categories, 0 and 1, the regression predictor of the item score from θ is given by

$$E(u \mid \theta) = 1P(u = 1 \mid \theta) + 0P(u = 0 \mid \theta) = P(u = 1 \mid \theta), \tag{2.37}$$

where all of the symbols have been defined previously. Equation (2.37) shows that the regression of the item score on θ is the same as the IRT function for the probability of correct response to the item when the test item has a score of 0 or 1. When test items have more than two score categories, the regression of the item score on θ is not quite as simple. For polytomously scored test items, the regression of the item score on θ is given by (2.31).

A traditional method for scoring tests has been to compute the sum of the item scores. This score is often called the total score, the raw score or the number-correct score. Because tests often have combinations of dichotomously and polytomously scored items, the term "number-correct" does not accurately describe these cases. The term "summed score" will be used here as a synonym for all of these terms that accurately reflects how these scores are produced. That is, the term "summed score" will refer to an unweighted sum of the item scores.

The regression of the summed score on θ is the expected value of the summed score conditional on θ. If the summed score for a person is represented by y_j, the regression predictor of y_j from θ_j is given by

$$E(y_j \mid \theta_j) = E\left(\sum_{i=1}^{n} u_{ij} \mid \theta_j\right) = \sum_{i=1}^{n} E(u_{ij} \mid \theta_j), \tag{2.38}$$

where n is the number of items on the test. For the special case of a test composed of items that are scored 0 or 1 the expression on the left of (2.38) is simply the sum of the item characteristic functions for the test items, $\sum_{i=1}^{n} P(u_{ij} \mid \theta_j)$.

The plot of the expected value of the summed score against θ is typically referred to as the test characteristic curve (TCC). Because classical test theory defines the true score on a test as the expected value of the observed score y_j (see Lord and Novick 1968), the TCC shows the relationship between the true score from classical test theory and the θ from item response theory. Lord (1980) considers true score and θ as representing the same concept, but being monotonic transformations of each other.

The TCC for a set of items appears in the psychometric literature in two different forms. One form is a plot with the horizontal axis representing θ and the vertical axes representing the expected summed score. This is a direct representation of (2.38). Sometimes, it is more useful to transform the TCC to use a proportion of maximum possible score (proportion correct for tests with items scored 0 or 1). That is, the expected summed score is divided by the maximum possible summed score. For that case, the vertical axis has a range from 0 to 1. This representation is more convenient when it is desired to compare TCCs from tests with different numbers of test items. Examples of the two representations of TCCs are given in Fig. 2.17. The item parameters used to produce the TCCs are given in Table 2.1. Table 2.1 contains item parameters for a set of 50 multiple choice and open ended items that are scored as either correct (1) or incorrect (0). The item parameters are for the three-parameter logistic model when the items are multiple-choice and for

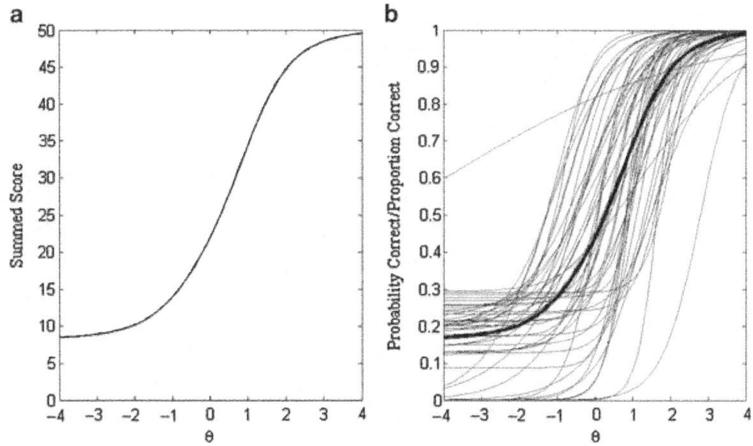

Fig. 2.17 Test characteristic curve (TCC) for items in Table 2.1

Table 2.1 Item parameters for 50 dichotomously score test items

Item number	*a*	*b*	*c*	Item number	*a*	*b*	*c*
1	1.83	0.91	0	26	1.44	0.58	0.27
2	1.38	0.81	0	27	2.08	0.82	0
3	1.47	0.06	0	28	0.81	−0.22	0.20
4	1.53	−0.80	0.25	29	1.10	1.82	0.23
5	0.88	0.24	0.21	30	0.66	0.26	0
6	0.82	0.99	0.29	31	0.91	−0.97	0.20
7	1.02	1.23	0.26	32	0.61	0.08	0.22
8	1.19	−0.47	0.19	33	0.67	0.54	0.17
9	1.15	2.78	0	34	0.43	1.22	0.20
10	0.18	−3.85	0.21	35	0.70	−1.27	0
11	0.70	1.49	0	36	0.83	1.02	0.13
12	1.36	0.56	0.20	37	1.30	1.50	0.18
13	1.53	0.80	0.21	38	2.01	1.19	0.28
14	1.17	−0.29	0.18	39	1.02	−0.68	0.20
15	1.14	−1.05	0.19	40	1.60	1.83	0.24
16	0.94	−0.25	0.15	41	1.02	−0.69	0.21
17	1.64	1.14	0.29	42	0.96	0.23	0.26
18	1.21	0.43	0.13	43	1.45	0.78	0.21
19	1.67	0.27	0.26	44	1.48	1.22	0.13
20	0.67	−0.32	0.19	45	2.23	1.64	0
21	1.74	1.99	0.29	46	1.51	0.24	0.17
22	0.74	0.59	0.19	47	0.88	0.58	0.12
23	0.79	−0.28	0.14	48	0.78	−0.06	0.24
24	1.38	1.06	0.15	49	0.52	−0.10	0
25	1.84	0.90	0.09	50	0.97	1.38	0

The zeros in the *c* columns indicate that short answer items were assumed to have a zero probability for guessing a correct response the two-parameter logistic model when the items are short-answer scored correct or incorrect. The c-parameters for the short-answer items are shown as 0 in the table because there was assumed to be no chance of guessing the answer to these items.

The left panel of Fig. 2.17 shows the TCC for this set of items with the summed score on the vertical axis. The appearance of this curve is similar to that of an ICC for a three-parameter logistic model, but the curve can not be modeled by that function unless all of the test items have the same item parameters. The possible forms of the TCC are quite varied. Lord and Novick (1968) provide informative examples in Chap. 16. The TCC in Fig. 2.17 has a lower asymptote that is equal to the sum of the c-parameters, 7.938. The TCC tends to be steepest for a value of the expected summed score of 29 that is half way between the lower asymptote and the maximum possible summed score. This is approximately the case for sets of test items that have a unimodal distribution of difficulty, but it is not a mathematical necessity. For sets of test items that have a bimodal distribution of difficulty, the TCC can have a lower slope in the middle range than for higher or lower values.

The right panel of Fig. 2.17 shows the TCC (dark line) using the proportion of maximum possible summed score as the vertical axis. The figure also contains the ICCs for all 50 items. When using the proportion of maximum possible as the vertical axis, the TCC is the average of all of the ICCs. A comparison of the two panels in the figure will show that the TCCs have exactly the same form – it is only the numerical values on the vertical axis that differ.

The TCC always shows a nonlinear relationship between θ and the expected summed score because the summed score has a finite range and θ has an infinite range. Where the TCC is fairly flat, the test is mapping a broad range of the θ-scale into a narrow range of the summed score scale. For example, the θ range from -4 to -2 is mapped into the summed score range from 8 to 10. Wherever the TCC is steep, the opposite is the case – the test provides a spread of summed scores for a fairly narrow range of the θ-scale. For the example given here, the θ-range from 1 to 1.5 is mapped into the range from 34 to 40 on the summed-score scale.

The TCC can be used to determine the shape of the expected summed-score distribution, that is, the true score distribution, when the θ-distribution is known. The TCC provides the transformation that maps the area within given boundaries on the θ-scale to the corresponding boundaries on the summed-score scale. Figure 2.18 provides an example of the estimation of the true score distribution. The TCC shown in the figure is computed from the item parameters in Table 2.1. The θ distribution is assumed to be normal with a mean 0 and standard deviation 1. The left panel of the figure shows the estimated true score distribution for the summed scores based on the assumed θ distribution and TCC. Note that the true score distribution is positively skewed because the majority of the b-parameters are positive indicating that the test is fairly difficult. Also, there are no scores below the sum of the c-parameters because this is a true score distribution – the scores are the expected scores for a particular level of θ and it is not possible to get a expected score less than the sum of the chance levels. Any assumed distribution of θ can be mapped through the TCC to determine the corresponding true score distribution. Lord and

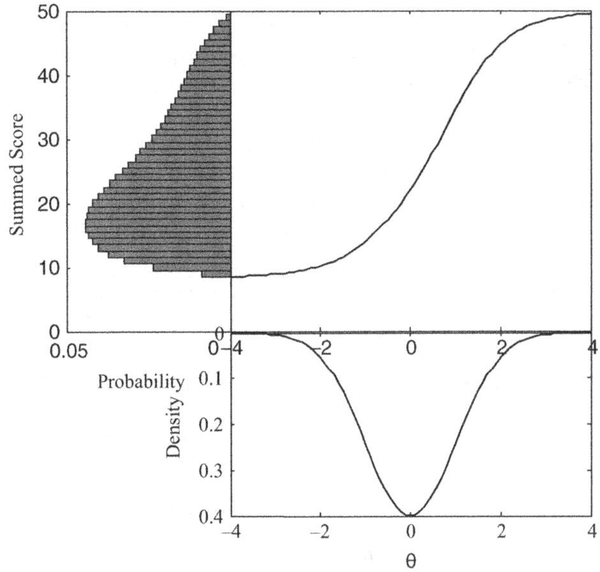

Fig. 2.18 True score distribution estimated from θ distribution using the TCC

Novick (1968, pp. 386–392) provide examples using a number of different TCCs and θ distributions. Lord (1980) shows how to estimate the observed summed-score distribution as well as the true summed-score distribution.

2.2.2 *Information Function*

The term "information" as it is used in IRT is a statistical indicator of the quality of the estimate of a parameter, usually the trait parameter that is the target for the test. Because item responses provide information for all levels of values on the θ-scale, information is usually represented as a function of the parameter being estimated rather than as a single value. The formula for information can be derived in a number of different ways. Birnbaum (1968) showed that the value of information is related to the length of the confidence interval around the trait estimate for a person. Kendall and Stuart (1961) indicated that the information function is related to the asymptotic standard error of the maximum likelihood estimate of the trait parameter. The approach taken here is to show that the information function is an indicator of the degree to which the reported score from a test or item differentiates between real differences in the trait of interest. In effect, the information function indicates how many standard errors of the trait estimate are needed to equal one unit on the θ-scale. When more standard errors are needed to equal one unit on the θ-scale, the standard errors are smaller indicating that the measuring instrument is sensitive enough to detect relatively small differences in θ. This approach to defining information is a combination of conceptual definitions of information provided by Lord (1980) and Hambleton and Swaminathan (1985).

Suppose the trait of interest can be assessed using a test composed of test items that can be accurately modeled by a unidimensional IRT model and that the true trait level for a person is given by θ_j. The true trait level of a person can not be observed. Rather, the observed score on a test for person j is represented by an estimate y_j. If it were possible to administer the test to the person repeatedly and get independent estimates of y_j, it would not be expected that all of the estimates would be the same. Instead, the y_j would vary and the full set of estimates could be collected together to form a distribution that would have a mean and standard deviation. The mean for a person with trait level θ_j is indicated by $\mu_{y\,|\,\theta_j}$. The standard deviation of the distribution is indicated by $\sigma_{y\,|\,\theta_j}$. This standard deviation is called the conditional standard error of measurement of test score y in classical test theory.

Now suppose that two individuals with different levels of θ are assessed using the same test and that the sensitivity of the test to differences in their trait level is of interest. A useful measure of the sensitivity of the test is given by

$$\frac{\mu_{y\,|\,\theta_2} - \mu_{y\,|\,\theta_1}}{\sigma_{y\,|\,\theta_1,\theta_2}}, \tag{2.39}$$

where $\sigma_{y\,|\,\theta_1,\theta_2}$ is the pooled standard error of measurement at the two θ values.

This measure of sensitivity indicates the distance between the means of the sampling distributions for the two individuals in terms of standard error units. If the result were 1.7, it would mean that the expected observed scores for the two individuals were 1.7 standard error units apart. Of course the value given by (2.39) is dependent on the distance between θ_1 and θ_2. If the distance between the two individuals is greater, the number of standard errors units they are apart will be greater as well. To compare the sensitivity of the test for distinguishing between individuals at different places in the θ-scale, an index is needed that is comparable – one that refers to the same distance on the θ-scale. Such an index can be developed by dividing the expression in (2.39) by the difference in θ-values. This results in a measure that tells the number of standard error units corresponding to one unit on the θ-scale. The resulting expression is

$$\frac{\frac{\mu_{y\,|\,\theta_2} - \mu_{y\,|\,\theta_1}}{\sigma_{y\,|\,\theta_1,\theta_2}}}{\theta_2 - \theta_1} = \frac{\mu_{y\,|\,\theta_2} - \mu_{y\,|\,\theta_1}}{\sigma_{y\,|\,\theta_1,\theta_2}(\theta_2 - \theta_1)}. \tag{2.40}$$

Thus, if the result from (2.39) was 1.7 and the two persons were .5 unit apart on the θ-scale, the result would be 3.4 – the projected number of standard error units for persons one unit apart on the θ-scale. This index is based on an assumption that the distance between individuals on the expected observed score scale increases linearly with increase in distance on the θ-scale. Although this is a good approximation when θ-values are close together, a review of typical test characteristic curves shows that it is not true in general. To avoid this assumption of a linear relationship, a measure of sensitivity for each value of θ is needed rather than one for each pair of θ-values. This measure can be obtained by taking the limit of the expression in (2.40) as θ_1 approaches θ_2. When θ_1 and θ_2 are very close to each other, the pooled standard error is approximately the same as the conditional standard error at that point on the θ-scale. Equation (2.40) then becomes

$$\lim_{\theta_1 \to \theta_2} \left(\frac{\mu_{y\,|\,\theta_2} - \mu_{y\,|\,\theta_1}}{\sigma_{y\,|\,\theta_1,\theta_2}(\theta_2 - \theta_1)} \right) = \frac{\frac{\partial \mu_{y\,|\,\theta}}{\partial \theta}}{\sigma_{y\,|\,\theta}}. \tag{2.41}$$

Values of the expression in (2.41) are functions of θ. They indicate how well differences in θ can be detected using the test items that produce the observed score, y. The value at a particular level of θ tells how far apart in standard error units are the observed scores that correspond to a one unit difference on the θ-scale at the point defined by the given value of θ.

Lord (1980), as well as other researchers, has shown that when the maximum likelihood estimator of θ is used as the reported score for a test, then the reciprocal of the square of the function given in (2.41) is equal to the asymptotic variance of the maximum likelihood estimate. The squared value of the function is called the amount of information provided by the estimate about the true value of θ. While some researchers initially preferred the values directly from (2.41) (e.g., Samejima 1982), most texts now call the square of the expression the information function for the scoring formula y. The function is indicated by

$$I(\theta, y) = \frac{\left[\frac{\partial E(y\,|\,\theta)}{\partial \theta}\right]^2}{\sigma^2_{y\,|\,\theta}}. \tag{2.42}$$

When the observed score of interest is the 0,1-score on a single dichotomous test item, the information function simplifies to

$$I(\theta, u_i) = \frac{\left[\frac{\partial P_i(\theta)}{\partial \theta}\right]^2}{P_i(\theta) Q_i(\theta)}, \tag{2.43}$$

where u_i is the score for Item i, $P_i(\theta)$ is the probability of correct response for the item, and $Q_i(\theta) = 1 - P_i(\theta)$. When the three-parameter logistic model accurately represents the interaction between the persons and test items, (2.43) becomes

$$I(\theta, u_i) = a_i^2 \frac{Q_i(\theta)}{P_i(\theta)} \left[\frac{P_i(\theta) - c_i}{1 - c_i}\right]^2. \tag{2.44}$$

When $c_i = 0$, this expression gives the information for the two-parameter logistic model, and in addition if $a_i = 1$, then the expression simplifies to the information function for the Rasch one-parameter logistic model. To show the effects of the parameters on the information function, the functions are shown graphically for

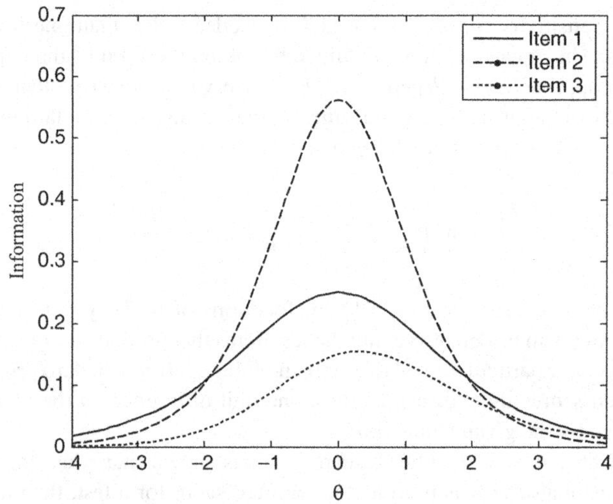

Fig. 2.19 Information functions for items following the Rasch, 2pl, and 3pl models

three items. All of the items have the same b parameter. Item 1 has $a_i = 1$ and $c_i = 0$. Item 2 has $a_i = 1.5$ and $c_i = 0$, and Item 3 has $a_i = 1$ and $c_i = .25$.

The solid curve shows the information function for the Rasch model. It has a maximum at $\theta = 0$ with a value of .25. Increasing the a-parameter to 1.5 increases the maximum of the curve by a^2, 2.25, to .5625. The inclusion of a nonzero lower asymptote reduces the information and shifts it to the higher levels of θ. Multiple-choice test items tend to have lower information than open-ended test items that are scored 0,1 because of the possibility of responding correctly by chance (Fig. 2.19).

Lord (1980, p. 70) shows that the information provided by the set of items in a test about the level of θ is equal to the sum of the information provided by each of the items. This is a consequence of the local independence assumption. Thus, the information from a test is given by

$$I(\theta) = \sum_{i=1}^{n} \frac{\left[\frac{\partial P_i(\theta)}{\partial \theta}\right]^2}{P_i(\theta)Q_i(\theta)}, \tag{2.45}$$

where n is the number of items on the test. Lord also shows that the test information given by (2.45) is an upper bound on the information that can be obtained by any method of scoring the test. Also, the reciprocal of the information is equal to the asymptotic sampling variance of the estimator of θ if the estimator is statistically unbiased as well. This is a characteristic of maximum likelihood estimators.

It is well known in the statistical literature (e.g., Cramér 1946, p. 500) that the maximum likelihood estimate of a parameter, in this case θ, is distributed with a mean equal to θ, and variance equal to

$$\sigma^2(\hat{\theta} \mid \theta) = \frac{1}{E\left[\left(\frac{\partial \ln L}{\partial \theta}\right)^2_\theta\right]}, \tag{2.46}$$

where L is the likelihood of the data given the parameter – in this case, the likelihood of the item responses given θ. Lord (1980) shows that the term in the denominator of (2.46) is equal to the test information when items are well fit by a dichotomous IRT model. The reciprocal of the variance of the maximum likelihood estimator was labeled as information by Fisher (1925) so the general formulation of information presented here is often called Fisher information (e.g., Baker and Kim 2004). Fisher (1925) considered the variance of the estimate as a measure of "intrinsic accuracy."

The concepts of information about θ have been generalized to tests composed of polytomous items that are well modeled by the graded response model or the generalized partial credit model. Muraki (1993) described the information function for the generalized partial credit model. Using the definition of terms provided in (2.31) and (2.33) and simplifying the notation to represent $\mathrm{P}(u_{ij} = k|\theta_j)$ by $\mathrm{P}_{ik}(\theta_j)$, the expression for the information from an item that is accurately modeled by the generalized partial credit model is

$$I(\theta_j, u_i) = D^2 a_i^2 \sum_{k=0}^{m_i} \left[k - E(u_{ij} \mid \theta_j)\right]^2 P_{ik}(\theta_j). \tag{2.47}$$

Note that the expression for information includes the constant, D, to make the results similar to that for the normal ogive version of the model. If a_i is set equal to .588 to that $Da_i = 1$, the expression gives the information function for the partial credit model. Plots of the item information corresponding to the test items represented in (2.11) are presented in Fig. 2.20.

The plot shows the dramatic effect of the change in a-parameter for the item. Because the information increases with the square of the a-parameter, the information is dramatically higher where the score characteristic curves are steepest. The peaks of the information function can be shifted to the right or left by changing the b-parameter for the item. An item with parameters like these would be best for measuring the trait level for a person in the area near 1.0 on the θ-scale. The variance of the error in the maximum likelihood estimate of the trait would be reduced substantially be administering the item to persons in that range of the scale.

The information function for the graded response model was derived by Samejima (1969). She showed that the information for a test item that is well modeled by the graded response model was a weighted sum of the information from each of the response alternatives. Using the simplified notation that $P^*_{ik}(\theta_j) = P^*(u_{ij} = k \mid \theta_j)$ and $Q^*_{ik}(\theta_j) = 1 - P^*_{ik}(\theta_j)$ (see (2.34)), the expression

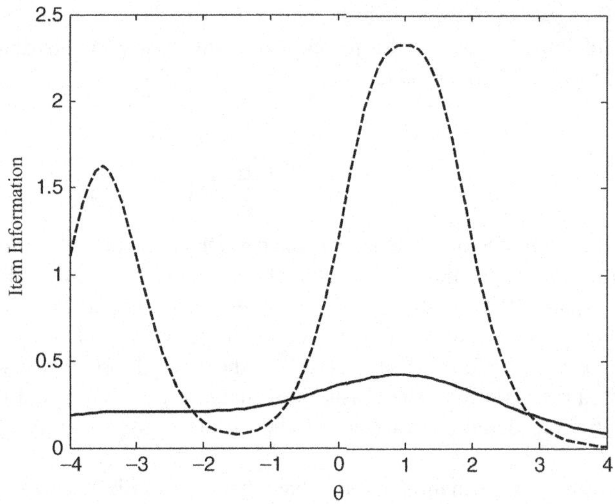

Fig. 2.20 Item information for the generalized partial credit model for items with parameters for $b = -.5$, $ds = 0, 3, -1, -2$, and $a = .5$ (*solid curve*) and 1.5 (*dashed curve*)

for the information provided by a test item is

$$I(\theta_j, u_i) = \sum_{k=1}^{m+1} \frac{[Da_i P^*_{i,k-1}(\theta_j) Q^*_{i,k-1}(\theta_j) - Da_i P^*_{ik}(\theta_j) Q^*_{ik}(\theta_j)]^2}{P^*_{i,k-1}(\theta_j) - P^*_{ik}(\theta_j)}. \quad (2.48)$$

Note that the terms in the numerator of (2.48) are the expressions for the information function for the two parameter logistic model. That model is used to define the cumulative category response functions for the graded response model. Also, this form of the information function includes the constant D so that the logistic form of the information function will yield similar results to the normal ogive form.

A plot of the information functions for the graded response test items used in Fig. 2.15 is presented in Fig. 2.21. The plot shows the clear effect of increasing the a-parameter and the shift in the b-parameters. The plot also shows that the information plot is not unimodal. This has important implications for item selection. For example, adaptive tests often select items that have maximum information at the current estimate of θ. When the information function is multimodal it is not clear how items should be selected to maximize information.

There is a growing literature on the use of IRT models for polytomous items. The reader is encouraged to seek out current articles on applications of polytomous IRT models for descriptions of recent work in this area. Also, Lord (1980) provides an extensive discussion of the concept of information in the IRT context. There is also an emerging literature on other forms of information functions in addition to the Fisher information described here. For example, there has been recent in-

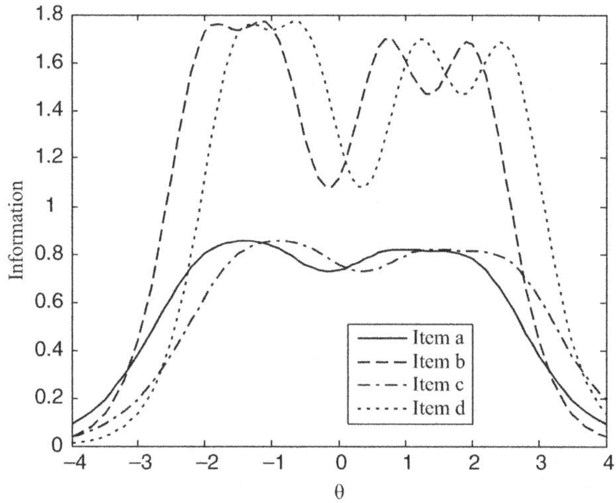

Fig. 2.21 Information functions for items modeled by the logistic version of the graded response model with (**a**) $a_i = 1$ (*solid line*) and (**b**) 1.5 (*dashed line*), and b_{ik}'s $= -2, -1, .7, 2$ and (**c**) $a_i = 1$ (*broken line*) and (**d**) 1.5 (*dotted line*), and b_{ik}'s $= -1.5, -.5, 1.2, 2.5$

terest in Kullback-Leibler information as an alternative to Fisher information (e.g., Savalei 2006; Chang and Ying 1996). A full discussion of alternative definitions for item and test information is beyond the scope of a summary chapter on unidimensional IRT.

2.3 Limitations of Unidimensional IRT Models

The previous sections of this chapter provide a summary of common unidimensional IRT models and the statistics used to describe the interactions of examinees with items and tests. These models have the advantages of having fairly simple mathematical forms, of having numerous examples of applications, and of having evidence that they are somewhat robust to violations of assumptions. Yet, it is likely that the actual interactions between persons and test items are not as simple as implied by these models. Examinees are likely to bring more than a single ability to bear when responding to a particular test item and the problems posed by test items are likely to require numerous skills and abilities to determine a correct solution. This is especially true for measures of achievement in complex areas such as the natural sciences. Thus, although unidimensional IRT models have proven to be useful under certain conditions, there is a need for more complex IRT models that more accurately reflect the complexity of the interactions between examinees and test items.

One way to increase the capability of IRT models to describe the interactions of persons and test items is to hypothesize that persons vary on a wide range of traits. Subsets of those traits or abilities are important for performance on specific test items. Further, test items may require multiple skills and abilities to arrive at the correct response. An extension of unidimensional IRT models to describe situations where multiple skills and abilities are needed to respond to test items will provide a more accurate representation of the complexity of tests. IRT models of this type describe the interaction of vectors of traits or abilities with the characteristics of test items rather than assuming a single trait parameter. Because these models have multiple parameters for the person, they are called multidimensional item response theory (MIRT) models. Careful development of MIRT models should lead to better descriptions of the interactions between persons and test items than can be provided by unidimensional IRT models. The next chapters of this book describe a number of MIRT models and procedures for applying the models to practical testing problems. The material in those chapters build on the framework provided by the development of unidimensional IRT models. The close parallels between related concepts should aid the conceptual understanding of new concepts.

2.4 Exercises

1. The item characteristic curve for a dichotomously scored item was shown to be a nonlinear regression function predicting the item score from θ. Typical regression analysis with continuous variables makes assumptions about the distribution of errors of prediction. Describe the error of prediction distributions that result from the application of dichotomous IRT models. Do the error of prediction distributions for an IRT model have the same distributional forms assumed by regression analysis procedures? How does the answer affect the use of the hypothesis tests used with regression analysis for IRT applications?

2. Plot the ICCs and the TCC for items 1 to 5 in Table 2.1. Use the proportion correct metric for the vertical axis of the plot. Where does the TCC have the steepest slope? How does the shape of the TCC compare to the logistic form for the items?

3. Plot the information functions for two items described by the graded response model. The parameters for the items are (1) $a_i = 1$, $b_{ik} = -1, 0, 1$ and (2) $a_i = 1$, $b_{ik} = -1, 0, 2$. Describe the effect of increasing the difference between the b-parameters on the information for the items.

4. TCCs can sometimes have a lower slope for scores in the middle of the score range than for scores in the low or high score range. Select a set of items from Table 2.1 that you believe will have this relationship between slope and range of scores. Verify that your selection will yield this relationship by plotting the TCC for the set of items.

5. Five dichotomously scored open-ended items were calibrated along with the items in a 50 item test. These items will be used to produce a subscore for the test. The items were calibrated using the two-parameter logistic model. The item parameters are provided in the following table.

Item number	a-parameter	b-parameter
1	.75	−1.25
2	1.05	.45
3	.90	−.50
4	.75	.90
5	1.30	1.15

Specify two different patterns of 0,1 scores for the items that would yield exactly the same maximum likelihood estimate for θ. Explain why these different score patterns will give the same estimate. What response patterns will give indeterminate estimates of θ? Why?

6. Assume that a test item is accurately modeled by the Rasch model with a b-parameter equal to .5. Determine the value of the slope of the ICC for this item at −.5, 0, .5, 1, and 1.5. At which of these values of θ is the slope the greatest? What is the value of the slope at that point? At which value of θ is the slope the least? At what value(s) of θ will the slope be 0?

7. The graded response model or the generalized partial credit model specify the probability of a response conditional on θ. Suppose that θ has a normal distribution with mean 0 and standard deviation 1. Describe how to compute the proportion of scores from examinees sampled from this distribution that will fall into each score category.

8. A carefully selected sample of examinees all with θs of 0 are administered two test items that are well fit by the Rasch model with $b = 0$. What is the expected correlation between the responses to the two items for this group of individuals? Explain how you determined that value. The same two test items are also administered to a sample of examinees half of whom have θ-values of $+1$ and half with θ-values of -1. What correlation between the item responses would be expected for the second group? Explain why the results are different.

9. Three persons with different θ-parameters, θ_1, θ_2, and θ_3, take the same test item. Their probabilities of correct response are .25, .5, and .75, respectively. If the test item is well modeled by the Rasch model with $b = 0$, what are the three θ values? If the item is well modeled by the 2PL model with $a = .9$ and $b = 0$, what are the three θ values? If the item is well modeled by the 3PL model with $a = .9$, $b = 0$, and $c = .2$, what are the three θ values? Are all the triples of θ values the same or different? Explain this result.

Chapter 3
Historical Background for Multidimensional Item Response Theory

Multidimensional item response theory (MIRT) is the result of the convergence of ideas from a number of areas in psychology, education, test development, psychometrics, and statistics. Two general themes underlie the influence of these ideas on the development of MIRT. The first theme is that as our understanding of these areas increases, it becomes clear that things are more complicated than originally thought. The second theme is that the complexity can be represented by models or theories, but these theories and models are idealizations of reality. Because they are idealizations, they can likely be proven false if tested using a large number of observations. Nevertheless, the models can give useful approximations with many practical applications.

It is common in the development of scientific theories to collect data about a phenomenon and then to develop an idealized model of the phenomenon that is consistent with the data. The idealized model is usually presented as a mathematical equation. An example of this approach to theory development is reported in Asimov (1972, p. 158). He describes Galileo in a church observing the swing of lamps hanging from the ceiling by long chains. These lamps were swinging like pendulums, and Galileo is reported to have recorded the length of time it took to make one full swing using his own pulse rate. From these observations, he developed a mathematical formula that related the length of the chain to the length of time for each swing (period) of a pendulum.

His model of the motion of pendulums was an idealization of reality in that it did not take into account such factors as wind resistance and the elasticity of the chain used to support the lamps. He also did not have a fully developed theory of the swing of a pendulum in three-dimensional space. The model did not give an absolutely precise description of the observed phenomenon, the swing of the pendulum. Yet, despite the lack of precision, the mathematical model was, and still is, useful as a description of the operational characteristics of pendulums.[1]

The same process of developing mathematical models to describe observed phenomenon was used by psychologists and statisticians such as Ebbinghaus (1885)

[1] The approximation formula for the period of an ideal simple pendulum is $p = 2\pi\sqrt{\frac{\text{length}}{g}}$, where g is the acceleration due to gravity. The approximation holds when the angle of swing is small.

M.D. Reckase, *Multidimensional Item Response Theory*, Statistics for Social and Behavioral Sciences, DOI 10.1007/978-0-387-89976-3_3,
© Springer Science+Business Media, LLC 2009

and Galton (1870). They observed various characteristics of individuals and developed idealized models of the relationships among those characteristics. Their models were far from precise representations of the observed phenomena, but in many cases they yielded useful representations of the phenomena.

For each of these examples, the researchers did not expect the idealized models to describe every nuance of the observed phenomenon. Galileo probably did not expect his mathematical equation to describe the period of swing for a pendulum with a very light weight and a large cross-sectional area because air resistance was not included as an element in his model. The focus of his work was to provide a model of the phenomenon for most practical applications of pendulums. Such models are idealizations of the relationships present among the observed phenomenon in that erratic features have been smoothed out along with components that have very minor effects on the relationships of interest. The same approach is followed when developing a mathematical model for the interactions between persons and test items. The focus is on the major features of the relationship, rather than on the components of the interaction that account for small perturbations. Even these idealized models can often yield information that helps understand the principles underlying observed phenomenon, in this case, the responses to test items.

A convenient way to represent idealized models is through mathematical expressions. The observed phenomena are quantified and the hypothesized model is stated as a functional relationship between the observations and characteristics of the situation. In general, these mathematical models take the following form:

$$y = f(\mathbf{x}), \tag{3.1}$$

where y is the observation of interest and $\mathbf{x}$ is a vector of variables that describe the conditions under which the observation was made.

When using idealized models, it is not expected that y will be predicted with absolute accuracy by the application of the function to the elements of the vector $\mathbf{x}$. It is only expected that a good approximation for y will be determined. Nor is the mathematical model thought to be "true" in an absolute sense. It is expected that as more observations are made, a more refined model will be developed. At best, it is expected that the model will be useful for describing the relationship between observations and the conditions of observation, or provide insights into the relationships among observed variables.

MIRT is a model or theory that is an idealization of reality. It gives only an approximation to the relationship between persons' capabilities and the responses to test items. The theory states that a particular mathematical expression can give a reasonably accurate representation of the relationship between persons' locations in a multidimensional space and the probabilities of their responses to a test item. At this stage in the development of MIRT, the mathematical expressions used to model the relationships are fairly simple. As more is learned about people and test items, it is likely that more complex mathematical expressions will be used that more closely represent the relationships between persons' abilities and the characteristics of test items. Despite the fact that MIRT models are a simplification of reality, they are still useful. Later chapters of this book will provide examples of the application of MIRT methodologies to practical testing problems.

In some cases, models for phenomenon do not work directly with the observation of interest. For example, when modeling the relationship between temperature and the pressure on a fixed amount of gas, the observation that is used is not the rate of molecular motion or the energy level of the gas. Rather, it is the height of the surface of a liquid in a glass tube such as a mercury thermometer, or the expansion of metals in a bimetal thermometer. The thermometers give a representation of temperature, but the expansion of liquid or metal is not really temperature or heat. Further, the height of the surface of the liquid or expansion of metal is measured on an arbitrary numerical scale such as the Celsius temperature scale.

Work in educational and psychological measurement has followed the same developmental path as other areas of science. Many idealized models have been hypothesized for the observed phenomenon, usually responses to test items, and characteristics of persons (see van der Linden and Hambleton 1997, for many examples). The characteristics of the persons are usually measures of hypothetical constructs. The models often relate the probability of a response to person characteristics rather than to the response itself. This is similar to using the height of liquid to represent temperature rather than measuring the energy in molecular movement. When modeling item/person interactions, working with probabilities allows simpler mathematical models and acknowledges the uncertainty in the hypothesized relationships. Because the models relate probabilities of test item responses to the characteristics of persons, they are called "item response theory" (IRT) models.

The later chapters of this book present a collection of mathematical models that are useful for describing the interactions between persons and test items. These models differ from many of the other IRT models in that they posit that multiple hypothetical constructs influence the performance on test items instead of only one hypothetical construct. Therefore, they are labeled MIRT models (Reckase et al. 1988). As with other IRT models, the actual observations that are the focus of the models are the responses to test items. In most cases, the models are for scored test items rather than the actual response. The most commonly used models are for items scored using two categories – correct and incorrect – although MIRT models for items with more than two score categories also exist (see Chap. 4 for some examples). MIRT models probabilities of responses rather than the actual responses. The basic form of the models considered here is

$$P(U = u|\boldsymbol{\theta}) = f(u, \boldsymbol{\theta}, \boldsymbol{\gamma}), \tag{3.2}$$

where U is the score on the test item for a particular person, u represents the value of the assigned score from among the possible scores to the test item, $\boldsymbol{\theta}$ is a vector of parameters describing the location of the person in the multidimensional space, and $\boldsymbol{\gamma}$ is a vector of parameters describing the characteristics of the test item.

The item score, u, is included on the right side of the expression because the form of the prediction equation may change depending on the score a person receives for his or her response to the test item. Of course, if the score on the item rather than the probability of the score were being predicted, the presence of the score on both sides of the equal sign would form a trivial tautology. Because the probability is being predicted, the presence of u on the right side of the expression is a convenient way to select the desired prediction equation.

None of the models presented here is believed to be a true representation of the psychological processes that underlie the interaction between a person and a test item. In all cases, it is expected that with the collection of enough data, all of the models can be shown to be false. However, one purpose of this book is to summarize the research that shows when these models provide useful idealizations of the relationship between hypothetical constructs and observed phenomena – latent traits and responses to test items. The criteria for usefulness are whether the models yield reasonably accurate predictions of actual observations or if they help reach an understanding of the interrelationships among variables of interest.

The remaining sections of this chapter will provide a historical context that underlies the development of the MIRT models. Both the psychological context that led to thinking about many dimensions of variation in the cognitive skills for people and the psychometric context that led to the development of multidimensional modeling procedures are presented. Although unidimensional IRT can legitimately be thought of as part of the psychometric context for MIRT, it is not included in this chapter. Rather, Chap. 2 gave a summary of the unidimensional IRT concepts that are helpful for understanding the development of MIRT concepts.

3.1 Psychological and Educational Context for MIRT

As with other areas of science and technology, psychological and educational testing first developed relatively simple theories and testing methods to obtain the quantitative variables needed to further develop those theories. Early models of atoms considered them as solid balls. Current models of the atom have numerous small particles and energy fields within the atom.

MIRT methodology developed in response to a realization that psychological and educational processes are very complex. This complexity became evident through the findings from many years of research. For example, in the 1950s, psychological research on memory focused on “immediate memory” and “chunking” (Deese 1958). The rule of thumb that individuals could remember about seven things after a single presentation was being investigated to determine what constitutes a “thing.” In contrast, the 1996 volume of the *Annual Review of Psychology* contains a 25 page summary on the topic of memory (Healy and McNamara 1996) that includes concepts such as primary and secondary memory stores, associative memory, permastore, and precategorical acoustic store. Current memory models are much more complex than those in the past, and they are likely to be more complex in the future.

The study of variation in the cognitive abilities of people shows a similar pattern of increase in complexity as greater understanding is attained. Vernon (1950,

p. 49) stated that "no intellectual faculties beyond *g* [general ability] and *v* [verbal ability] are yet established as having much educational or vocational importance." In contrast to this relatively simple conception of abilities, Carroll (1993, p. 147) identifies 15 factors related to language ability. Many of those factors have many "token" factors. For example, verbal or printed language comprehension (*V* in Carroll's notation) has 150 token factors. Clearly, the psychological conceptualization of cognitive abilities has become much more complex as the result of continuing research. Other achievement and aptitude areas have equally complex structures. Further, research in cognitive sciences (e.g., Frederikson et al. 1990) shows that many skills are needed to respond correctly to single test items.

There is a similar pattern in the development of educational concepts. The early conception of reading comprehension was "How much did the child get out of what he read?" (Burgess 1921, p. 18). Reading skill was assessed by having students read a story and write as much as they could remember (Kallon 1916). The current conception of reading comprehension is much more complex. The 2005 National Assessment of Educational Progress (NAEP) describes fourth grade reading in this way (Perie et al. 2005).

> "reading . . . includes developing a general understanding of written text, thinking about texts, and using texts for different purposes. In addition [the Governing Board] views reading as an interactive and dynamic process involving the reader, the text, and the context of the reading experience." (p. 24)

NAEP assesses reading skill and knowledge using a complex set of item types including multiple-choice, open-ended, and extended response items. The implication is that the different item types are needed to assess the breadth of skills that encompass "reading." The reading passages on NAEP also vary in a number of different ways including the type of content, the structure of the writing (i.e., narrative, argumentative, etc.), and the length. The conceptual understanding of reading has changed in dramatic ways since 1921. The trend has been to consider it a more complex process requiring multiple skills.

3.2 Test Development Context for MIRT

The process for developing tests has become more complicated over the years. Early tests consisted of sets of tasks that were selected in unspecified ways. Whipple (1910, p. 460) describes the procedures for administering and scoring many early tests. One example is an assessment of size of a student's vocabulary. Students were given a list of 100 words and they were asked to write a definition for each. The results were scored by counting the number of correct definitions. The results were converted to a proportion correct and that number was multiplied by 28,000 to give an estimate of the size of the student's vocabulary. The number 28,000 was used because it was assumed to be the maximum size for a person's vocabulary. No information was given about how the words were selected, but they included some interesting choices like "amaranth" and "eschalot."

Current test development processes are much more complex, not only because of more elaborate conceptions of the constructs to be measured, but also because of the level of detail provided in test specifications. Millman and Greene (1989) provide a thorough description of the test development process. Their 32 page chapter includes substantial discussions of the development of test specifications and the match of item types to the specific content. More recent work demonstrates even more dramatically the complexity of current test development procedures. van der Linden (2005) indicates that computerized test assembly procedures sometimes have hundreds of constraints that must be met when selecting items for a test.

There is a certain irony in the evolution of the scoring of tests. Thorndike (1904) found it obvious that different test items required different amounts of skill and knowledge and they should be scored to reflect their complexity. Yet, the major tests that were developed in the early 1900s treated items as equal units. The Army Alpha Tests (Yoakum and Yerkes 1920) clearly indicated that each item is scored either right or wrong and the score is the number right. The tests based on the work of Binet and Simon (1913) used very complex items, but Stern (1914) indicates that responding correctly to five tests (his label for items) increased the mental age by 1 year. The advice from McCall (1922, pp. 249–250) was to produce a test that did not have zero scores or perfect scores and that had at least seven reporting categories. He further advised that there be at least 13 reporting categories if correlations were going to be computed. Although unstated, the implication was that the score on a test was the sum of the points allocated for each item. Different test items could have different numbers of allocated points. By 1950, little had changed about the scoring of tests. Gulliksen (1950) does not raise the issue of what the test is measuring but only assumes that "the numerical score is based on a count, one or more points for each correct answer and zero for each incorrect answer" (p. 4). Everything in his book on test theory is built on the characteristics of that type of score. He also laments that for most item analysis methods "no theory is presented showing the relationship between the validity or reliability of the total test and the method of item analysis" (p. 363).

With the implementation of item response theory methods, scoring has become more complex. Methods based on the two and three-parameter logistic models (see Chap. 2) give items different weights depending on the discriminating power of the items. The use of the three-parameter logistic model also reduces the relative impact of correct responses to that of incorrect responses on the estimates of proficiency because of the possibility that they may have been obtained by chance. The process of scoring tests using these models is called "pattern scoring" because different patterns of responses to the set of items on a test give different scores, even when the number of correct responses is the same. The book edited by Thissen and Wainer (2001) provides an extensive discussion of test scoring methodology.

The trend in test design and development, and test scoring is to consider the test item as the basic component of test design rather than the test as a whole. This is the basic difference between item response theory and true score theory. The former focuses on characteristics of test items and how they combine to make tests. The later assumes that a test has been constructed and focuses on the characteristics of test scores. MIRT continues the trend toward treating the test item as the fundamental unit of test construction. It extends the work from unidimensional IRT to give a more thorough description of the characteristics of test items and how the information from test items combines to provide a description of the characteristics of persons.

3.3 Psychometric Antecedents of MIRT

Depending on a psychometrician's background, MIRT may be considered as either a special case of multivariate statistical analysis, especially factor analysis or structural equation modeling, or as an extension of unidimensional IRT. These two conceptualizations of MIRT color the way that the methodology is applied and the way that the results of MIRT analyses are interpreted. Because of the strong connection of MIRT to both of these psychometric traditions, it is helpful to review the precursors to MIRT from both of these areas. The next sections of this chapter will summarize both perspectives and highlight the differences.

3.3.1 Factor Analysis

A review of the mathematical procedures used for factor analysis and MIRT will reveal that there are numerous similarities in the statistical underpinnings of the methods. Both methods define hypothetical scales that can be used to reproduce certain features of the data that are the focus of the analysis. For both of the procedures, the scales have arbitrary zero points (origins) and units of measurement. They also specify systems of coordinate axes that can be rotated to emphasize certain characteristics of the data. MIRT differs from most implementations of factor analysis in that the varying characteristics of the input variables (the items), such as difficulty level and discrimination, are considered to be of importance and worthy of study. Factor analysis implementations typically consider the differences in the characteristics of input variables as nuisances to be removed through transformations that standardize the variables to have common means and standard deviations. Because of the lack of interest in the characteristics of the variables in the analysis, most factor analysis texts begin with the analysis of a correlation matrix, a data source that ignores differences in means, and standard deviations of the variables. For example, Harman's (1976) classic work on factor analysis describes the purpose of the analysis as follows:

> "The principal concern of factor analysis is the resolution of a set of variables linearly in terms of (usually) a small number of categories or 'factors.' This resolution can be accomplished by the analysis of the correlations among the variables." (p. 4)

Even when factor analysis is applied to item scores, usually 0 or 1, the characteristics of the variables, such as difficulty and discrimination, are not considered.

In fact, a major motivation for some of the variations in factor analysis procedures described later is dealing with difficulty factors. These were factors that resulted from variation in difficulty of dichotomously scored test items. The difficulty factors were a consequence of the relationship between proportion correct for the test items and the magnitude of the Pearson product-moment correlation between test items. Only test items with proportions correct of .5 can have correlations of 1. Similarly, tetrachoric correlations have more unstable estimates when the cells of a two-by-two table of scores on test items have near zero frequencies.

Another issue related to the characteristics of test items is the possibility that a person might guess the correct answer. Factor analysis does not usually have any way to adjust for the possibility of guessing on multiple-choice test items. Rather, guessing is considered as another nuisance feature of the data that should be removed through a correction to the process of computing the correlations (Carroll 1945).

As with any scientific endeavor, experts in a field do not always agree on an approach or basic philosophy. This is also true for those developing the factor analysis methodology. Several researchers chose to address the problem of how to identify hypothetical variables that would allow the reproduction of the relationships in the data from a slightly different perspective than most others. The contributions of five researchers are described here because their work contributed to the foundations for MIRT. These individuals should be considered as representatives of a set of contributors rather than the sole proponents of a point of view. Many others, no doubt, had similar perspectives on factor analysis. These five were selected because they were the most visible in the literature and were most active in advancing their perspective over a period of years.

Horst

Paul Horst was one of the early contributors to the field of factor analysis who foreshadowed the development of MIRT. The major distinction between his approach and that of other factor analysts is that he advocated developing factor models that could reproduce the full data matrix rather than the correlation matrix. This perspective is described in detail in his book *Factor Analysis of Data Matrices* (Horst 1965). His perspective is summarized as follows.

> "It should be observed at the outset that most treatments of factor analysis do not, however, begin with a consideration of the x matrix [the matrix of observed scores] as such and the determination of the u matrix [the matrix of true scores]. These treatments usually begin with the correlation matrices derived from the x matrix. This approach has led to much misunderstanding because the analyses applied to the correlation matrix sometimes imply that there is more information in the correlation matrix than in the data matrix x. This can never be the case. For this reason, as well as others, it is much better to focus attention first on the data matrix, as such, in considering the problems and techniques of factor analysis." (p. 96)

Because Horst worked from the observed score matrix, he had to confront issues related to the characteristics of the variables. His book contains extended discussions of the issues of origin and unit of measurement and the effects of scaling transformations on factor analysis results. More importantly for this discussion of MIRT, he argued against trying to standardize the variables when factor analyzing a binary data matrix. Rather, he suggested partialing out the effects of variation in item difficulty, or as he called it, the "dispersion of item preferences." This procedure is called "partialing out the simplex" and it is conceptually similar to estimating the difficulty parameters of the items and using the estimates to model the data.

Although there are many similarities between Horst's work and current conceptions of MIRT, he did not quite get to the point of developing MIRT models. He was attempting to recover the actual data rather than the probability of a response and he did not consider factor loadings as item parameters. The emphasis of the analysis was on the factors – the coordinate system, rather than item characteristics and person locations.

Christoffersson and Muthén

The methodologies developed by Christoffersson (1975) and Muthén (1978) are conceptually closer to current thinking about MIRT than those presented by Horst (1965). They produced probabilistic models for the relationship between item responses and vectors of person parameters. Both used a normal ogive model to obtain estimates of threshold parameters for items. The threshold parameters are the normal deviate values that specified the area beneath the normal curve equal to the proportion of incorrect responses to the items. These parameters are essentially the same as the item difficulty parameters for a MIRT model.

Christoffersson (1975) states: "we see that the model $[p = \pi + \varepsilon]^2$ expresses the observed proportions p in terms of the threshold levels $z_i, i = 1, 2, \ldots, n$, the loadings $\mathbf{A}$, the factor correlations $\mathbf{R}$ and a random component ε." π is given by the following equation involving the integral of the normal density

$$\pi_i = P(u_i = 1) = \int_{z_i}^{\infty} \frac{1}{\sqrt{2\pi}} \mathrm{e}^{-\frac{t^2}{2}} \mathrm{d}t, \tag{3.3}$$

where u_i is the item score on Item i, and z_i is the threshold parameter for Item i.

Christoffersson's formulation of the relationship between item responses and hypothetical latent variables uses factor loadings and threshold estimates as item

[2] The original presentations of factor analytic and IRT models used a wide variety of symbols to represent the parameters of the models. To make comparisons of the models easier, the symbols have been changed to a common set. This means that the symbols used here may not match those in the original article.

parameters. These parameters are very similar to those used to describe the characteristics of test items in MIRT. The major differences between Christoffersson's representation and MIRT are that he focused on modeling continuous item scores underlying the dichotomous observed scores rather than the locations of individuals in a multidimensional space. Further, the probabilities of correct response in the model are not conditional on the location of a person in the multidimensional space as they are in current MIRT models (see Chap. 4). Instead, the focus is on the probability of correct responses for the entire population of examinees.

Muthén (1978) expanded on Christofferson's work. He developed a model that included both the probability of correct response for a single item for the examinee population and the probability that the examinee population would give correct responses to pairs of items. These probabilities were included in a single vector, **p**, with the first n elements containing the probabilities for single items and the next $n(n-1)/2$ elements containing the probabilities for correct responses to each possible pair of items. Muthén's model is

$$\mathbf{p} = f(\eta) + \boldsymbol{e}, \tag{3.4}$$

where η is partitioned into two parts, (η_1', η_2'), η_1' is an n-dimensional vector of thresholds, η_2' is a $n(n-1)/2$ element vector of population tetrachoric correlations between items, and **e** is a matrix of errors in predicting the probabilities. The function, $f\,()$, relates the probabilities using the univariate or bivariate normal density function to the descriptive characteristics of the test items. As in the work of Christofferson, the population probabilities of correct responses were modeled rather than the conditional probabilities for persons with specified vectors of location parameters.

Both Christofferson and Muthén came very close to presenting the current formulation for MIRT. However, neither of their models was based on the conditional probability of correct response to each item as a function of a person's location in a multidimensional space. Rather, they modeled the probability of correct response for the full population of examinees.

McDonald

The nonlinear factor analysis methodology proposed by McDonald (1967) is probably the presentation of factor analysis that is most similar to the current conception of MIRT. McDonald addressed the problem of factor analyzing variables that have values of 0 or 1. He indicated that concerns about the appearance of difficulty factors when dichotomous data are analyzed could be overcome if the relationship between the observed data and the hypothetical factors is allowed to be nonlinear. McDonald also clearly specified the important concept of local independence as the basis for the analysis of test items.

The general form of the principle of local independence is

$$h(\mathbf{x}|\boldsymbol{\theta})\prod_{i=1}^{n} h_i(x_i|\boldsymbol{\theta}), \tag{3.5}$$

where $\mathbf{x}$ is the vector of observed responses, $\boldsymbol{\theta}$ is the vector of latent"characterizations," and $h(\mathbf{x}|\boldsymbol{\theta})$ is the conditional density of the observed response vector given the latent "characterizations." In current terminology, McDonald's "characterizations" are abilities or proficiencies needed to respond correctly to the test item.

McDonald also represented the basic form of the relationship between the probability of correct response to an item and the coordinates of the location of persons in the ability space as the regression of the item score on ability. He also noted that the connection between the regression function and the conditional probability of correct response is

$$P_i(\boldsymbol{\theta}) \equiv E(u_i|\boldsymbol{\theta}), \tag{3.6}$$

where $P_i(\boldsymbol{\theta})$ is the probability of correct response to Item i.

The difference between McDonald's (1967) formulation and current MIRT representations is that he used a polynomial model to represent the interaction of persons with a test item rather than the logistic or normal ogive models. The polynomial model was used as an approximation to the normal ogive model. Also, he did not provide any interpretation for the item parameters. The focus was on estimating the factors rather than understanding the characteristics of the items or the interactions between persons and items. More recent work by McDonald (1985, 1999) makes the relationship between factor analysis and MIRT very clear. In fact, McDonald considers factor analysis as a special case of latent trait theory. "The view taken here is that common factor analysis is really a special case of latent trait theory, based on the principle of local independence, but one in which for convenience only the weak zero-partial-correlation version of the principle is typically tested" (McDonald 1985).

Bock and Aitkin

The methodology presented in Bock and Aitken (1981) provided the convergence of ideas from IRT and factor analysis that resulted in MIRT. They defined a normal ogive model for a multidimensional ability space that included characterizations of test items using both factor analytic and IRT representations. Their model is given by

$$P(x_{ij} = 1|\boldsymbol{\theta}_j) = \frac{1}{\sqrt{2\pi}} \int_{-z_i(\boldsymbol{\theta}_j)}^{\infty} e^{-\frac{t^2}{2}} \mathrm{d}t, \tag{3.7}$$

where $z_i(\boldsymbol{\theta}_j) = d_i + \mathbf{a_i}\boldsymbol{\theta}_\mathbf{j}'$, $\mathbf{a}_i$ is the $1 \times m$ vector of item discrimination parameters for Item i, d_i is a scalar parameter related to the difficulty of Item i, and $\boldsymbol{\theta}_\mathbf{j}$ is a $1 \times m$ vector of proficiencies for Person j. The parameters of the model have the same meaning and interpretation as the current MIRT parameterization.

Bock and Aitken demonstrated the use of this model through an analysis of test items from the *Law School Admissions Test (LSAT)* Section 7. The item difficulty and discrimination parameters were estimated, but they were labeled as slopes and intercepts. The only distinction between the Bock and Aitken (1981) analysis and a full MIRT conceptualization was the interpretation of the item parameters as descriptive measures that were useful for describing the interactions of persons and test items. The item parameters were still used in a factor analytic sense as a means to help label the factors.

Although the model presented in Bock and Aitken (1981) is essentially a MIRT model, its major use was as a factor analytic model as shown in Bock, Gibbons, and Muraki (1988). The emphasis was still on defining factors rather than investigating the interactions between persons and items.

3.3.2 Item Response Theory

The focus of item response theory (IRT) is quite different than that of factor analysis. Rather than trying to determine the minimum number of factors that can reproduce the data in a matrix of item responses, IRT analyses try to model the relationship between persons' characteristics and the features of test items. Lord (1980) expressed the goal of IRT this way.

> "We need to describe the items by item parameters and the examinees by examinee parameters in such a way that we can predict probabilistically the response of any examinee to any item, even if similar examinees have never taken similar items before."

Early work in IRT was based on the assumption that the parameter that describes the examinees varies on only one dimension (Lord and Novick 1968; Rasch 1960), but it quickly became apparent that the unidimensionality assumption was often violated. Work still continues on determining the consequences of violating the unidimensionality assumption (e.g., Camilli et al. 1995; Kirisci et al. 2001; Wang and Wilson 2005).

The remainder of this section presents some early attempts to consider multidimensionality in IRT. The final section of this chapter provides a direct comparison of the IRT perspective with the factor analysis perspective.

Rasch

The earliest published work of Rasch (1960) dealt only with unidimensional IRT models. However, in 1962 he presented a generalization of his initial models that included the possibility that the ability of the examinee could be represented by a vector or proficiencies rather than by a scalar (Rasch 1962). The general Rasch model is given by

$$P(u_{ij}|\boldsymbol{\theta}_\mathbf{j}, \boldsymbol{\eta}_\mathbf{i}) = \frac{1}{\gamma(\boldsymbol{\theta}_\mathbf{j}, \boldsymbol{\eta}_\mathbf{i})} e^{f(u_{ij})'\boldsymbol{\theta}_\mathbf{j} + g(u_{ij})'\boldsymbol{\eta}_\mathbf{i} + \boldsymbol{\theta}_\mathbf{j}'h(u_{ij})\boldsymbol{\eta}_\mathbf{i} + \ell(u_{ij})}, \tag{3.8}$$

where *f*, *g*, *h*, and ℓ are scoring functions for the item. That is, the functions indicate how the items are scored for each proficiency dimension, each dimension of sensitivity of the items, and the interaction of the two types of dimensions. The function "*f*" indicates the score that corresponds to each item response for each dimension in $\boldsymbol{\theta}$. For the unidimensional Rasch model, only two scores are given to the item – 1 for a correct response and 0 for an incorrect response. The function "*g*" indicates the weights given to the item parameters for each dimension for each item. For the unidimensional model, these are 1 for a correct response and 0 for an incorrect response. The function "*h*" gives weights for the interaction between person and item parameters. The value of this function is 0 for all responses for the unidimensional model. The function "ℓ" allows for a fixed constant term for the item. This function is set to 0 for all responses for the unidimensional model. All of these functions are fixed in advance of the application of the model rather than estimated from the data. Fixing these functions maintains the critical property of the Rasch model of having observable sufficient statistics for the person and item parameters. The function "γ" generates a normalizing constant that is the sum of all of the possible exponential terms. Dividing by this function causes the probabilities for the possible responses to sum to 1.0.

The different functions in the general Rasch model have been used by Fischer and Molenaar (1995) to develop complex linear logistic model. Reckase (1972) and Kelderman (1994) used the scoring functions to apply the model to what are now called "testlets" or for items with more than two score categories. Glas (1992) used the scoring functions to indicate the content dimensions measured by the items. More recent work, such as Rijmen and De Boeck (2005), also used this approach. Glas and Vos (2000) have used this model in an adaptive testing context. This model is described in more detail in Chap. 4.

Lord and Novick

The basic requirements for a MIRT model were presented in Chap. 16 of Lord and Novick (1968), although a complete MIRT model was not presented. The chapter includes definitions of a complete latent space and the assumption of local independence.

> Local independence means that within any group of examinees all characterized by the same values $\theta_1, \theta_2, \ldots, \theta_k$, the (conditional) distribution of the item scores are all independent of each other. (p. 361)

The vector $\boldsymbol{\theta}$ defines the complete latent space.

Lord and Novick (1968) also presented the relationship between the unidimensional normal ogive IRT model and the common factor model. It is notable, however, that the major portion of Chap. 16 is a discussion of the meaning of the item parameters and their use for solving practical testing problems. The focus is not on the meaning of factors resulting from the common factor model.

Samejima

Samejima (1974) gave another early presentation of a proposed MIRT model. Although most IRT models have been developed for items that are scored either dichotomously or polytomously, it is also possible to have items with scores on a continuous scale. Samejima generalized her continuous response model to the case with a $\boldsymbol{\theta}$ - vector. The model is given by

$$P_{z_i}(\boldsymbol{\theta}_\mathbf{j}) = \frac{1}{\sqrt{2\pi}} \int_{-\infty}^{\mathbf{a_i}'(\boldsymbol{\theta}_\mathbf{j}-\mathbf{b}_i)} \mathrm{e}^{-\frac{t^2}{2}} \mathrm{dt}, \tag{3.9}$$

where z_i is the continuous response to Item i, P is the probability of obtaining a score of z or better on Item i, $\mathbf{b}_i$ is a vector of difficulty parameters, with other parameters as previously defined.

Although the Samejima (1974) model is one of the first formal presentations of a MIRT model, it has not been widely used. Bejar (1977) provided the only application of the model that could be found. The lack of use is probably related to the rarity of applications for continuous response items.

3.3.3 Comparison of the Factor Analytic and MIRT Approaches

Factor analysis and MIRT have virtually identical statistical formulations when they are applied to matrices of item responses. This can be noted from a comparison of the models presented by Bock and Aitken (1981), Samejima (1974), and McDonald (1967). In fact, the software for the full information factor analysis methodology presented by Bock et al. (1988) can be used for either factor analysis or MIRT.

If the statistical procedures are virtually identical, what is the difference in the two types of methodology? First, factor analysis is thought of as a data reduction technique. The goal is usually to find the smallest number of factors that reproduces the observed correlation matrix. MIRT is a technique for modeling the interaction between persons and test items. Reckase and Hirsch (1991) have shown that using too few dimensions might degrade the modeling of the item/person interactions, but using too many dimensions does not cause serious problems. Thus, MIRT may be a better analysis tool when it is not thought of as a data reduction technique. It is a method for modeling the meaningful contributors to the interactions of people with test items.

Second, factor analysis typically ignores the characteristics of the input variables while MIRT focuses on them. Analyzing the correlation matrix implies that differences in means and variances of variables is of little or no consequence. On the one hand, newer versions of factor analysis, such as structural equation modeling, do consider means, variances, and covariances, but not for the purpose of getting a better understanding of the input variables. MIRT, on the other hand, focuses on the differences in means and variances of the item scores because they are directly related to important characteristics of test items such as difficulty and discrimination. These item characteristics are actively used in MIRT applications.

Finally, MIRT analyses actively work to find solutions that use the same latent space across tests and samples. The goal is to keep a common coordinate system for all analyses so that the items will have parameter estimates on common metrics. Having item parameters on a common metric support their storage in an item bank for use in test forms construction and computerized adaptive testing. Factor analysis procedures have developed some procedures for putting the solutions into common coordinate systems, but those methods are not widely used. Instead, factor analysis methods now emphasize confirmatory methods and structural equation modeling. The methods developed for factor analysis like Procrustes rotations are now being used to place MIRT solutions onto common scales. Such methods are an extension of unidimensional IRT methods for test equating and linking of calibrations. Developing methods for linking calibrations from different tests and examinee samples is a major part of the research on MIRT. These methods will be described in detail in Chap. 9 of this book.

3.4 Early MIRT Developments

In the late 1970s and early 1980s, a number of researchers were actively working to develop practical MIRT models. In addition to the work by Reckase (1972) on the multidimensional Rasch model (see (3.8)), Mulaik (1972), Sympson (1978), and Whitely (1980a,b) suggested multidimensional models for the item/person interaction.

The Mulaik (1972) model is given by

$$P(u_{ij}|\boldsymbol{\theta}_{\mathbf{j}},\boldsymbol{\eta}_{\mathbf{i}}) = \frac{\sum_{k=1}^{m} \mathrm{e}^{(\theta_{jk}-\eta_{ik})u_{ij}}}{1+\sum_{k=1}^{m} \mathrm{e}^{(\theta_{jk}-\eta_{ik})u_{ij}}}, \tag{3.10}$$

where the symbols have the meaning defined previously and $u_{ij} = 0$ or 1. This model has an interesting property. For fixed values of the exponent, the probability

Table 3.1 Relation of size of exponent to the number of dimensions for the Mulaik model, $P = .5$

Number of dimensions	Exponent of e
1	0
2	−.69
3	−1.10
4	−1.39
5	−1.61
6	−1.79
7	−1.95
8	−2.08
9	−2.20
10	−2.30

of a correct response increases with an increase in the number of dimensions. For example, if the person and item parameters are equal giving an exponent of 0, the probability of correct response is .5 if $m = 1$, but it increases to .67 for $m = 2$, and .75 for $m = 3$. In general, for an exponent of 0 for all dimensions, the probability of correct response is $m/(m + 1)$. This property of the model implies that if the probability of correct response is fixed, the values of the exponents will have to change as the number of dimensions increases. For example, Table 3.1 gives the value of the exponent x for the case where e^x is the same for each of the m dimensions and the probability of correct response is .5. Note that the exponent gets progressively smaller as the number of dimensions increases.

A model with a relationship between the number of dimensions and the size of the exponent that is in the opposite direction than the Mulaik (1972) model was proposed by Sympson (1978) and Whitely[3] (1980a). For this model, for fixed values of the exponent, the probability of correct response decreases with an increase in the number of dimensions. The version of the model presented by Sympson (1978) is given by

$$P(u_{ij} = 1|\boldsymbol{\theta}_\mathbf{j}, \mathbf{a}_\mathbf{i}, \mathbf{b}_\mathbf{i}, c_i) = c_i + (1 - c_i)\prod_{k=1}^{m} \frac{e^{a_{ik}(\boldsymbol{\theta}_{jk} - b_{ik})}}{1 + e^{a_{ik}(\theta_{jk} - b_{ik})}}, \tag{3.11}$$

where c_i is a scalar parameter that indicates the probability of correct response for persons with very low proficiency on all dimensions and the other parameters are as defined above. When the exponent for all of the terms in the product is 0, the probability of correct response is $c_i + (1 - c_i)(.5)^m$. As m increases, this expression converges to c_i.

As with the Mulaik (1972) model, the scaling of the item parameters changes with change in number of dimensions. Table 3.2 shows the value of the exponent of e as the number of dimensions increases for the special case when $c_i = 0$ and all of the exponents are equal. Because the probability of a correct response is based on

[3] Whitely now publishes under the name Embretson.

Table 3.2 Relation of size of exponent to the number of dimensions for the Sympson model, $P = .5$

Number of dimensions	Exponent of e
1	0
2	.9
3	1.3
4	1.7
5	1.9
6	2.1
7	2.3
8	2.4
9	2.5
10	2.6

the product of m terms and the terms are all less than 1.0, the terms must increase in value with increase in m to yield the same probability of correct response.

Reckase (1972) investigated the use of the general Rasch model given in (3.8) and determined that it was not possible to model multidimensional data from dichotomously scored items with that model unless the scoring functions were defined in advance of the estimation of the parameters. Instead, he grouped together sets of items to form what are now called testlets to allow the estimation of the scoring functions. Recent work (e.g., Wilson and Adams 1995) using the model in (3.8) has been based on fixing the scoring functions prior to estimating the model parameters. The scoring function is defined based on characteristics of the items such as relation to a common stimulus or having a common content framework.

McKinley and Reckase (1982) further considered variations on the model given in (3.8) and determined that the current multivariate form of the linear logistic model was the most useful and practical for exploratory analyses of data from tests composed of dichotomous items. The model as they presented it is given by

$$P(u_{ij} = 1|\boldsymbol{\theta}_\mathbf{j}, \mathbf{a}_\mathbf{i}, d_i) = \frac{\mathrm{e}^{\sum\limits_{k=1}^{m} a_{ik}\theta_{jk}+d_i}}{1 + \mathrm{e}^{\sum\limits_{k=1}^{m} a_{ik}\theta_{jk}+d_i}}, \tag{3.12}$$

where the symbols have the same meaning as in previous definitions. This model was labeled as a multivariate extension of the two-parameter logistic model because it has two item parameters – a vector of **a**-parameters (discrimination parameters) and a d−parameter. The two-parameter logistic model is described in the Chap. 2.

The model in (3.12) does not change scales for the parameters with the number of dimensions like those presented in (3.10) and (3.11) because the combination of dimensions is in the exponent of e. As long as the sum of the terms in the exponent has the same value, the probability of correct response stays the same. The number of dimensions does not have a direct effect on the probability. For example, if the exponent sums to 0, the probability of correct response is .5. Adding more terms to the sum in the exponent (i.e., adding more dimensions) without changing the value of the sum will not change the probability of a correct response.

3.5 Developing Applications of MIRT

The applications of MIRT have evolved since the early developments of the models. Initial applications focused on investigating the structure of relationships among item responses (e.g., Bock and Aitken 1981; McDonald 1967). The applications have evolved in a number of different ways since that time. A brief summary of some of the applications of MIRT is given here. The details of methodology for those applications are given in Chaps. 8–10. MIRT is a very active area of current research. Additional applications will no doubt appear in the research literature before the publication of this book. The journals *Psychometrika* and *Applied Psychological Measurement* often publish research articles on MIRT. Other journals that publish research on educational and psychological measurement are likely to have occasional articles on applications of the methodology.

Following the initial developments that followed the factor analytic tradition, Reckase (1985) and Reckase and McKinley (1991) developed ways of describing the results of a MIRT analysis that were more consistent with IRT conceptualizations. They developed graphic ways of describing the combinations of dimensions that are assessed by a test item, and ways of describing the difficulty and discrimination of items in a multidimensional context. These methods will be described in detail in Chap. 5 of this book.

The focus of MIRT analysis on the interaction of the characteristics of test items and those of examinees has naturally led to fine grained studies of the skills and abilities need to respond correctly to test items, and to determine the dimensions of sensitivity for test items. Miller and Hirsch (1992), for example, have analyzed a number of different tests using a combination of MIRT and cluster analysis to identify sets of test items that measure the same combination of skill and knowledge dimensions. The particular dimensions of sensitivity of the items were determined through detailed content analysis of the item text for the identified clusters of items. In some cases, the clusters of items accounted for less variance than would typically be considered meaningful through traditional factor analysis. Yet, the clusters were replicable over multiple samples of examinees and different tests. In some cases, these small clusters of items that accounted for small proportions of variance in a full sample were very important for identifying specific subsamples with special characteristics such as scholarship candidates. Since that early work, there have been numerous studies on the detailed structure of item response data. This area of research shows the importance of a thorough understanding of the ways that tests function.

MIRT analysis clearly shows that test items can be sensitive to examinee differences on multiple dimensions. If these differences are on dimensions that are goals of the assessment, the test is said to yield results that are valid indicators of the target dimensions. But items may be sensitive to other dimensions that are not the goals of the assessment. If subgroups of the examinee population differ on the dimensions that are other than the goal dimensions, sometimes called nuisance dimensions, then the reported results may include test bias. MIRT analyses can help identify group differences and item sensitivities that contribute to test and item bias. The results of MIRT analyses can help clarify the reasons for large differential item functioning (DIF) statistics. Ackerman (1992) provided a clear representation of DIF using MIRT models.

MIRT procedures have also been used to support the selection of items for a test so that the assumptions of unidimensional IRT will be met even when the items clearly require multiple skills and knowledge to determine the correct answer. This use of MIRT makes it possible to support the use of unidimensional IRT for a wide range of testing applications, such as measuring achievement in school subjects. Reckase et al. (1988) demonstrated the process of item selection that meets unidimensional IRT requirements. These results show that the unidimensionality assumption is not as restrictive as was once thought.

Another example of MIRT applications is the problem of putting calibrations of different sets of items into the same multidimensional coordinate system. This process is typically called linking of calibrations and it is closely related to the equating of test forms. Davey and Oshima (1994) and others have addressed this problem. Their work shows that it is possible to put the parameter estimates from multiple calibrations into the same coordinate system. This allows performance on different sets of items to be reported as profiles on multiple dimensions that are on the same scales. It is also possible to develop large pools of calibrated items that can be used for computerized adaptive testing and the construction of test forms that are multidimensionally parallel.

These and other applications are described in later chapters of this book. The application of MIRT to practical testing problems is a very active area of research, so the descriptions of these applications will necessarily be incomplete. New work is appearing with nearly every issue of journals such as *Applied Psychological Measurement* and *Psychometrika*. The reader is encouraged to read current issues of those journals to learn about recent work on MIRT applications.

3.6 Influence of MIRT on the Concept of a Test

This chapter has summarized the development of MIRT from its factor analytic and UIRT roots to the current conceptualization. The path of that development has lead to an increase in the emphasis on accurately modeling the item/person interaction and a reduced emphasis on simplification and data reduction as the goal of multidimensional analyses. The MIRT models define a complex multidimensional space for the purpose of describing individual differences in the target traits. Once defined, the multidimensional space can be used to study the effects of education and the functioning of cognitive processes. Items are considered as multidimensional probes for obtaining information about a person's location in a complex person space. Items need to be carefully crafted to be sensitive to the desired combinations of skills and knowledge, and then be carefully selected to help refine estimates of a person's vector of coordinates in the multidimensional space. Items are not interchangeable pieces that sum to a total test score.

MIRT analysis is still fairly early in its development. The goal of this book is to provide basic information about this important psychometric perspective and analysis methodology. But, the best is yet to come. Those who grasp these procedures likely will make important advances into the understanding of the ways that tests function. The prospect of that future work is indeed exciting.

3.7 Exercises

1. There are many situations in the application of statistical methodology where simplifying assumptions are made. For example, it is often assumed that distributions of observed variables follow the normal (Gaussian) distribution. Consider linear regression analysis. What assumptions are often made when applying linear regression that are not absolutely true in practice? List at least two such assumptions and explain what effects the assumptions likely have on the results of the analysis.

2. The following test item is an example from the 12th grade Science Assessment from the National Assessment of Educational Progress.

The table below gives information about the planets: their periods of revolution about the Sun and rotation about their axes.

Planet	Mean distance from the Sun (million kilometers)	Period of revolution (Earth time)	Period of rotation (Earth time)
Mercury	58	88 days	59 days
Venus	108	225 days	243 days
Earth	150	365 days	23.9 hs
Mars	228	687 days	24.6 hs

Which planet has the longest year in Earth time?

A. Mercury
B. Venus
C. Earth
D. Mars

Carefully analyze this test item to determine all of the skills and knowledge that are needed to arrive at the correct answer. List the skills and knowledge and consider how they are likely to be related to each other. That is, will they be correlated in the population of 12th grade examinees?

3. Items on a test analyzed using Christofferson's model (3.3) have the following threshold values. For each of those threshold values, what is the estimated proportion correct for the population of examinees?

z_i	π_i
−2	
−.8	
0	
1.2	

4. The probability of correct response for each item on a three item test for a person with ability $\boldsymbol{\theta}$ is given below. What should the probability of the response pattern 110 be for this person if local independence holds for this set of items?

Item	$P(u_i\,\|\,\boldsymbol{\theta})$
1	.80
2	.65
3	.44

5. Equation (3.10) shows the form of one of several possible mathematical models for the probability of correct response given person and item parameters. Suppose the probability of correct response for a person located at (θ_1, θ_2) is .5 for an item with η-parameters on both dimensions equal to 0. Determine the equation for the set of (θ_1, θ_2) points that will yield the probability of .5 and plot that equation over the range of θ-values from −4 to 4 for both coordinates. Describe the form of the plot.

6. Consider the models in (3.11) and (3.12) for the special case where all of the a-parameters are 1 and all other item parameters are 0. Suppose for the model in 3.12, θ_1 is 2. What must the θ_2 value be for the probability of correct response to be .5? For this (θ_1, θ_2) point, what is the corresponding probability of correct response for the model in (3.11)? Why are these results different and what implications do the results have for evaluating the usefulness of the two models?

Chapter 4
Multidimensional Item Response Theory Models

As the previous chapters suggest, it is not difficult to conceive of test items that require more than one hypothetical construct to determine the correct response. However, when describing multidimensional item response theory (MIRT) models, care should be taken to distinguish between dimensions as defined by MIRT models, which represent statistical abstractions of the observed data, and the hypothetical constructs that represent cognitive or affective dimensions of variation in a population of examinees. The earlier chapters present some of those distinctions. This chapter will elaborate on the distinctions between coordinates and constructs and the distinctions will be given additional treatment in Chaps. 6 and 7.

There are two major types of multidimensional item response theory models. The types are defined by the way the information from a vector of θ-coordinates is combined with item characteristics to specify the probability of responses to the item. One type of model is based on a linear combination of θ-coordinates. That linear combination is used with a normal ogive or logistic form to specify the probability of a response. The linear combination of θ-coordinates can yield the same sum with various combinations of θ-values. If one θ-coordinate is low, the sum will be the same if another θ-coordinate is sufficiently high. This feature of this type of model has been labeled as compensation and models with this property are typically called *compensatory models* to emphasize that property. Because of its common use, that terminology will be used here as a short-hand description for that type of model.

The second type of model separates the cognitive tasks in a test item into parts and uses a unidimensional model for each part. The probability of correct response for the item is the product of the probabilities for each part. The use of the product of probabilities results in nonlinear features for this class of models. Also, the fact that the probability of correct response can not exceed the highest of the probabilities in the product reduces the compensation of a high θ-coordinate for a low θ-coordinate. These models are often called *noncompensatory models* in the MIRT literature, but the term *partially compensatory* will be used here because a high θ-coordinate on one dimension does yield a higher probability of response than a low value on that dimension. Therefore, some compensation does occur.

Within these two major types of MIRT models, there are a number of model variations. This chapter describes both of these model types and their characteristics. The type based on the linear combination of θ-coordinates (compensatory models)

M.D. Reckase, *Multidimensional Item Response Theory*, Statistics for Social and Behavioral Sciences, DOI 10.1007/978-0-387-89976-3_4,
© Springer Science+Business Media, LLC 2009

is described first because of its close connection to factor analysis and because models of this type are more prevalent in the research literature.

A major component of variation within MIRT model type is the number of possible score points for the test items that are being modeled. The historic antecedents of MIRT presented in Chap. 3 dealt solely with models for items with two response categories. More recent work (e.g., Adams et al. 1997; Kelderman and Rijkes 1994; Muraki and Carlson 1993; Yao and Schwarz 2006) has extended unidimensional models for test items with more than two score categories to the multidimensional case. At this time, the MIRT models for polytomous items all fall within the category of compensatory models, but it is certainly possible that partially compensatory models for more than two score categories will be developed.

To provide a context for the MIRT models that will be presented in this chapter, two examples of dichotomously scored test items are provided. For these examples, it is assumed that all of the test items written for a test depend strictly on two underlying skill constructs that are labeled (1) arithmetic problem solving, and (2) algebraic symbol manipulation. These test items might also be considered to require skill in reading English, but that construct will be ignored for these examples to allow simple tabular presentation of the examples.

The fact that the items require capabilities on two constructs to determine the correct response to the items suggests that a trait space with two coordinate axes is needed to describe the variation in examinee responses to the set of items on the test. The coordinates for a specific examinee j for this space are indicated by $(\theta_{j1}, \theta_{j2})$. Further, the function P $(\theta_{j1}, \theta_{j2})$ will be used to indicate the probability of correct response to an item given the location of examine j in the space. In general, the coordinates $(\theta_{j1}, \theta_{j2})$ need not be associated with any hypothetical constructs, such as those listed earlier. Under some circumstances, however, it may be possible to align the coordinate axes with the hypothetical constructs. In such cases, estimation of the location of an examinee will also provide estimates of the levels on the constructs of interest. For example, θ_{j1} could be an estimate of the examinee's level on arithmetic problem solving and θ_{j2} could be an estimate of the examinee's level on algebraic symbol manipulation. For most of the MIRT models, estimates of the constructs range from $-\infty$ to $+\infty$ along the coordinate axes. Larger values indicate a greater capability on the construct than smaller values.

An example test item that requires both of the hypothesized constructs is given below.

1. A survey asked a sample of people which of two products they preferred. 50% of the people said they preferred Product A best, 30% said they preferred Product B, and 20% were undecided. If 1,000 people preferred Product A, how many people were undecided?

   A. 200
   B. 400
   C. 800
   D. 1,200
   E. 2,000

Table 4.1 Proportions of correct responses to Item 1 for 4,114 examinees

Midpoints θ_{j1}	Midpoints of θ_{j2} intervals							
	−1.75	−1.25	−.75	−.25	.25	.75	1.25	1.75
−1.75								
−1.25	.20		.09					
−.75	.06	.18	.39	.47	.19	.67		
−.25	.18	.25	.30	.45	.54	.50	.61	.82
.25	.19	.40	.39	.53	.45	.46	.77	.57
.75	.24	.34	.49	.53	.50	.65	.76	.71
1.25	.30	.35	.54	.55	.47	.63	.78	.55
1.75	.51	.55	.57	.62	.60	.71	.71	.65

The empty cells have frequencies of less than 10 so proportions were not computed for those cells

An examination of this test item might suggest that it requires some level of proficiency on both hypothetical constructs. It clearly requires some arithmetic computation. It could also require some algebraic symbol manipulation because the examinees must solve for some unknown values. If some level of skill on both constructs is required to determine the correct solution, then differences in responses of examinees with various combinations of knowledge or skill for the two constructs would be expected.

Suppose this test item is administered to a large number of examinees with known θ coordinates. The empirical proportions of correct response for the test item at $(\theta_{jl}, \theta_{j2})$ points can be calculated. Table 4.1 presents the proportions of 4,114 examinees who responded correctly to a single test item. These data are from a random sample of examinees who have taken a college entrance examination in the United States. Eight intervals are used to summarize the θ-coordinates. Each interval is .5-unit wide. The midpoints of the intervals are shown in the table. The proportion correct values for combinations of θ-coordinates that had frequencies of less than 10 are not shown. Overall, the tabled results present a pattern that as the values of either θ-coordinate increases, the proportion of correct responses tend to increase. Furthermore, the proportion of correct responses tends to be low when both θ_l and θ_2 are low and high when both are high. There are also combinations of θ_l and θ_2 that give approximately the same proportions of correct response. For example, if θ_l is 1.75 and θ_2 is −1.75, the proportion of correct responses is .51. Similarly, if θ_l is −.25 and θ_2 is .75, the proportion of correct responses is .50. A series of cells from lower left to upper right tend to have the same proportion of correct responses.

The classical test theory statistics for this item are a proportion correct of .54 and a point-biserial correlation with the total score of .49. A unidimensional IRT analysis with the three-parameter logistic model yields an item discrimination parameter estimate of 1.11, difficulty parameter estimate of .01, and pseudo-guessing parameter estimate of .08. Also, the unidimensional model did not yield good fit to the item response data from this test item. The chi-square fit statistic from the BILOG MG program (Zimowski et al. 2003) was 60.4 with 8 degrees of freedom. This is not a surprising result because the test item violates the assumption that only a single trait is needed to determine the correct response.

The general pattern of the response function for Item 1, $\mathbf{P}_1(\theta_1, \theta_2)$, tends to follow a monotonically increasing pattern of proportions of correct response across the $\boldsymbol{\theta}$-space. Further, the fairly consistent pattern of increasing proportions conditional on θ_1 and θ_2 shows that the test item is sensitive to differences on each coordinate dimension. If those coordinate dimensions align with the hypothetical constructs arithmetic problem solving and algebraic symbol manipulation, the test item is sensitive to differences on each of the constructs.

Consider a second test item that involves only a small amount of the hypothetical construct arithmetic problem solving, but requires a substantial amount of the hypothetical construct algebraic symbol manipulation. An example test item of this type is:

2. For all x, $(2x + 3)^2 + 2(2x + 4) - 2$ equals which of the following expressions?
   A. $4x^2 + 4x + 11$
   B. $(4x + 15)(x + 1)$
   C. $(2x + 5)(2x + 3)$
   D. $(2x + 5)(2x + 2)$
   E. $(2x + 5)(2x - 1)$.

Table 4.2 presents the proportions of correct response for Item 2 for the same 4,114 examines that responded to Item 1. For this test item, the proportion of correct responses increases quite dramatically with an increase in θ_2, but there is little change with an increase in θ_1. The test item is relatively insensitive to changes on one coordinate dimension, while it is very sensitive to changes on the other coordinate dimension. The overall proportion correct for this test item is .38 and it has a point-biserial correlation with the number-correct score of .26. The unidimensional IRT parameter estimates for this test item are $a = 1.175$, $b = .933$, and $c = .12$. As with the previous test item, the unidimensional IRT model did not fit the item response data for this item very well. The chi-square goodness of fit statistic had a value of 68.4 with 8 degrees of freedom. This statistic indicates that the probability

Table 4.2 Proportion of correct responses to Item 2 for 4,114 examinees

Midpoints θ_{j1}	Midpoints of θ_{j2} intervals							
	−1.75	−1.25	−.75	−.25	.25	.75	1.25	1.75
−1.75								
−1.25	.10		.18					
−.75	.06	.00	.22	.33	.31	.40		
−.25	.14	.18	.36	.28	.25	.36	.28	.91
.25	.10	.19	.18	.21	.29	.37	.65	.86
.75	.20	.29	.30	.37	.31	.43	.55	.88
1.25	.11	.11	.23	.36	.43	.43	.59	.97
1.75	.07	.15	.15	.19	.36	.60	.76	.99

The empty cells have frequencies of less than 10, so proportions were not computed for those cells was well below .001 that the data were generated from the unidimensional model. The poor fit is present even though the item mainly assesses the single construct of ability to perform algebraic manipulations. The lack of fit is due to the fact that the construct measured by the test item does not match the dominant construct measured by the full set of test items.

The unidimensional discrimination parameter estimates for these two test items are approximately the same, but they differ in difficulty. However, more than a shift in difficulty is indicated by the results in the two tables. A comparison of two cells in Tables 4.1 and 4.2 illustrates the differences. In Table 4.1, cells (1.75, −1.75) and (−.25, .75) had proportions correct of approximately .5. In Table 4.2, the corresponding values are .07 and .36. These results show that the interactions of the two items with the locations of persons in the coordinate space are quite different. In Sect. 4.1 of this chapter, these differences will be shown to indicate that the test items are sensitive to different combinations of skill dimensions along with having different difficulty.

The estimated proportions of correct response in Tables 4.1 and 4.2 provide two types of information. First, they give approximations of the probability of correct response for examinees with locations given by specified $\boldsymbol{\theta}$-vector. The values in the table could be smoothed and probabilities could be estimated by interpolation for any $\boldsymbol{\theta}$-vector. Second, the pattern of increase in the proportions for each test item indicates the general characteristics of the item for assessing the constructs that define the coordinate axes. Some of those characteristics are the direction in the $\boldsymbol{\theta}$-space that yields the greatest increase in proportion of correct response for a change of location in that direction and information about the difficulty of the test item for examinees at locations specified by a $\boldsymbol{\theta}$-vector. The direction of greatest increase in the space indicates the sensitivity of the test item to changes in levels of the hypothesized constructs. These characteristics suggest possible parameters for a function that models the relationship between the coordinates for an examinee and the probability of correct response to the test item.

In MIRT, the intent is to specify a model that provides a reasonable representation of data like that presented in Tables 4.1 and 4.2 and estimate the parameters of the model. The term *structural* is used to describe the parameters that describe the functioning of the test items. The term *incidental* is used to describe the vector of coordinates describing the locations of individuals (Hambleton and Swamination 1983; Neyman and Scott 1948). In this text, the vector, $\boldsymbol{\theta}$, represents the incidental parameters, and Roman letters are used to represent the structural parameters.

The mathematical function chosen as the MIRT model is fit to the observed proportions of correct response. When the fit is reasonably good, the resulting model provides estimates of the conditional probability of correct response given the coordinates $\boldsymbol{\theta} = (\theta_1, \theta_2, \ldots, \theta_m)$ for the m-dimensional space, where m is the number of dimensions used to model the data. The MIRT model is assumed to be a continuous probability function relating the location specified by $\boldsymbol{\theta}$ to the probability of correct response to a test item i with specified structural parameters. This model can be represented in the following ways for a test item scored 1 for a correct response and 0 for an incorrect response.

$$P_i(\theta_1, \ldots, \theta_m) = \Pr(u_i = 1|\theta_1, \ldots, \theta_m) \equiv P_i(\boldsymbol{\theta}). \tag{4.1}$$

In these expressions, the subscript i indicates the item and there is an implied set of structural parameters for the item, even though they are not explicitly listed. In the next section of this chapter, the structural parameters will be defined for several different models.

A more general representation of a MIRT model is given in (4.2). In this equation, $\boldsymbol{\eta}$ represents a vector of structural parameters that describe the characteristics of the test item, U represents the score on the test item and u is a possible value for the score, and f is a function that describes the relationship between the locations of persons specified by $\boldsymbol{\theta}$ and the probability of the response.

$$P_i(U = u|\boldsymbol{\theta}) = f(\boldsymbol{\theta}, \boldsymbol{\eta}_i, u). \tag{4.2}$$

The item score, u, may appear on both sides of the equation if the test item is scored either correct (1) or incorrect (0) to change the form of the function depending on the value of the score. When more than two score categories are present for the item, this mathematical convenience is not used.

Most MIRT models assume that the probability of selecting or producing the correct response to a test item scored as either correct or incorrect increases as any element in the $\boldsymbol{\theta}$-vector increases. This assumption is usually called the *monotonicity assumption*. In addition, examinees are assumed to respond to each test item as an independent event. That is, the response by a person to one item does not affect the response to an item produced by another person. Also, the response by a person to one item does not change that person's tendencies to respond in a particular way to another item. The response of any person to any test item is assumed to depend solely upon the person's $\boldsymbol{\theta}$-vector and the item's vector of parameters, $\boldsymbol{\eta}$. The practical implications of these assumptions are that the testing process needs to be controlled so that examinees do not share information during the test, and that tests must be constructed so that information in one test item does not increase or decrease the chances of correctly responding to another test item. Collectively, the assumption of independent responses to all test items by all examinees is called the *local independence assumption*.

The term "local" in the local independence assumption is used to indicate that responses are assumed independent at the level of individual persons with the same $\boldsymbol{\theta}$-vector, but the assumption does not generalize to the case of variation in $\boldsymbol{\theta}$-elements. For groups of individuals with variation in the constructs being assessed, responses to different test items typically are correlated, because they are all related to levels of the individuals' traits. If the assumptions of the MIRT model hold, the correlation between item scores will be due to variation in elements in the person parameter vector.

Because of the local independence assumption, the probability of a collection of responses (responses from one person to the items on a test or the responses from many people to one test item) can be determined by multiplying the probabilities of each of the individual responses. That is, the probability of a vector of item responses, **u**, for a single individual with trait vector $\boldsymbol{\theta}$ is the product of the probabilities of the individual responses, u_i, to the items on an I-item test.

$$P(U_1 = u_1, \ldots U_I = u_I | \boldsymbol{\theta}) = \prod_{i=1}^{I} P(U_i = u_i | \boldsymbol{\theta}). \tag{4.3}$$

McDonald (1967, 1981) indicates that sometimes a weaker assumption than (4.3) can be used to develop estimation procedures for the models. The weaker assumption is that the conditional covariances between all pairs of items are zero. That is

$$E(\text{cov}(U_i, U_j)|\boldsymbol{\theta}) = 0, \quad i \neq j, \tag{4.4}$$

for all values of the $\boldsymbol{\theta}$-vector.

The following sections of this chapter will describe the characteristics of individual MIRT models. These models use a number of functional forms and they include models for both dichotomously and polytomously scored items.

4.1 Multidimensional Models for the Interaction Between a Person and a Test Item

As was the case for UIRT models, MIRT comprises a set of models (item response theories), which have as a basic premise that the interaction between a person and a test item can be modeled reasonably accurately by a specific mathematical expression. Many different mathematical expressions have been developed for MIRT models. Some of them have already been presented in Chap. 3. This section will provide descriptions of the MIRT models that most commonly appear in the research literature. The MIRT models for items with two score categories will be presented first. These models have a relatively long history in the psychometric literature, and there is more experience with their application. The models for items with more than two score categories are described next. Chapter 5 presents statistical ways for representing characteristics of test items that are sensitive to differences on multiple dimensions. These statistical measures parallel those presented for UIRT models in Chap. 2.

4.1.1 MIRT Models for Test Items with Two Score Categories

Some of the stimulus for the development of MIRT came from attempts to addressing the problem of factor analyzing dichotomous data. For that reason, MIRT models for dichotomous items have appeared in the research literature since the 1980s (e.g., Bock and Aitken 1981). Because of the importance of this early work, the MIRT models for dichotomous items (those with two score categories) are presented first, beginning with the model that is an extension of the two-parameter logistic UIRT model. That model is used to show basic MIRT concepts. Then, alternatives to that model with the same basic form are presented. These include models based on the normal ogive rather than the logistic function and models that have fewer or greater numbers of item parameters. A different extension of UIRT models is presented next, followed by comparisons of the different types of models.

4.1.1.1 Compensatory Extensions of the UIRT Models

Multidimensional extension of the two-parameter logistic model. The two-parameter logistic model (see (2.10)) has an exponent of the form $a(\theta - b)$. Multiplying through by a results in $a\theta - ab$. If $-ab$ is replaced by d, the expression is in what is called slope/intercept form, $a\theta + d$. One way of extending the two-parameter logistic model to the case where there are multiple elements in the $\boldsymbol{\theta}$-vector is to replace the simple slope/intercept form with the expression $\mathbf{a}\boldsymbol{\theta}' + d$, where $\mathbf{a}$ is a $1 \times m$ vector of item discrimination parameters and $\boldsymbol{\theta}$ is a $1 \times m$ vector of person coordinates with m indicating the number of dimensions in the coordinate space. The intercept term, d, is a scalar. The form of the multidimensional extension of the two-parameter logistic (M2PL) model is given by

$$P(U_{ij} = 1|\boldsymbol{\theta}_\mathbf{j}, \mathbf{a}_\mathbf{i}, d_i) = \frac{\mathrm{e}^{\mathbf{a}_\mathbf{i}\boldsymbol{\theta}_\mathbf{j}' + d_i}}{1 + \mathrm{e}^{\mathbf{a}_\mathbf{i}\boldsymbol{\theta}_\mathbf{j}' + d_i}}. \tag{4.5}$$

The exponent of e in this model can be expanded to show the way that the elements of the $\mathbf{a}$ and $\boldsymbol{\theta}$ vectors interact.

$$\mathbf{a}_\mathbf{i}\boldsymbol{\theta}_\mathbf{j}' + d_i = a_{i1}\theta_{j1} + a_{i2}\theta_{j2} + \cdots + a_{im}\theta_{jm} + d_i = \sum_{\ell=1}^{m} a_{i\ell}\theta_{j\ell} + d_i. \tag{4.6}$$

The exponent is a linear function of the elements of $\boldsymbol{\theta}$ with the d parameter as the intercept term and the elements of the $\mathbf{a}$-vector as slope parameters. The expression in the exponent defines a line in an m-dimensional space. This results in an interesting property for this model. If the exponent is set to some constant value, k, all $\boldsymbol{\theta}$-vectors that satisfy the expression $k = \mathbf{a}_\mathbf{i}\boldsymbol{\theta}_\mathbf{j}' + d_i$ fall along a straight line and they all yield the same probability of correct response for the model.

This relationship can be shown graphically if the number of coordinate axes is assumed to be two. For example, suppose that $k = 0$. For this value of the exponent, the probability of correct response is .5 because $\mathrm{e}^0 = 1$. The expression on the right of (4.5) simplifies to $1/2$. For a test item with $\mathbf{a}$-vector equal to [.75 1.5] and d-parameter equal to $-.7$, the exponent of the model for this item is $.75\theta_1 + 1.5\theta_2 - .7 = 0$. Rearranging terms to put this expression into the usual slope/intercept form for a line results in

$$\theta_2 = -.5\theta_1 + \frac{.7}{1.5}. \tag{4.7}$$

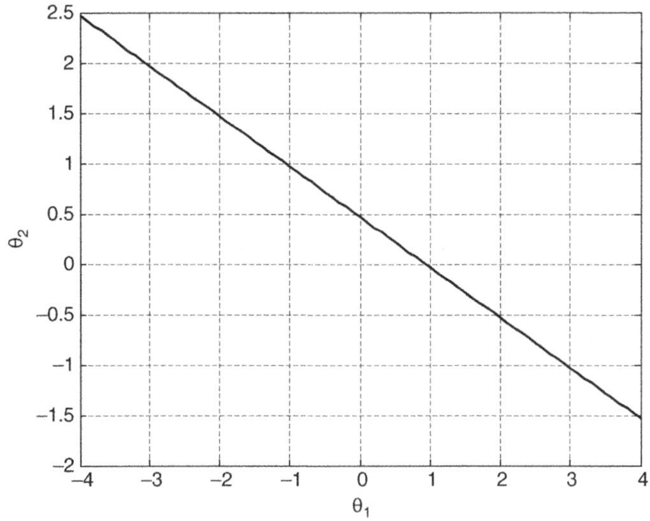

Fig. 4.1 Plot of θ-vectors that yield exponents of $k = 0$ for a test item with parameters $a_1 = .75$, $a_2 = 1.5$, $d = -.7$

This is the equation for a line with slope $-.5$ and intercept $.7/1.5 = .467$. This line is shown in Fig. 4.1.

This plot shows an interesting property of this MIRT model. The model indicates that all persons with $\boldsymbol{\theta}$-vectors that fall on the line have a probability of correct response of .5. Persons with $\boldsymbol{\theta}$-vectors of [0 .5], moderate values on both sets of coordinates, and [−4 2.5], a very low value on the first coordinate and a high value on the second coordinate, have predicted probabilities of .5. When the coordinates are interpreted as abilities, this feature of the model has been used to indicate that a high ability on one dimension can compensate for a low ability on another dimension. This is also shown by the fact that a $\boldsymbol{\theta}$-vector of [4 −1.5] also falls on the line yielding a probability of correct response of .5. Because of this feature of the model, it has been labeled as a *compensatory* MIRT model. Of course, the compensatory nature of the model also holds for higher dimensional cases. Low values of any coordinate, or any combinations of coordinates, can be compensated for by a high value on another coordinate, or combinations of coordinates, to yield the same probability of response as more moderate values.

Graphs of the model for the two-dimensional case clearly show the linear form of the exponent and the compensatory nature of the model. Figure 4.2 shows the form of the model in two ways. The left panel shows the probability of correct response to the item as the height above the (θ_1, θ_2)-plane. This shows the item response surface (IRS) for the item. The right panel shows the probabilities as contours of the surface shown in the left panel. The example uses the same item parameters as used in Fig. 4.1.

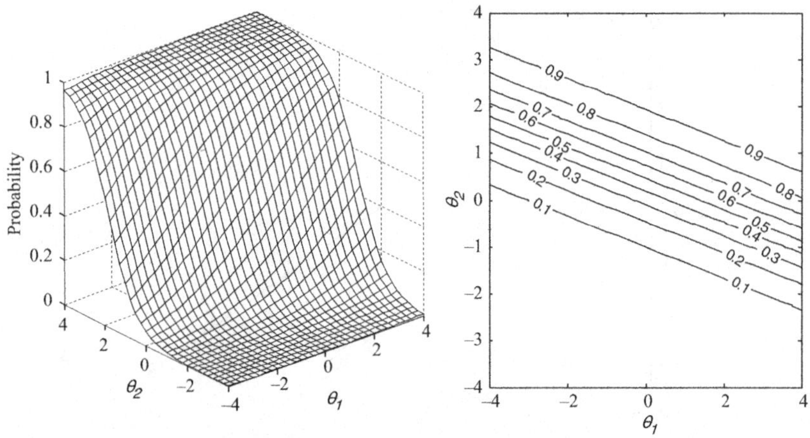

Fig. 4.2 Surface plot and contour plot for probability of correct response for an item with $a_1 = .5$, $a_2 = 1.5$, $d = -.7$

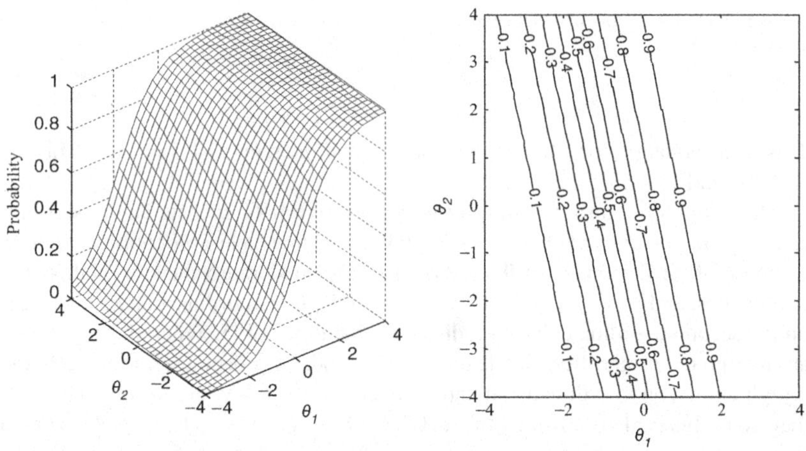

Fig. 4.3 Surface plot and contour plot for the probability of correct response for an item with $a_1 = 1.2$, $a_2 = .3$, $d = 1$

The plots show the way the model represents the characteristics of the test item. Both representations show that the probability of correct response increases monotonically with an increase in one or both elements of the $\boldsymbol{\theta}$-vector. Further, it is clear that the contours of equal probability form straight lines. These lines show the compensatory nature of the model. The plots also show that the probability of correct response increases more quickly with changes in location parallel to the θ_2-axis than changes parallel to the θ_1-axis. The rate of change of the probabilities with changes in location corresponds to the difference in the respective a-parameters. For comparison purposes, Fig. 4.3 shows the corresponding plots for an item with $a_1 = 1.2$,

$a_2 = .3$, and $d = 1.0$. The orientation of the surface for the second test item is quite different than for the first test item because the second test item increases in probability more quickly along the θ_1 coordinate axis and the first test item increases more quickly along the θ_2 coordinate axis.

Some intuitive meaning for the parameters of the model can be determined from careful inspection of Figs. 4.2 and 4.3. First, the scales for θs are from −4 to 4 for the plots. In the standard forms of the models, θs generally fall in this range, but the actual range is from $-\infty$ to ∞ for each coordinate dimension. The zero point and unit of measurement for each coordinate dimension is arbitrary. The values of these features of the θs are usually constrained to be the mean and standard deviation of the sample first used to calibrate a set of test items, but they can be transformed to match other characteristics of the sample of examinees or the characteristics of the items. The possible transformations of parameters will be described in Chap. 8.

The a-parameters indicate the orientation of the equiprobable contours and the rate that the probability of correct response changes from point to point in the $\boldsymbol{\theta}$-space. This can be seen by taking the first partial derivative of the expression in (4.5) with respect to a particular coordinate dimension, θ_ℓ. To simplify the presentation of the results $\mathrm{P}(U_{ij} = 1|\boldsymbol{\theta}_\mathbf{j}, \mathbf{a}_\mathbf{i}, d_i) = \mathrm{P}$ and $\mathrm{Q} = (1 - \mathrm{P})$.

$$\frac{\partial P}{\partial \theta_\ell} = a_\ell P(1 - P) = a_\ell PQ. \tag{4.8}$$

This result shows that the slope of the IRS parallel to a coordinate axis has the same form as for the two-parameter logistic model shown in (2.11). The slope is greatest, $\frac{1}{4}a_\ell$, when the probability of correct response is .5. Because the a-parameters are related to the slope of the surface and the rate of change of the probability with respect to the coordinate axes, the **a**-parameter is usually called the *slope* or *discrimination parameter*.

The probability of correct response for a test item is .5 when the exponent in (4.5) is 0. That is $\mathrm{e}^0/(1 + \mathrm{e}^0) = 1/(1 + 1) = \frac{1}{2}$. When the exponent of e is 0, the exponent takes the form $\mathbf{a_i}\boldsymbol{\theta}_\mathbf{j}' + d_i = 0$. This equation is the expression for the line in the $\boldsymbol{\theta}$-space that describes the set of locations in the space that have a .5 probability of a correct response. If all of the elements of $\boldsymbol{\theta}$ are equal to 0 except one, say θ_ℓ, then the point where the line intersects the θ_ℓ-axis is given by $-d_i/a_\ell$. This is usually called the intercept of the line with that axis. For that reason, d is usually called the *intercept parameter*.

The d-parameter is not a difficulty parameter in the usual sense of a UIRT model because it does not give a unique indicator of the difficulty of the item. Instead, the negative of the intercept term divided by an element of the discrimination parameter vector gives the relative difficulty of the item related to the corresponding coordinate dimension. For example, Fig. 4.4 shows the .5 line for the item shown in Fig. 4.2 as line AC extended. The intersection of the line AC with the θ_1 coordinate axis is $-d/a_1 = -(-.7)/.5 = 1.4$. This is the location of C on the graph. Similarly, the location of A on the θ_2 axis is $-(-.7)/1.5 = .47$. This indicates that if θ_2 were 0,

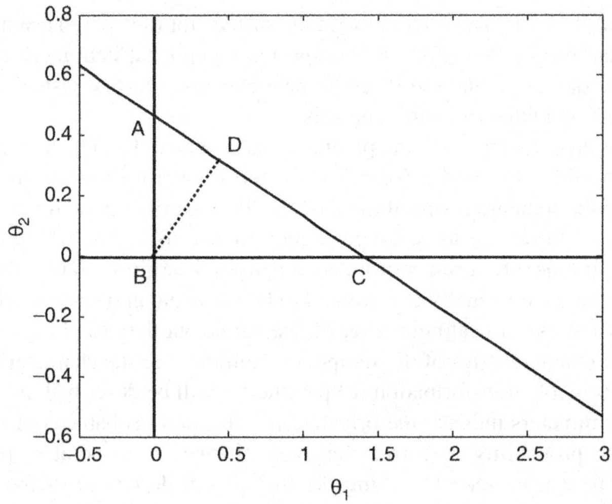

Fig. 4.4 Relationship of the .5 probability line with the coordinate axes for an item with $a_1 = .5$, $a_2 = 1.5$, and $d = -.7$

then a person would need a value of θ_1 of 1.4 to have a probability of .5 of a correct response. But, if θ_1 were 0, then a person would need only .47 on the θ_2 dimension to have a .5 probability of correct response. The conditional nature of these statements makes the actual intercepts awkward indicators of the item difficulty. A useful alternative is the distance of the line from the origin of the space. This is indicated by the dotted line BD on the figure.

The distance between the origin and the line can be derived from the properties of similar triangles. The complete derivation is left to the reader. If the length of BD is represented by b, the general expression for the distance of the line from the origin is given by

$$b = \frac{-d}{\sqrt{\mathbf{aa}'}} = \frac{-d}{\sqrt{\sum\limits_{v=1}^{m} a_v^2}}. \tag{4.9}$$

The value of b has the same interpretation as the b-parameter for UIRT models. To avoid confusion with the UIRT models, b is often called MDIFF in the MIRT literature. When MDIFF is 0, the .5 contour line goes through the origin of the space. This means that one of the vectors of $\boldsymbol{\theta}$-parameters that will yield a .5 probability of response is the 0-vector (a vector with all m elements equal to 0). Of course, any point on the .5 probability line also yields the same probability of response, so there are many other $\boldsymbol{\theta}$-vectors that will yield a .5 probability.

There are many variations on the M2PL model that have very similar properties. They all have equiprobable contours that are straight lines. They are also compensatory in the sense described above. Several variations and extensions of the M2PL model are described in the next sections of this chapter.

Multidimensional extension of the three-parameter logistic model. A fairly straightforward extension of the M2PL model provides for the possibility of a non-zero lower asymptote to the model. This is a multidimensional extension of the three-parameter logistic UIRT model described in Chap. 2. This model is typically labeled the M3PL model. The mathematical expression for the model is given in (4.10) using the symbols as previously defined.

$$P(U_{ij} = 1|\boldsymbol{\theta}_\mathbf{j}, \mathbf{a_i}, c_i, d_i) = c_i + (1 - c_i)\frac{e^{\mathbf{a_i}\boldsymbol{\theta}_\mathbf{j}' + d_i}}{1 + e^{\mathbf{a_i}\boldsymbol{\theta}_\mathbf{j}' + d_i}}. \tag{4.10}$$

The M3PL model was designed to account for observed empirical data such as that provided in Lord (1980), which shows that examinees with low capabilities have a nonzero probability of responding correctly to multiple-choice items. Because the process of selecting a correct response for individuals with low capabilities does not seem to be related to the constructs assessed by the test item, the model contains a single lower asymptote, or pseudo-guessing, parameter, c_i, to specify the probability of correct response for examinees with very low values in $\boldsymbol{\theta}$.

The item response surface for item response data that can be modeled with two coordinate dimensions is presented in Fig. 4.5. The graph of the model shows that the lines of equal probability are straight lines as was the case for the M2PL model and the form of the surface is basically the same. The major difference is that the surface asymptotes to c_i rather than continuing down to a probability of response of 0.

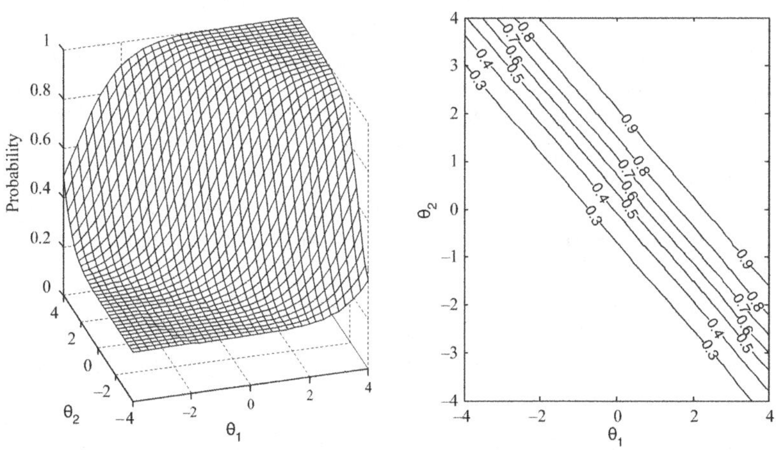

Fig. 4.5 Surface plot and contour plot for probability of correct response for an item with $a_1 = 1.3$, $a_2 = 1.4$, $d = -1$, $c = .2$

Multidimensional extension of the Rasch model. It is tempting to consider the multidimensional extension of the Rasch model as simply the M2PL model with all of the a-parameters set to 1.0. This would be equivalent to the relationship between the Rasch one-parameter logistic model and the two-parameter logistic model for the UIRT case. However, an analysis of the consequences of setting all of the a-parameters in the M2PL model to 1.0 shows that this type of generalization of the UIRT case does not give a useful result.

The general form of the exponent of the M2PL model is given by

$$a_{i1}\theta_{j1} + a_{i2}\theta_{j2} + \ldots + a_{im}\theta_{jm} + d_i. \tag{4.11}$$

If all of the a-parameters are set equal to the same value, say a_{i*}, they can be factored from the expression in (4.11) to yield

$$a_{i*}(\theta_{j1} + \theta_{j2} + \ldots + \theta_{jm}) + d_i. \tag{4.12}$$

For Person j at any given moment, the θ-coordinates are fixed and the sum of them takes on a particular value that can be represented as θ_*. Substituting the sum of the θ-coordinates into (4.12) yields $a_{i*}\theta_{j*} + d_j$. Finally, if $b_i = -d_i/a_{i*}$, the exponent can be represented as

$$a_{i*}(\theta_{j*} - b_i). \tag{4.13}$$

If all of the a_{i*} values are set to one, the exponent has the same form as the simple UIRT Rasch model. The only difference is that the ability parameter is a value that is the sum of coordinates rather than what is usually interpreted to be the level on a single construct. Trying to create a multidimensional version of the Rasch model by setting the a-parameters to 1.0 only yields a UIRT version of the Rasch model with a more complex definition for the person parameter.

The multidimensional generalization of the Rasch model is more complex. The approach that currently appears in the psychometric literature (Adams et al. 1997) is an adaptation of the general Rasch model presented in Chap. 3 (3.8). The model as specified in Adams et al. (1997) is for the general case that includes both dichotomously and polytomously scored test items. The general form of the model is presented first using the notation from the original article. Then the simpler case for dichotomously scored items is presented using the same notation as the other models presented in this book.

The expression for the full model is presented in (4.14). This model is for a test item that has the highest score category for Item i equal to K_i. The lowest score category is 0. This implies that the number of score categories is $K_i + 1$. For the dichotomous case, $K_i = 1$ and there are two score categories, 0 and 1. The score category is represented by k. The random variable X_{ik} is an indicator variable that indicates whether or not the observed response is equal to k on Item i. If the score is k, the indicator variable is assigned a 1 – otherwise, it is 0. For the dichotomous case, if $X_{i1} = 1$, the response to the item was a correct response and it was assigned a score of 1.

$$P(X_{ik} = 1|\mathbf{A},\mathbf{B},\boldsymbol{\xi},\boldsymbol{\theta}) = \frac{e^{\mathbf{b_{ik}}\boldsymbol{\theta}+\mathbf{a_{ik}}'\boldsymbol{\xi}}}{\sum_{k=0}^{K_i} e^{\mathbf{b_{ik}}\boldsymbol{\theta}+\mathbf{a_{ik}}'\boldsymbol{\xi}}}, \tag{4.14}$$

where $\mathbf{A}$ is a design matrix with vector elements $\mathbf{a_{ik}}$ that select the appropriate item parameter for scoring the item; $\mathbf{B}$ is a scoring matrix with vector elements $\mathbf{b_{ik}}$ that indicate the dimension or dimensions that are required to obtain the score of k on the item; $\boldsymbol{\xi}$ is a vector of item difficulty parameters; and $\boldsymbol{\theta}$ is a vector of coordinates for locating a person in the construct space.

For the dichotomous case, using the same notation as the other models, the multidimensional Rasch model is given by

$$P(U_{ij} = 1|\mathbf{a_i}, d_i, \boldsymbol{\theta_j}) = \frac{e^{\mathbf{a_i}\boldsymbol{\theta_j}'+d_i}}{1 + e^{\mathbf{a_i}\boldsymbol{\theta_j}'+d_i}}, \tag{4.15}$$

where $\mathbf{a_i}$ is a vector such that $\mathbf{a_i} = \mathbf{b_{ik}}$ and d_i is a scalar value equal to $\mathbf{a}'_{\mathbf{ik}}\boldsymbol{\xi}$. Note that when $k = 0$ in (4.14) the exponent of e is 0 so that term of the sum in the denominator is equal to 1.

Equation (4.15) and (4.5) appear to be identical. The difference between the two is the way that the $\mathbf{a_i}$ vector is specified. In (4.5), $\mathbf{a_i}$ is a characteristic of Item i that is estimated from the data. In (4.15), $\mathbf{a_i}$ is a characteristic of Item i that is specified by the test developer. In the case of the model in (4.5), statistical estimation procedures are used to determine the elements of $\mathbf{a_i}$ that will maximize some criterion for model/data fit. Except for the usual monotonicity constraint that requires the values of the elements of $\mathbf{a_i}$ be positive, the elements can take on any values. For the model in (4.15), the values are specified by the analyst and they typically take on integer values. Adams et al. (1997) specified two variations for the model – between item and within item dimensionality. For between item dimensionality, the $\mathbf{a_i}$-vector has elements that are all zeros except for one element that specifies the coordinate dimension that is measurement target for the item. That is, the test developer specifies the dimension that is the target for the item. In a sense, the test developer estimates the elements of the $\mathbf{a_i}$-vector rather than obtaining estimates through the usual statistical estimation procedures.

For within item dimensionality, the $\mathbf{a_i}$-vector has more than one nonzero element. The test developer can indicate that performance on the test item is influenced by more than one of the coordinate dimensions. For the two-dimensional case, $\mathbf{a_i}$-vectors of [1 0] or [0 1] would indicate between item dimensionality. The first vector would specify that the item was only affected by level on coordinate dimension 1 and the second vector specifies that the item is only affected by level on coordinate dimension 2. A specification for within item dimensionality might have a vector such as [1 1] indicating that the item is affected equally by both coordinate dimensions. Other alternatives such as [1 2] or [3 1] are possible. The quality of the fit of the model to the data will depend on how well the test developer specifies the values of the $\mathbf{a_i}$-vector.

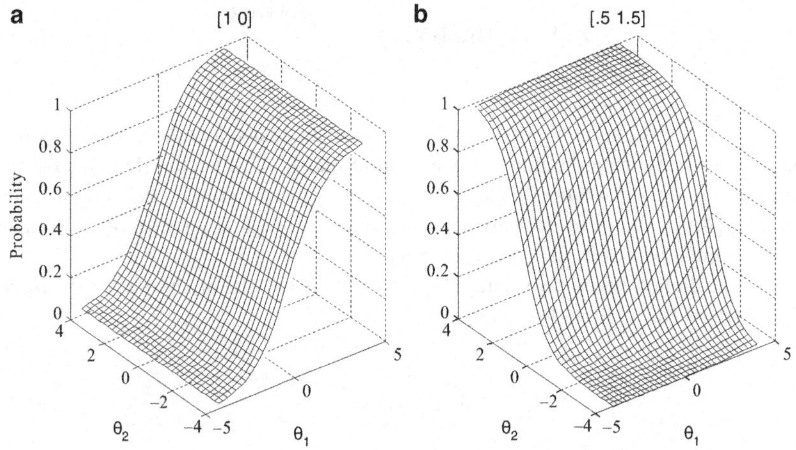

Fig. 4.6 Two-dimensional Rasch model surfaces with $\mathbf{a}_i = [1\ 0]$ and $[.5\ 1.5]$ and $d_i = 0$

The reason for specifying the $\mathbf{a}_i$-vector rather than using statistical estimation methods to determine the values is that the model then has observable sufficient statistics for the person and item parameters (Rasch 1962). The sufficient statistic for the $\boldsymbol{\theta}$-vector for a person is the sum of the $\mathbf{a}_i$-vectors for the items a person answers correctly. The sufficient statistic that is related to the d_i-parameter is the sum over people of the $\mathbf{a}_i$-vectors for the correct responses to Item i. This is simply the number of times Item i is answered correctly times $\mathbf{a}_i$.

The form of the item response surface for the multidimensional Rasch model for dichotomously scored items is the same as that shown in Fig. 4.3, but the orientation of the surface is dependent on the specification of values in the $\mathbf{a}_i$-vector. Figure 4.6 shows surfaces for the two-dimensional case with $\mathbf{a}_i$-vectors [1 0] and [.5 1.5] and $d_i = 0$ for both examples. The surface in panel a does not differentiate at all in probability for differences along θ_2 – the item only measures θ_1. The item represented in panel b has changes in probability for changes in θ_2 and slight changes along θ_1.

The model given in (4.14) has many other variations. Some of those will be described later in this chapter when multidimensional models for polytomously scored items are presented. The reader is referred to Adams et al. (1997) for a more detailed description of other variations of the model.

Multidimensional extension of the normal ogive model. As indicated in Chap. 3, much of the original work on MIRT was done using the normal ogive form to represent the relationship between the location in the multidimensional space and the probability of a correct response to a test item. The normal ogive form is still used as the basis of statistical estimation programs. These programs and the underlying statistical methods are described in Chap. 6.

The general form for the multidimensional extension of the normal ogive model (Bock and Schilling 2003; McDonald 1999; Samejima 1974) is given by

$$P(U_{ij} = 1|\boldsymbol{\theta}_\mathbf{j}, \mathbf{a}_\mathbf{i}, c_i, d_i) = c_i + (1 - c_i)\frac{1}{\sqrt{2\pi}} \int\limits_{-z_i(\boldsymbol{\theta}_\mathbf{j})}^{\infty} e^{\frac{-t^2}{2}} dt, \tag{4.16}$$

where $z_i(\boldsymbol{\theta}_\mathbf{j}) = \mathbf{a}_\mathbf{i}\boldsymbol{\theta}'_\mathbf{j} + d_i$ and the other symbols have been previously defined. If $c_i = 0$, the result is the normal ogive version of the multidimensional two-parameter logistic model. That form of the model defines the probability of correct response for an item as the area under a standard normal distribution from $-z_i(\boldsymbol{\theta}_\mathbf{j})$ to infinity. Because of the symmetry of the normal distribution, this is the same as the area below $z_i(\boldsymbol{\theta}_\mathbf{j})$.

The form of the surface defined by (4.16) is essentially the same as that defined by (4.10). Camilli (1994) summarized the work on comparing the normal ogive and logistic functions. He included the mathematical proof by Haley (1952) showing that the normal distribution function and the logistic function differ by less than .01 in probability when the constant 1.702 is included in the exponent of the logistic function. More explicitly, for z as defined above,

$$|\Phi(z) - \Psi(1.702z)| < .01 \quad \text{for} \ -\infty < z < \infty, \tag{4.17}$$

where Φ is the cumulative normal ogive function and Ψ is the cumulative logistic function.

For the parameters in (4.10) and (4.16) to have essentially the same meaning, the exponent of (4.10) has to be changed to $1.702(\mathbf{a}_\mathbf{i}\boldsymbol{\theta}'_\mathbf{j} + d_i)$. Multiplying by the constant 1.702 changes the scale for the parameters in the logistic model, but has no other effect on the form of the surface. Figure 4.7 shows examples of the surfaces for

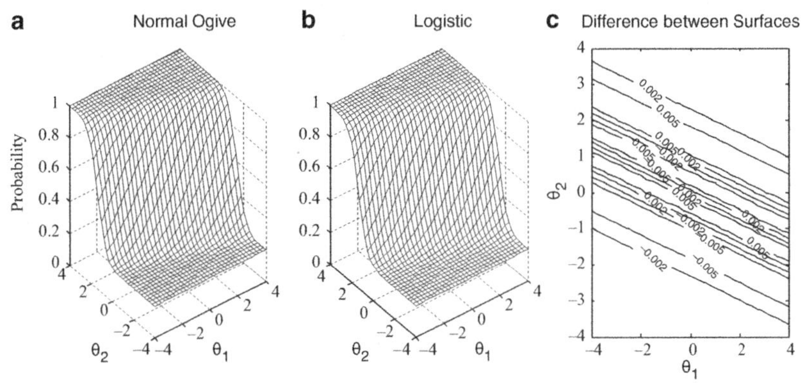

Fig. 4.7 Normal ogive and logistic surfaces, and difference between the surfaces for a test item with $a_1 = .5, a_2 = 1.5, d = 0, c = .2$. Note that $D = 1.702$ is included in the exponent of the logistic model

an item that can be modeled in two-dimensions using both the logistic and normal ogive models. The difference in the two surfaces is also shown.

The surfaces shown in panels a and b are virtually indistinguishable. The contour plot of the differences between the two surfaces has less than .01 in all cases, and the differences were the same along the lines of equal probability. This indicates that the surfaces have the same orientation to the coordinate axes – the lines of equal probability are the same. Because of the close similarity of the surfaces defined by the two models, the parameters estimated from the models are often used interchangeably as long as the 1.702 is included in the exponent of the logistic model.

All of variations of the logistic model presented in this chapter can also be implemented for the normal ogive model by modifying (4.16). If $c_i = 0$, the result is the multivariate generalization of the two-parameter normal ogive model. The z-function can also be defined with prespecified $\mathbf{a_i}$ vectors to yield a confirmatory model that is like the multivariate version of the Rasch model.

4.1.1.2 Partially Compensatory Extensions of UIRT Models

One of the continuing theoretical issues raised about the model presented in (4.5) is the compensatory nature of the model. If any $m - 1$ coordinates for a person are very low, the person can still have a very high probability of correct response if the mth coordinate is sufficiently high. Sympson (1978) argued that this hypothesized compensation is not realistic for some types of test items. He presents an example of a mathematics test item that requires both arithmetic computation skills and reading skills. His example has similar characteristics to the test item presented at the beginning of this chapter. Sympson (1978) hypothesizes that a person with reading skill that is very low will not be able to determine the problem that needs to be solved. The contention is that even if such a person had very high mathematics computation skills, they would not be able to determine the correct answer because of lack of understanding of the problem. To model the situation he considered, Sympson (1978) proposed the following expression for the interaction between the person and the test item, where all of the symbols have the same meaning as in previous equations.

$$P(U_{ij} = 1|\boldsymbol{\theta}_\mathbf{j}, \mathbf{a_i}, \mathbf{b_i}, c_i) = c_i + (1 - c_i)\left(\prod_{\ell=1}^{m} \frac{e^{1.7a_{i\ell}(\theta_{j\ell} - b_{i\ell})}}{1 + e^{1.7a_{i\ell}(\theta_{j\ell} - b_{i\ell})}}\right). \tag{4.18}$$

The expression in (4.18) has two main parts. The term on the far right is the product of terms that have the form of the 2PL UIRT model that was described in Chap. 2. In a sense, each of these terms gives the probability of being successful on one component of the item – for example, the reading or the mathematics components of the example item. These components of the test item are considered as independent activities so that the probability of doing all of them correctly is the product of the probabilities of doing each part correctly. The other part of the expression to the right of the equal sign provides a nonzero lower asymptote for the model, c_i. This part of the model has the same function as in (4.10). There is only one c_i-parameter for each item. Sympson (1978) did not believe that there was a lower asymptote for each task in the item, but only for the item overall.

The form of the surface defined by (4.18) can be investigated by considering the case when $c_i = 0$ and the probability of correct response to the test item is some constant value, k. Further, if the 2PL terms in the product are represented by p_ℓ, where ℓ is the dimension of interest, the simplified version of the model becomes

$$k = \prod_{\ell=1}^{m} p_\ell. \tag{4.19}$$

For the simple case of only two dimensions, the expression is simply $k = p_1 p_2$. This is the equation for a hyperbola with values in the probability metric. The hyperbolas defined by this function are shown in the left panel of Fig. 4.8 for $k = .25$, .50, and .75. The hyperbolas do not continue on to the asymptotic values because the probabilities are constrained to the range from 0 to 1. As a result, only segments of the hyperbolas are shown.

The pairs of probabilities that are specified by each point along one of the parabolas can be transformed to the θ scale through the item characteristic curve for the item. This process results in a pair of θ coordinates for each point on a hyperbola. These points can be plotted in the θ-space to show the sets of coordinates that yield the specified probability of correct response to a test item that is well modeled by (4.18). Note that for a specified probability of correct response to a test item, only one hyperbola is defined for a specific number of dimensions. If $k = .5$ and the item is modeled with two dimensions, the corresponding hyperbola is the one shown by the dashed line in Fig. 4.8. The θ-vectors that correspond to the probability pairs represented by the hyperbola are dependent on the item parameters for the item. For

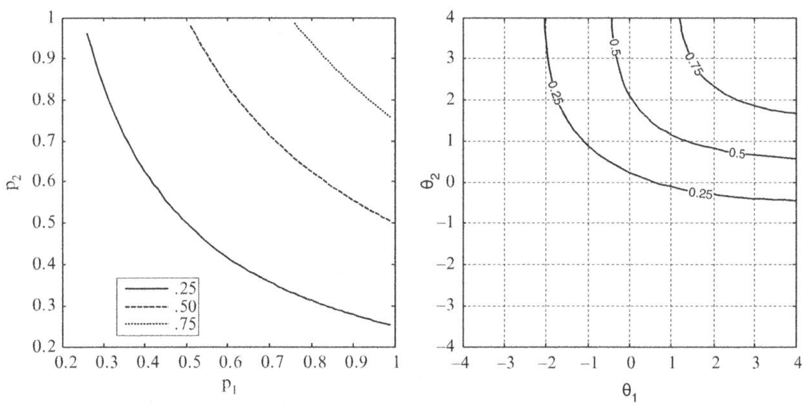

Fig. 4.8 Curves of equal probability of correct response for the noncompensatory model with two coordinates and $c_i = 0$

example, if the item parameters for an item modeled in two dimensions are $c_i = 0$, $a_{i1} = .7$, $a_{i2} = 1.1$, $b_{i1} = -.5$, and $b_{i2} = .5$, the curves in the θ-space that correspond to the hyperbolas in the left panel of Fig. 4.8 are shown in the right panel of the same figure.

The curves in the right panel of Fig. 4.8 are not true hyperbolas, although they do asymptote to specific values. The .5 curve asymptotes to the values of the b-parameters, -.5 and .5. This is a result of the partially compensatory nature of the model. If θ_1 is equal to -.5, then the probability of correctly responding to the first component of the item is .5. The actual probability of correct response to the item as a whole depends on the probability of the second component. For example, if θ_2 were equal to .5, then the probability of responding correctly to the second component of the item would be .5, and the overall probability of correct response would be only .25, that is, the product $p_1 p_2$. As θ_2 increases, the probability of correct response increases. But, even if θ_2 is positive infinity yielding a probability of 1 for the second component, the overall probability of correct response would only be .5. Thus, the probability of correct response for an item that follows this model can never be greater than the probability for the component with the lowest probability.

The item response surface for the item with the parameters given above and $c_i = .2$ is shown in Fig. 4.9. Inspection of the figure will show that the surface has a lower asymptote to the value of the c-parameter. Also, the curvature of the surface shows the partially compensatory nature of the model. The probability of correct response for low values of either θ_1 or θ_2 or both is close to the lower asymptote

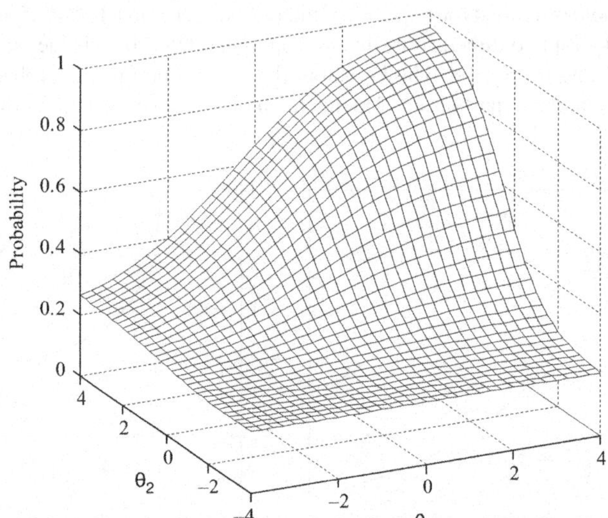

Fig. 4.9 Item response surface for the partially compensatory model when $a_1 = .7$, $a_2 = 1.1$, $b_1 = -.5$, $b_2 = .5$, and $c = .2$

value. Only when both θ-values are high does the model yield a high probability of correct response.

Another unique feature of this model is that the interpretation of the item parameters changes as the number of dimensions increase. Those familiar with UIRT probably know that when θ is equal to the difficulty parameter for the item, b, the probability of correct response to the test item is .5 if there is no lower asymptote parameter in the model. A simple example is if $\theta = 0$ and $b = 0$, the probability of correct response is .5. The same is true for the compensatory model. If the $\boldsymbol{\theta}$-vector is 0 and the d-parameter is 0, the probability of correct response to the item is .5 when there is no lower asymptote parameter. However, that is not the case for the partially compensatory model. If the $\boldsymbol{\theta}$-vector and the $\mathbf{b}$-vector are both 0 for the two-dimensional case, the probability of correct response is .25. For the three dimensional case, it is .125. In general, for the case when both the $\boldsymbol{\theta}$ and $\mathbf{b}$-vectors are 0, the probability of correct response is $.5^m$, where m is the number of dimensions used in the model.

The value of a common b-parameter that yields a .5 probability of correct response depends on the corresponding a-parameter. However, it is useful to consider the special case when $\boldsymbol{\theta}$ is the zero vector, all a-parameters are .588 (note that the constant 1.7 is in the model), and the c-parameter is 0. If all the b-parameters are the same, what must they be for the probability of correct response for the test item to equal .5 for different numbers of dimensions? To get the answer, the left side of (4.18) is set to .5 and the equation is solved for $\mathbf{b}$ under the above constraints. The results are provided in Table 4.3.

The results in Table 4.3 show that as the number of dimensions increases, the value of the b-parameter must be reduced to maintain the same probability of correct response. This is a direct result of the fact that the model contains a product of the probabilities of success on each component. Whenever the probability of success is less than 1.0, adding another component results in multiplying by a number less than 1.0. This reduces the overall probability of a correct response. To compensate for this, the components must be easier as reflected by the reduced magnitude of the b-parameters.

The model presented in (4.18) is a multidimensional extension of the three-parameter logistic UIRT model. Whitely[1] (1980b) suggested using a simplified version of (4.18) to model the cognitive processes in test items. Maris (1995) also

Table 4.3 b-parameter required for a probability of correct response of .5 for different numbers of dimensions

Number of dimensions	b-parameter
1	0
2	−.88
3	−1.35
4	−1.66
5	−1.91
6	−2.10

[1] Whitely now publishes under the name Embretson

suggested this model and labeled it the conjunctive Rasch model. The model is an extension of the one-parameter logistic model. This model is presented in (4.20). Although the terms in the product are equivalent to the Rasch UIRT model, the multidimensional model does not match the requirements for a Rasch model because there is not an observable sufficient statistic for the person parameter vector. Adams et al. (1997) indicate that the model in (4.20) can be considered as a Rasch model if it is considered as an item with 2^m possible response categories. A vector of 0 s and 1 s is developed to describe the success on each cognitive component of the model, and each of the possible vectors is considered as a response to the full item. This approach is based on the assumption that success on the various cognitive components is independent. Whitely (1980b) also suggested a model of the same general form that assumed that success on component ℓ was dependent on success on component $\ell - 1$.

$$P(U_{ij} = 1|\boldsymbol{\theta}_\mathbf{j},\mathbf{b}_\mathbf{i}) = \prod_{k=1}^{m} \frac{\mathrm{e}^{(\theta_{jk}-b_{ik})}}{1 + \mathrm{e}^{(\theta_{jk}-b_{jk})}}. \tag{4.20}$$

4.1.1.3 Comparison of Compensatory and Partially Compensatory Models

The models that combine the effect of multiple θs using a linear function in the exponent of the model (compensatory models) as in (4.5) and the ones that combine the θs through a product of terms (partially compensatory models) as in (4.18) are quite different in their philosophical underpinnings and in mathematical form. Some researchers (e.g., Maris 1995) may prefer one model over the other because it better matches hypotheses about how persons interact with the test items. The partially compensatory product models are consistent with the hypothesis that test items have different parts related to different skills or knowledge and that overall success requires success on each part. The compensatory models are more consistent with a more holistic view of the interaction of persons and test items. Persons bring all of their skills and knowledge to bear on all aspects of the items. Ultimately, the usefulness of the models will be determined by how accurately they represent the responses from actual test items. Only a few studies were available at the time this book was written that compared the fit of the two types of models to the same data. One study that was identified, Bolt and Lall (2003), found that the compensatory model fit item response data from an English usage test better than the partially compensatory model in (4.20). Note that this model does have all of the a-parameters set equal to 1. That study also compared the models on the fit to data generated from the other model. The compensatory model fit partially compensatory data almost as well as the partially compensatory model. The partially compensatory model did not fit the compensatory data very well.

The results reported by Spray et al. (1990) may provide some insight into the Bolt and Lall (2003) results. They carefully selected parameters for the compensatory model in (4.15) so that generated item response data would have the same characteristics such as internal consistency reliability, item difficulty distribution, and item discrimination as real test data. They then generated 2,000 $\boldsymbol{\theta}$-vectors and

Table 4.4 Item parameters for the partially compensatory and compensatory models for the same test item

Partially compensatory model		Compensatory model	
Parameters	Values	Parameters	Values
a_1	1.26	a_1	.90
a_2	1.60	a_2	1.31
b_1	−.92	d	−.67
b_2	−.15		

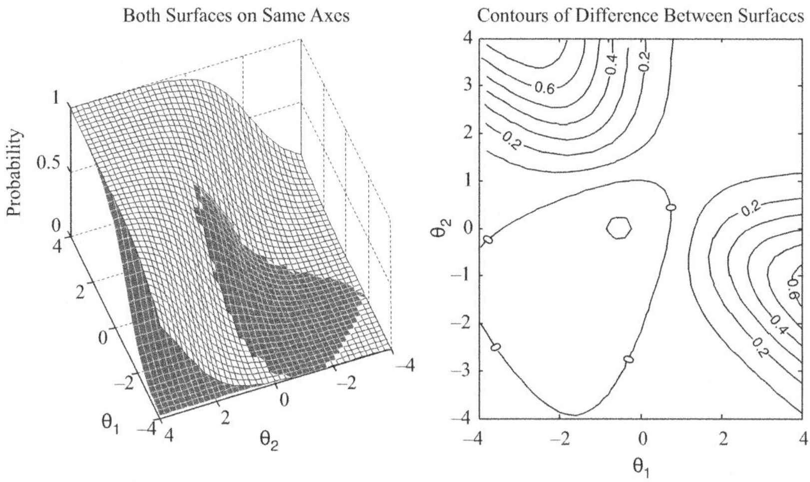

Fig. 4.10 Comparison of partially compensatory and compensatory item response surfaces

computed the probability of correct response for each vector and the compensatory parameters for each item. Then, assuming $\boldsymbol{\theta}$-vectors known, the parameters of the partially compensatory model were estimated that minimized the squared differences in probabilities of correct response. The results were item response surfaces that gave the same p-values for each item assuming a standard bivariate normal distribution of $\boldsymbol{\theta}$.

Table 4.4 gives the item parameters for the two models that gave best match to the item response surfaces. The c_i parameter was set to zero for the item. Figure 4.10 shows the differences in the representation of the interaction between persons and the test item in two different ways. The left panel of Fig. 4.10 shows the item response surfaces for the models on the same set of axes. The dark gray surface is for the partially compensatory model and the white surface is for the compensatory model. The graph shows that the two surfaces intersect, with higher probabilities for the partially compensatory surface $\boldsymbol{\theta}$-vectors when both elements are below 0.

The right panel in Fig. 4.10 shows a contour plot for the differences between the two surfaces. The enclosed curve labeled "0" represents the intersection of the two surfaces. The probability of correct response is the same for the two models for $\boldsymbol{\theta}$-vectors that fall on that curve. The other curves are labeled with the difference in probability of correct response for the two surfaces. Those contours show that the models give quite different probabilities of correct response for $\boldsymbol{\theta}$-vectors near $(-3, 4)$ and $(4, -1)$. In both of these regions of the $\boldsymbol{\theta}$-space, the compensatory model gives probabilities of correct response that are over .6 higher than the partially compensatory model.

The two comparisons of the item response surfaces show that for $\boldsymbol{\theta}$ vectors along the diagonal from $(-4, -4)$ to $(4, 4)$ there is little difference in the probability of correct response for the two models. For real tests with θ-elements that may be positively correlated, the two models may give very similar results. It is only when the elements of the $\boldsymbol{\theta}$-vector are very different that the models predict different rates of responding correctly to the test item.

The results for the test analyzed by Bolt and Lall (2003) suggest that the θ-coordinates tend to function in a compensatory way for the items on the test. However, for other tests, the partially compensatory model may be more appropriate. Ultimately, empirical studies of the usefulness of the models for representing the item response data are needed to determine which form of the model more accurately represents the interactions between persons and test items.

4.1.2 MIRT Models for Test Items with More Than Two Score Categories

Although test items that are scored using more than two score categories have been used for a long time, the development of item response theory models for these item types is a relatively new development. Chapter 2 provides a summary of some of these IRT models under the category polytomous IRT models (see Sect. 2.3). The polytomous IRT models have been extended to allow the person characteristics to be represented by $\boldsymbol{\theta}$-vectors. Muraki and Carlson (1993) produced an extension of the graded response model, and there have been recent extensions of the generalized partial credit model (Yao and Schwarz 2006). The following sections of this chapter describe the extensions of the generalized partial credit, partial credit, and graded response models. These models all fall under the label of compensatory models. At the time of the writing of this book, no partially compensatory polytomous models have been proposed.

4.1.2.1 Multidimensional Generalized Partial Credit Model

The multidimensional extension of the generalized partial credit (MGPC) model is designed to describe the interaction of persons with items that are scored with more than two categories. The maximum score for Item i is represented by K_i. To be consistent with the way dichotomous items are scored, the lowest score is assumed to be 0 and there are $K_i + 1$ score categories overall. The score assigned to a person on the item is represented by $k = 0, 1, \ldots, K_i$. The mathematical representation of the MGPC model is given by the following equation,

$$P(u_{ij} = k|\boldsymbol{\theta}_j) = \frac{e^{k\mathbf{a_i}\boldsymbol{\theta}_\mathbf{j}' - \sum\limits_{u=0}^{k} \beta_{iu}}}{\sum\limits_{v=0}^{K_i} e^{v\mathbf{a_i}\boldsymbol{\theta}_\mathbf{j}' - \sum\limits_{u=0}^{v} \beta_{iu}}}, \tag{4.21}$$

where β_{iu} is the threshold parameter for score category u, β_{i0} is defined to be 0, and all other symbols have there previously defined meaning. The representation of the model given here is a slight variation of the form given in Yao and Schwarz (2006).

There are two important differences between the equation for the MGPC model and that for the GPC model given in (3.33). First, the model does not include separate difficulty and threshold parameters. Second, because $\boldsymbol{\theta}$ is a vector and the βs are scalars, it is not possible to subtract the threshold parameter from $\boldsymbol{\theta}$. Instead, the slope/intercept form of the generalized partial credit model is used as the basis of the multidimensional generalization, $a\theta + d$, but with the sign of the intercept reversed. The result is that the βs cannot be interpreted in the same way as the threshold parameters in the UIRT version of the model. This will be discussed in more detail after presenting the form of the item response surface.

The item response surfaces for the MGPC model for the case when the item/person interaction can be represented in a space with two coordinate dimensions is presented in Fig. 4.11. The test item represented here has scores from 0 to 3. The item parameters for the model are $\mathbf{a_i} = [1.2\ .7]$ and $\beta_{iu} = 0, -2.5, -1.5, .5$.

Figure 4.11 presents four surfaces – one for each possible item score. The darkest surface to the left is for the score of 0. The probability of that score decreases as the

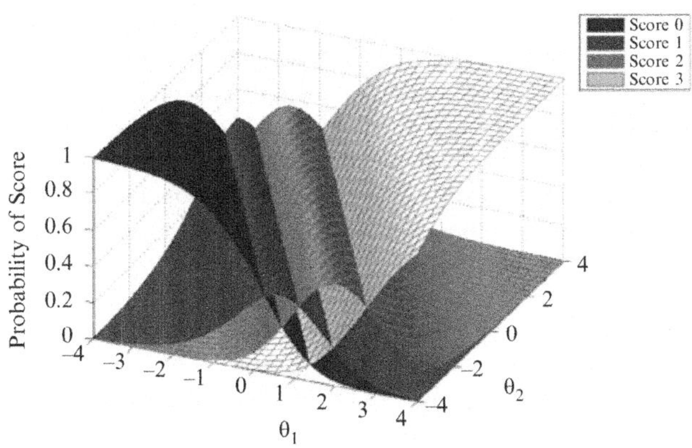

Fig. 4.11 Item response surfaces for MGPC with item parameters $\beta_{iu} = 0, -2.5, -1.5, .5$, and $\mathbf{a_i} = [1.2\ .7]$

θ-coordinate increases on either dimension. The surfaces for scores 1 and 2 first increase and then decrease as the θ-coordinates increase. The surface for the score of 3 increases with an increase in any of the θ-coordinates. The surfaces for the scores of 0 and 3 have upper asymptotes of 1 and lower asymptotes of 0. The other two surfaces have ridge-shaped forms with lower asymptotes of 0.

The intersections between the surfaces for adjacent score categories are over a straight line in the $\boldsymbol{\theta}$-plane. In general, the line is the set of points in the $\boldsymbol{\theta}$-plane where the probabilities of obtaining the adjacent scores are equal. This set of points can be obtained by finding the solution to (4.22). This equation is specified by setting the exponents in the numerator of (4.21) for adjacent score categories equal to each other.

$$k\mathbf{a_i}\boldsymbol{\theta_j}' - \sum_{u=0}^{k} \boldsymbol{\beta}_{iu} = (k+1)\mathbf{a_i}\boldsymbol{\theta_j}' - \sum_{u=0}^{k+1} \boldsymbol{\beta}_{iu}. \tag{4.22}$$

Some algebraic manipulation results in the following solution for the intersection between the kth and $(k+1)$th surfaces. This is the equation for a line in the m-dimensional space used to represent the item. Note that the only part of this expression that changes for different adjacent score categories is the intercept term, β. As was the case for the UIRT version of the generalized partial credit model, this parameter controls the location of the thresholds between score categories.

$$0 = \mathbf{a_i}\boldsymbol{\theta_j}' - \boldsymbol{\beta}_{i,k+1}, \quad k = 0,\ldots,k-1. \tag{4.23}$$

Equation (4.21) gives the expression for the probability of each score for a test item. A surface that defines the expected score on the test item for a person with a particular $\boldsymbol{\theta}$-vector is given by

$$\boldsymbol{E}(u_{ij}|\boldsymbol{\theta_j}) = \sum_{k=0}^{K_i} \boldsymbol{k}\boldsymbol{P}(u_{ij} = \boldsymbol{k}|\boldsymbol{\theta_j}). \tag{4.24}$$

The surface defined by (4.24) for the item shown in Fig. 4.11 is given in Fig. 4.12.

This surface has the appearance of the item response surface for a dichotomously scored item for a compensatory model, but the upper asymptote for the surface is 3, the maximum score on the item. The MGPC is a compensatory model in the same sense as the UIRT version of the model in that a high value on θ_v can compensate for a low value on θ_w resulting in a high expected score on the item. This effect can be seen in the figure for the point (4, –4) that has an expected score near 3.

4.1.2.2 Multidimensional Partial Credit Model

There are a number of simplifications of the multidimensional version of the generalized partial credit model that have the special properties of the Rasch model. That is, they have observable sufficient statistics for the item- and person-parameters. Kelderman and Rijkes (1994) present the general form for one multidimensional extension of the Rasch model to the polytomous test item case. Their model is

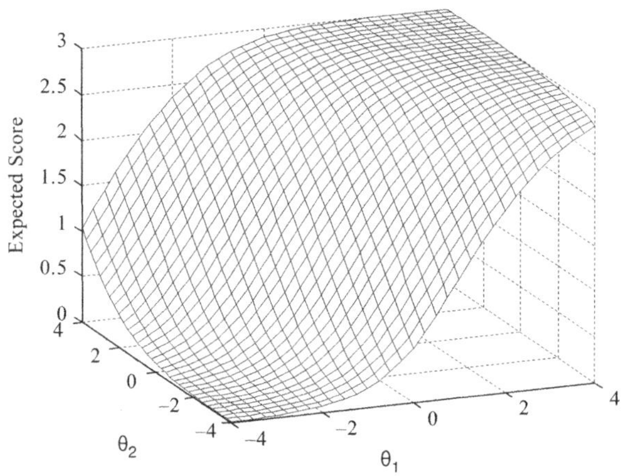

Fig. 4.12 Expected score surface for the item in Fig. 4.11

presented below (4.25) using slightly different symbols than their original presentation to facilitate comparisons with the other models presented in this book. A very similar model is presented by Adams et al. (1997).

$$P(u_{ij} = k|\boldsymbol{\theta}_j) = \frac{e^{\sum_{\ell=1}^{m}(\theta_{j\ell}-b_{i\ell k})W_{i\ell k}}}{\sum_{r=0}^{K_i} e^{\sum_{\ell=1}^{m}(\theta_{j\ell}-b_{i\ell r})W_{i\ell r}}}, \tag{4.25}$$

where $b_{i\ell k}$ is the difficult parameter for Item i on dimension ℓ for score category k, and $W_{i\ell k}$ is a predefined scoring weight for Item i related to dimension ℓ and score category k. The other symbols have the same meaning as in previous equations.

The key to the functioning of this model is the specification of the matrix of weights, $W_{i\ell k}$. Suppose that a test item has $K_i = 3$ score categories: 0, 1, and 2. Also assume that the item is sensitive to differences on two dimensions. The weight matrix for such an item might be specified as $\begin{bmatrix} 0 & 0 \\ 1 & 0 \\ 1 & 1 \end{bmatrix}$. In this matrix, the rows represent the score categories, k, and the columns represent the dimensions, ℓ. This matrix indicates that a 0 response to the item indicates a 0 score on both dimensions, a 1 response indicates that the part of the item related to Dimension 1 was correct but that on Dimension 2 was incorrect, and a score of 2 indicated that the examinee successfully performed the components of the item that are related to both of the dimensions.

For this special case, when $k = 0$, the term in the numerator of (4.25) is $e^0 = 1$. For the other values of k, (4.25) simplifies to

$$P(u_{ij} = k|\boldsymbol{\theta}_j) = \frac{e^{\sum_{\ell=1}^{k}(\theta_{j\ell} - b_{i\ell k})}}{1 + \sum_{r=1}^{K_i} e^{(\theta_{j\ell} - b_{i\ell r})}}, \quad k = 1, \ldots, K_i. \tag{4.26}$$

The developers of this model note that there is an indeterminacy in the estimation of the $b_{i\ell k}$ parameters so they set the parameters equal across the response categories, $k = 1, 2, \ldots, K_i$. The items have different difficulty parameters for the different dimensions, but the same for response categories within a dimension. This means that the item functions as a series of dichotomous items for each dimension with a difficulty for that dimension.

The item response surfaces for each score category for a test item scored 0, 1, or 2 using this model are shown in Fig. 4.13. This is for the two-dimensional case with the scoring matrix given on the previous page. The $b_{i\ell k}$ parameters for the item are -1 for dimension 1 and $+1$ for dimension 2. Careful study of Fig. 4.13 will show that the surface for a score of zero is highest for $\boldsymbol{\theta}$-vector $(-4, -4)$ and lowest for the vector (4, 4). That score surface intersects with the surface for the score of 1 along the line $\theta_1 = -1$. The surface for a score of 1 is near 1 when the $\boldsymbol{\theta}$-vector is $(4, -4)$ and it is near zero for the vector $(-4, 4)$. It intersects with the surface for a score of 2 along the line $\theta_2 = 1$. Thus, for the region with θ_l greater than -1 and θ_2 greater than 1, the score of 2 is the most likely score.

The expected score surface for this test item is obtained by multiplying the score category by the probability and summing over score categories. The expected score surface for the score response surfaces shown in Fig. 4.13 is presented in Fig. 4.14.

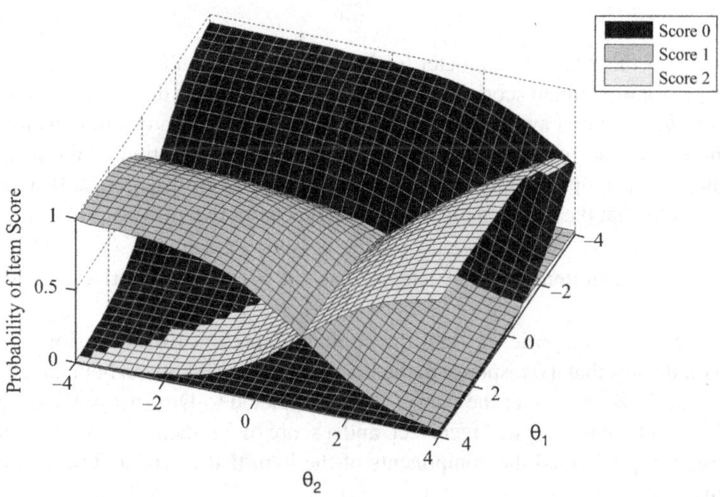

Fig. 4.13 Item response surfaces for a Kelderman and Rijkes model for a test item that requires capabilities on two dimensions to obtain a correct response – score categories of 0, 1, 2 – difficulty parameters -1 for dimension 1 and $+1$ for dimension 2

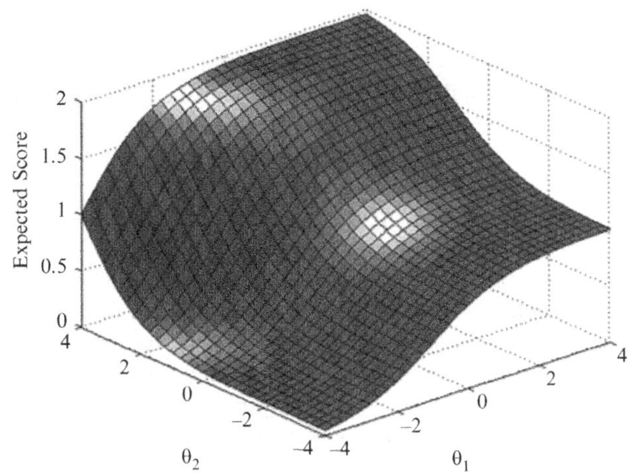

Fig. 4.14 Expected score surface for the Kelderman and Rijkes model for the test item in Fig. 4.13

This surface has an expected score near 2 when levels on both θ-coordinates are 4. The expected score drops as either θ coordinate is reduced, but there is a leveling of the surface in the region around (4, −4). Examinees in this region have mastered the first task in the test item, but have very low proficiency on the second task. Therefore, their expected score is 1.

This is a very interesting model because it acknowledges that the skills and knowledge needed to achieve the highest score on a test item may be different than those needed to achieve lower scores. The user of the model must confront the challenge of identifying the particular skills and knowledge needed for each score category. This might not be too great a problem for one item, but those skills and knowledge categories need to generalize across the set of test items on a test. At this time there is not much in the research literature on the effect of misidentifying the required skills and knowledge for a test item.

4.1.2.3 Multidimensional Graded Response Model

Another approach to the multidimensional modeling of the responses to test items with more than two score categories was presented by Muraki and Carlson (1993). This model is a generalization of the unidimensional graded response model and it uses response functions that have the normal ogive form. As with the unidimensional version of this model, the multidimensional model assumes that successful accomplishment of the task specified by the test item requires a number of steps and reaching step k requires success on step $k - 1$. This type of model is also appropriate for rating scales where a rating category subsumes all previous categories. An example is rating scale for the amount of time spent on a project. If a rating category indicating one hour was spent on a project is selected, which means that all rating categories specifying less than one hour also apply.

The parameterization of the model given here considers the lowest score on Item i to be 0 and the highest score to be m_i. The probability of accomplishing k or more steps is assumed to increase monotonically with an increase in any of the hypothetical constructs underlying the test as represented by the elements of the $\boldsymbol{\theta}$-vector. This is equivalent to dichotomizing the scale at k and scoring k or higher as a 1 and below k as 0 and fitting a dichotomous model to the result. The probability of accomplishing k or more steps is modeled by a two-parameter normal ogive model with the person parameter defined as a linear combination of the elements in the $\boldsymbol{\theta}$-vector weighted by discrimination parameters. The probability of receiving a specific score, k, is the difference between the probability of successfully performing the work for k or more steps and successfully performing the work for $k + 1$ or more steps. If the probability of obtaining an item score of k or higher at a particular $\boldsymbol{\theta}$-level is $P^*(u_{ij} = k \mid \boldsymbol{\theta}_j)$, then the probability that an examinee will receive a score of k is

$$P(u_{ij} = k \mid \boldsymbol{\theta}_j) = P^*(u_{ij} = k \mid \boldsymbol{\theta}_j) - P^*(u_{ij} = k + 1 \mid \boldsymbol{\theta}_j), \tag{4.27}$$

where $P^*(u_{ij} = 0 \mid \boldsymbol{\theta}_j) = 1$ because doing the work for step 0 or more is a certainty for all examinees and $P^*(u_{ij} = m_i + 1 \mid \boldsymbol{\theta}_j) = 0$ because it is impossible do work representing more than category m_i. The latter probability is defined so that the probability of each score can be determined from (4.27). Samejima (1969) labels the terms on the right side of the expression as the cumulative category response functions and those on the left side of the expression as the category response function.

The normal ogive form of the graded response model is given by

$$P(u_{ij} = k \mid \boldsymbol{\theta}_j) = \frac{1}{\sqrt{2\pi}} \int_{\mathbf{a}_i'\boldsymbol{\theta}_j + d_{i,k+1}}^{\mathbf{a}_i'\boldsymbol{\theta}_j + d_{ik}} e^{\frac{-t^2}{2}} \mathrm{d}t, \tag{4.28}$$

where k is the score on the item, 0, 1, ..., m_i, $\mathbf{a}_i$ is a vector of item discrimination parameters, and d_{ik} is a parameter related to ease with which a person will reach the kth step of the item.

Note that the d_{ik} parameter has high positive values when it is relatively easy to obtain a particular score and large negative values when it is difficult to obtain a particular score. The d_{ik} parameters have an inverse relationship with the scores for the item. For score category 0, $d_{i0} = \infty$ and when the score category is $m_i + 1$, a value that is a point higher than actually exists on the score scale for the test item, $d_{i,m_i+1} = -\infty$. Only the values of d_{ik} from $k = 1$ to m_i are estimated in practice.

The probability of response category k can also computed from the difference of two integral expressions. This representation of the model is given in (4.29).

$$P(u_{ij} = k \mid \boldsymbol{\theta}_j) = \frac{1}{\sqrt{2\pi}} \int_{-\infty}^{\mathbf{a}_i'\boldsymbol{\theta}_j + d_{ik}} e^{\frac{-t^2}{2}} dt - \frac{1}{\sqrt{2\pi}} \int_{-\infty}^{\mathbf{a}_i'\boldsymbol{\theta}_j + d_{i,k+1}} e^{\frac{-t^2}{2}} dt. \quad (4.29)$$

This representation of the model makes it clear that it is based on dichotomizing the score scale for the item at different score values and using the normal ogive model to describe the probability of obtaining a score at or above that value. The probability of a particular score value, k, is the difference between the probability of being k or higher and $k + 1$ or higher.

Plots of the category response functions for a test item with four response categories, 0, 1, 2, 3, are shown in Fig. 4.15. This test item has item parameters $a_{i1} = 1.2$, $a_{i2} = .7$, $d_{i1} = .5$, $d_{i2} = -1.5$, and $d_{i3} = -2.5$. Careful study of the figure reveals that as the θs increase, the probability of the score of 0 decreases and the score of 3 increases. The intermediate scores of 1 and 2 increase, then decrease, as the θs increase.

The expected score on the item is computed by multiplying the score by the probability of the score. The expected score surface for the item shown in Fig. 4.15 is presented in Fig. 4.16. The expected score is near 0 when the elements of the $\boldsymbol{\theta}$-vector are both near -4 and it increases to near 3 when the elements of the $\boldsymbol{\theta}$-vector are both near 4. Because the multidimensional graded response model is based on a compensatory multidimensional model, each of the response probability surfaces has parallel equal probability contours. Therefore, the expected score surface also has parallel equal score contours.

The slope of this surface is dependent on both the magnitude of the elements of the **a**-parameter vector and the amount of variation on the d-parameters. The

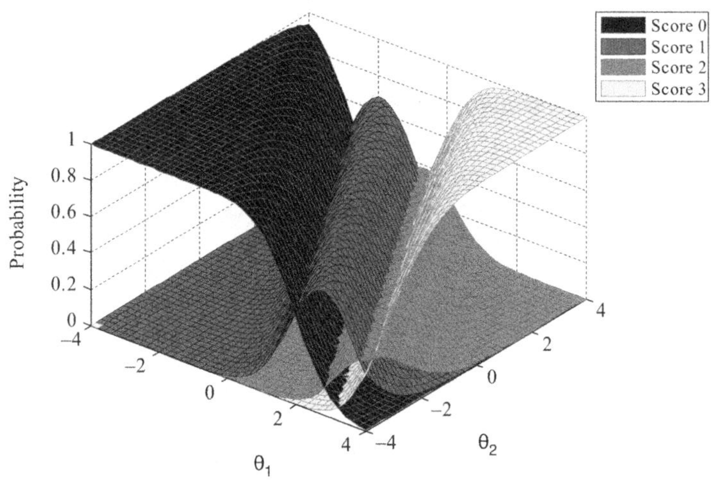

Fig. 4.15 Category response surfaces for an item with four score categories modeled by the graded response model

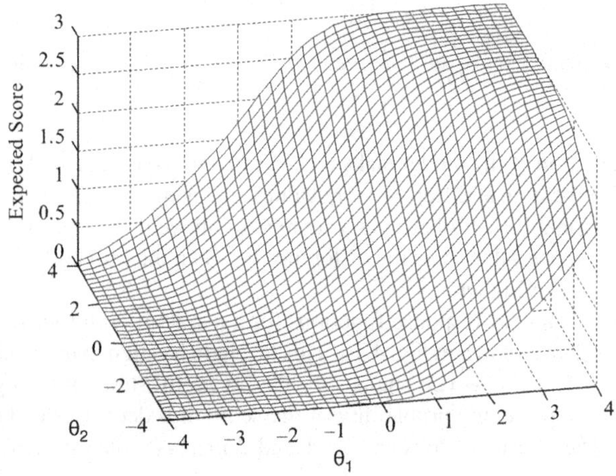

Fig. 4.16 Expected score surface for the item shown in Fig. 4.15

expected response surface is steeper when the variation in d-parameters is reduced. If the d-parameters are all equal, the item functions as a dichotomous item with scores of 0 and m.

The multidimensional graded response model has category response functions that appear similar to those from the multidimensional generalized partial credit model. A comparison of Figs. 4.11 and 4.15 will show the apparent similarity. Although, the models appear similar, they have different underlying scoring processes and work by van der Ark (2001) on the unidimensional versions of the models show that it is possible to distinguish between data sets generated from the two models.

4.2 Future Directions for Model Development

Although many different kinds of MIRT models have been proposed, it is likely that more models will be proposed as the interactions between persons and items become better understood. For example, it is likely that persons scoring performance assessments such as writing samples consider different combinations of skills and knowledge when they assign scores representing different levels of performance. It may be that the difference between 0 and 1 on the rubric for scoring a writing sample may focus on simple writing mechanics, while differences between the top score categories likely reflect differences in organization and style of writing. Such shifts in the focus of the scoring rubrics suggest that there should be vectors of **a**-parameters for each score boundary rather than a single **a**-parameter vector for the item. A merger of the Kelderman and Rijkes (1994) model and the multidimensional versions of the generalized partial credit or graded response models may be needed to accurately represent scores from such rubrics.

It is also hypothesized that for some dichotomously scored items different examinees have different solution strategies. A student who has recently studied the topic that is the focus of the test item may be generating a response based on memory of recent assignments. Another student may need to use problem solving skills to determine how to approach the item. If situations can be identified where such hypotheses can be supported, it may be necessary to merge latent class models and MIRT models. The latent class would define the solution strategy and the vectors of θ-elements would specify the skills and knowledge needed by each strategy. Model development is continuing and it is likely that new models or variations on the existing models will appear in the research literature.

4.3 Exercises

1. Select a test item that you believe would be well modeled by a compensatory model and another test item that would be will modeled by a partially compensatory model. Describe why you believe each of the two items would be best represented by the different types of models.

2. A test item has three score categories and it is well fit by the multidimensional graded response model. The item has been calibrated assuming a three-dimensional $\boldsymbol{\theta}$-space. The item parameter estimates for the item are given in the table below. Compute the probability of each score category for persons with the following two $\boldsymbol{\theta}$-vectors – [−.5 .2 1] and [1.5-.7 0].

a_1	a_2	a_3	d_1	d_2
.5	1	1.2	.8	−1.2

3. A dichotomously scored test item is well modeled by the compensatory logistic model using three coordinate dimensions. The **a**-parameter vector for the item is [.8 1.2 .3] and the d parameter is .5. What is the slope of the item response surface parallel to each coordinate axis at the point [0 0 0] in the $\boldsymbol{\theta}$-space?

4. A dichotomously scored test item is well modeled by the compensatory logistic model using two coordinate dimensions. The **a**-parameter vector for the item is [1.5 .5] and the d parameter is −1. Draw the lines in the $\boldsymbol{\theta}$-plane where the probability of correct response for the item is .2 and .7. Determine the perpendicular distance between the two lines. Do the same for an item with the same d parameter, but with **a**-parameter vector [1.2 1.2]. For which item are the two lines closer together? Explain why there is a difference in the distance for the two items.

5. A short quiz with five test items has been modeled using a MIRT model and the probability of correct response for each item is predicted for a student in the class. The probabilities for the five items are .9, .75, .60, .55, .5. After the quiz was administered the following scores were recorded for that student – 1 1 0 1 0. The item score vector and the probability vector have the items in the same order. What is the probability of the set of item scores for this student based on the MIRT model? What assumption of the model was important for computing the probability of the set of item scores?

6. Using the parameters for the two test items given in 4 above, compute the distance from the origin of the $\boldsymbol{\theta}$-space to the .5 equiprobable contour for each item.

7. Does the data presented in Table 4.1 support the use of a compensatory or partially compensatory MIRT model? Give the reasons for your conclusion using specific information from the table.

8. For a compensatory MIRT model with a lower asymptote parameter, c, that is not zero, what probability of correct response corresponds to $\boldsymbol{\theta}$-vectors that meet the condition $\mathbf{a}'\boldsymbol{\theta} + d = 0$?

9. A test item is well modeled by the Rasch version of the partially compensatory model. The number of elements in the $\boldsymbol{\theta}$-vector is four and all of the b-parameters for the item are equal. The observed probability of correct response for the item is .41 for a group of persons who all have $\boldsymbol{\theta}$-vectors equal to the 0 vector. What value of the b-parameters is consistent with this information?

Chapter 5
Statistical Descriptions of Item and Test Functioning

The MIRT models in Chap. 4 provide mathematical descriptions of the interactions of persons and test items. Although the parameters of these models summarize the characteristics of the items, the vectors of item parameters sometimes lack intuitive meaning. This chapter provides other statistical ways of describing the functioning of test items that may more clearly indicate the value of the test items for determining the location of individuals in the multidimensional $\boldsymbol{\theta}$-space. The ways of describing test item characteristics given here are direct extensions of the descriptive information for UIRT models described in Chap. 2.

5.1 Item Difficulty and Discrimination

The UIRT measures of item difficulty and discrimination are directly related to the characteristics of the item characteristic curve (ICC). The difficulty parameter indicates the value of θ that corresponds to the point of steepest slope for the ICC. The discrimination parameter is related to the slope of the ICC where it is steepest. These two descriptive statistics for test items can be generalized to the MIRT case, but there are some complexities to the process. The slope of a surface is dependent on the direction of movement along the surface so the point of steepest slope depends on the direction that is being considered. For example, the contour plot of the item response surface for a test item that is well modeled by the multidimensional extension of the two-parameter logistic (M2pl) model is shown in Fig. 5.1. The solid arrow in the figure shows a direction that is parallel to the equi-probable contours for the surface, the set of points in the $\boldsymbol{\theta}$-space that yield the same probability of correct response to the test item. Over the length of the arrow, there is no change in probability so the slope in that direction is zero. The dashed arrow is in a direction with substantial change in probability – .4 over the length of the arrow. Because the length of the arrow is about one unit, the slope in that direction is about .4.

At each point in the $\boldsymbol{\theta}$-space, there is a direction that has the maximum slope from that point. If the entire $\boldsymbol{\theta}$-space is considered and the slopes in all directions at each point are evaluated, there is a maximum slope overall for the test item. The value of the maximum slope would be a useful summary of the capabilities of the

M.D. Reckase, *Multidimensional Item Response Theory*, Statistics for Social and Behavioral Sciences, DOI 10.1007/978-0-387-89976-3_5,

© Springer Science+Business Media, LLC 2009

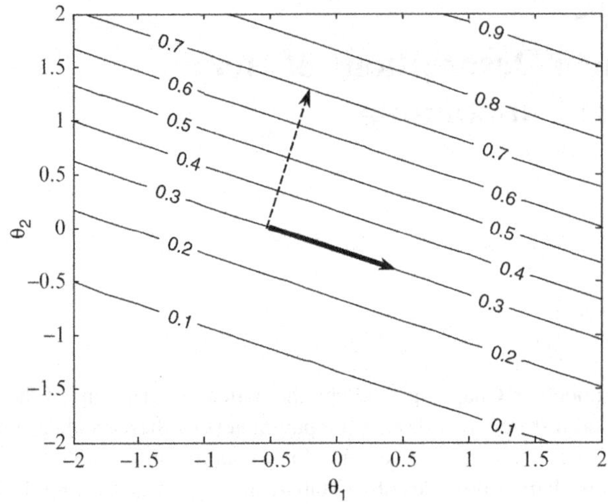

Fig. 5.1 *Arrows* showing differences in slope for an M2pl item with parameters $a_1 = .5, a_2 = 1.2, d = -.6$

test item for distinguishing between $\boldsymbol{\theta}$-points in the direction of greatest slope. It would also be helpful to know the relationship between the **a**-parameter vector and the values of the slopes at a point in the $\boldsymbol{\theta}$-space. Knowing the relationship will allow the evaluation of the usefulness of the test item for differentiating between $\boldsymbol{\theta}$-points at different locations in the space using estimates of the item parameters.

The b-parameter in UIRT is a measure of the distance from the 0-point of the θ-scale to the value on the scale that is below the point of steepest slope for the ICC. The sign of the b-parameter indicates the direction from the 0-point of the θ-scale to the location of the point of steepest slope. By convention, negative signs indicate distances to the left of the 0-point and positive signs indicate distances to the right of the 0-point (see Sect. 2.1.1 for a discussion of the difficulty in UIRT models). It would be useful to have a similar indicator for test items that are described using multidimensional models. The parallel measure of item difficulty would be the distance from the origin of the $\boldsymbol{\theta}$-space (i.e., the $\mathbf{0}$-vector) to the $\boldsymbol{\theta}$-point that is below the point of steepest slope for the surface. The sign associated with this distance would indicate the relative position of the $\boldsymbol{\theta}$-point to the origin of the $\boldsymbol{\theta}$-space. Also, it would be useful if the distance to this point were related to the d-parameter in the model.

The statistics that correspond to the a and b-parameters for the UIRT models are derived here for the M2pl model. A similar derivation can be used for other compensatory models, but they do not generalize to the partially compensatory models. The basic concepts apply to the partially compensatory models, but the corresponding statistical summaries do not result in simple mathematical expressions.

The goal of developing these statistics is to determine the point of steepest slope for the surface and the distance from the origin of the $\boldsymbol{\theta}$-space to that point. Because

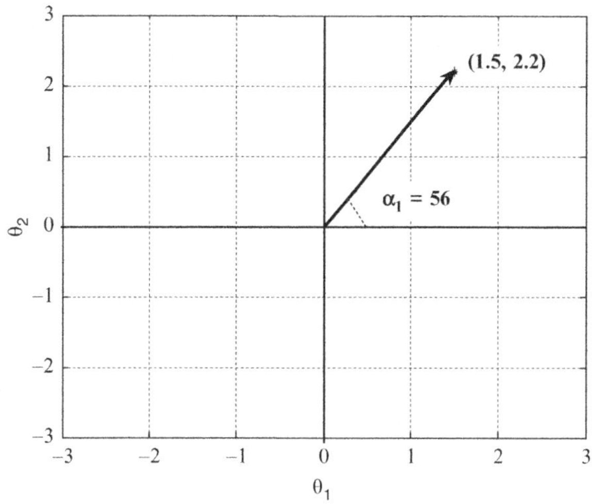

Fig. 5.2 Polar coordinate representation of a point in a two-dimensional $\boldsymbol{\theta}$-space – the length of *arrow* is 2.66 θ-coordinate units

this conceptualization uses the distance from the origin of the $\boldsymbol{\theta}$-space as a reference point for the measure of item difficulty, it is helpful to reparameterize the M2pl model using a polar coordinate representation. That is, instead of representing each point in the $\boldsymbol{\theta}$-space by a vector of θ-coordinates, each point is represented by a vector of angles from each coordinate axis and a distance from the origin. A two-dimensional representation of this reparameterization is given in Fig. 5.2. The same conceptual framework can be used to generalize the reparameterization to an n-dimensional space.

In Fig. 5.2, the location of a point in the $\boldsymbol{\theta}$-space is indicated by the two coordinates, $\theta_1 = 1.5$ and $\theta_2 = 2.2$. That same point can also be represented by a distance (i.e., the bold arrow) of 2.66 θ-units and a direction of 56° from the θ_1-axis. The distance is computed using the standard distance formula and the angle is determined from the right triangle trigonometric formula for the cosine of an angle. In this two-dimensional case, the angle between the arrow and the θ_2-axis can be determined by subtraction as $90 - 56 = 34°$. In m dimensions, $m - 1$ angles can be computed from the θ-coordinates using trigonometric relationships. The mth angle is mathematically determined because the sum of squared cosines must equal 1. Given the distance to the point and the directions from the axes, the values of the coordinates of the point on each of the axes can be recovered using the trigonometric relationship

$$\theta_v = \zeta \cos \alpha_v, \tag{5.1}$$

where θ_v is the coordinate of the point on dimension v, ζ is the distance from the origin to the point, and α_v is the angle between the vth axis and the line from the origin to the point.

The expression on the right side of (5.1) can be substituted for the θ-coordinates in the exponent of the M2pl model. After the substitution, the model is given by

$$P\left(U_{ij}=1|\zeta_j,\mathbf{a_i},\boldsymbol{\alpha}_\mathbf{j},d_i\right)=\frac{\mathrm{e}^{\left(\zeta_j\sum\limits_{\ell=1}^{m}a_{i\ell}\cos\alpha_{j\ell}\right)+d_i}}{1+\mathrm{e}^{\left(\zeta_j\sum\limits_{\ell=1}^{m}a_{i\ell}\cos\alpha_{j\ell}\right)+d_i}}, \tag{5.2}$$

where ζ_j is a scalar parameter for Person j that indicates the distance from the origin to the location of the person, $\boldsymbol{\alpha}_\mathbf{j}$ is the vector of angles between the coordinate axes and the line from the origin to the point representing the location of Person j in the solution space, and the other symbols have the same meaning as for the M2pl model. The $\boldsymbol{\alpha}_\mathbf{j}$ vector has m elements, but only $m-1$ of them need to be estimated because the squared cosines must sum to 1.

The form of the model given in (5.2) is useful because the slope in a direction specified by the $\boldsymbol{\alpha}$-vector can be determined by taking the partial derivative of the model equation with respect to the single scalar variable, ζ_j. This partial derivative is given in (5.3).

$$\frac{\partial P\left(U_{ij}=1|\zeta_j,\mathbf{a_i},\boldsymbol{\alpha}_\mathbf{j},d_i\right)}{\partial\zeta_j}=P_{ij}Q_{ij}\sum_{\ell=1}^{m}a_{i\ell}\cos\alpha_{j\ell}. \tag{5.3}$$

In (5.3), the P_{ij} and Q_{ij} symbols are abbreviated notation for the probability of correct and incorrect response, respectively, for Person j on Item i. This result shows that the slope at a location in the solution space is dependent on the probability of correct response at that location, the elements of the **a**-parameter vector, and the angles with the axes indicated by the $\boldsymbol{\alpha}$-vector. If the angle with an axis is 0°, the corresponding cosine is 1 and all of the other cosines are 0. The slope along an axis simplifies to $P_{ij}Q_{ij}a_{i\ell}$, for coordinate axis ℓ.

To determine the steepest slope in the direction specified by the $\boldsymbol{\alpha}$-vector, the second derivative of the item response function is taken with respect to ζ_j and the result is set equal to zero and solved for the value of ζ_j. The second derivative is given in (5.4).

$$\frac{\partial^2 P\left(U_{ij}=1|\zeta_j,\mathbf{a_i},\boldsymbol{\alpha}_\mathbf{j},d_i\right)}{\partial\zeta_j^2}=\left(\sum_{\ell=1}^{m}a_{i\ell}\cos\alpha_{j\ell}\right)^2 P_{ij}\left(1-3P_{ij}+2P_{ij}^2\right). \tag{5.4}$$

There are three solutions when (5.4) is set equal to 0, but only one of them results in a finite value of ζ_j. That solution is when $P_{ij}=.5$. The probability is .5 when the exponent of (5.2) is 0. Solving for the value of ζ_j that results in 0 gives the location along the line in the direction specified by the $\boldsymbol{\alpha}$-vector where the surface has maximum slope. The result is

$$\frac{-d_i}{\sum_{\ell=1}^{m} a_{i\ell} \cos \alpha_{j\ell}}, \tag{5.5}$$

where all of the symbols have been previously defined. The location of the point of maximum slope along a particular axis is simply $-d/a_{i\ell}$ because all of the cosines will be 0 except for the axis ℓ being considered. For that axis, the cosine is 1.

Substituting the expression in (5.5) for ζ_j in (5.2) results in a probability of a correct response of .5 for a person located along the line from the origin at the point that gives the steepest slope. As a result, the value of the slope at the point of steepest slope in the direction specified by the $\boldsymbol{\alpha}$-vector is

$$\frac{1}{4}\sum_{\ell=1}^{m} a_{i\ell} \cos \alpha_{j\ell}. \tag{5.6}$$

To determine the direction of steepest slope from the origin of the $\boldsymbol{\theta}$-space, the expression in (5.6) is differentiated with respect to cos $\boldsymbol{\alpha}$ and solved for 0. This is done under the constraint that the sum of the squared cosines is equal to 1. The result is the system of equations given in (5.7).

$$a_{i\ell} - a_{im}\frac{\cos \alpha_{i\ell}}{\cos \alpha_{im}} = 0, \quad \text{for } \ell = 1, 2, \ldots, m-1, \tag{5.7}$$

where $\cos^2 \alpha_{im} = 1 - \sum_{k=1}^{m-1} \cos^2 \alpha_{ik}$. The solution for the system of equations is given by

$$\cos \alpha_{i\ell} = \frac{a_{i\ell}}{\sqrt{\sum_{k=1}^{m} a_{ik}^2}}. \tag{5.8}$$

The corresponding angles are given by taking the arccosine of the cosine of α. These angles and cosines are characteristics of the item. They indicate the direction from the origin of the $\boldsymbol{\theta}$-space to the point in the $\boldsymbol{\theta}$-space that has the greatest slope considering all possible directions. The cosines specified by (5.8) are sometimes called *direction cosines*.

The distance from the origin to the point of steepest slope in the direction specified by (5.8) can be obtained by substituting the results of (5.8) for the cos α in (5.5). The result is

$$B_i = \frac{-d_i}{\sqrt{\sum_{k=1}^{m} a_{ik}^2}}. \tag{5.9}$$

The symbol B_i is used here to represent the multidimensional difficulty of the test item. Sometimes this item characteristic is represented by MDIFF, but B is used here to more clearly make the connection to the unidimensional b-parameter because it has an equivalent interpretation to that of the b-parameter in UIRT models. That is, high positive values of B indicate difficult items (i.e., those that require high values of the elements of $\boldsymbol{\theta}$ to yield a probability of a correct response greater than .5). Low values of B indicate items with a high probability of correct response for the levels of $\boldsymbol{\theta}$ that are usually observed.

This interpretation of B applies only to the direction specified by the $\boldsymbol{\alpha}$-vector. Thus, this analysis of the characteristics of a test item results in two descriptive measures. One is an indication of the difficulty of the test item (i.e., B) and the other is a description of the combination of the coordinate axes that is most differentiated by the test item (i.e., $\boldsymbol{\alpha}$). This combination is indicated by the direction of steepest slope from the origin of the $\boldsymbol{\theta}$-space.

A value that is analogous to the discrimination parameter from the UIRT model can also be defined. In UIRT, the discrimination parameter is related to the slope at the point of steepest slope for the ICC. The equivalent conceptualization for the discrimination parameter in the MIRT case is the slope of the item response surface at the point of steepest slope in the direction from the origin of the θ-space. This slope can be determined by substituting (5.8) into (5.6). The slope is $1/4$ the value presented in (5.10). As with the unidimensional IRT models, the constant $1/4$ is not included in the expression resulting in a multidimensional discrimination index of

$$A_i = \sqrt{\sum_{k=1}^{m} a_{ik}^2}. \tag{5.10}$$

A_i is the multidimensional discrimination for Item i. In some articles, the term MDISC_i is used instead of A_i. Here, A_i is used to emphasize the connection to the a-parameter in the unidimensional models. Note that A_i has the same mathematical form as the term in the denominator of (5.9). Therefore, another expression for the multidimensional difficulty is $B_i = -d_i / A_i$.

Two examples are provided to give intuitive meaning to these descriptive indices of multidimensional items. Figure 5.3 provides the equi-probable contours for two test items that are described in a two-dimensional coordinate system. The parameters for the two items are given in Table 5.1 along with the multidimensional discrimination and difficulty, and the angles with the coordinate axes for the direction of maximum slope. Several features can be noted from the plots. First, the contour lines are closer together for Item 1 than for Item 2. This shows that Item 1 is more discriminating than Item 2 because the probabilities are changing more quickly with change in location of $\boldsymbol{\theta}$-points. This is also shown by the value of A_i for the two items. Item 1 has a larger value for the multidimensional discrimination.

A second feature of the contour plots is that the contour lines have different orientations to the coordinate axes. Each plot also contains an arrow that shows the direction of steepest slope from the origin of the $\boldsymbol{\theta}$-space. The angles with the coordinate axes for the arrows are given by the α-values. For Item 1, the arrow is about 23° from the θ_1-axis and about 67° from the θ_2-axis. The angles are quite different for the arrow for Item 2. Note that the arrows are also pointing in different directions.

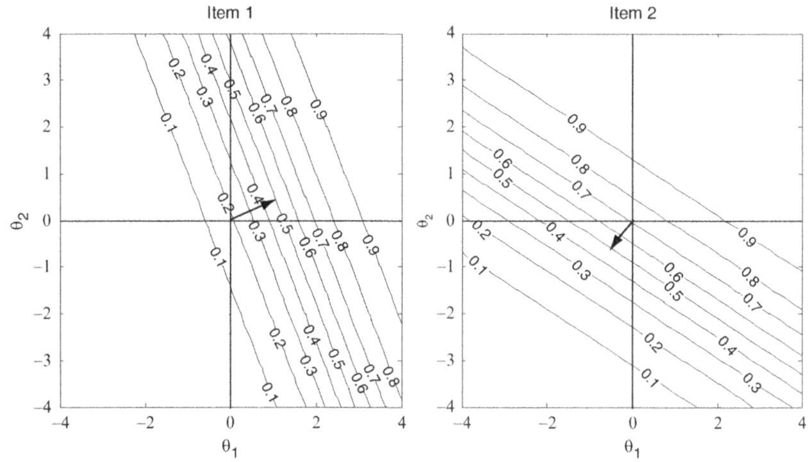

Fig. 5.3 Representation of the characteristics of the items with parameters in Table 5.1

Table 5.1 Item parameters and multidimensional statistics for two test items

Item	a_1	a_2	d	A	B	α_1	α_2
1	1.2	.5	−1.5	1.30	1.15	22.62	67.38
2	.6	1	.9	1.17	−.77	59.04	30.96

The arrows stretch from the origin of the $\boldsymbol{\theta}$-space to the line of the .5-probability contour. When the arrow is in the lower left quadrant of the space, the item is fairly easy. When the arrow is in the upper right quadrant, the item is fairly hard. The only way that the arrow will point in the direction of one of the other quadrants is if one of the a-parameters is negative. The length and direction of the arrow is given by B_i. Negative values generally indicate easy items and positive values hard items.

If the item response surfaces for multiple items are plotted as equi-probable contour plots on the same set of axes, the characteristics of the individual items will be difficult to discern because of the number of intersecting equi-probable lines. One way to show the same information in a less cluttered way is to represent each item by an arrow with the base of the arrow at the point of maximum slope along a line from the origin of the $\boldsymbol{\theta}$-space. The arrow points up slope in the direction along the line from the origin. The length of the arrow can be used to represent the discriminating power, A_i, for the item. The distance from the origin to the base of the arrow indicates the difficulty, B_i, for the item and the direction, $\boldsymbol{\alpha}_i$, of the arrow shows the direction of greatest positive change in slope for the item. This type of representation for the two items in Table 5.1 is given in Fig. 5.4. Using these conventions, a number of items can be displayed graphically when the number of coordinate axes is two or three. Figure 5.5 gives the arrow representation for 45 items in a three-dimensional space. This representation of the items makes it clear that the items form three fairly distinct sets that tend to have the steepest slope in the same direction.

Fig. 5.4 Representation of items with parameters in Table 5.1 as *arrows*

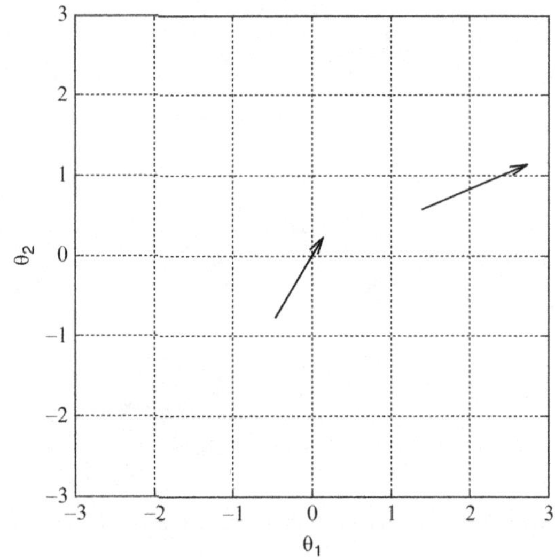

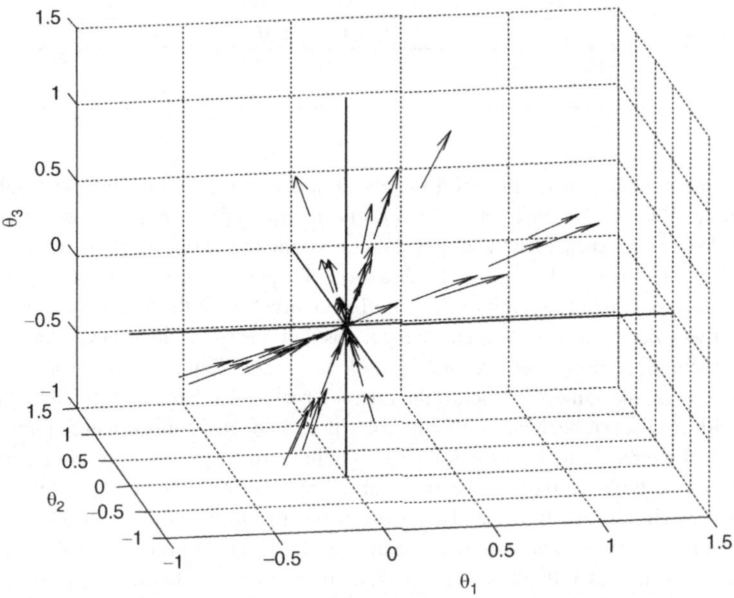

Fig. 5.5 Representation of 45 items by *arrows* in a three-dimensional space

The description of test items using the concepts of multidimensional difficulty, multidimensional discrimination, and direction of steepest slope in the multidimensional space can also be used with polytomous test items. Muraki and Carlson (1993) derive these statistics for the multidimensional graded response model. The development results in the same expressions for multidimensional discrimination, A_i, and the vector of angles, $\boldsymbol{\alpha}$. They also developed the equivalent to (5.9) for the step difficulty for an item (see (4.28)).

$$B_{ik} = \frac{-d_{ik}}{\sqrt{\sum_{\ell=1}^{m} a_{i\ell}^2}}, \tag{5.11}$$

where B_{ik} is the step difficulty for the kth step of the graded response item and d_{ik} is the step parameter as defined in the model. The other terms have been previously defined.

The same procedures can be used to define the multidimensional statistics for the item whenever the exponential term in the model is in the form $\mathbf{a}\boldsymbol{\theta}' + d$. This is also the case when the limits of integration for a normal ogive model have the same form. Partially compensatory models do not have this form; therefore, these statistical descriptions of characteristics of the test items do not apply to test items that are described by partially compensatory models. It may be possible to derive similar statistics for test items model by the partially compensatory models, but they have not been developed at the time this book was written.

5.2 Item Information

The concept of item information that is used in UIRT can also be generalized to the multidimensional case. The definition of information in the multidimensional case is the same as that given in (2.42) for the unidimensional case – the squared slope of the regression of the item score on the $\boldsymbol{\theta}$ divided by the variance of the item score at θ. There is a complication, however. At each point in the $\boldsymbol{\theta}$-space, the slope of the multidimensional item response surface differs depending on the direction of movement from the point. The two arrows in Fig. 5.1 give examples of the differences in slope for movements in different directions. The solid arrow shows movement in a direction that has a slope of 0. The dashed arrow has a much higher positive slope. This implies that the information provided by a test item about the difference between nearby points in the $\boldsymbol{\theta}$-space depends on the orientation of the points (i.e., the direction of movement from one point to the other).

To accommodate the change in slope with direction taken from a point in the $\boldsymbol{\theta}$-space, the definition of item information is generalized to

$$I_{\boldsymbol{\alpha}}(\boldsymbol{\theta}) = \frac{[\nabla_{\boldsymbol{\alpha}} P(\boldsymbol{\theta})]^2}{P(\boldsymbol{\theta})Q(\boldsymbol{\theta})}, \tag{5.12}$$

where $\boldsymbol{\alpha}$ is the vector of angles with the coordinate axes that defines the direction taken from the $\boldsymbol{\theta}$-point, $\nabla_{\boldsymbol{\alpha}}$ is the directional derivative or gradient, in the direction $\boldsymbol{\alpha}$, and the other symbols as previously defined. Equation (5.12) represents the information for one item at one location in the $\boldsymbol{\theta}$-space, so the item and person subscripts have not been included to more clearly show the general structure of the expression.

The directional derivative for the item response surface is given by

$$\nabla_{\alpha} P(\boldsymbol{\theta}) = \frac{\partial P(\boldsymbol{\theta})}{\partial \theta_1} \cos \alpha_1 + \frac{\partial P(\boldsymbol{\theta})}{\partial \theta_2} \cos \alpha_2 + \cdots + \frac{\partial P(\boldsymbol{\theta})}{\partial \theta_m} \cos \alpha_m. \tag{5.13}$$

If the MIRT model being considered is the multidimensional extension of the two-parameter logistic model given in (4.5), the directional derivative is

$$\begin{aligned} \nabla_{\alpha} P(\boldsymbol{\theta}) = a_1 P(\boldsymbol{\theta}) Q(\boldsymbol{\theta}) \cos \alpha_1 \\ + a_2 P(\boldsymbol{\theta}) Q(\boldsymbol{\theta}) \cos \alpha_2 + \cdots + a_m P(\boldsymbol{\theta}) Q(\boldsymbol{\theta}) \cos \alpha_m. \end{aligned} \tag{5.14}$$

This expression can be presented more compactly as

$$\nabla_{\alpha} P(\boldsymbol{\theta}) = P(\boldsymbol{\theta}) Q(\boldsymbol{\theta}) \sum_{v=1}^{m} a_v \cos \alpha_v. \tag{5.15}$$

Substituting (5.15) into (5.12) yields

$$I_{\alpha}(\boldsymbol{\theta}) = \frac{\left[P(\boldsymbol{\theta}) Q(\boldsymbol{\theta}) \sum_{v=1}^{m} a_v \cos \alpha_v \right]^2}{P(\boldsymbol{\theta}) Q(\boldsymbol{\theta})} = P(\boldsymbol{\theta}) Q(\boldsymbol{\theta}) \left(\sum_{v=1}^{m} a_v \cos \alpha_v \right)^2. \tag{5.16}$$

When the MIRT model contains only two dimensions, the information in the direction specified by the $\boldsymbol{\alpha}$-vector can be represented by an information surface. The height of the surface above the θ-plane indicates the amount of information at each location in the plane. Information surfaces for the test item represented in the contour plot shown in Fig. 5.1 are shown in Fig. 5.6. The surfaces show the information in three directions – angles of 0, 67.38, and 90° with the θ_l-axis.

The angle of 67.38° is the direction from the θ_l-axis when the item response surface has the steepest slope along a line from the origin of the space. In all three cases, the information surfaces have the shape of a ridge that has its highest region over the .5 equiprobable contour line for the test item. That is the line in the $\boldsymbol{\theta}$-space where the slope of the item response surface is the greatest as well. Of all of the possible directions in the space, the direction of steepest slope has the highest ridge for the information function. The low maximum height for the ridge in the panel on the left of Fig. 5.6 shows that the test item is relatively ineffective at distinguishing nearby points when the direction between the points is parallel to the θ_l-axis. However, the test item is quite effective at distinguishing points on either side of the .5 equiprobable contour in the direction of steepest slope for the item response surface – 67.38° to the θ_l-axis. This is shown by the high ridge in the middle panel

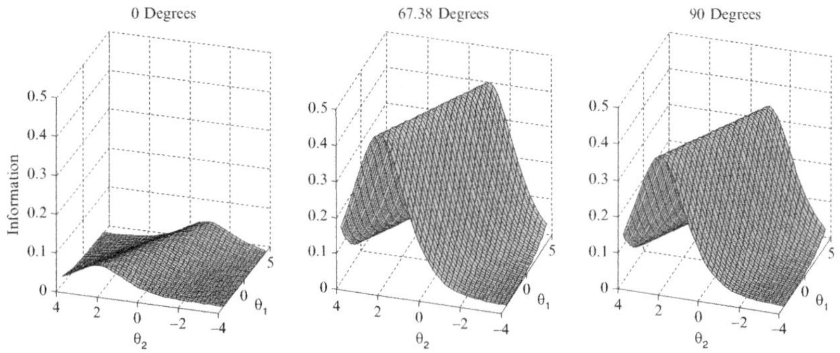

Fig. 5.6 Information surfaces for a M2PL test item with $a_1 = .5$, $a_2 = 1.2$, and $d = -.6$ in three directions

of Fig. 5.6. The capability of the item for distinguishing in a direction parallel to the θ_2-axis is between the other two directions as shown by the right panel in the figure. The maximum height of the surface is between the maximum heights of the surfaces for the other two directions.

If the direction of steepest slope from (5.8) is substituted for the $\cos \alpha_k$ in (5.16), the result is the information for the test item in the direction of maximum slope. That expression is given by

$$I_{\alpha\ \max}(\boldsymbol{\theta}) = P(\boldsymbol{\theta})Q(\boldsymbol{\theta})\sum_{k=1}^{m} a_k^2 = P(\boldsymbol{\theta})Q(\boldsymbol{\theta})A^2, \tag{5.17}$$

where A is the multidimensional discrimination for the item. In this case, the information function has exactly the same form as that for the two-parameter logistic model described in Chap. 2. For the example in Fig. 5.6, $A = 1.3$ and because the term $P(\boldsymbol{\theta})Q(\boldsymbol{\theta})$ has its maximum when $P(\boldsymbol{\theta}) = .5$, the maximum information is $.5 \times .5 \times 1.3^2 = .425$.

Because the information surface is different in every direction that is selected, it is difficult to get a sense of the overall information provided by an item. One approach to addressing this issue was given by Reckase and McKinley (1991). For a grid of points selected in the $\boldsymbol{\theta}$-space, the information was determined in directions from the θ_1-axis in 10° increments. The results were plotted as lines radiating from the $\boldsymbol{\theta}$-points in the selected directions with the length of the line indicating the amount of information. These plots have sometimes been labeled "clam shell" plots because the sets of lines often look like the back of a clam shell. Figure 5.7 shows a clam shell plot for the information provided by the test item shown in Fig. 5.6.

Careful examination of Fig. 5.7 will show that the lines are longest for $\boldsymbol{\theta}$-points that fall near the .5 equiprobable contour line and that the longest line in each set of lines is at 70°, the angle closest to the direction of maximum slope from the origin of the $\boldsymbol{\theta}$-space. When the $\boldsymbol{\theta}$-points are far from the .5 contour line, the information is very low and the amount is represented by a point on the graph. Clam shell

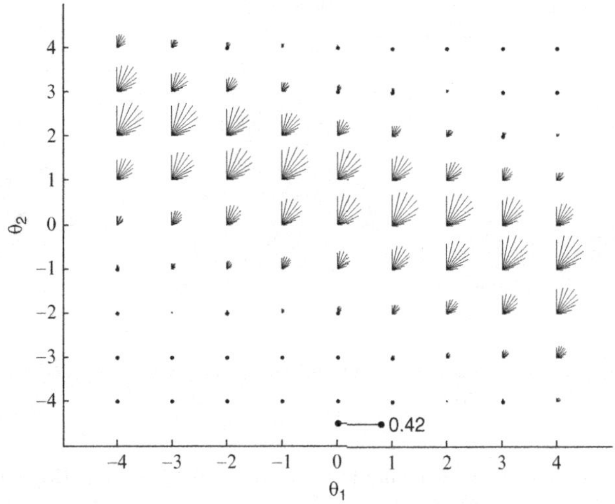

Fig. 5.7 Information for a M2PL test item with $a_1 = .5$, $a_2 = 1.2$, and $d = -.6$ at equally spaced points in the $\boldsymbol{\theta}$-space for angles from 0° to 90° at 10° intervals

plots can be used to represent information in many directions from each point in the $\boldsymbol{\theta}$-space for any of the MIRT models. Unfortunately, the plots can only be produced for two-dimensional solutions. Three-dimensional plots are possible, but the information pattern is difficult to see from such plots because lines from one point cover those from another point. There is not yet a satisfactory solution for graphically representing the information from items when the number of coordinate dimensions is greater than two. Although not solving the problem of representing test characteristics in high dimensions, Ackerman (1996) and Ackerman et al. (2003) provide other ways to graphically represent the characteristics of tests and test items when they are modeled using two or three-dimensional MIRT models.

5.3 MIRT Descriptions of Test Functioning

The UIRT procedure used to represent the functioning of sets of items that are scored together to represent the performance of a person, usually called tests, can be used when the tests are analyzed using MIRT models. Most of these procedures can be represented graphically when the item response data are modeled with two θ-coordinates. The procedures are the same for higher numbers of coordinate dimensions, but graphic representations are not available.

A common UIRT approach for showing the characteristics of a test is the *test characteristic curve* (see Sect. 2.2.1). This curve is the regression of the sum of the item scores on θ. This regression function can easily be generalized to the multidimensional case. The *test characteristic surface* (TCS) is the regression of the sum of the item scores on the $\boldsymbol{\theta}$-vector. The mathematical expression for the test characteristic surface, or TCS, is exactly the same as for UIRT models (see (2.38)) except that the expectation is conditioned on the $\boldsymbol{\theta}$-vector instead of the unidimensional value of θ. The MIRT expression for the TCS for a test composed of dichotomously scored test items is given by

$$E\left(y_j|\boldsymbol{\theta}_\mathbf{j}\right) = E\left(\sum_{i=1}^{n} u_{ij}|\boldsymbol{\theta}_\mathbf{j}\right) = \sum_{i=1}^{n} E\left(u_{ij}|\boldsymbol{\theta}_\mathbf{j}\right) = \sum_{i=1}^{n} P\left(u_{ij}|\boldsymbol{\theta}_\mathbf{j}\right). \tag{5.18}$$

The TCS is simply the sum of the item characteristic surfaces for the items in the test. For tests composed of polytomously scored items, or mixtures of dichotomously and polytomously scored items, all of the terms in (5.18) still hold except the one at the far right. The TCS is the sum of the expected scores on the test items included in the test conditional on the $\boldsymbol{\theta}$-vectors.

An example of the TCS for a test is given using the item parameter estimates provided in Table 5.2. These parameter estimates were obtained from a two-dimensional solution using the program NOHARM. Detailed information about this program is given in Chap. 6. The TCS for this set of items is shown using two different graphic representations, (a) and (b), in Fig. 5.8. For points in the $\boldsymbol{\theta}$-space near $(-4, -4)$, the expected number-correct score on the set of test items is near 0. With increase in either θ-coordinate, the expected number-correct score increases until it approaches the maximum of 20 near $(4, 4)$. The surface appears similar to an item characteristic surface (see panel a), but the equal score contours are not straight lines (see panel b) as they are for an item characteristic surface (Fig. 4.5).

Another way of summarizing the characteristics of the set of test items in a test is to indicate the orientation of the unidimensional θ-scale in the multidimensional

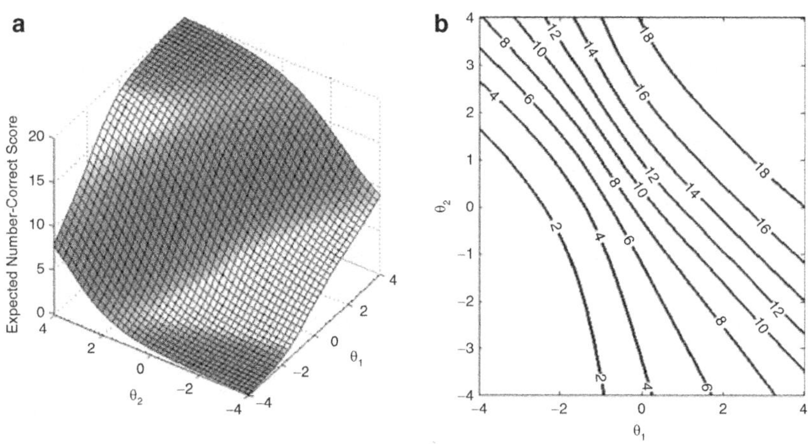

Fig. 5.8 Test characteristic surface for the test items in Table 5.2. Plot (**a**) shows the surface and plot (**b**) shows the equal score contours for the surface

Table 5.2 Item parameter estimates from a two-dimensional compensatory model

Item number	a_1	a_2	d
1	.79	1.36	−.90
2	.93	1.38	−1.20
3	.58	.38	1.00
4	.87	.87	−.97
5	.83	.79	−1.08
6	.31	.99	−1.53
7	.60	.48	−.61
8	.60	.87	−.60
9	1.64	.15	1.24
10	1.11	1.30	−.69
11	.53	.97	−1.31
12	1.26	.39	.92
13	2.37	.00	2.49
14	1.17	1.76	−.06
15	.96	1.26	−.48
16	.56	.46	−.82
17	1.17	.20	1.11
18	.63	.26	.66
19	1.01	.47	−.15
20	.81	.77	−1.08

space. This is the line in the multidimensional space that represents the unidimensional scale. The projections of the $\boldsymbol{\theta}$-points in the multidimensional space gives an estimate of the unidimensional θ that would result if the response data from the test items were analyzed using a unidimensional IRT model. Wang (1985, 1986) derived that the unidimensional θ-line corresponding to the θ-estimates from a set of test items was related to the characteristics of the matrix of discrimination parameters for the compensatory MIRT model, **a**. The orientation of the unidimensional line in the $\boldsymbol{\theta}$-space is given by the eigenvector of the $\mathbf{a}'\mathbf{a}$ matrix that corresponds to the largest eigenvalues of that matrix. Wang labeled the unidimensional θ that is estimated in this way as the *reference composite* for the test.

For the **a**-matrix specified by the middle two columns of Table 5.2, $\mathbf{a}'\mathbf{a}$ results in the matrix $\begin{bmatrix} 21.54 & 12.82 \\ 12.82 & 15.87 \end{bmatrix}$. The diagonal values in this matrix are the sum of the squared a-elements from the columns of the **a**-matrix. The off-diagonal values are the sums of the cross-products of the a-elements from different columns. The eigenvalues for this matrix are 31.84 and 5.57. Note that the sum of the eigenvalues is the same as the sum of the diagonal elements. The eigenvector that corresponds to the larger of the two eigenvalues is $\begin{bmatrix} .7797 \\ .6292 \end{bmatrix}$. The sum of the squared elements of the eigenvector is equal to 1; therefore, the elements of the eigenvector can be considered as direction cosines. These direction cosines give the orientation of the reference composite with the coordinate axes of the $\boldsymbol{\theta}$-space.

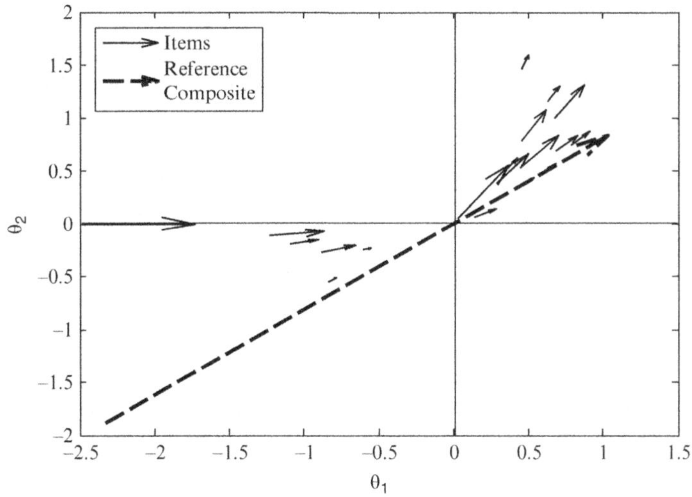

Fig. 5.9 Item *arrows* and reference composite for the item parameters in Table 5.1

Because the test items represented in the **a**-matrix were calibrated assuming a two-dimensional coordinate space, the relationship between the reference composite and the arrow representation of test items can be shown graphically. Figure 5.9 shows the arrows representing each item and the large, bold, dashed arrow representing the reference composite.

The angle between the reference composite and the coordinate axes can be determined by taking the arccosine of the elements of the eigenvector. In this example, the reference composite has an angle of approximately 39° with the θ_1 axis and 51° with the θ_2 axis. This orientation results from the slightly higher **a**-parameters related to dimension 1 than dimension 2. It is useful to compare the orientation of the reference composite with the contour plot in Fig. 5.8. The reference composite tends to be oriented along the direction of steepest slope from the origin of the $\boldsymbol{\theta}$-space for the test characteristic surface. This is not a formal relationship like that for individual test items modeled with a compensatory MIRT model because the form of the test characteristic surface is much more complex than the item characteristic surface.

Another way of showing the relationship between the unidimensional estimates of θ and the multidimensional solution is to determine the orthogonal rotation of the unidimensional θs that best matches the multidimensional $\boldsymbol{\theta}$s. The more general case of rotating one set of multidimensional $\boldsymbol{\theta}$s to match a corresponding set in another solution space will be discussed in detail in Chap. 7. The solution can be found in a number of ways. An approach with a convenient conceptual framework is used here. Suppose that a sample of two-dimensional $\boldsymbol{\theta}$-vectors used to generate item response data using the parameters given in Table 5.2 is represented by the 2,000 × 2 matrix of coordinates, $\boldsymbol{\theta}_t$. These are the "true" coordinates for the examinees. From these $\boldsymbol{\theta}$-vectors and the item parameters in Table 5.2, a 2,000 × 20 item response matrix is generated by comparing the matrix of computed probabilities of correct response for each person to each item to a matrix of uniform random numbers. If the random number is less than the computed probability, an item score of 1 is assigned. Otherwise, a 0 item score is assigned. The matrix of item scores is then used to calibrate the items and estimate θs using the unidimensional two-parameter logistic model (in this case using BILOG-MG). Those θs are used to create a 2,000 × 2 matrix of the form $\begin{bmatrix} \theta_1 & 0 \\ \theta_2 & 0 \\ \vdots & \vdots \\ \theta_{2,000} & 0 \end{bmatrix}$, where the index of the θs represent an examinee identification number. This matrix is represented by $\boldsymbol{\theta}_{\mathbf{e}}$.

To determine the orthogonal rotation that best matches the estimates in $\boldsymbol{\theta}_{\mathbf{e}}$ to the generating values, $\boldsymbol{\theta}_{\mathbf{t}}$, the singular value decomposition of the $\boldsymbol{\theta}_{\mathbf{t}}'\boldsymbol{\theta}_{\mathbf{e}}$ is determined as shown in (5.19).

$$\boldsymbol{\theta}_{\mathbf{t}}'\boldsymbol{\theta}_{\mathbf{e}} = \mathbf{U}\boldsymbol{\Sigma}\mathbf{V}', \tag{5.19}$$

where $\mathbf{U}$, $\boldsymbol{\Sigma}$, and $\mathbf{V}$ are orthogonal matrices. The rotation matrix, $\mathbf{R}$, is given by $\mathbf{VU}'$ and the rotated solution is $\boldsymbol{\theta}_{\mathbf{e}}\mathbf{R}$.

An example of the rotation of the unidimensional estimates to best match the two dimensional solution is shown in Fig. 5.10. The results in the figure show a scatter plot of the θ-coordinates for the two-dimensional $\boldsymbol{\theta}$-vectors used to generate the item response data and the corresponding line for the unidimensional θs after

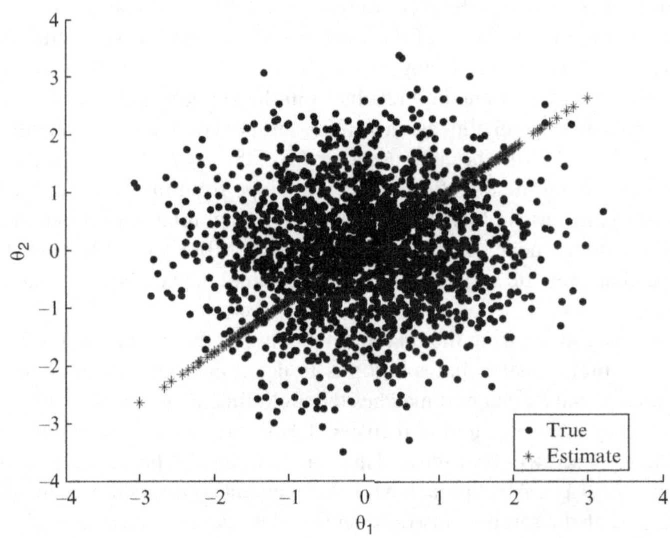

Fig. 5.10 Relationship between unidimensional estimates and two-dimensional $\boldsymbol{\theta}$-points

rotation. The rotation matrix is given by $\begin{bmatrix} .75 & .66 \\ -.66 & .75 \end{bmatrix}$. This matrix corresponds to an angle of 42° with the θ_1 axis after rotation and 48° with the θ_2 axis. These values are slightly different than the theoretical values of 39° and 51° respectively because of estimation error in the unidimensional θ estimates. Note that this rotation gives the same result as the projection of the two-dimensional points onto the unidimensional θ estimates. The rotation minimizes the sum of squared distances between the θ-estimates and the $\boldsymbol{\theta}$-points used to generate the data.

As was the case for the unidimensional IRT models, the precision of a test can be determined by summing the information available from each item. MIRT models have one additional complication. The sum of the information estimates must be for the same direction in the $\boldsymbol{\theta}$-space. Figure 5.11 shows the information surfaces in two dimensions for three different directions the space for the items described in Table 5.2. The leftmost figure shows the information from the 20 item test in a direction parallel to the θ_1 axis. The rightmost figure shows the information in a direction parallel to the θ_2 axis. The middle figure shows the information at a 45° angle to both axes. Note that the vertical axis is not the same for the three figures because there is more information in the center figure than for the ones on either side.

Beyond the fact that the high points of the three figures are in different places in the $\boldsymbol{\theta}$-space, it is important to recognize that the shapes of the test information surfaces are different. For estimating θ_1, the information surface shows that the most information is available between 0 and -2 on the θ_1 scale. The estimation of θ_2 is most accurate along a diagonal from $(-4, 4)$ to $(4, -2)$. The best estimation of an equally weighted combination of θ_1 and θ_2 is at about $(-2, 2)$ in the $\boldsymbol{\theta}$-space. These plots of the information surfaces do not provide a very clear picture of the information provided by the test because of the need to simultaneously attend to

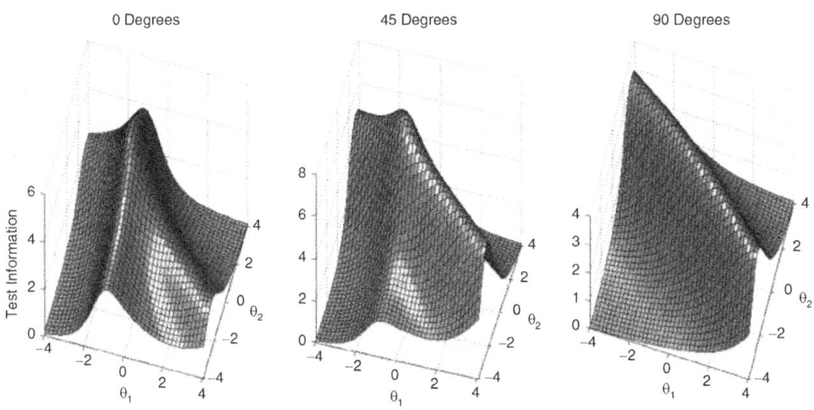

Fig. 5.11 Information surfaces for the test composed of items in Table 5.2 in three directions in the $\boldsymbol{\theta}$-space

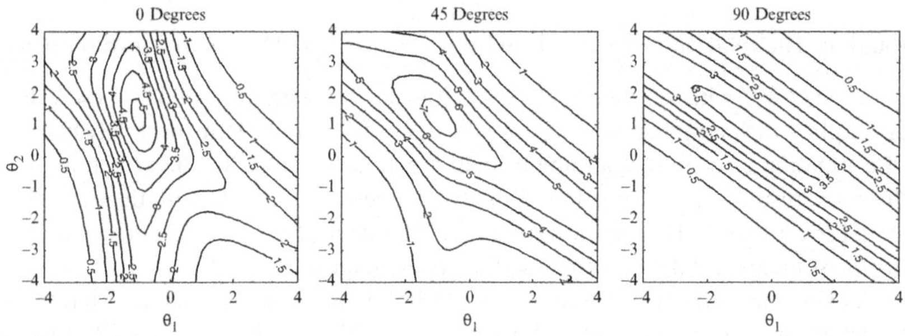

Fig. 5.12 Contour plots of information for the test composed of items in Table 5.1 in three directions in the $\boldsymbol{\theta}$-space

the features of multiple surfaces. Other alternative ways of to show the information available to estimate the θ-coordinates are to present the information as contour plots or the clam shell plots shown in Fig. 5.7.

The contour plots of the information for the same 20-item test are shown in Fig. 5.12. The contour plots make the location of the areas of highest information more evident and they also make it easier to determine which direction provides the most information. In this case, the 45° direction yields peak information over 7 and the other two directions are lower in the most informative areas. It is also clear that the test is most informative in all three directions near $(-1, 1.5)$ in the $\boldsymbol{\theta}$-space.

The clam shell plot of the test information for the same 20-item test is given in Fig. 5.13. In this case, the total test information is shown by the length of the line at each point in the direction indicated by the line. At the bottom of the plot is a line segment with the value 7.33 next to it. The line segment shows the length of line in the plot that represents 7.33 units of information. The clam shell plot shows the same pattern of information as the other plots, but now it is all included in one plot.

All of these representations of the information provided by a test are only practical when the functioning of the test items can be represented in a two-dimensional coordinate system. Although this limits the applicability of the graphic procedures for representing information, these examples still show that the amount of information provided by a test is a complex function of the location in the $\boldsymbol{\theta}$-space. There are portions of the space where estimation of an examinee's location would be very poor. For example, at $(-3.5, -.5)$ the information is almost zero for the test modeled here. At $(-1, -2.5)$, there is a small amount of information, but it is mainly useful for estimating θ_1. The test provides the most information in a variety of directions slightly below 0 on θ_1 and slightly above 0 on θ_2.

The complexity of the form of the test information surface suggests that it would be useful to search the $\boldsymbol{\theta}$-space to determine where the information is greatest and in what direction at that point. At the time of the writing of this book, there was no convenient procedure for finding the location and direction of maximum information for a test analyzed with several dimensions. With the current generation of

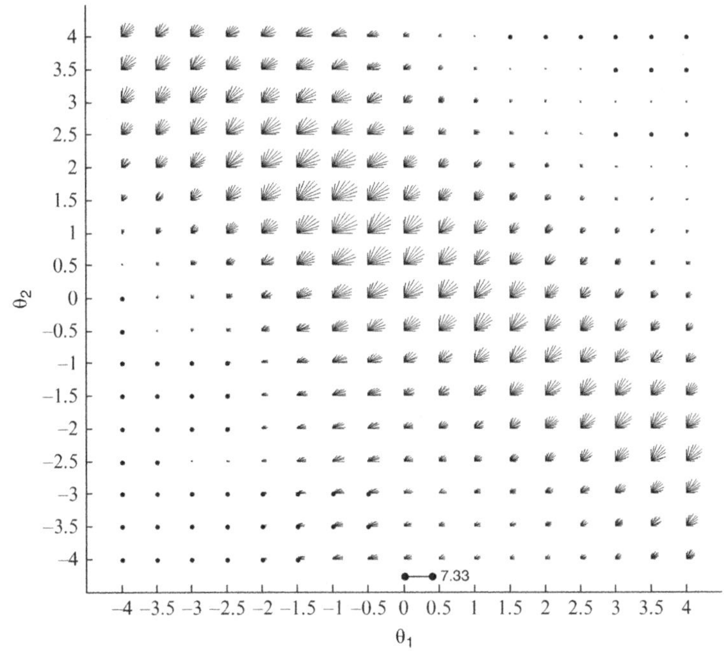

Fig. 5.13 Clam shell plot for the test information from the 20 items in Table 5.1

computers, it seems practical to search a grid of points in the space for the maximum information in each dimension, but software for that process has not been developed.

Another way to represent test results using MIRT is by tracking the multidimensional meaning of other types of scores computed from the item score vectors. For example, even tests that have very complex content structures often report scores that are based on the sum of item scores. MIRT procedures can be used to determine the meaning of this supposedly simple score type. The *centroid* plot is a way to show how the meaning of a single score derived from a test that requires multiple dimensions for successful performance changes with the level of the score. This form of representation was first used to check the multidimensional parallelism of test scores from different test forms (Reckase et al. 1988; Davey et al. 1989).

Centroid plots are formed by sorting the reporting scores into order from low to high. Then the sorted scores are divided into groups of equal size. For each group, the mean and standard deviation of the elements of the corresponding $\boldsymbol{\theta}$-vectors are computed. The resulting mean vectors are called group centroids. The standard deviations of the elements of the $\boldsymbol{\theta}$-vectors are used to put error ellipses around the centroids. One way to specify the error ellipses is to have the axes of the ellipses be equal to two times the standard error of the means for each dimension of the $\boldsymbol{\theta}$-vector.

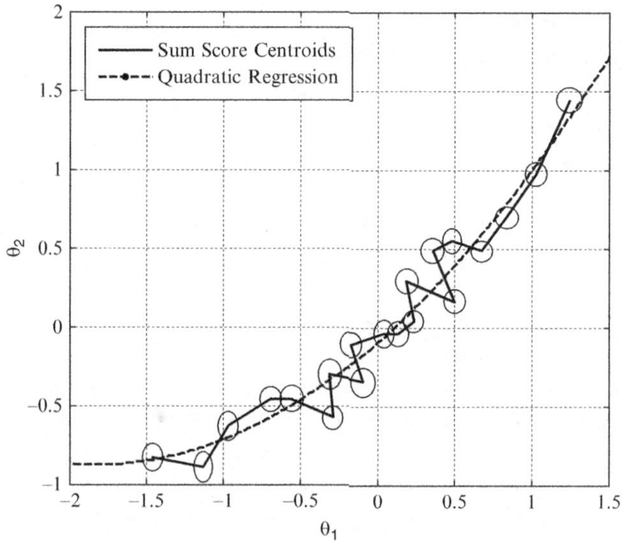

Fig. 5.14 Centroid plot based on number-correct scores for the test using items in Table 5.1

Figure 5.14 shows the centroid plot for the test composed of the items in Table 5.2 and a standard bivariate normal distribution of **θ**-coordinates with the identity matrix as the covariance matrix. The solid line on the graph connects each of the group centroids. Twenty groups were used in this case with a sample size of 100 for each group. The ellipses are located at each centroid and their axes are defined by the standard error of the mean of the corresponding coordinate. Ellipses that would overlap if they were on the same line indicate that the centroids are not significantly different from each other on that dimension. The plot also includes the quadratic regression line for the centroids showing that the centroids shift in the direction of change from the lower score levels to the higher score levels. The lower level centroids change in location mainly along θ_1. Higher centroids shift more along θ_2.

If θ_1 were aligned with a construct like arithmetic computation and θ_2 were aligned with a construct like problem solving, these results would indicate that differences in number-correct scores near the bottom end of the score scale are due to differences in arithmetic computation skills. Differences in problem solving skills have little effect at that level. At the high end of the score scale, problem solving skills are a major component in differences in the scores.

Centroid plots can be produced for any reported score for the test. For example, the UIRT θ-estimates could be used in place of the number-correct scores in the previous example. Centroid plots can also be produced for tests that are modeled in three dimensions. In that case, the mean vectors for each group define points in three-space and the standard errors of the means are used as the axes of an ellipsoid. Figure 5.15 shows a three-dimensional centroid plot using the number-correct score as the unidimensional variable.

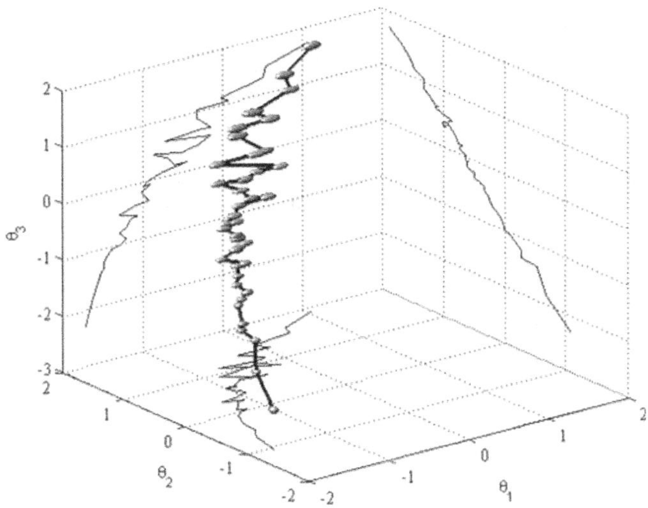

Fig. 5.15 Three-dimensional centroid plot with standard error of the mean ellipsoids and projections onto θ-planes

The plot in Fig. 5.15 is based on an analysis of 4,000 cases divided into 40 groups of 100 using the number-correct score for the test. The test is composed of 70 dichotomously-scored test items. The error ellipsoids for each centroid are fairly small indicating that the successive centroids are usually significantly different from each other. The plot also contains the projections of the lines connecting the centroids onto the side panels of the plot – the planes formed by pairs of θs. The projection onto the θ_2, θ_3 plane is close to linear while the projections onto the other planes are nonlinear. A two-dimensional analysis of this test based on θ_2 and θ_3 would indicate that the meaning of the differences on the number-correct score scale is the same over the range of the scale, but the full analysis of the data indicate that the meaning of differences on the number-correct score scale change with the level of performance on the scale.

5.4 Summary and Conclusions

This chapter provides ways for representing the characteristics of test items and tests when MIRT models are used to describe the interaction between persons and test items. Some of the statistical indices and graphical representations show the usual IRT item characteristics of difficulty and discrimination. Because MIRT models consider the functioning of items in a multidimensional space, there is also a need to indicate the direction in the space that the item provides the best discrimination. This is done by representing an item as an arrow or vector in the multidimensional space.

This type of representation shows the direction of greatest discrimination and helps show the relationships among items and the connection between unidimensional and multidimensional models.

The chapter also presents methods for describing the information provided by items and tests that can be used for estimating the location of a person in the $\boldsymbol{\theta}$-space. The information about a person's location in the space is shown to differ by the direction taken from that location. Items and tests are not equally good at differentiating individuals that differ from each other along different coordinate axes. The concept of information will prove useful in later chapters when test design issues are considered.

Finally, the chapter describes the relationship between unidimensional estimates of a construct and multidimensional representations. The results from unidimensional IRT models are shown to be weighted combinations of the estimated coordinates from the MIRT solution. The weights are related to the discrimination parameters for the items. Centroid plots are used to show that the meaning of reported scores may be different at different points along the score scale. These multidimensional representations were designed to help develop greater conceptual understanding of the way MIRT models represent test items and clarify the meaning of the results of the application of unidimensional models to multidimensional data.

5.5 Exercises

1. A set of test items require three coordinate axes to represent the interaction between the examinees and the test items. The parameters for two of the test items are provided in the following table.

Item number	a_1	a_2	a_3	d
1	1.2	.5	.4	−1
2	.35	.9	.9	1

For each item, compute the distance from the origin of the space to the point of steepest slope in the space. Which of the two items would be easier for a population of examinees who are distributed as a standard bivariate normal distribution with $\rho = 0$? What is the distance along the coordinate axes from the origin of the space to the point of steepest slope in that direction? Determine that distance for each item along each coordinate axes.

2. A person is located at a distance of 2 units from the origin of a three-dimensional space along a line with the following angles with each of the coordinate axes: [33.2 63.4 71.6]. The angles are in degrees with axes θ_1, θ_2, and θ_3, respectively, and the person has positive coordinates on each axis. Give the person's location as a $1 \times m$ vector of $\boldsymbol{\theta}$ coordinates.

3. Draw the arrow representation for the two items described by the parameters in Exercise 1.

4. Figure 5.14 is a centroid plot for the scores from a test that shows differences mostly along θ_1 for low scoring examinees and differences with more of a θ_2 component for high scoring examinees. Describe how you would select items for a test using the items' MIRT parameters so that both low and high scores show differences along θ_2 and mid-range scores show differences along θ_1. Give your reasons for the approach to selecting test items.

Chapter 6
Estimation of Item and Person Parameters

The MIRT models presented in this book are useful from a theoretical perspective because they provide a model for the interaction between persons and test items. The different kinds of models represent different theoretical perspectives. For example, the compensatory and partially compensatory models provide two different conceptions of how levels on hypothetical constructs combine when applied to items that require some level on the constructs to determine the correct response. Although the theoretical models are interesting in their own right, the practical applications of the models require a means of estimating the item and person parameters for the models. Without practical procedures for parameter estimation, the usefulness of the models is very limited.

This chapter describes the procedures that are currently used for estimating the item and person parameters for the models. These procedures are necessarily embedded within computer programs for carrying out the steps in the estimation methodology. It is difficult to separate the estimation procedures from the programs used to implement them. An excellent estimation methodology may perform poorly because it is improperly programmed or programmed in an inefficient way. A method with poorer theoretical properties may perform better overall because the programming of the method was done in a more creative way. Because of this close tie between estimation methodology and the computer programs used to implement them, they will be described together in the later sections of this chapter. Before getting into the details of estimation procedures, a general overview is provided. This overview is designed to give a conceptual framework for understanding the estimation procedures without getting into the technical details.

This chapter is reasonably up to date about programs and methods as of 2008. However, computer software becomes obsolete and computer systems change fairly rapidly. For that reason, this chapter does not go into the details of running specific programs. Those may change by the time this book is published. Rather, the basic estimation model is described for commonly used programs and differences in constraints used in estimation procedures are presented. These are the features of the estimation methods and programs that explain why different programs applied to the same item response data give different parameter estimates. Chapter 7 describes some methods for determining if the parameter estimates from different programs are simple transformations of each other.

M.D. Reckase, *Multidimensional Item Response Theory*, Statistics for Social and Behavioral Sciences, DOI 10.1007/978-0-387-89976-3_6,
© Springer Science+Business Media, LLC 2009

6.1 Background Concepts for Parameter Estimation

The estimation of the values of parameters for MIRT models is challenging for a number of reasons. First, the models contain parameters for both persons and test items and generally it is not possible to estimate the two sets of parameters independent of each other. The consequences of the need to jointly estimate person- and item-parameters are shown in the next section of this chapter. A second reason that the estimation of parameters is challenging is that many parameters need to be estimated. For the compensatory model described in Chap. 4, if m is the number of coordinate axes, n is the number of test items, and N is the number of people, then there are $n\,(m+1) + m \times N$ parameters to be estimated. For a 50 item test modeled with four dimensions calibrated with 2,000 examinees, 8,250 parameters need to be estimated using 100,000 item responses. A third reason the estimation is challenging is that there are indeterminacies in the models such as the location of the origin of the space, the units of measurement for each coordinate axis, and the orientation of the coordinate axes relative to the locations of the persons. All of these issues must be addressed in the construction of a computer program for estimating the parameters.

The next sections of this chapter describe the parameter estimation process as separate pieces – the estimation of person locations with item parameters known, and the estimation of item parameters with person locations known – to highlight the general methods that are used and the problems that must be addressed when the methods are combined. Following those preliminary descriptions of estimation procedures, the methods used in commonly available estimation programs will be described. There is no attempt to give a formal mathematical description of statistical estimation procedures because that would double the length of this book. Interested individuals should look at texts such as Baker and Kim (2004) and Gamerman and Lopes (2006) for a more complete exposition of statistical estimation procedures.

6.1.1 Estimation of the $\boldsymbol{\theta}$-vector with Item Parameters Known

Suppose that there is a large set of test items available that have already been analyzed with a high quality computer program for estimating their parameters. These items have parameter estimates that are based on a large, appropriate sample of examinees. Initially, the item parameters for these items are assumed known without error (the estimation error is assumed to be very small) and the problem of estimating the location of examinees with these items is addressed.

Suppose further that an examinee has been selected and the test items are administered to this person to estimate his or her location in the $\boldsymbol{\theta}$-space. The results from the administration are the scored responses to the test items. The information available for estimating the location of the examinee is the string of item scores and the item parameters for the items that have been administered. When computing a location estimate, consideration must first be given to the characteristics of a good estimate. These characteristics provide criteria for choosing one estimate of location over another. Three different criteria are considered here – the maximum likelihood criterion, the maximum a posteriori Bayesian criterion, and the least squares criterion. Estimation of an examinee's location is first described using the maximum likelihood criterion and then estimation procedures using the other two criteria are described and compared to maximum likelihood procedure.

The maximum likelihood criterion is basically that the estimate of the examinee's location is the $\boldsymbol{\theta}$-vector that results in the highest probability for the observed string of item scores. The term *likelihood* is used for the probability of the string of item scores for any candidate value of the $\boldsymbol{\theta}$-vector. The particular $\boldsymbol{\theta}$-vector that yields a likelihood for the response string that is higher than all other $\boldsymbol{\theta}$-vectors is the maximum likelihood estimate for the given set of items and the observed string of item scores. A few examples are provided to show how maximum likelihood estimation works in practice and to identify some problems with the methodology. The examples begin with the simple two-dimensional case with the compensatory model so that graphic representations of the likelihoods of the item score string can be used. Later examples consider higher dimensional cases.

The first item presented to an examinee has item parameters for the compensatory model given in (4.5) of $a_{11} = .8$, $a_{12} = .5$, and $d_1 = -.6$ and the examinee answers the item correctly so the item score $u_1 = 1$. Figure 6.1 shows the item response surface for this item as an equi-probable contour plot. In this case, the plot is shaded from black for low probabilities to white for probabilities near 1.0 so that the region of highest probability is easy to identify. For the one item case, the item

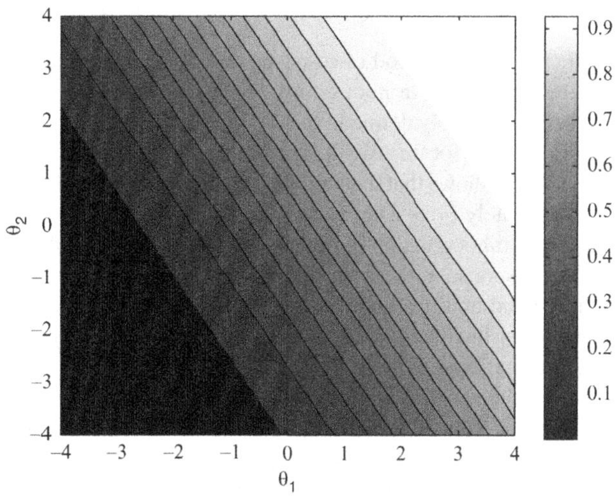

Fig. 6.1 Likelihood surface for a correct response to the one item test with $a_{11} = .8$, $a_{12} = .5$, and $d_1 = -.5$. The *bar* at the *right* indicates the relationship between shade of *gray* and probability

response surface is the same as the surface showing the likelihoods for the response string because it shows the probability of the single item score for various locations in the $\boldsymbol{\theta}$-space.

Study of the plot shows that the highest probabilities for a correct response occur in the upper right corner where the graph is white. In fact, the probability of a correct response is highest at (4, 4) for the region of the $\boldsymbol{\theta}$-space included on this plot. The probability there is .99 and is higher than at any other $\boldsymbol{\theta}$ location shown in the plot. If the surface were not constrained to the region between −4 and 4 on each axis, the maximum would be at (∞, ∞) because the surface is monotonically increasing. The undefined point, (∞, ∞), is the maximum likelihood estimator of the location for the person based on the one item test and a correct response to the test item.

This result is inconvenient because infinite proficiency on the skills required to respond to the test item is difficult to justify as a reasonable estimate. However, it is consistent with the maximum likelihood criterion because a person with infinite ability would be able to answer the item correctly with certainty and no other location would give that high a probability. This result also emphasizes that one item tests do not do a very good job of locating a person in a multidimensional $\boldsymbol{\theta}$-space.

The second item presented to an examinee is more difficult with parameters $a_{21} = .2$, $a_{22} = 1.1$, and $d_2 = -1.2$ and the examinee responds incorrectly to the item. The item score vector is now [1 0]. The likelihood of this response string is given by the product of the probability of a correct response to Item 1 and the probability of an incorrect response to Item 2. In general, the likelihood for a response string for a particular location in the $\boldsymbol{\theta}$-space is given by the following equation:

$$L\left(\mathbf{U}_j \mid \boldsymbol{\theta}_j\right) = \prod_{i=1}^{n} P\left(u_{ij} \mid \boldsymbol{\theta}_j\right)^{u_{ij}} Q\left(u_{ij} \mid \boldsymbol{\theta}_j\right)^{1-u_{ij}}, \tag{6.1}$$

where $L\left(\mathbf{U}_j|\boldsymbol{\theta}_j\right)$ is the likelihood of response string $\mathbf{U}_j$ for a person j located at $\boldsymbol{\theta}_j$, and u_{ij} is the item score on item i for person j on the n-item test. The other symbols have been previously defined.

The likelihood surface for this two-item test with the response string 10 is shown in Figure 6.2. This plot shows that the likelihood for the 10 response string is greatest in value at approximately (4, −2) for the region of the $\boldsymbol{\theta}$-space covered by the plot. At that point, the likelihood is approximately .77, the product of .83 for the probability of a correct response to the first item and .93, the probability of an incorrect response to the second item for an examinee at that location. All other $\boldsymbol{\theta}$-values in this region have lower likelihood values. If the entire $\boldsymbol{\theta}$-space is unlimited, then the location of the maximum likelihood value would be at $(\infty, -\infty)$ because infinitely low proficiency on the second dimension of the space would predict an incorrect response to the second item with certainty. The likelihood of the response string 10 at this undefined point in the space is 1.

After two responses, the maximum likelihood estimate of the examinees location is still not very meaningful. The concept of infinitely low proficiency is difficult to comprehend. A two-item test is not very useful for locating an examinee in a two-dimensional $\boldsymbol{\theta}$-space.

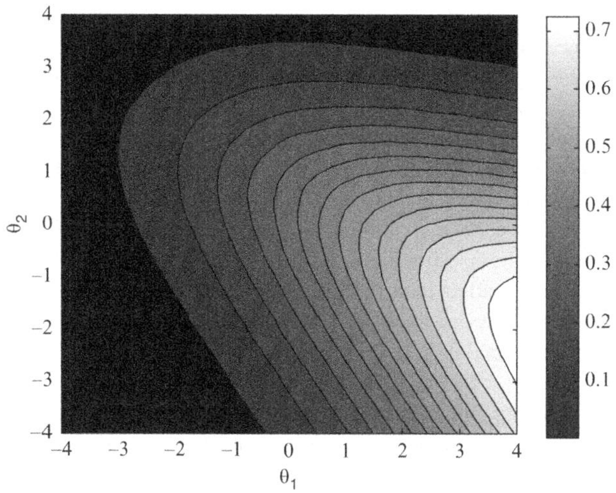

Fig. 6.2 Likelihood surface for a two-item test with response string 10. The *bar* at the *right* indicates the relationship between the shade of *gray* and the likelihood at each $\boldsymbol{\theta}$-point

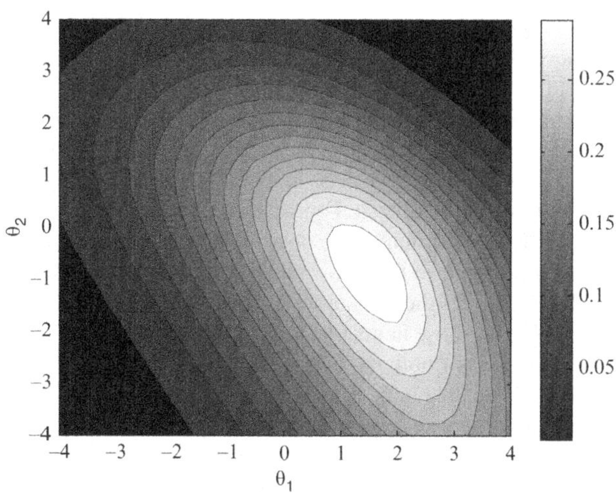

Fig. 6.3 Likelihood surface for the response string 100

The third item presented to an examinee has parameters $a_{31} = 1.0$, $a_{32} = .2$, and $d_3 = -2$. The examinee answers this test item incorrectly so the resulting response string is 100. The likelihood surface for this response string is given in Figure 6.3. For the three-item test with the specified item parameters and the observed item scores, there is now a location for the maximum of the likelihood function with finite values for both coordinates. That location is at approximately (1.5, $-.75$) in the $\boldsymbol{\theta}$-space. The likelihood value at that point is .3101 and it is larger than any other likelihood value. However, its magnitude is less than the maximum likelihood for the two-item case. With each additional item, the magnitude of the maximum of the likelihood is smaller because another probability term is added to the product in (6.1). As the number of items in the test increases, the value of the likelihood at the maximum gets very small. For example, if the probability of the observed response for each item on a 40 item test were .8, the likelihood of that response pattern would be $.8^{40} = .000133$, a very small number. To avoid problems that result from working with very small numbers, estimation programs often search for the maximum of the log of the likelihood rather than the likelihood. The log likelihood surface has its maximum at the same location as the likelihood surface.

When unidimensional item response theory models are used, finite estimates of the person parameters are usually found when item scores of both 0 and 1 are present in the response string. The exception is for some unusual response strings for the three-parameter logistic model where the lower asymptote to the model yields maximums at $-\infty$ even when there are both correct and incorrect responses. This result generally indicates that the examinee has been answering questions correctly at less than that specified by the lower asymptote parameter. In most cases, however, the presence of both a correct and incorrect response results in a finite estimate for the person parameter.

In the example given here, it is clear that having both a correct and incorrect response was not sufficient to guarantee that the location of the maximum likelihood point would have finite values for all coordinates. This raises questions of the conditions under which the maximum likelihood estimation procedure yields finite estimates of coordinates for MIRT models. To give some insight into this question, the .5 contour lines are plotted for each of the items used in the example. These contour lines are shown in Figure 6.4. For each line, an arrow shows the direction of increasing probability for the item score obtained from the examinee. The response to the first item was correct, so the arrow points in the increasing direction for both θs from the solid line that is the .5-contour for that item. The other two-item scores were 0, so the arrows for those items (dashed and dotted contour lines) are pointing in the negative direction for both θs. The lines and the associated directions of increasing slope contain an area in the $\boldsymbol{\theta}$-space that forms a triangle. The maximum of the likelihood surface is enclosed within that triangle. Interestingly, the only other pattern that gives a finite location for the maximum of the likelihood function is obtained by taking the response string 100 and changing all of the ones to zeros and zeros to ones – 011. There are no other response strings that yield locations for the maximum of the likelihood function that have finite coordinates.

The use of the .5-contour lines in this way suggests that there are many cases when the likelihood function will not have a useful maximum value. Suppose for example, four test items all have the same a-parameter vector of [1.2 .8], but have d-parameters of -2, -1, 0, 2. The .5-contours for these items will form a parallel set of lines in the $\boldsymbol{\theta}$-space – it is not possible to enclose a space with the lines. If an examinee answers the two easier items correctly and the two hard items incorrectly, the likelihood surface for that response string is given in Figure 6.5. This surface has

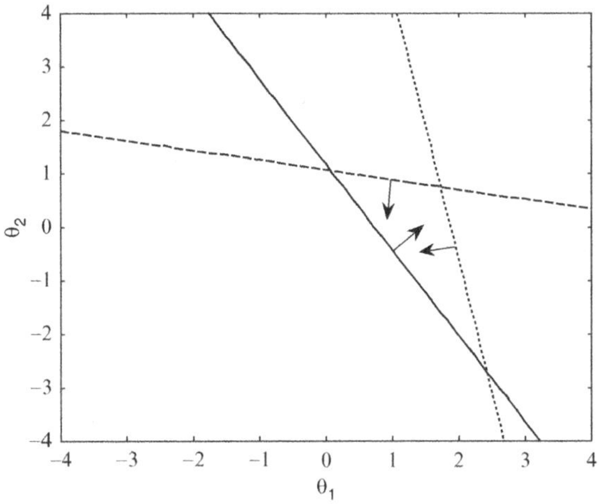

Fig. 6.4 .5-contours for the item response surfaces for the items used in the example

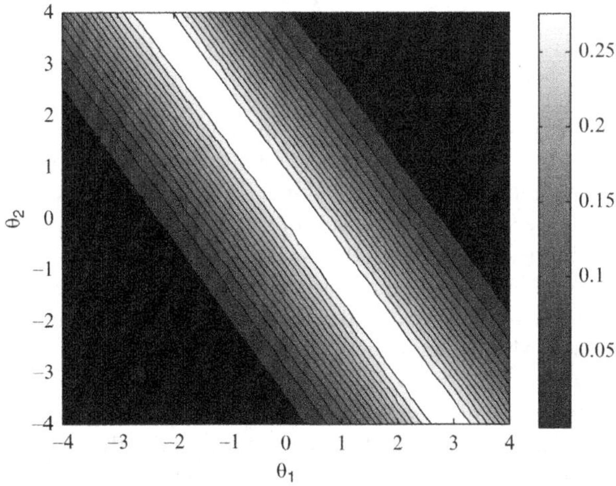

Fig. 6.5 Likelihood surface for the response string 1100 for items with parallel contours

a clear region of higher likelihood along a line from upper left to lower right, but there are many $\boldsymbol{\theta}$-points along that line that have the same likelihood value equal to the maximum. That is, the use of the maximum likelihood criterion does not yield a unique estimate for the $\boldsymbol{\theta}$-point. Because of the orientation of the item response surfaces, there is no information from the items to distinguish among positions along the line of maximum likelihood.

The examples presented here have been generated to show anomalous cases. For typical test lengths with relatively small numbers of dimensions, the vast majority of response strings will yield maximum likelihood estimates that have finite estimates for the $\boldsymbol{\theta}$-vector. When maximum likelihood estimation does not yield finite estimates, it is usually a symptom that the test was not well designed to determine the location in the multidimensional space of the examinee in question. It may have been too easy or difficult, or not have enough test items that are sensitive to differences along one of the coordinate axes.

When maximum likelihood estimates yield values that are infinite, the pragmatic solution is to assign values that are as extreme as those that are typically observed in practice. These might be coordinate values such as 4 or −4. This suggests that the researcher has other information that indicates that it is not believable to have an estimate of −50 or 100 on a scale with a mean 0 and standard deviation of 1. The beliefs of the researcher can be taken into account in a more formal way by using Bayesian estimation procedures.

Bayesian estimation is based on a theorem about the relationship among certain conditional probabilities that was published in 1763 (Bayes 1763). Originally, the theorem dealt with the probabilities of discrete events. Using modernized notation, Bayes' Theorem is given by (Stigler 1986, p. 103)

$$P(A_i \mid E) = \frac{P(E \mid A_i)P(A_i)}{\sum_j P(E \mid A_j)P(A_j)}, \tag{6.2}$$

where E is an observed event and A_i is a possible cause for the event. The summation is over all of the possible causes for the event. The denominator of the expression on the right is the sum of all of the possible numerators. Dividing by that term ensures that the terms on the left side of the expression will sum to 1.0 as is required for probabilities. The term $P(A_i)$ is called the prior probability for the cause and the full set of those probabilities form the prior distribution for the cause of the event E. The term $P(A_i|E)$ is called the posterior probability of the cause given that the event occurred. The full set of these probabilities forms the posterior distribution of the causes of E.

Bayes' theorem gives the probability that each possible cause is the cause for the event given the probability of the event if the cause is the correct one, and the probability of observing a particular cause. In the context of IRT, the event is the observed string of item scores and the possible causes are the possible values of θ. If the possible values of θ were discrete points, (6.2) could be used for Bayesian estimation of the $\boldsymbol{\theta}$-vector. A criterion for selecting the best estimate of the $\boldsymbol{\theta}$-vector is the one that has the highest probability given the observed string of item scores. This estimation criterion is analogous to the maximum likelihood criterion used with (6.1).

Because $\boldsymbol{\theta}$ is usually considered to be a continuous rather than a discrete variable, a different version of Bayes' theorem is used for estimation of the $\boldsymbol{\theta}$-vectors. This continuous version of Bayes' theorem is given in many statistics texts (e.g., Degroot 1970, p. 28). It is presented here using the same notation used when describing maximum likelihood estimation.

$$h(\boldsymbol{\theta} \mid \mathbf{U}_j) = \frac{L(\mathbf{U}_j \mid \boldsymbol{\theta}) f(\boldsymbol{\theta})}{\int\limits_{\theta} L(\mathbf{U}_j \mid \boldsymbol{\theta}) f(\boldsymbol{\theta}) d\boldsymbol{\theta}}, \tag{6.3}$$

where $f(\boldsymbol{\theta})$ is the prior probability density function for $\boldsymbol{\theta}$, $\mathbf{U}_j$ is the item score string for Examinee j, $L(\mathbf{U}_j|\boldsymbol{\theta})$ is the probability of the item score string given $\boldsymbol{\theta}$, and $h(\boldsymbol{\theta}|\mathbf{U}_j)$ is the posterior probability density of $\boldsymbol{\theta}$ given the item scores string.

Note that the probability of the item score string given $\boldsymbol{\theta}$ is the same as the likelihood of the item score string given in (6.1).

Because the denominator of the right side of (6.3) is the same for all values of θ, Bayes' theorem is sometimes written as

$$h(\boldsymbol{\theta}|\mathbf{U}_j) \propto L(\mathbf{U}_j|\boldsymbol{\theta}) f(\boldsymbol{\theta}). \tag{6.4}$$

This form of the theorem indicates that the posterior probability of $\boldsymbol{\theta}$ is proportional to the likelihood times the prior distribution. The implication is that finding the maximum of the right side of the expression will also yield the maximum of the left side of the expression.

Bayesian estimation procedures can use a number of different statistics to estimate $\boldsymbol{\theta}$. Those used most frequently are the mode and mean of $h(\boldsymbol{\theta}|\mathbf{U}_j)$. Using the mode is called maximum a posteriori estimation, or MAP. Using the mean is called expected a posteriori estimation, or EAP. If the posterior distribution of $\boldsymbol{\theta}$ is symmetric, these two types of estimates of $\boldsymbol{\theta}$ will yield the same value.

When using Bayesian estimation, the prior distribution of $\boldsymbol{\theta}$ needs to be specified. The form of this distribution may be specified based on previous analyses of test data or from general knowledge about the form of distributions typically found in educational or psychological settings. The form of this distribution is required before the estimation of $\boldsymbol{\theta}$, hence the name given to it is the prior distribution.

When there is little empirical information about the form of the distribution of $\boldsymbol{\theta}$-points, the standard multivariate normal distribution with an identity matrix for the variance/covariance matrix is often used as the prior distribution for Bayesian analyses. This selection is supported by years of successful use of the multivariate normal distribution as a default distributional assumption for the analysis of educational and psychological data.

To show the difference between Bayesian and maximum likelihood estimation, the same item score strings that have been used earlier are used to estimate $\boldsymbol{\theta}$ using the bivariate normal prior with a zero mean vector and an identity matrix for a variance/covariance matrix. Also, MAP estimation is used. After one item with a correct response, the equi-density plot for the prior and posterior distributions are presented in Fig. 6.6.

The plot shows that the posterior distribution of $\boldsymbol{\theta}$ has shifted to the upper right relative to the prior distribution. The maximum point on the prior distribution was at (0, 0) in the $\boldsymbol{\theta}$-space. After the correct response to one item, the maximum of the posterior distribution is approximately (.5, .25). This is the MAP estimate of $\boldsymbol{\theta}$ after the response to the single item. In contrast to the maximum likelihood estimate that

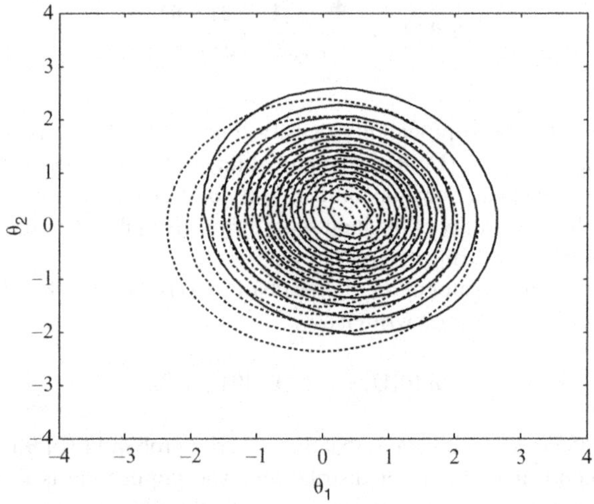

Fig. 6.6 Prior (*dotted lines*) and posterior (*solid lines*) probability density functions for a bivariate normal prior density and a correct response to an item with parameters with $a_{11} = .8$, $a_{12} = .5$, and $d_1 = -.5$

had maximums approaching infinite values for the θ elements, the Bayesian estimate has finite coordinates. This is usually seen as a major advantage for Bayesian estimation.

The Bayesian estimate for the item score string of 100, using the same items as for the maximum likelihood procedure shown in Fig. 6.3, is obtained from the posterior density shown in Fig. 6.7. The highest point for the posterior density function for this item score string is located at $(.25, 0)$, a location that is quite different than that for the maximum of the likelihood function for the same item score string – $(1.5, -.75)$. The reason for this large difference is that the bivariate normal prior distribution dominates the posterior distribution when the number of test items is small. As the number of test items increases, the maximum likelihood estimate and the MAP estimate become closer to each other.

The fact that the Bayesian estimate is closer to the location of the mean vector for the prior distribution than is the maximum likelihood estimate is known as a regression effect. Bayesian estimates are acknowledged to have regression effects that result in statistically biased estimates of the $\boldsymbol{\theta}$-vector. When an estimator has statistical bias the mean of the estimator is not equal to value of the model parameter. The statistical bias in the estimation of the location of the $\boldsymbol{\theta}$-vector is often considered as a reasonable trade off for insuring finite estimates of the elements of the $\boldsymbol{\theta}$-vector.

The maximum likelihood and Bayesian estimation procedures can be used to estimate the item parameters as well as the $\boldsymbol{\theta}$-vectors. For item parameter estimation, the $\boldsymbol{\theta}$-vectors are assumed known and the item parameter space is searched to find the set of parameters that yields the maximum of the likelihood function or the Bayesian posterior distribution. The maximum of the functions cannot be shown here as points on surfaces because even when there are only two $\boldsymbol{\theta}$-coordinates,

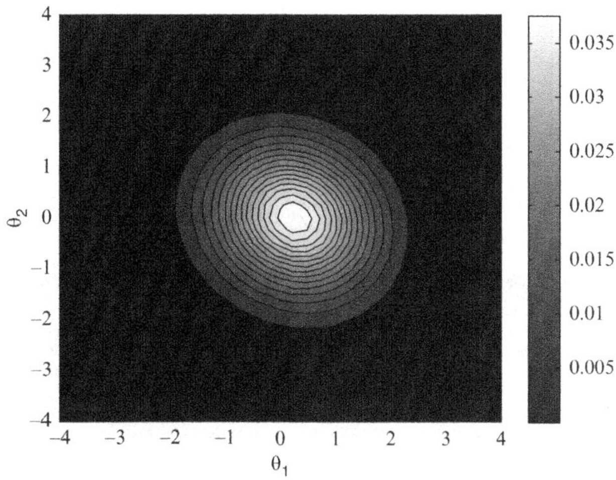

Fig. 6.7 Posterior distribution for the item score string 100

there are three item parameters – a_1, a_2, and d. The likelihood or the height of the Bayesian posterior would need a fourth coordinate axis to show where the height of the surface is maximum for a set of item parameters. As a result, graphic methods cannot be used to find the estimates for the item parameters.

The two estimation criteria presented earlier identify the estimate for the $\boldsymbol{\theta}$-vector by searching for the maximum of the likelihood function of the posterior density distribution. It is also possible to specify a criterion for estimation that is based on minimizing the difference between predictions from the MIRT model and the observed data. A common predictor for an observation is the expected value of the observation, in this case $E\,(u\,|\,\boldsymbol{\theta},\ \mathbf{a},\ d)$. Minimizing the squared difference between the observed value and the predicted value is called the *least squares* criterion for an estimator. The expected value of the item score is simply $P\,(u = 1|\,\boldsymbol{\theta},\ \mathbf{a},\ d)$, so a least squares method for finding the estimate of $\boldsymbol{\theta}$ is to find the vector $\boldsymbol{\theta}$ that results in a minimum value for the following expression.

$$SS_\theta = \sum_{i=1}^{n} \left(u_i - P\,(u_i = 1\,|\,\boldsymbol{\theta}, \mathbf{a}_i, d_i)\right)^2, \tag{6.5}$$

where SS_θ is the sum of squared differences for a particular value of $\boldsymbol{\theta}$, and u_i is the 0 or 1 item score for Item i.

The sum of squared differences can be computed for each $\boldsymbol{\theta}$-point. The $\boldsymbol{\theta}$-point that yields the smallest value for SS_θ is the least squares estimator for $\boldsymbol{\theta}$. The sum-of-squares surface for the item score string 100 is presented in Fig. 6.8. In contrast to Figs. 6.3 and 6.7, the estimator is given by the low point for this surface rather than the high point. In this case, the least squares estimate of $\boldsymbol{\theta}$ is $(1.5, -.5)$, a point close to the maximum likelihood estimator $(1.5, -.75)$. Least squares estimators based

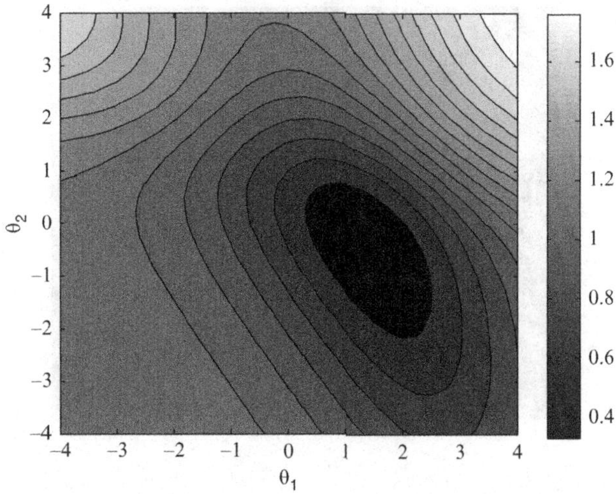

Fig. 6.8 Least squares surface for the item score string 100

on (6.5) are not often used for the estimation of MIRT parameters, but variations on this approach are used in the NOHARM estimation program. The details of that least-squares approach are given later in the chapter.

All of the estimation procedures described earlier select a criterion and then search for the parameter vector that best satisfies the criterion. Three criteria were described: (a) maximum likelihood, (b) Bayesian maximum a posteriori, and (c) least squares. These are not the only criteria that can be used. For example, as was noted earlier, the mean vector for the posterior distribution can be used instead of the vector of maximum values. The former estimation criterion is called expected a posteriori. Other estimation criteria are available as well.

When these approaches are used in practice, graphic procedures for finding the parameter vector are not used. Instead, mathematical search procedures for the maximum or minimum of a function are used. The details of these search procedures are provided in the next section of this chapter.

6.2 Computer Programs for Estimating MIRT Parameters

A number of computer programs have been developed for estimating the values of the parameters in MIRT models. The programs use a variety of estimation procedures and sometimes they include more than one option. A sampling of the computer programs that are available are described here. It is not possible to provide a complete list of computer programs or even to accurately describe the procedures in any one computer program. Computer methodology changes very rapidly and the information presented here may be dated by the time this book is published. Also, new and better computer programs may become available. For all of these reasons, the inclusion of a computer program here is not an endorsement. Rather, the computer program is used as a practical example of the ways that estimation procedures are implemented in practice. Those who wish to estimate the values of the parameters of MIRT models should review the current literature to determine the best of the currently available programs.

6.2.1 TESTFACT

TESTFACT (Bock, Gibons, Schilling, Muraki, Wilson, and Wood 2003) is a computer program for performing factor analysis of interitem tetrachoric correlations and what the authors label "modern methods of item factor analysis based on item response theory." The modern methods of item factor analysis include the estimation of the item and person parameters for the multidimensional extension of the two-parameter normal ogive model. The user can also input lower asymptote parameters so that the program can use the multidimensional generalization of the three-parameter normal ogive model. The program does not estimate the lower asymptote parameter for the items.

The program estimates the MIRT model item parameters using a variation of the maximum likelihood method called marginal maximum likelihood (Bock and Aitken 1981). Estimates of the $\boldsymbol{\theta}$-vectors are obtained using a Bayesian estimation method. The method of estimation is described in some detail in Bock, Gibbons, and Muraki (1988). That method is briefly described here. Some recent enhancements are described in Bock and Schilling (2003).

The estimation of the item parameters is based on the likelihood of an item score string given in (6.1). That likelihood is used to specify the probability of observing the item score string in the population of examinees. This overall probability of the item score string is obtained by weighting the likelihood by the probability density of the $\boldsymbol{\theta}$-vectors and then integrating over the $\boldsymbol{\theta}$-space. The equation for the probability of the score response string for the population of examinees is given by

$$P\left(\mathbf{u}=\mathbf{u}_{\ell}\right)=\int_{\boldsymbol{\theta}} L\left(\mathbf{u}_{\ell} \mid \boldsymbol{\theta}\right) g\left(\boldsymbol{\theta}\right) \mathrm{d}\boldsymbol{\theta}, \tag{6.6}$$

where $P\left(\mathbf{u}=\mathbf{u}_{\ell}\right)$ is the probability of item score string $\mathbf{u}_{\ell}$ for the population of examinees, $L\left(\mathbf{u}_{\ell}|\boldsymbol{\theta}\right)$ is the likelihood of the item score string given a particular $\boldsymbol{\theta}$-vector (see (6.1)), and $g\left(\boldsymbol{\theta}\right)$ is the probability density function for $\boldsymbol{\theta}$.

The integral in (6.6) is evaluated through an integral approximation procedure. When the number of dimensions is five or less, Gauss–Hermite quadrature is used for the evaluation of the integral. For more dimensions, adaptive quadrature is used (Schilling and Bock 2005). The expression for the evaluation of the integral using quadrature is

$$P(\mathbf{u} = \mathbf{u}_\ell) = \sum_{qm=1}^{Q} \cdots \sum_{q2=1}^{Q} \sum_{q1=1}^{Q} L(\mathbf{u}_\ell \mid X) A(X_{q1}) A(X_{q2}) \cdots A(X_{qm}), \tag{6.7}$$

where $\mathbf{X}$ is the vector of values that specify the quadrature point, X_{qk} is the value of a quadrature point for dimension k, $A\left(X_{qk}\right)$ is a weight that is related to the height of the normal density function at the value of the quadrature point for dimension k and the distance between the quadrature points, and qk is the index of the Q quadrature points for dimension k.

Note that the integral is evaluated using the product of unidimensional normal densities. This means that the elements of $\boldsymbol{\theta}$ are assumed to be uncorrelated. Thus, it is a property of the estimates of $\boldsymbol{\theta}$ from TESTFACT that the coordinates of the $\boldsymbol{\theta}$-points are uncorrelated in the initial solution. The program includes options to rotate the solution to PROMAX criterion if nonorthogonal solutions are desired.

The expression in (6.7) gives an estimate of the probability of observing a particular item score string in the population of examinees represented by the multivariate density function $g(\boldsymbol{\theta})$. The probability of the full set of item score strings, $\mathbf{U}$, is given by

$$L(\mathbf{U}) = \frac{N!}{r_1! r_2! \cdots r_s!} P(\mathbf{u} = \mathbf{u}_1)^{r_1} P(\mathbf{u} = \mathbf{u}_2)^{r_2} \cdots P(\mathbf{u} = \mathbf{u}_s)^{r_s}, \tag{6.8}$$

where N is the number of examinees in the sample, s is the number of distinct item score strings, and r_w is the frequency of occurrence of item score string w.

The goal of the estimation procedure is to find the set of parameters that will maximize $L(\mathbf{U})$. Note that the expression in (6.8) does not contain any person parameters, $\boldsymbol{\theta}$. These have been replaced by the quadrature points in (6.7) to integrate out the person distribution from the estimation of the item parameters. Only the item parameters can be estimated using this likelihood function.

In a sense, the likelihood in (6.8) is computed by summing over the distribution of $\boldsymbol{\theta}$s using the quadrature approximation. For that reason, the likelihood is called the marginal likelihood and the use of it for estimation is called marginal maximum likelihood estimation (MML). The elements of the $\boldsymbol{\theta}$-vector are not estimated from this likelihood function because they have been eliminated using the quadrature procedure. Instead, the $\boldsymbol{\theta}$-vector is estimated using the Bayesian method described earlier after the item parameters have been estimated.

In the examples given at the beginning of this chapter, the maximum value of the likelihood function was determined through inspection. The estimate of the parameter vector was determined from the direct evaluation of the surface. When the number of dimensions is above two, a graphic approach to estimation is impractical. In all cases, using graphs to estimate the parameters lacks precision. The alternative is to use a mathematical search procedure to find the maximum of the likelihood function. TESTFACT uses a procedure based on expectation/maximization (EM) algorithm developed by Dempster, Laird, and Rubin (1977).

The estimation procedure in TESTFACT is based on the common mathematical notion that the maximum of a surface is the place where the tangent plane to the surface has slope of zero in all directions. The point where the tangent plane touches the surface is the maximum of the surface. This is the place where the partial derivatives of the surface with respect to the parameters of interest are zero. Bock, Gibbons, and Muraki (1988) give a general expression for the derivative of the likelihood function given in (6.8). The expression uses v to represent one of the item parameters, the elements of the **a**-vector or the d parameter. Using the notation from (6.8), the expression for the derivative is given in (6.9).

$$\begin{aligned}\frac{\partial \log L(\mathbf{U})}{\partial v_i} &= \sum_{\ell=1}^{s} \frac{r_\ell}{P(\mathbf{u}=\mathbf{u}_\ell)}\left(\frac{\partial P(\mathbf{u}=\mathbf{u}_\ell)}{\partial v_i}\right) \\ &= \int_{\boldsymbol{\theta}} \frac{\overline{r}_i - \overline{N}\Phi_i(\boldsymbol{\theta})}{\Phi_i(\boldsymbol{\theta})\left[1-\Phi_i(\boldsymbol{\theta})\right]} \frac{\partial \Phi_j(\boldsymbol{\theta})}{\partial v_i} g(\boldsymbol{\theta})\mathrm{d}\boldsymbol{\theta},\end{aligned} \tag{6.9}$$

where

$$\overline{r}_i = \sum_{\ell=1}^{s} \frac{r_\ell u_{\ell i} L\left(\mathbf{u}_\ell \mid \boldsymbol{\theta}\right)}{P\left(\mathbf{u}=\mathbf{u}_\ell\right)}$$

is the number of correct responses to item i estimated from the MIRT model and the estimated item parameters, and

$$\overline{N} = \sum \frac{r_\ell L\left(\mathbf{u}_\ell \mid \boldsymbol{\theta}\right)}{P\left(\mathbf{u}=\mathbf{u}_\ell\right)}$$

is the total frequency estimated from the MIRT model and the estimated item parameters. Note that $\Phi_j\left(\boldsymbol{\theta}\right)$ is the normal ogive version of the MIRT model. That is the model used in the TESTFACT program.

The estimation of the number of correct responses using the MIRT model with the estimated item parameters constitutes the E-step (estimation step) of the EM algorithm. These estimates are substituted into (6.9) to obtain the maximum likelihood estimates of the item parameters in the M-step (maximization step). Because the estimates of frequencies depend on estimates of item parameters, the process must be iterated to get to a solution that gives a close approximation to the observed frequencies of response patterns.

Equation (6.9) specifies $n\,(m+1)$ nonlinear equations that are simultaneously set to 0 and solved. The simultaneous solution of all of these equations requires a substantial amount of computation and various methods have been used to speed up the process. Constraints have also been placed on the item parameter estimates to facilitate convergence. Details of these techniques are provided in Bock, Gibbons, and Muraki (1988) and the TESTFACT manual. The results of the process are estimates of the a-parameters (m per item) and the d-parameter (one per item) for each of the n items. The solution process is fairly slow. Even with the current generation of fast computers, the solution time is typically in tens of minutes. Of course, by the time this book is published, the speeds of computers will have increased, reducing the computing time.

To obtain unique solutions for the item parameters, several indeterminacies in the MIRT model must be dealt with through constraints. These indeterminacies include the location of the origin of the $\boldsymbol{\theta}$-space, the units of measurement for each coordinate axis, and the rotation of the solution relative to the points in the space. The first two indeterminacies are dealt with through the assumption of a multivariate normal distribution for the $\boldsymbol{\theta}$-vectors with a mean vector containing all 0 elements and an identity matrix for the variance/covariance matrix. The initial solution for the model used in TESTFACT deals with the rotational indeterminacy by setting the a_{ik} parameters to 0 when $k > i$. This solution is not presented in the output from the program. Instead, the output includes the solution after it is rotated to the principal factor solution.

Once the item parameters have been estimated, an option is available to estimate the $\boldsymbol{\theta}$-vectors. The procedure for estimating the $\boldsymbol{\theta}$-vectors is described in Muraki and Englelhard (1985). A Bayesian expected a posteriori (EAP) is used so that estimates of coordinates from item score string from short tests will not tend toward infinite values. That is, the estimate of the coordinates in the $\boldsymbol{\theta}$-space for a person is the expected value of the posterior distribution for each coordinate in $\boldsymbol{\theta}$. The basic mathematical expressions for the estimates are

$$\hat{\theta}_{jv} = E\left(\theta_{jv}\,|\,\mathbf{u}_i\right) = \int_{\boldsymbol{\theta}} \theta_v P\left(\boldsymbol{\theta}\,|\,\mathbf{u}_j\right) \mathrm{d}\boldsymbol{\theta} = \int_{\boldsymbol{\theta}} \frac{\theta_v f\left(\mathbf{u}_j\,|\,\boldsymbol{\theta}\right) g\left(\boldsymbol{\theta}\right)}{h\left(\mathbf{u}_j\right)} \mathrm{d}\boldsymbol{\theta}, \tag{6.10}$$

where $\hat{\theta}_{jv}$ is the estimate of the coordinate on dimension v for person j, $f\left(\mathbf{u}_j|\boldsymbol{\theta}\right)$ is the likelihood function for the item score string based on the MIRT model, $g\left(\boldsymbol{\theta}\right)$ is the prior distribution for $\boldsymbol{\theta}$, and $h\left(\mathbf{u}_j\right) = \int_{\boldsymbol{\theta}} f\left(\mathbf{u}_j|\boldsymbol{\theta}\right) g\left(\boldsymbol{\theta}\right) \mathrm{d}\boldsymbol{\theta}$.

The integral in (6.10) is evaluated using Gauss–Hermite quadrature assuming that the parameters for the items are known. The standard deviation of the posterior distribution is reported as the standard error of measurement for the coordinate estimate.

Two data sets with known characteristics are used here to demonstrate the functioning of the estimation procedures. The same data sets are used with all of the procedures described in this chapter so that they can be directly compared. The item parameters for the data sets are shown in Table 6.1. A test consisting of 30 dichotomously scored test items is assumed to be accurately modeled in a three dimensional space using the compensatory logistic model shown in (4.5). The table contains the three a-parameters for each item and the d-parameter as well as the multidimensional discrimination estimate A, the multidimensional difficulty estimate B, and the angles of the direction of best measurement, α_v, for each item with the coordinate axes for the space.

The set of test items was developed to approximate simple structure in that each test best measures along one of the coordinate axes. However, the set of test items

Table 6.1 Item parameters and descriptive statistics for 30 test items in three dimensions

Item number	a_1	a_2	a_3	d	α_1	α_2	α_3	A	B
1	0.7471	0.0250	0.1428	0.1826	11	88	79	0.76	−0.24
2	0.4595	0.0097	0.0692	−0.1924	9	89	81	0.46	0.41
3	0.8613	0.0067	0.4040	−0.4656	25	90	65	0.95	0.49
4	1.0141	0.0080	0.0470	−0.4336	3	90	87	1.02	0.43
5	0.5521	0.0204	0.1482	−0.4428	15	88	75	0.57	0.77
6	1.3547	0.0064	0.5362	−0.5845	22	90	68	1.46	0.40
7	1.3761	0.0861	0.4676	−1.0403	19	87	71	1.46	0.71
8	0.8525	0.0383	0.2574	0.6431	17	88	73	0.89	−0.72
9	1.0113	0.0055	0.2024	0.0122	11	90	79	1.03	−0.01
10	0.9212	0.0119	0.3044	0.0912	18	89	72	0.97	−0.09
11	0.0026	0.2436	0.8036	0.8082	90	73	17	0.84	−0.96
12	0.0008	0.1905	1.1945	−0.1867	90	81	9	1.21	0.15
13	0.0575	0.0853	0.7077	0.4533	85	83	8	0.72	−0.63
14	0.0182	0.3307	2.1414	−1.8398	90	81	9	2.17	0.85
15	0.0256	0.0478	0.8551	0.4139	88	87	4	0.86	−0.48
16	0.0246	0.1496	0.9348	−0.3004	89	81	9	0.95	0.32
17	0.0262	0.2872	1.3561	−0.1824	89	78	12	1.39	0.13
18	0.0038	0.2229	0.8993	0.5125	90	76	14	0.93	−0.55
19	0.0039	0.4720	0.7318	1.1342	90	57	33	0.87	−1.30
20	0.0068	0.0949	0.6416	0.0230	89	82	8	0.65	−0.04
21	0.3073	0.9704	0.0031	0.6172	72	18	90	1.02	−0.61
22	0.1819	0.4980	0.0020	−0.1955	70	20	90	0.53	0.37
23	0.4115	1.1136	0.2008	−0.3668	70	22	80	1.20	0.30
24	0.1536	1.7251	0.0345	−1.7590	85	5	89	1.73	1.02
25	0.1530	0.6688	0.0020	−0.2434	77	13	90	0.69	0.35
26	0.2890	1.2419	0.0220	0.4925	77	13	89	1.28	−0.39
27	0.1341	1.4882	0.0050	−0.3410	85	5	90	1.49	0.23
28	0.0524	0.4754	0.0012	0.2896	84	6	90	0.48	−0.61
29	0.2139	0.4612	0.0063	0.0060	65	25	89	0.51	−0.01
30	0.1761	1.1200	0.0870	0.0329	81	10	86	1.14	−0.03

was designed to be fairly realistic in that the angles with the coordinate axes are not all close to 0 or 90°. The B estimates are in a reasonable range and the A estimates are not too large.

These item parameters were used to generate data sets with two different variance/covariance matrices for the coordinates for simulated examinees. Data Set 1 was generated assuming a mean vector of $\mathbf{0}$ and an identity matrix for the variance/covariance matrix. Data Set 2 was designed to represent more realistic conditions. The mean vector was set to $[-.4\ -.7\ .1]$ and the variance/covariance matrix was set to

$$\begin{bmatrix} 1.21 & .297 & 1.232 \\ .297 & .81 & .252 \\ 1.232 & .252 & 1.96 \end{bmatrix}.$$

Table 6.2 Descriptive statistics and reliability estimates for the number-correct scores from the two simulated data sets

	Data Set 1	Data Set 2
Mean	14.75	12.71
Standard deviation	4.75	6.09
Reliability	.71	.84

This matrix is consistent with standard deviations for the coordinates of [1.1 .9 1.4] and a correlation matrix of

$$\begin{bmatrix} 1 & .3 & .8 \\ .3 & 1 & .2 \\ .8 & .2 & 1 \end{bmatrix}.$$

The reason for using these values to generate the data is to show the parameter estimates that result when the data do not match the assumptions built into the estimation program. These assumptions are often a multivariate normal distribution with mean vector $\mathbf{0}$ and identity matrix for the variance/covariance matrix.

The analysis data were generated by first randomly selecting 2,000 $\boldsymbol{\theta}$-vectors from each of the two specified population distributions. The two sets of $\boldsymbol{\theta}$-vectors were then used to generate item score strings using the item parameters shown in Table 6.1. The results were two 2000×30 matrixes of item scores. The means, standard deviations, and coefficient α estimates of internal consistency reliability for the number-correct scores computed from these data sets are presented in Table 6.2.

The differences in the number-correct score distributions and reliabilities for the two simulated tests reflect the differences in the $\boldsymbol{\theta}$-distributions used to generate the data. The $\boldsymbol{\theta}$-distribution for Data Set 1 had means of 0 on the three coordinates so the mean number-correct score is approximately half of the total possible. The reliability is moderate because the dimensionality of the generated data violates the assumptions of the internal consistency reliability measure.

Data Set 2 has a lower mean number-correct score because the means for two of the $\boldsymbol{\theta}$-coordinates are below 0. The standard deviation and reliability are higher because the $\boldsymbol{\theta}$-coordinates are correlated resulting in a more internally consistent test. The differences in the analyses of the two data sets reinforce the sample specific nature of these descriptive statistics. These differences exist because of differences in the $\boldsymbol{\theta}$-distributions. The same item parameters were used to generate the two data sets.

The item score matrices from the two data sets were analyzed using TESTFACT specifying three dimensions using the default options. Item parameter estimates for Data Set 1 converged in 14 cycles. The estimation for the item parameters for Data Set 2 did not converge in 200 cycles. The item parameter estimates obtained from the two data sets are shown in Table 6.3.

The analysis of Data Set 1 shows that the order of the dimensions in the TESTFACT output does not match that of the generating data. Dimension 1 of the generating parameters corresponds to Dimension 3 from TESTFACT. Dimension 3 of the generating parameters corresponds to Dimension 1 for the estimates and Dimension 2 in the generating parameters remains as Dimension 2 for the estimates. Another feature of the Data Set 1 estimates is that the values of the a-parameters are

Table 6.3 Item parameter estimates for Data Set 1 and Data Set 2

Item number	Data Set 1				Data Set 2			
	a_1	a_2	a_3	d	a_1	a_2	a_3	d
1	.04	.09	***.50***	.08	***.52***	.06	.33	−.08
2	.02	−.00	***.27***	−.09	***.31***	.04	.17	−.26
3	.15	.07	***.58***	−.29	***.64***	.14	.31	−.43
4	−.09	.08	***.67***	−.29	***.46***	.22	.33	−.49
5	.16	.03	***.33***	−.22	***.38***	.11	.19	−.36
6	.16	.10	***.67***	−.31	***1.23***	.27	.49	−.73
7	.20	.16	***.89***	−.63	***.98***	.19	.42	−.83
8	.12	.03	***.51***	.40	***.66***	.17	.38	.19
9	.12	.04	***.60***	.04	***.76***	.09	.44	−.22
10	.06	.05	***.54***	.05	***.71***	.11	.30	−.20
11	***.47***	.14	.07	.45	***.68***	.22	.07	.43
12	***.63***	.02	.14	−.14	***.93***	.17	−.11	−.16
13	***.42***	.04	.11	.23	***.58***	.04	.05	.23
14	***1.09***	.03	.17	−1.02	***1.53***	.30	.03	−.94
15	***.51***	.02	.08	.23	***.69***	.11	−.06	.29
16	***.55***	.01	.05	−.16	***.79***	.11	−.02	−.16
17	***.85***	.05	.05	−.16	***1.06***	.28	−.02	−.17
18	***.54***	.16	.12	.31	***.75***	.10	−.05	.34
19	***.56***	.18	.06	.71	***.59***	.25	.01	.55
20	***.39***	−.00	.05	.03	***.53***	.06	−.04	−.03
21	.05	***.65***	.06	.38	.18	***.54***	.17	−.17
22	−.01	***.27***	.11	−.12	.10	***.29***	.10	−.39
23	.16	***.65***	.15	−.17	.41	***.61***	.14	−.78
24	.12	***1.08***	.01	−1.07	.11	***.81***	.15	−1.67
25	.01	***.37***	.01	−.14	.14	***.39***	.05	−.47
26	.08	***.73***	.04	.29	.20	***.67***	.10	−.26
27	.06	***.91***	.06	−.21	.13	***.68***	−.02	−.86
28	.03	***.35***	−.02	.16	.08	***.29***	.03	−.10
29	.04	***.30***	.08	.00	.11	***.32***	.18	−.24
30	.11	***.65***	.05	.06	.26	***.54***	.05	−.52

Note: The largest a-parameter for each item is shown in bold italics.

less than the corresponding generating parameters. This is also true for the estimates of the d-parameters. This is a result of the fact that the data were generated with the logistic compensatory MIRT model without the 1.7 constant in the exponent that improves the match to the normal ogive model. Because TESTFACT assumes the normal ogive model, the parameter estimates for a are approximately the generating values divided by 1.7. The actual ratios of the means of the generating a-parameters to the estimated a-parameters are 1.62, 1.59, and 1.88, respectively. The average of these three values is 1.7. Also, the ratio of the standard deviations of the generating d-parameters (.657) to the estimated d-parameters (.386) is 1.7.

If the data had been generated with the 1.7 multiplier in the exponent of the model, the parameter estimates should more closely match the parameters used to

Table 6.4 Item parameter estimates for Data Set 1a

Item Number	a_1	a_2	a_3	d
1	.10	.16	***.73***	.18
2	.02	.05	***.48***	−.19
3	.28	.12	***.88***	−.48
4	−.00	.14	***.97***	−.45
5	.07	.13	***.51***	−.41
6	.29	.11	***1.38***	−.61
7	.22	.32	***1.21***	−1.05
8	.14	.21	***.82***	.61
9	.12	.08	***.89***	.07
10	.22	.13	***.82***	.12
11	***.79***	.14	.05	.78
12	***1.11***	.07	.19	−.19
13	***.69***	.04	.11	.44
14	***1.73***	.19	.23	−1.62
15	***.80***	−.03	.16	.40
16	***.91***	.05	.10	−.32
17	***1.36***	.18	.15	−.21
18	***.84***	.12	.15	.54
19	***.62***	.37	.01	1.06
20	***.59***	.01	.10	.03
21	.02	***.90***	.24	.58
22	.02	***.48***	.18	−.15
23	.12	***1.15***	.28	−.36
24	.12	***1.41***	−.04	−1.55
25	.09	***.65***	.08	−.27
26	.10	***1.22***	.07	.61
27	.12	***1.47***	−.06	−.31
28	−.04	***.47***	.05	.35
29	.03	***.45***	.15	−.01
30	.15	***1.00***	.07	.01

Note: The largest a-parameter for each item is shown in bold italics.

generate the data. To demonstrate that situation, a third data set was generated (Data Set 1a) using the item parameters in Table 6.1, the zero vector for means, the identity matrix as the variance covariance matrix, but with 1.7 in the model. The results of the estimation of the item parameters for that data set are given in Table 6.4. These results show a much closer recovery of the generating item parameters than was the case for Data Set 1. Even though the results appear to be different, they are really a change of scale. The corresponding parameter estimates from the two data sets correlate in the high .90s.

The relationships between the parameter estimates from Data Set 2 and the generating item parameters are not as clear as those for Data Sets 1 and 1a. Because the coordinates of simulated examinees on Dimensions 1 and 3 were correlated .8 when the data were generated, the a-parameters for the 20 items that are sensitive

Table 6.5 Summary information about $\boldsymbol{\theta}$-estimates for the Data Sets 1, 1a, and 2

	Data Set 1			Data Set 1a			Data Set 2		
	θ_1	θ_2	θ_3	θ_1	θ_2	θ_3	θ_1	θ_2	θ_3
Mean	.01	.01	.01	.00	.01	.01	.01	.02	.00
SD	.82	.83	.80	.82	.83	.80	.94	.74	.54
Reliability	.66	.67	.63	.78	.78	.76	.83	.53	.29
θ_1	1			1			1		
θ_2	.24	1		.20	1		.44	1	
θ_3	.32	.23	1	.30	.31	1	.74	.50	1

Note: The values in the bottom three rows of the table are the correlations between the PROMAX rotated factors.

to differences on those two dimensions are all high for estimated Dimension 1. The last 10 items were sensitive to differences on Dimension 2 and continue to have high a-parameters for estimated Dimension 2. The d-parameters are also shifted to show that the test items are more difficult for this calibration sample because the means on the first two coordinates were $-.4$ and $-.7$, respectively. Clearly, the characteristics of the sample of individuals who take the test affect the recovery of the item parameters. In this case, TESTFACT is providing what is essentially a two-dimensional solution because of the correlations between two of the sets of coordinates used to generate the data. It may be possible to rotate and translate this set of estimates to better match the generating item parameters. Methods for converting one set of item parameters to the scale of another set are considered in Chap. 7.

The calibration analyses reported earlier also used the TESTFACT program option for estimating the $\boldsymbol{\theta}$-vectors for each examinee. Table 6.5 presents the descriptive statistics and internal consistency reliability estimates for the $\boldsymbol{\theta}$-estimates obtained from the three data sets. For all of the data sets, the estimation procedure sets the mean values of the $\boldsymbol{\theta}$-estimates to 0. It is interesting to note, however, that the standard deviations of the estimates are not 1.0 for any of the estimates. Bock and Schilling (2003) indicate that sum of the factor score variance and the mean-square error should be close to 1.0 (p. 589). For all of the cases considered here, the sum of the variance of the coordinate estimates and the mean-square error was close to 1.0. The θ_1 standard deviation was closest to 1.0. That $\boldsymbol{\theta}$ was estimated using 20 of the 30 items on the simulated test because the highly correlated coordinates resulted in a merging of two dimensions. That $\boldsymbol{\theta}$ also had the highest reliability while the reliabilities for the other two θs were notably lower. As a result, the mean-square error for θ_1 is small. The correlations between the coordinates for Data Set 2 are recovered fairly well from the PROMAX rotation of the solution.

The results for Data Sets 1 and 1a are comparable except for the reliability estimates. Data Set 1a has higher estimates because the inclusion of the 1.7 in the generating model effectively increases the discriminating power of all of the items.

An important implication of these examples is that the estimates of the item parameters from TESTFACT are affected by the match between the generating model and the generating distribution of person coordinates and those assumed by the program. TESTFACT was programmed assuming a standard multivariate normal distribution of coordinates with zero intercorrelations. That assumption places constraints on the estimation of the model parameters. A second implication is that the parameter estimates for a set of data are not unique and they may not match those used to generate data. Even when the item parameters are well estimated, they may be reported on scales that are different than the generating parameters. This is a result of the indeterminacies in the origin, rotation, and units of measurement for the parameters in the models. Each estimation program uses different methods for dealing with the indeterminacy.

6.2.2 NOHARM

NOHARM (Fraser 1998) is a program for estimating the item parameters of the same normal ogive form of MIRT model that is used by TESTFACT. This is the form of MIRT model given in (4.16). NOHARM (Normal-Ogive Harmonic Analysis Robust Method) uses a procedure for estimating the parameters of test items for MIRT models that is quite different than that used by TESTFACT. The estimation procedure is described here along with some examples using the same data sets as were analyzed using TESTFACT. The symbol set used in the other sections of this book are used to present the NOHARM estimation method. These are different than the presentations by Fraser (1998) and McDonald (1997).

The estimation methodology in NOHARM fits the multidimensional normal ogive version of the compensatory MIRT model to the person-by-item matrix of item scores. However, rather than fit that matrix using the MIRT model, it first fits specific features of the matrix using a polynomial approximation to the normal ogive model. McDonald (1997) argues that a polynomial up to the cubic term provides sufficient accuracy for most applications. The characteristics of the item score matrix that are used for estimating the item parameters for the model are the estimate of the population probability of correct response for each item, $\hat{\pi}_i$, and the estimate of the population probability of correctly responding to both items in a pair of items, $\hat{\pi}_{ik}$. The estimation procedure does not use the higher order interactions between items. The use of these two features of the item score matrix is roughly equivalent to using the means of scores on the items and the tetrachoric correlations between pairs of items McDonald (1997, p. 262).

The polynomial approximation to the normal ogive MIRT model is given by

$$P(u_{ij} = 1 \mid \boldsymbol{\theta}_j) = \sum_{p=0}^{\infty} \gamma_{ip} h_p \left[\frac{\mathbf{a}_i \boldsymbol{\theta}'_j}{\sqrt{\mathbf{a}_i \mathbf{P} \mathbf{a}'_i}} \right], \tag{6.11}$$

where h_p is the normalized Hermite–Tchebycheff polynomial of degree p, γ_{ip} is the coefficient for the pth term of the polynomial for Item i, and $\mathbf{P}$ is the covariance matrix for $\boldsymbol{\theta}$.

In practice, only the first four terms of the polynomial are used to estimate the item parameters. Note that the covariance matrix **P** is present in (6.11). For the calibration of test items, **P** is usually assumed to be an identity matrix. This assumption is not a formal part of the MIRT model, but it is used when estimating parameters. NOHARM allows the user to specify other forms for **P** than the identity matrix.

If, for convenience $z_j = \mathbf{a}_i \boldsymbol{\theta}'_j / \sqrt{\mathbf{a}_i \mathbf{P} \mathbf{a}'_i}$, the form of the first four terms of $h_p(z_j)$ are: $h_0(z_j) = 1, h_1(z_j) = z_j, h_2(z_j) = (z_j^2 - 1)/\sqrt{2}$, and $h_3(z_j) = (z_j^3 - 3z_j)/\sqrt{6}$. The estimate of the proportion answering the item correctly is given by the coefficient of the first term of the series. That is,

$$\hat{\pi}_i = \gamma_{i0} = \Phi \left[\frac{d_i}{\sqrt{1 + \mathbf{a}_i \mathbf{P} \mathbf{a}'_i}} \right]. \tag{6.12}$$

The estimate of the probability of correctly responding to both test items, i and k, in a pair is given by

$$\hat{\pi}_{ik} = \sum_{p=0}^{\infty} \gamma_{ip} \gamma_{jp} \left[\frac{\mathbf{a}_i \mathbf{P} \mathbf{a}'_k}{\sqrt{\mathbf{a}_i \mathbf{P} \mathbf{a}'_i \mathbf{a}_k \mathbf{P} \mathbf{a}'_k}} \right]^p. \tag{6.13}$$

In practice, only the first few terms of the summation are used to approximate the proportion of correct responses to both items in the i, j-pair (McDonald 1997, p. 261).

The actual estimation of the item parameters is done using unweighted least squares methodology. The following criterion (6.14) is minimized relative to the item parameters,

$$SS_{ik} = \sum_{i \neq k} (p_{ik} - \hat{\pi}_{ik})^2 \quad \text{for all } i, k, \tag{6.14}$$

where p_{ik} is the observed proportion correct for both items in the i, k pair. In NOHARM, the parameters that minimize (6.14) are found using a quasi-Newton algorithm.

To demonstrate the results of applying this methodology for the estimation of item parameters, NOHARM was run in exploratory mode on the same data-sets that were analyzed using TESTFACT. The item parameters used to generate the data are given in Table 6.1. Both Data Set 1 and 2 were analyzed to show the results when the data were generated meeting the assumptions of the estimation program and when they were not.

Table 6.6 contains the item parameter estimates for the two data sets. For both data sets, some of the a-parameter estimates are set to 0 to fix the orientation of the coordinate axes. For the examples, a_2 and a_3 are set to 0 for Item 1 and a_3 is set to 0 for Item 2. These fixed values are defaults in the program. Fixing these a-parameters in this way sets the θ_1-axis to align with the direction of maximum discrimination for Item 1 and the direction of maximum discrimination of Item 2 is set to fall within the θ_1, θ_2-plane. The directions for the other items are determined from their

Table 6.6 Item parameter estimates for Data Set 1 and Data Set 2

Item number	Data Set 1				Data Set 2			
	a_1	a_2	a_3	d	a_1	a_2	a_3	d
1	***.62***	.00	.00	.09	***1.20***	.00	.00	−.09
2	***.25***	.04	.00	−.08	.25	***.35***	.00	−.26
3	***.56***	.18	.02	−.28	***.54***	.34	.35	−.42
4	***.58***	.07	−.11	−.27	.32	.29	***.39***	−.47
5	***.34***	.16	.05	−.22	***.32***	.19	.25	−.35
6	***.63***	.20	.01	−.30	***.97***	.73	.68	−.71
7	***.77***	.24	.03	−.58	***.76***	.60	.51	−.80
8	***.54***	.15	.02	.41	***.54***	.37	.38	.19
9	***.56***	.17	−.02	.04	***.61***	.42	.34	−.20
10	***.52***	.14	−.04	.06	***.59***	.45	.31	−.19
11	.15	***.35***	.27	.45	***.47***	.40	.42	.44
12	.20	***.39***	.19	−.12	***.59***	.53	.40	−.15
13	.16	***.30***	.15	.23	***.42***	.33	.22	.23
14	.25	***.50***	.34	−.79	***1.00***	.86	.73	−.87
15	.15	***.33***	.16	.22	***.50***	.36	.32	.29
16	.14	***.36***	.15	−.14	***.57***	.42	.36	−.15
17	.17	***.45***	.25	−.13	***.68***	.64	.58	−.16
18	.18	***.38***	.29	.30	***.50***	.42	.32	.33
19	.20	***.42***	.39	.71	.36	***.39***	.38	.56
20	.11	***.26***	.11	.03	***.35***	.28	.23	−.03
21	−.03	.14	***.55***	.36	−.11	.22	***.56***	−.16
22	.06	.02	***.25***	−.12	−.06	.09	***.32***	−.38
23	.04	.18	***.58***	−.16	.09	.34	***.66***	−.75
24	.06	.31	***.75***	−.91	−.04	.22	***.46***	−1.40
25	−.07	.04	***.34***	−.14	−.10	.17	***.40***	−.46
26	−.03	.15	***.61***	.28	−.14	.26	***.64***	−.24
27	−.05	.15	***.67***	−.18	−.17	.19	***.54***	−.80
28	−.08	.05	***.32***	.16	−.12	.14	***.31***	−.10
29	.03	.06	***.28***	.01	−.06	.14	***.36***	−.23
30	−.02	.15	***.58***	.06	−.04	.24	***.57***	−.50

Note: The largest a-parameter for each item is shown in bold italics.

relationships with Items 1 and 2. This pattern of constraints on the estimation of the $\mathbf{a}$-parameters is placed on the parameters for the first $m - 1$ items where m is the number of dimensions in the solution.

This approach to dealing with the rotational indeterminacy of the solution has some potential problems. Because both Item 1 and Item 2 have similar directions in the space, these constraints may not provide a stable orientation for the θ_2 and θ_3 axes. This seems to be a particular problem for Data Set 2 that had a fairly high correlation between θ_1 and θ_3. As was the case for the application of TESTFACT to Data Set 2, those two dimensions are merged in the analysis, but for NOHARM there is some inconsistency in the estimates of the a-parameters for the items used to anchor the coordinate axes.

To show the effects of the items selected to anchor the axes when using NOHARM, Data Set 2 was analyzed a second time, but with the items rearranged so that different items were in the second and third positions in the file. The column of responses for Item 12 were interchanged with those for Item 2 and the column of responses for Item 23 were interchanged with those for Item 3. This rearrangement put items that were sensitive to differences along the three different coordinate axes in the first three locations in the data set. These three items then set the orientation of the coordinate axes because of the constraints placed on the a-parameters. The results from this calibration are shown in Table 6.7.

Table 6.7 Item parameter estimates for Data Set 2 with items rearranged

Item number	Item parameter estimates			
	a_1	a_2	a_3	d
1	***1.02***	.00	.00	−.09
12	.64	***1.16***	.00	−.19
23	.16	.31	***.71***	−.77
4	***.42***	.21	.40	−.48
5	***.35***	.18	.23	−.35
6	***1.07***	.70	.61	−.71
7	***.83***	.58	.46	−.80
8	***.64***	.27	.42	.20
9	***.70***	.34	.36	−.21
10	***.65***	.37	.32	−.19
11	.46	***.51***	.32	.44
2	***.30***	.13	.16	−.25
13	***.43***	.38	.16	.23
14	1.04	***1.10***	.50	−.91
15	.46	***.55***	.16	.29
16	.54	***.56***	.24	−.15
17	.67	***.82***	.43	−.16
18	.48	***.55***	.21	.34
19	.37	***.42***	.33	.56
20	.32	***.44***	.13	−.03
21	.01	.15	***.58***	−.16
22	.02	.05	***.34***	−.38
3	***.60***	.31	.33	−.42
24	−.11	.18	***.69***	−1.54
25	−.03	.16	***.40***	−.46
26	−.09	.25	***.71***	−.25
27	−.17	.19	***.65***	−.84
28	−.07	.15	***.28***	−.10
29	.05	.07	***.38***	−.23
30	−.00	.28	***.55***	−.50

Note: The largest a-parameter estimate in each row is shown in bold italics. The item number matches the items in Table 6.6.

These results show that using appropriate items to anchor the axes provides much better recovery of the structure of the data. Although a-parameter estimates for a_1 and a_2 are often similar in magnitude, the largest a-parameter estimate for each item very closely matches the pattern for the true parameters used to generate the data. The analysis was able to detect the differences in sensitivity of the items to the different dimensions even though two of the dimensions are highly correlated.

NOHARM does not provide an option for estimating the elements of the $\boldsymbol{\theta}$-vector. Therefore, it is not possible to directly estimate the location of individuals or the correlations between $\boldsymbol{\theta}$-estimates. However, the item parameters from NOHARM can be entered into TESTFACT as fixed parameters and $\boldsymbol{\theta}$-estimates can be obtained using that program and the item score strings.

6.2.3 ConQuest

ConQuest (Wu, Adams, and Wilson 1997) is a general purpose program for estimating the parameters of a family of models that fall under the categorization of Rasch models. This means that the models have an exponential form and they have observable sufficient statistics for the parameters that describe the test items and persons. The description given here focuses on the use of the program for estimating the parameters of the Rasch version of MIRT. The program has many other options and the interested reader should refer to the manual that accompanies the software to get a full list of applications.

The general model that underlies ConQuest is given in (4.14) with the version for dichotomous data given in (4.15). An important feature of the model is that the user needs to specify the scoring matrix, **A**, and the design matrix, **B**, when using the program to estimate parameters. For the analysis of dichotomous test items that are scored as either correct (1) or incorrect (0), only the design matrix needs to be specified to indicate which test items are sensitive to differences in which coordinate of the $\boldsymbol{\theta}$-vector.

When analyzing real test data, it is unlikely that the elements of the **B** matrix will be known with certainty. Instead, the data analyst will use best judgment to identify the elements of the $\boldsymbol{\theta}$-vector that are likely to influence the probability of a correct response for the test items. ConQuest will allow any values in the **B** matrix. Adams, Wilson, and Wang (1997) distinguish between design matrices that have a single nonzero value in each row of **B** indicating a simple-structure solution that they call a between-item solution and matrices that have multiple nonzero values in the rows of the matrix that they call a within-item solution.

A comparison of (4.14) and (4.15) shows that the **B** matrix is equivalent to the matrix of discrimination parameters for the multidimensional extension of the two-parameter logistic model, **a** in the notation used in this book. In a sense, ConQuest requires that the discrimination parameters be estimated separately from the computer program by the persons analyzing the test. These estimates are then fixed so the solution will have Rasch model properties. That is, there will be computable sufficient statistics for the person- and item-parameters.

Table 6.8 Design matrix for the analysis of three-dimensional simulated data

1	0	0
1	0	0
1	0	0
1	0	0
1	0	0
1	0	0
1	0	0
1	0	0
1	0	0
1	0	0
0	1	0
0	1	0
0	1	0
0	1	0
0	1	0
0	1	0
0	1	0
0	1	0
0	1	0
0	1	0
0	0	1
0	0	1
0	0	1
0	0	1
0	0	1
0	0	1
0	0	1
0	0	1
0	0	1
0	0	1

For the set of items used in the examples in this chapter, each set of ten items (1 – 10, 11 – 20, and 21 – 30) is most sensitive to a different dimension. If the test developer designed the test that way, or can identify the test items as measuring different constructs, then they could produce a design matrix of the form shown in Table 6.8.

This design matrix was used for the analysis of Data Set 1 that was used in the examples of the application of the TESTFACT and NOHARM programs.

ConQuest uses maximum likelihood estimation implemented in two different ways – a quadrature approach and a Monte Carlo approach. These methods are described in detail in Volodin and Adams (2002). The quadrature approach is used when the number of $\boldsymbol{\theta}$-dimensions is one or two. The Monte Carlo approach is used when the number of $\boldsymbol{\theta}$-dimensions is three or more. The manual for the ConQuest (Wu, Adams, and Wilson 1997), indicates that the program can estimate up to 15 dimensions.

Because ConQuest is a very general program that can estimate the parameters for many different types of models, issues of model identification are very important.

Volodin and Adams (2002) give informal proofs that show that the model is generally not identified (unique estimators of the parameters are not available). To address this problem in the multidimensional case, either the sum of the difficulty parameters of the items are constrained to be zero for items related to each dimension, or the means of the elements of the $\boldsymbol{\theta}$-vector are constrained to be zero. It is also possible to specify identified solutions through appropriate selection of the scoring and design matrices. The selection of appropriate constraints is important, especially if calibration results from different programs are being compared. The results of different constraints on the parameter estimates will be discussed in more detail when the results of the calibration of the data sets are presented.

The estimation procedure using quadrature is very similar to that described for TESTFACT earlier in this chapter. Extending (4.15) to give the likelihood of an item score string, the basic likelihood equation is

$$L\left(\mathbf{u}_{\ell} \mid \boldsymbol{\theta}\right) = P\left(\mathbf{u}_{\ell} \mid \mathbf{A}, \mathbf{d}, \boldsymbol{\theta}\right) = \left\{\sum_{\mathrm{z}\in\Omega} \mathrm{e}^{\mathrm{z}'(\mathrm{A}\theta'+\mathrm{d})}\right\}^{-1} \mathrm{e}^{\mathbf{u}'_{\ell}(\mathrm{A}\theta'+\mathrm{d})}, \tag{6.15}$$

where $L\left(\mathbf{u}_{\ell}|\boldsymbol{\theta}\right)$ is the likelihood of the item score string ℓ for a particular $\boldsymbol{\theta}$-vector, $\mathbf{A}$[1] is the prespecified scoring matrix for the set of items in the test, $\mathbf{d}$ is a vector of intercept terms for the items in the test, $\mathbf{z}$ is one of the possible item score strings from the test, and Ω is the set of all possible item score strings.

The likelihood of the item score string $\mathbf{u}_{\ell}$ for a randomly sampled examinee is very similar to that in (6.6),

$$P\left(\mathbf{u} = \mathbf{u}_{\ell}\right) = \int_{\boldsymbol{\theta}} L\left(\mathbf{u}_{\ell}|\boldsymbol{\theta}\right) g\left(\boldsymbol{\theta}|\boldsymbol{\mu}, \boldsymbol{\Sigma}\right) \mathrm{d}\boldsymbol{\theta}, \tag{6.16}$$

where $P\left(\mathbf{u} = \mathbf{u}_{\ell}\right)$ is the probability of item score string $\mathbf{u}_{\ell}$ over the population of examinees, and $g\left(\boldsymbol{\theta}|\boldsymbol{\mu}, \Sigma\right)$ is the probability density function for $\boldsymbol{\theta}$ with a specified mean vector and covariance matrix.

Equations (6.16) and (6.6) are essentially the same. However, the probability of the entire item score matrix is computed slightly differently in ConQuest than in (6.8). The likelihood of the full matrix of responses is simply

$$L\left(\mathbf{U}\right) = \prod_{j=1}^{N} P\left(\mathbf{u} = \mathbf{u}_{j}\right), \tag{6.17}$$

where $\mathbf{U}$ is the matrix of item scores, j is the index for examinees, and N is the total number of examinees in the sample. When estimating item parameters for the

[1] In the manual for ConQuest, the scoring matrix is denoted a $\mathbf{B}$. Here $\mathbf{A}$ is used to be consistent with the notation for discrimination parameters in this book.

model, the logarithm of the likelihood of the full matrix of item scores is differentiated with respect to the item parameter vector, $\boldsymbol{\gamma}$. The result for the dichotomous case is

$$\frac{\partial \log L(\mathbf{U})}{\partial \boldsymbol{\gamma}} = \sum_{j=1}^{N} \left[\mathbf{u}_j - \int_{\boldsymbol{\theta}_j} E\left(\mathbf{z} \,|\, \boldsymbol{\theta}_j\right) h\left(\boldsymbol{\theta}_j \,|\, \mathbf{u}_j, \boldsymbol{\gamma}\right) \mathrm{d}\boldsymbol{\theta}_j \right] = 0, \tag{6.18}$$

where $h()$ is the marginal posterior density of $\boldsymbol{\theta}_j$ given the item score string $\mathbf{u}_j$ and the other symbols have been previously defined. Note that the expectation of $\mathbf{z}$ gives a vector of proportion correct values that are the means of the item scores in the dichotomous case. The expression in (6.18) is used to find the estimates of the item parameters that minimizes the difference between the expected item scores and the observed item scores over the entire matrix of item scores $\mathbf{U}$. Similar expressions are developed to estimate the mean $\boldsymbol{\theta}$-vector and the variance/covariance matrix for the $\boldsymbol{\theta}$s. The full set of estimation equations is given in Adams, Wilson, and Wang (1997) or in the ConQuest manual. The set of equations is solved using the EM-algorithm (Dempster, Laird, and Rubin 1977) using a method similar to that of Bock and Aitken (1981).

The distribution used in the estimation procedure is approximated using either quadrature or a Monte Carlo procedure. In either case, a set of nodes are defined, Θ_q, $q = 1, \ldots, Q$ with a set of weights, $W_q(\gamma, \Sigma)$ corresponding to each node. The integrals are then approximated by

$$P(u = u_\ell) = \sum_{q=1}^{Q} L\left(u_\ell \,|\, \Theta_q\right) W_q(\gamma, \Sigma) \tag{6.19}$$

and

$$h\left(\Theta_q \,|\, u_\ell, \gamma\right) = \frac{L\left(u_\ell \,|\, \Theta_q\right) W_q(\gamma, \Sigma)}{\sum_{q=1}^{Q} L\left(u_\ell \,|\, \Theta_q\right) W_q(\gamma, \Sigma)}. \tag{6.20}$$

Volodin and Adams (2002) indicate that Gauss–Hermite quadrature is used for the one and two-dimensional cases with weights that are a function of the height of the standard normal distributions at each node. The ConQuest manual indicates that 20 nodes are used for each dimension and higher dimensional solutions use 2000 nodes as a default. For higher dimensional cases, the nodes are randomly sampled from a standard normal distribution of the appropriate dimensionality and are then transformed to have a mean vector of $\boldsymbol{\gamma}\mathbf{W}_n$, where n references the particular response string, and variance/covariance matrix $\boldsymbol{\Sigma}$. The weights for the nodes are $1/Q$. Generally, several hundred nodes are used for the Monte Carlo based estimation.

ConQuest was used to estimate the item and person parameters for the same set of data analyzed with NOHARM and TESTFACT. The results for Data Set 1 are shown in Table 6.9. The table shows the results from two different analyses of Data Set 1 – one with the default constraints on the item parameters and the other with constraints on the $\boldsymbol{\theta}$-estimates. As a default, ConQuest sets the means of the item

Table 6.9 d-parameter estimates from ConQuest for Data Sets 1 and 2

Item number	Data Set 1		Data Set 2
	Item parameter constraint	$\boldsymbol{\theta}$-distribution constraint	$\boldsymbol{\theta}$-distribution constraint
1	−.32	−.14	.12
2	−.02	.15	.49
3	.27	.45	.70
4	.26	.44	.84
5	.20	.38	.67
6	.29	.47	.85
7	.67	.85	1.12
8	−.84	−.67	−.32
9	−.25	−.07	.32
10	−.27	−.09	.31
11	−.65	−.79	−.77
12	.35	.21	.23
13	−.28	−.42	−.44
14	1.43	1.28	1.03
15	−.26	−.40	−.53
16	.39	.24	.24
17	.36	.21	.21
18	−.38	−.53	−.59
19	−1.04	−1.18	−1.02
20	.07	−.07	.04
21	−.69	−.60	.25
22	.13	.22	.67
23	.16	.25	1.12
24	1.26	1.34	2.41
25	.16	.25	.79
26	−.54	−.45	.37
27	.18	.27	1.28
28	−.37	−.29	.17
29	−.10	−.02	.40
30	−.19	−.10	.80

Note: The Item Parameter Constraint is that the item parameters for items 1–10, 11–20, and 21–30 sum to 0. The $\boldsymbol{\theta}$-distribution Constraint is that the mean of the θ-elements for each dimension is 0. The a-parameters for the items are those specified in Table 6.8.

parameters on each dimension to 0 when a between-item, simple structure solution is requested. Another option is to constrain the solution by setting the mean of the $\boldsymbol{\theta}$-estimates on each dimension to be 0. The results of both types of constraints are shown in Table 6.9 so the differences in parameter estimates are clearly evident.

From a review of the results in Table 6.9, it is obvious that the parameter estimates using the different constraints are different. A comparison with the results from TESTFACT and NOHARM will also show that the signs of the parameter estimates are opposite those of the estimates from the other programs. The reason for this difference in sign is not clear from the expressions for the model in (4.14) and (4.15). To be consistent with the results, the exponent of the model used in the estimation program should be $\mathbf{a}\boldsymbol{\theta}' - d$ instead of the form used by the other estimation programs $-\mathbf{a}\boldsymbol{\theta}' + d$. There seems to be an inconsistency between the published description of the estimation procedure and the model that is implemented in the program. The correlation between the estimates of the d-parameter used with those from the other programs is .99 when the θ-means are constrained to 0 and Data Set 1 is used, but the slope of the regression line predicting the other parameter estimates from the ConQuest estimates is $-.69$ and $-.62$ for TESTFACT and NOHARM, respectively. The reason the slope is not closer to 1.0 is that ConQuest uses the logistic form of the model while the other programs use the normal ogive form of the model. The slope predicting the generating d-parameters that are for the logistic model is 1.2 showing that the estimates are slightly regressed toward the mean compared to the true parameters.

The results from the analysis of Data Set 2 are similar to those from Data Set 1. The d-parameter estimates from ConQuest were correlated .99 with those from NOHARM and TESTFACT, but the slope of the regression lines are $-.66$ and $-.61$ respectively, showing the difference between the scales for the normal ogive and logistic models. The slope would be $-1/1.7 = -.58$ if the shift of scale were due solely to the differences between the normal ogive and logistic forms of the models. The remaining differences are probably because of differences in the ways that constraints are implemented in the programs and estimation error.

ConQuest also provides maximum likelihood estimates of the $\boldsymbol{\theta}$-vectors. The estimates are different depending on the constraints used to deal with the indeterminacy in the solution. For the constraint that the mean θ-elements for each dimension is 0 for Data Set 1, the mean of the estimates is very close to 0, but the standard deviations of the estimates are 1.31, 1.37, 1.32 for three dimensions, respectively. These standard deviations are the result of fixing the a-parameters for each dimension at 1 with perfect simple structure.

Table 6.10 provides summary statistics for the $\boldsymbol{\theta}$-estimates for each of the dimensions from the analysis of Data Sets 1 and 2. The table presents both the estimates of population parameters for the $\boldsymbol{\theta}$-distributions given in the ConQuest output, and the values computed from the maximum-likelihood estimates of the θs. Table 6.11 presents the correlations among the $\boldsymbol{\theta}$-estimates for each data set and the correlations with the θ-values used to generate the simulated data.

From a comparison of the summary statistics from the estimated θs and those that are estimates of the population parameters in the model, it is clear that these are not the same. The ConQuest manual emphasizes that point. The population correlation estimates are estimates of the correlations corrected for attenuation while the calculated correlations are affected by the estimation error in the θs. The estimates of the standard deviations are similarly affected. The important point is that the values reported in the output from the program should not be interpreted as being the same as values computed from the maximum-likelihood estimates.

Table 6.10 Summary statistics for $\boldsymbol{\theta}$-distribution estimates for Data Sets 1 and 2

	Data Set 1			Data Set 2		
	θ_1	θ_2	θ_3	θ_1	θ_2	θ_3
Mean	0 (−.02)	0 (.02)	0 (−.01)	0 (−.05)	0 (.02)	0 (−.07)
SD	.90 (1.31)	.98 (1.37)	.92 (1.32)	1.21 (1.53)	1.33 (1.67)	.85 (1.25)
Reliability	.60	.62	.60	.62	.68	.85
θ_1	1			1		
θ_2	.32 (.20)	1		.90 (.64)	1	
θ_3	.21 (.14)	.23 (.14)	1	.53 (.34)	.53 (.33)	1

Note: The values in parentheses are computed from the estimated θ-values. The other values are the estimated population parameters from the ConQuest output. The bottom three rows give the correlations for θs within the analysis of a data set.

Table 6.11 Correlations of estimated and generating θs for Data Sets 1 and 2

Generating values	Data Set 1 Estimates			Data Set 2 Estimates		
	θ_1	θ_2	θ_3	θ_1	θ_2	θ_3
θ_1	.75	.03	.19	.82	.71	.41
θ_2	.00	.17	.76	.25	.26	.73
θ_3	.23	.79	.03	.73	.86	.31

Note: Correlations are within the same data set. The generating values for Data Sets 1 and 2 are not the same.

The correlations in Table 6.10 do not recover the correlations between the generating θs very well. The θs used to generate Data Set 1 had intercorrelations that were very close to 0. The θs used to generate Data Set 2 had correlations of about .3, .8, and .2. The ConQuest correlations for neither data set approximates the generating correlations. Further information is provided in Table 6.10. The relationship between the generating θs and estimated θs are clearly identified for Data Set 1, but the pattern in Data Set 2 is not as evident. This result is partially because of the specification of all a-parameters as 1 in the analysis and partially because of the correlations between the generating θs in Data Set 2. A comparison of Tables 6.5 and 6.11 indicates that neither TESTFACT nor ConQuest provides accurate estimates of the correlations used to generate the data. This topic will be addressed in more detail in Chap. 7 when issues of the indeterminacy of the $\boldsymbol{\theta}$-space are discussed.

6.2.4 BMIRT

Another approach to estimating the parameters of the MIRT models has been implemented in a computer program called BMIRT[2] (Bayesian Multivariate Item

[2] BMIRT is proprietary and trade secret software developed by CTB/McGraw-Hill LLC, a subsidiary of the McGraw-Hill Companies, Inc. Used with permission.

Response Theory) (Yao 2003). This program implements Markov chain Monte Carlo (MCMC) methods using the Metropolis–Hastings sampling algorithm to estimate the item, examinee, and population distribution parameters for a set of MIRT models for both dichotomously and polytomously scored test items.

MCMC methods are a way of generating samples from the posterior distribution of the item and person parameters given the observed item response matrix. The generation is done through computer simulation. That is, observations are sampled from probability distributions with known properties. This is the Monte Carlo part of the process. Monte Carlo methods are quite common for generating simulated data to test the functioning of estimation programs. The data used for the examples in this chapter where generated using Monte Carlo simulation methods. The key to estimation using MCMC methods is generating samples from complex distributions using samples generated from known, convenient distributions. This is known as acceptance–rejection sampling (Chib and Greenberg 1995) or simply rejection sampling (Gamerman and Lopes 2006).

The Markov Chain part of the process is based on a statistical procedure for modeling the probability of transition from one state in a domain to another state in the domain. Suppose that there are n states – $S_1, S_2, \ldots, S_n$. These states are assumed to include all possible states in the domain. For example, the states could represent the 48 states in the continental USA. If a person were limited to travel within the 48 continental USA, then those states would be the full set of possible locations for the person. At any given point in time, k, the person is located in one of the states, S_j^k, and they have a probability of moving to another state or staying in the same one at time $k + 1$. If the probability of moving to a state at time $k + 1$ is only dependent on the state at time k, then the string of locations over time is labeled a Markov chain. The probability of moving from state to state in a Markov chain can be represented by a transition matrix,

$$\mathbf{p} = \begin{bmatrix} p(1,1) & p(1,2) & \cdots & p(1,n) \\ p(2,1) & p(2,2) & \cdots & p(2,n) \\ \vdots & \vdots & \ddots & \vdots \\ p(n,1) & p(n,2) & \cdots & p(n,n) \end{bmatrix}, \tag{6.21}$$

where $p(i,j)$ gives the probability of moving from S_i at time k to state S_j at time $k + 1$. Because the person cannot move out of the domain, the values in the rows must sum to 1. The probability of being in state S_j after n units of time is given by $\mathbf{p}^n$. If the rows of $\mathbf{p}^n$ converge to the same vectors as n becomes large, the Markov chain is said to be stationary. That is, no matter what the starting state is, the probability of being in state S_j is the same if enough steps are taken through the Markov chain.

Stationary Markov chains provide a way of simulating the data from the stationary probability distribution. If the locations in the states are recorded after each step of the Markov chain, then those locations provide a sample from the stationary distribution. Those observations can be analyzed to determine characteristics of the stationary distribution. A simple example should help clarify these points.

Suppose that the transition matrix for a Markov chain is given by

$$\begin{bmatrix} .5 & .4 & .1 \\ .1 & .7 & .2 \\ .2 & .3 & .5 \end{bmatrix}. \tag{6.22}$$

This transition matrix indicates that, for example, if a person starts in S_2 at time $k = 0$, then they would have a probability of remaining in S_2 of .7 at time $k = 1$, and small probabilities of .1 and .2 of moving to S_1 and S_3, respectively. Note that each row of the transition matrix has probabilities that sum to 1.

This transition matrix defines a stationary Markov chain. After 11 steps through the chain, the probability of being in each state for each starting state is

$$\mathbf{p}^{11} = \begin{bmatrix} .2093 & .5349 & .2558 \\ .2093 & .5349 & .2558 \\ .2093 & .5349 & .2558 \end{bmatrix}. \tag{6.23}$$

Thus, no matter which state is the starting state, the probability distribution for the location in a state after 11 time periods is the same and it remains at those values for additional time periods as well.

The states at each time period for this Markov chain can be simulated by selecting an initial starting state and then determining the next state by comparing a uniform random number to the cumulative probabilities of being in the successive states. That is, using the original transition matrix, if the starting state is S_1 and the uniform random number is between 0 and .5, the state at time $k = 1$ remains S_1. If the random number is greater than .5, but less than $.5 + .4 = .9$, then the state changes to S_2. If the uniform random number is greater than .9, then the state changes to S_3. The state at each time period is recorded as an observation from the stationary distribution.

For the transition matrix in (6.22), a string of the first ten states for a Markov chain beginning in S_1 is $S_1S_2S_3S_1S_3S_3S_1S_1S_2S_3$. From this starting state, the proportion of times in S_1 is .4, in S_2 is .2, and S_3 is .4. This is not a very good match to the stationary distribution given in (6.23) because of the dominance of the starting state and the short nature of the chain. However, if the chain continues on for a 1,000 time periods, the proportions are now .236, .550, and .214 – a better match to stationary distribution over states. After 10,000 time periods, the proportions of times in each state are .2108, .5282, and .2610. After 100,000 time periods, the distribution over states is .2094, .5353, and .2554. The proportion of times in each state is converging to the stationary distribution, but convergence is not particularly fast.

The use of Markov chain Monte Carlo (MCMC) for MIRT estimation uses a process that is conceptually the same as this example. The goal is to simulate observations from a stationary distribution. For estimation purposes, the Markov chain is defined so that the stationary distribution is the posterior distribution of the model parameters given the observed item score matrix.

$$P(\boldsymbol{\theta}, \mathbf{a}, \mathbf{d}, \boldsymbol{\mu}, \boldsymbol{\sigma} \mid \mathbf{X}) \propto P(\mathbf{X} \mid \boldsymbol{\theta}, \mathbf{a}, \mathbf{d})\, P(\boldsymbol{\theta} \mid \boldsymbol{\mu}, \boldsymbol{\sigma})\, P(\mathbf{a}, \mathbf{d})\, P(\boldsymbol{\mu}, \boldsymbol{\sigma}), \tag{6.24}$$

where

$$P(\mathbf{X} \mid \boldsymbol{\theta}, \mathbf{a}, \mathbf{d}) = \prod_{j=1}^{N} \prod_{i=1}^{I} P\left(X_{ij} \mid \boldsymbol{\theta}_j, \mathbf{a}_i, d_i\right) \tag{6.25}$$

and

$$P(\boldsymbol{\theta} \mid \boldsymbol{\mu}, \boldsymbol{\sigma}) = \prod_{j=1}^{N} P\left(\boldsymbol{\theta}_j \mid \boldsymbol{\mu}, \boldsymbol{\sigma}\right). \tag{6.26}$$

In these equations, the $\boldsymbol{\theta}$, $\mathbf{a}$, and $\mathbf{d}$ parameters are those of the compensatory MIRT model and $\boldsymbol{\mu}$ and $\boldsymbol{\sigma}$ are the parameters of the assumed multivariate distribution for the $\boldsymbol{\theta}$-vectors. The equations are used to model the item responses for N individuals to an I-item test.

In this case, the states are vectors of the model parameters – the $\boldsymbol{\theta}$-vectors for the examinees and the item parameter vectors for the full set of items. Unlike the example given earlier, these are continuous variables rather than discrete states. This means that there is a density function that shows the transitions between states rather than a discrete probability distribution. The density function is called the transition kernel $t\,[\,]$ and it gives the conditional density of being in a state given the current values of the parameters:

$$t\left[\left(\boldsymbol{\theta}^k, \mathbf{a}^k, \mathbf{d}^k\right), \left(\boldsymbol{\theta}^{k+1}, \mathbf{a}^{k+1}, \mathbf{d}^{k+1}\right)\right] = P\left[\left(\boldsymbol{\theta}^{k+1}, \mathbf{a}^{k+1}, \mathbf{d}^{k+1}\right) \mid \left(\boldsymbol{\theta}^k, \mathbf{a}^k, \mathbf{d}^k\right)\right], \tag{6.27}$$

where the superscripts indicate time k and time $k + 1$.

The BMIRT program uses a transition kernel that is based on an approach called Gibbs samplers (Geman and Geman 1984). This approach specifies the transition kernel as the product of two conditional distributions. In this case, the transition kernel is

$$\begin{aligned} t&\left[\left(\boldsymbol{\theta}^k, \mathbf{a}^k, \mathbf{d}^k\right), \left(\boldsymbol{\theta}^{k+1}, \mathbf{a}^{k+1}, \mathbf{d}^{k+1}\right)\right] \\ &= P\left(\boldsymbol{\theta}^{k+1} \mid \mathbf{X}, \mathbf{a}^k, \mathbf{d}^k\right) P\left(\mathbf{a}^{k+1}, \mathbf{d}^{k+1} \mid \mathbf{X}, \boldsymbol{\theta}^{k+1}\right). \end{aligned} \tag{6.28}$$

Because the transition kernel is partitioned into two components, the sampling of observations can be done in two steps. First a $\boldsymbol{\theta}$ can be drawn from its conditional distribution; then the sampled value can be used to specify the conditional distribution for the item parameters.

The conditional distributions for the parameters are difficult to compute, so further refinements are added to the process. The Metropolis–Hastings algorithm (Metropolis, Rosenbluth, Rosenbluth, Teller and Teller 1953; Hastings 1970) is used to specify a more convenient transition kernel and then uses acceptance-rejection sampling to obtain observations from the desired transition kernel. Further, parameters are dealt with in blocks based on independence assumptions to simplify the computation. The complete description of the estimation process is beyond the scope of this chapter. Patz and Junker (1999) give a fairly complete description of the estimation methodology as applied to unidimensional IRT models.

If the transition kernel can be specified and used to simulate the steps in the Markov chain, then the observations from each step can be saved as a sample from the stationary distribution for the Markov chain. As with the example provided earlier, long chains are needed before the characteristics of the sample approximate the characteristics of the stationary distribution. Also, the initial starting states affect the results for some time. Therefore, the initial observations from the Markov chain are discarded. Those observations are collected during what is called a "burn in period" for the Markov chain.

The observations collected after the burn in period can be used to estimate the parameters of the stationary distribution. For example, the mean of the $\boldsymbol{\theta}$ vectors can be used to estimate the proficiency vectors for the examinees. These would be approximations to the EAP estimators of proficiency. The standard deviation of the distributions can be used as estimates of the standard errors for the parameter estimates. The same procedure can be used to get estimates of the item parameters.

The BMIRT computer program for estimating the parameters of the compensatory MIRT model uses a transition kernel designed to give the stationary distribution specified in (6.24). The states specified by the transition kernel are the full set of item parameters, the vectors of person parameters, and vector for the mean person parameters and the variance/covariance matrix for the person parameters. Although the MCMC approach implemented in BMIRT is very powerful, it still requires user specified constraints to address the indeterminacy of the origin, scale, and rotation for the model. BMIRT addresses these issues requiring that the user specify a population mean vector and variance for each dimension, and identify at least one item to anchor each scale. The anchor item approach is the same as is used by the NOHARM program. The user is also asked to specify the number of observations to discard as "burn in" before using the sampled observations to estimate the parameters. The sample size for estimating the parameters also needs to be specified.

The BMIRT program was used to estimate the parameters for the same two data sets used as examples for TESTFACT and NOHARM. For the analyses, the mean vector for $\boldsymbol{\theta}$ was specified as the $\mathbf{0}$-vector and the variances were specified as 1.0. Also, the first item of each of the ten item sets related to a dimension was used to anchor the axes of the coordinate space to deal with the rotational indeterminacy for the model. The program was run with 10,000 samples discarded as burn in and 20,000 iterations used to generate the sample for estimating the parameters. The program took approximately 45 min to converge on the estimates on a notebook computer with a Pentium 1,400 MHz processor. The item parameter estimates from the program are given in Table 6.12. The b-parameter estimates have the signs reversed relative to the generating parameters because the dichotomous item responses were analyzed as a special case of the partial credit model with two score categories. That model has a "$-d$" in the exponent instead of the "$+d$" used in the generating model.

Table 6.12 Item parameter estimates for Data Set 1 and Data Set 2

Item number	Data Set 1				Data Set 2			
	a_1	a_2	a_3	d	a_1	a_2	a_3	d
1	.22	.00	.00	−.12	***1.19***	.00	.00	.12
2	.21	.21	***.46***	.14	***.55***	.24	.22	.40
3	.24	.35	***1.04***	.47	***1.20***	.40	.30	.70
4	.25	.21	***1.19***	.48	***.91***	.28	.44	.78
5	.22	.33	***.59***	.36	***.67***	.29	.25	.57
6	.27	.39	***1.22***	.52	***2.24***	.97	.53	1.22
7	.40	.50	***1.62***	1.06	***1.80***	.73	.42	1.39
8	.22	.30	***.87***	−.66	***1.26***	.37	.35	−.34
9	.22	.31	***1.12***	−.07	***1.48***	.36	.29	.34
10	.23	.24	***.96***	−.09	***1.28***	.49	.27	.31
11	.30	***.85***	.00	−.75	***1.01***	.80	.00	−.75
12	.22	***1.15***	.27	.23	1.14	***1.25***	.25	.25
13	.22	***.76***	.24	−.38	***.80***	.60	.22	−.39
14	.27	***2.14***	.34	1.79	***2.15***	1.90	.48	1.59
15	.22	***.91***	.23	−.38	***.88***	.85	.23	−.50
16	.22	***.99***	.22	.25	***1.06***	.90	.24	.25
17	.26	***1.56***	. 22	.27	***1.42***	1.37	.45	.25
18	.39	***.98***	.26	−.52	.91	***.98***	.23	−.59
19	.40	***1.03***	.24	−1.19	***.80***	.72	.40	−.95
20	.21	***.69***	.21	−.06	.64	***.66***	.22	.04
21	***1.22***	.23	.22	−.65	.34	.26	***.91***	.25
22	***.49***	.21	.24	.20	.23	.22	***.50***	.62
23	***1.18***	.34	.31	.27	.71	.44	***1.09***	1.27
24	***2.10***	.30	.24	1.87	.30	.30	***1.51***	2.88
25	***.66***	.21	.21	.23	.25	.25	***.65***	.75
26	***1.34***	.24	.23	−.50	.33	.33	***1.17***	.39
27	***1.68***	.24	.24	.34	.24	.30	***1.14***	1.39
28	***.62***	.21	.21	−.26	.21	.22	***.49***	.15
29	***.53***	.21	.23	−.01	.26	.22	***.57***	.37
30	***1.18***	.26	.23	−.11	.39	.36	***.92***	.83

Note: The largest a-parameter for each item is shown in bold italics.

The a-parameter estimates clearly recover the structure of the data for the simple structure case. There are two interesting anomalies in the solution. First, even though Item 1 was used to anchor one of the axes, that item is not correctly estimated as sensitive to differences on the same dimension as the other items in the first ten. It has a 0 a-parameter on the third coordinate axis. This poor estimation of the parameters for Item 1 did not seem to interfere with the estimation of the parameters for the other items. To check the functioning of the program, the parameters for this data set were estimated a second time starting with a different random seed number. This analysis gave a .88 a-parameter for the first item and similar item parameter estimates for all of the other items. This result suggests that the BMIRT program should be run more than once on a set of data using different starting values to determine if the parameter estimates are stable.

Table 6.13 Summary statistics for $\boldsymbol{\theta}$ distribution estimates for Data Sets 1 and 2

	Data Set 1			Data Set 2		
	θ_1	θ_2	θ_3	θ_1	θ_2	θ_3
Mean	.001	−.001	.001	−.007	−.004	−.008
SD	.79	.79	.75	.81	.63	.71
θ_1	1.00			1.00		
θ_2	−.04	1.00		.48	1.00	
θ_3	−.02	.02	1.00	.10	.10	1.00

Table 6.14 Correlations of estimated and generating θs for Data Sets 1 and 2

Generating values	Data Set 1 Estimates			Data Set 2 Estimates		
	θ_1	θ_2	θ_3	θ_1	θ_2	θ_3
θ_1	.14	−.03	.76	.84	.51	.27
θ_2	.79	.09	−.08	.20	.23	.74
θ_3	−.03	.81	.13	.81	.74	.14

Note: Correlations are within the same data set. The generating values for Data Sets 1 and 2 are not the same.

The second anomaly is that none of the a-parameter estimates are below .2 even when the generating item parameters are close to 0. This was true for both analyses of the data set of the first data set and for the second data set. This may be a result of the priors specified in the program. Despite these unusual results, the parameter estimates for the first data set provide a close match to the generating parameters. The a-parameter estimates for the second data set tend to be over-estimates and the program tends to merge the two dimensions that have generating θs correlated .8. This result is similar to that found for TESTFACT (Table 6.3) and NOHARM (Table 6.6). All of these programs have difficulty separating the dimensions when the θs on those dimensions are highly correlated.

Table 6.13 presents the descriptive statistics for the $\boldsymbol{\theta}$-estimates from the BMIRT program for the two data sets. The mean θs are very close to 0, but the standard deviations are not 1.0. The standard deviations in Data Set 2 are not equal and tend to reflect the differences in standard deviations used to generate the data. The correlations between θs for Data Set 1 match the uncorrelated θs used to generate the data. The correlations for Data Set 2 do not recover the correlational structure used to generate the data. To further investigate the relationships between the generating and estimated θs, these variables were correlated with each other. The results are presented in Table 6.14.

The correlations of the $\boldsymbol{\theta}$-estimates with the generating θs show that BMIRT recovered the underlying structure of the data well for Data Set 1, the data set generated with uncorrelated θs. The correlation between the estimated θs and the generating θs is as high as can be expected from a test with ten items sensitive to differences on each dimension. The correlational structure underlying Data Set 2 was not well recovered by BMIRT. Dimensions 1 and 2 for the estimated θs were both correlated with Dimension 3 from the generating θs. This is because of the high correlation between Dimensions 1 and 3 for the θs used to generate the data. BMIRT gave what is essentially a two-dimensional solution for the data set with the two highly correlated $\boldsymbol{\theta}$-dimensions used to generate the data being estimated as a single common dimension. It is possible that the Data Set 2 solution can be rotated and translated to better match the parameters used to generate the data. This possibility will be address in Chap. 7.

6.3 Comparison of Estimation Programs

The application of MIRT procedures is dependent on the quality of parameter estimates that are obtained from the estimation programs. The programs that are available vary in the estimation procedures used and the way that they address the indeterminacy issues of the MIRT models. The programs also differ in the types of models that they support and whether they estimate the person parameter vectors. Further, the programs differ in the number of dimensions that they can estimate and the computer resources needed to implement the estimation procedure. Some programs are very fast, but have limited capabilities. Others take substantial amounts of computer time to converge on estimates, but can handle a wide variety of applications. While different statistical estimation methods can be compared on theoretical characteristics such as whether the estimators are unbiased, efficient, etc., in practice the estimation methods cannot be evaluated independently of the computer software used to implement them. A theoretically optimal estimation method may not have such properties in practice because approximations were used when developing the estimation software. Because of the interconnectedness of the statistical estimation methodology and the software used to implement it, methods are often evaluated using parameter recovery studies based on computer simulations. The results of some parameter recovery studies are summarized here. This summary should be used with some caution because some programs are updated regularly and the results may no longer apply. The information provided here was collected in July 2007.

Because it is impossible to know how soon the information about programs will become dated, the information presented here will only cover general trends rather than the details about specific estimation programs. It is also recommended that new estimation software be investigated as it becomes available. New estimation methods may supersede those presented here.

The majority of comparative studies that were available at the time this chapter was written consider the NOHARM and TESTFACT software. These programs have been available much longer than the others. The general finding of the comparative studies (Béguin and Glas 2001, Gosz and Walker 2002, Maydeu-Olivares 2001, Miller 1991, Stone and Yeh 2006) was that neither NOHARM nor TESTFACT is clearly superior to the other when considering the recovery of item parameters. Each program performs better than the other for specific situations, but the results are for a particular number of examinees administered a test of a specified number of items with a specific item structure and pattern of correlations between θs used to generate data. It is difficult to generalize these results to the analysis of new data sets.

There are practical differences in the two software packages. NOHARM does not provide estimates of the $\boldsymbol{\theta}$-vectors – a clear limitation. TESTFACT does provide estimates of the $\boldsymbol{\theta}$-vectors. NOHARM requires less computer time than TESTFACT, but with the speed of current computers, the differences in computational time are not of practical importance. TESTFACT is limited in the number of dimensions that can be estimated because of the way the full information aspect of the program uses computer storage. NOHARM does not have that limitation and special versions of the program have been used to estimate as many as 50 dimensions.

In contrast to the comparative studies for NOHARM and TESTFACT, only one study was found comparing ConQuest to another program and that was to a new procedure with limited availability (Moulton 2004). There have also been a few studies that compare ConQuest and other programs for estimating the parameters of the unidimensional Rasch model, but those are not the focus of this chapter.

Research articles have begun to appear comparing MCMC procedures with NOHARM or TESTFACT (Bolt and Lall 2003). The results of these studies have indicated that the MCMC procedures tend to have larger standard errors for the parameter estimates than NOHARM. It is difficult to judge the generalizability of these studies because the results depend on the particular implementation of a MCMC procedure. The Bolt and Lall (2003) study used their own implementation of MCMC using WinBUGS software (Spiegelhalter, Thomas, and Best 2000) and the results may not generalize to the BMIRT software described earlier in this chapter.

At the time this chapter was written, NOHARM or TESTFACT still seem to be the programs of choice if the test data consists of dichotomous item responses. NOHARM is a free program that gives quick estimates of item parameters. TESTFACT is a more flexible program that provides estimates of $\boldsymbol{\theta}$-vectors as well as item parameters. Because TESTFACT is not a free, it has the advantage of having updated versions and more complete documentation. This chapter did not review all software that is available for MIRT calibration. Other programs may be available and some of them may function very well.

6.4 Exercises

1. The example on p. 141 of this chapter considers the likelihood function for item score vector [1 0]. Using the item parameters for the same test items given in that example, consider the likelihood function for the item score vector [0 1]. Where in the region of the $\boldsymbol{\theta}$-space defined by the range from -4 to 4 on each coordinate axes will the likelihood be the greatest for the item score vector [0 1]?

2. A test item is modeled with two coordinate axes. When the normal ogive version of the compensatory model is used the item parameters are $a_1 = .5$, $a_2 = .5$, and $d = -1.7$. Assuming that the two discrimination parameters are equal for a logistic version of the model, what logistic model item parameters will give the item characteristic surface that gives the closest match to the normal ogive version?

3. For each program described in this chapter, indicate whether it uses maximum likelihood, marginal maximum likelihood, generalized least squares, Bayes modal estimation, Bayes expected a posteriori estimation, or Markov chain Monte Carlo estimation.

4. A gambler suspects that a coin has been tampered with so that it will land "heads" 75% of the time when flipped. Suppose the coin was flipped one time and landed "heads." The belief before the coin flip was that there were even chances that the coin was tampered with or fair. What is the posterior probability that the coin is a "fair" coin (.5 probability of a head) or the tampered with coin?

5. Which of the constraint options in ConQuest is consistent with an assumption that sets of items that measure different constructs are of equal difficulty on average? Summarize the rationale for your answer.

6. Which two of the MIRT model calibration programs described in the chapter use the most similar statistical estimation procedure? Briefly summarize that procedure and indicate how the two programs differ in the implementation of the methodology.

7. Use the item parameters used to create Fig. 6.4 to determine the maximum likelihood estimator for the item score string 011. How does this estimate differ from the maximum likelihood estimate for the item score string 100?

8. What computer program would you select if you wanted to estimate the item parameters for a test specifying fixed guessing parameters and aligning 12 content dimensions with coordinate axes? Summarize the features of the program that lead to its selection.

9. How does NOHARM remove the rotational indeterminacy in the estimates of item parameters? Give a practical example of how you would implement this system of constraints if a test contains 40 items with 10 items written to be sensitive to differences along each of four different constructs.

10. The a-parameters were estimated for the items on a simulated test using the TESTFACT program. The item score data for the test were generated using (4.5) and a multivariate normal distribution with an identity matrix for the correlations among θs. What relationship is expected between the estimated a-parameters and those used to generate the data?

11. Suppose that a third data set was generated using the item parameters in Table 6.1. The third data set has a zero mean vector for the θs and standard deviations of 1.0, and all the intercorrelations are .8. How would the statistical analysis results for this data set compare to those given in Table 6.2? Explain the reasoning behind your prediction.

12. If both item and person parameters are estimated, how many parameters need to be estimated for the model presented in (4.5) for a four-dimensional solution for a test of 50 items administered to 5,000 persons?

Chapter 7
Analyzing the Structure of Test Data

One of the common uses of MIRT is the analysis of the structure of the item response data that results from the administration of a set of test items to a sample of examinees. This type of analysis can be done in either an exploratory or confirmatory way. The exploratory analysis of item response data is used when either there is no clear hypothesis for the structure of the item response data, or when an unconstrained solution is seen as a strong test of the hypothesized structure. Confirmatory analyses require a clear hypothesis for the structure of the item response data. That is, there must be hypotheses about the number of coordinate dimensions needed to model the data and the relationship of the item characteristic surface to the coordinate axes. The types of confirmatory analyses that are typically done specify the relationship of the direction best measured by a test item (the direction of maximum discrimination) with the coordinate axes. It is also possible to have hypotheses about the difficulty of test items, but such hypotheses are seldom checked with the MIRT models. The difficulty parameters are typically left as parameters to be estimated without constraints.

In many cases, what is labeled as an exploratory analysis also has a confirmatory analysis component because the number of coordinate dimensions is selected prior to estimating the item and person-parameters. The resulting measures of fit of the model to the data are a test of a hypothesis about the number of dimensions. Because the number of coordinate dimensions is a critical component of both exploratory and confirmatory analyses, this issue will be addressed first. After consideration of the number-of-dimensions problem, procedures are described for determining the structure of item response data using exploratory and confirmatory procedures.

7.1 Determining the Number of Dimensions for an Analysis

Approaches for determining the number of dimensions for a multidimensional analysis of test data has a long history in the literature on factor analysis. For example, Holzinger and Harman (1941, pp. 64–68) determined the number of variables needed to support the estimation of the factor loadings for m independent factors.

M.D. Reckase, *Multidimensional Item Response Theory*, Statistics for Social and Behavioral Sciences, DOI 10.1007/978-0-387-89976-3_7,

© Springer Science+Business Media, LLC 2009

The following expression gives the number of variables, n, needed to support the estimation of m independent factors.

$$n \geq \frac{(2m+1)+\sqrt{8m+1}}{2}. \tag{7.1}$$

This expression was derived assuming no error in the estimation of correlations. Thurstone (1947) suggested that the number of variables needed for a convincing analysis with m factors should be "two or three times greater" than this number. For a solution with three coordinate axes, a minimum of six variables is needed, but Thurstone recommends 12–18 to yield a convincing result.

Thurstone (1947) also specified a principal of factor analysis that has carried forward to this day and is also used by many who perform MIRT analyses. "The scientific problem is to account for as much as possible of the relations between tests by the smallest possible number of common factors" (p. 82). Although many subscribe to this principal, the position taken in a later section of this chapter is that the number of coordinate axes should be more than the minimum needed to account for the relationships in the data so that solutions are not misleading in certain ways. A thorough discussion of this topic is given in Sect. 7.1.1.

The seminal work on factor analysis done by Thurstone also made the important point that the factor analysis solutions are dependent both on the set of variables in the analysis and the selection of persons that are measured on these variables. Even for the case of simple structure (each variable loading on a single coordinate axis), the correlations between the factors are dependent on the characteristics of the persons in the sample (Thurstone 1947, p. 440). This is an extremely important point that will be elaborated upon in the next pages of this chapter.

The concept of simple structure will be referenced a number of times in this chapter so it is useful to give it a formal definition here. Thurstone (1947) gave this concept a very specific meaning.

> "The combination of a test configuration and the co-ordinate axes is called a *structure*. The co-ordinate axes determine the co-ordinate planes. If each test vector is on one or more of the co-ordinate planes, then the combination of the configuration and the co-ordinate axes is called *simple structure*. The corresponding factor pattern will then have one or more zero entries in each row." p. 181 (Italics in the original)

This definition of simple structure is more general than current usage because it allows test items to have nonzero a-parameters on more than one dimension. Only one zero a-parameter is needed for Thurstone to label the solution as simple structure. Current usage is more restrictive in that it tends to allow only one nonzero a-parameter for each item. Approximate simple structure is used when test items have one large a-parameter and the others are near zero. When this is the case, the item arrows point along the coordinate axes. In this chapter, the more restrictive definition of simple structure is used.

The early work on factor analysis was more concerned with specifying the amount of data for an analysis with a specified number of dimensions than with the problem of determining the number of dimensions needed to model the data.

This probably reflects the problems of obtaining factor analytic solutions at a time when work was done on large main-frame computers or mechanical calculators. As computing power increased, the issue of number of dimensions has become more important, but the solution to the number of dimensions problem seems to be unsolved. Reise et al. (2000) summarize the research on selecting number of dimensions and conclude that it is better to overestimate the number of dimensions than underestimate them and that scree plots, parallel analysis, and analysis of the residual correlation matrix are as good as more elaborate procedures for determining the dimensionality needed to model a matrix of test data. Econometricians have started to notice this problem and have addressed it using fit indexes based on the AIC and BIC measures (Bai and Ng 2002). It is interesting that Bai and Ng (2002) see the problem as determining the "true number of factors." The position taken here is that a true number of dimensions does not exist, but that a sufficient number of dimensions is needed to accurately represent the major relationships in the item response data. If the fine details of the relationships in the data are of interest, more dimensions are needed to accurately show those details. Using too few dimensions results in projecting the complexities of the relationships into a smaller space than is necessary to show the relationships. The result is that people and items can appear similar when they differ on important features. The next section provides some empirical examples to set the stage for later development.

7.1.1 Over and Under-Specification of Dimensions

Item response data from real tests is generated through a very complex interaction between people and the test tasks. The people vary in a large number of ways and the test tasks require numerous skills including decoding of language and other specialized symbols such as mathematical or chemical notation. As a result, all data matrices from the administration of real tests are likely to require a large number of dimensions to accurately represent the relationships in the data. At the most extreme, each test item can be considered to measure a somewhat different construct and an n-item test can be thought of as requiring n-dimensions to represent all of the relationships.

The extreme position is probably correct in a purely mathematical sense because all $N \times n$ data matrices, where N is the number of examinees, n is the number of test items, and $N > n$, have a rank that is very likely n. However, there is still value in determining if a smaller number of dimensions can be used to represent major relationships in the data. This means the ignoring dimensions needed to model minor relationships that are incidental to the main purpose of the test is not seen as a deficiency. For example, not being able to determine that some portion of the performance on a test item is related to the location of a test item on the page of a test booklet is acceptable when the purpose of the test is to measure skills in mathematics. Of course, that is only true if the effect of location on the page is very small relative to the influence of mathematical skills.

When the number of dimensions used to model an item response matrix is purposely minimized to only identify the major features of the data matrix, there is a danger that the meaning of constructs will be confused rather than clarified. This can happen because the locations of persons and items are projected from a high dimensional space to a lower dimensional space. This can make person locations seem close when they are not or test items seem to be sensitive along the same dimensions when they are not. This can happen because person locations or item vectors may be projected on top of each other when they really have large distances between them in the higher dimensional space. This is a common phenomenon when we look at stars in the night sky. Two stars may appear to be close to each other when they are really far apart. The illusion of proximity results from the star locations being on the same line of sight from the location of the observer. Their three-dimensional locations are being projected onto a two-dimensional plane. The stars may be far apart on the third dimension, even though their two-dimensional projections are close to each other.

One way to avoid the problem of projecting persons or test items in a way that makes them appear similar when they are not is to use more dimensions for analysis than is thought to be necessary to accurately represent the data. The relative locations of points stay the same when they are analyzed in more than enough dimensions. However, there is a price to be paid for using more than enough dimensions. More person and item parameters must be estimated and that may result in increased estimation error.

An underlying premise of this chapter is that number of dimensions needed to accurately model the relationships in the item response matrix is dependent on two aspects of the data collection process – the number of dimensions on which the people taking the test differ and the number of dimensions on which test items are sensitive to differences. In the most extreme cases, it is possible to imagine a group of individuals who have been carefully selected to be identical on all dimensions except one. Because this set of individuals only varies on one dimension, the item response matrix that results from administering any test to them can represent differences on only one dimension, no matter what the test items are designed to measure. Similarly, if the set of test items used in a test are only sensitive to differences along one of the dimensions of variability of the examinee population, the resulting data will be well fit by a model with a single θ, even though the examinees differ in many different ways. Thus, the position taken here is that the number of dimensions needed to accurately model a matrix of item response data is the smaller of the dimensions or variation for the people and the dimensions of sensitivity for the test items.

The literature on assessing the number of dimensions needed to accurately model item response data is somewhat imprecise in the way that the term "dimensionality" is used. For example, Mroch and Bolt (2006) take the following position: "Due to the multidimensional nature of many psychological and educational tests, procedures that identify test dimensional structure can be helpful for test practitioners" (p. 67). This statement implies that dimensionality is solely a feature of the test. No mention is made of the dimensions of variability of the examinees. The authors probably mean to focus on the dimensions of sensitivity of the test items, but this is not clearly stated. It is also important when evaluating the sensitivity of test items that the examinees in the sample vary on dimensions that are the focus of the items. The number of dimensions needed to model the item response matrix may be different depending on the amount of variability on the dimensions in different samples of examinees.

The next part of this section demonstrates the main points of the introductory comments using the analysis of simulated item response data. Two cases are considered. The first case is that test items are sensitive to examinee differences on a number of dimensions (three for the example), and the amount of variation on the dimensions for the examinees is manipulated when generating the simulated item response data. The simulated examinees are either well spread on all the three dimensions or are distributed along a single composite of the dimensions, falling along a line in the three-dimensional space.

The second case is that the items are sensitive to a single composite of dimensions, but the examinee sample varies on all three dimensions. This case does not require that the test items measure a single construct, but that they all measure the same weighted combination of a set of constructs. It is shown that the data generated in this case is indistinguishable from data that are generated using a model with a single θ.

Case 1: Items Sensitive to Variation on Three Dimensions

The parameters for the test items used for this example are the same as those used for the demonstration of estimation procedures in Chap. 6. These item parameters are listed in Table 6.1. This test is composed of three sets of ten test items, each with their direction of greatest discrimination along one of the three coordinate axes. The item arrows for these items are shown in Fig. 7.1.

The item parameters were used with $\boldsymbol{\theta}$-vectors randomly sampled from two distributions to generate item response data. In both cases, 5,000 $\boldsymbol{\theta}$-vectors were sampled from the distributions. The first distribution of $\boldsymbol{\theta}$s was the three-dimensional multivariate normal distribution with mean vector $\mathbf{0}$ and the identity matrix for the variance/covariance matrix. For convenience, the data set generated with the items and these $\boldsymbol{\theta}$-vectors is labeled 3d. The second distribution also has a mean vector of $\mathbf{0}$, but the variance/covariance matrix is $\begin{bmatrix} .1670 & .2362 & .2892 \\ .2362 & .3340 & .4091 \\ .2892 & .4091 & .5010 \end{bmatrix}$. This matrix yields a correlation matrix with 1s in all locations indicating that the matrix is of rank 1. All the $\boldsymbol{\theta}$-vectors have three values, but the points they define fall along a line in the $\boldsymbol{\theta}$-space. The data set generated using the item parameters and these $\boldsymbol{\theta}$-vectors is labeled 3d1 because the items are sensitive to differences along three dimensions, but the people vary along a single composite score. In all cases, the data were generated assuming the multidimensional generalization of the two-parameter logistic model.

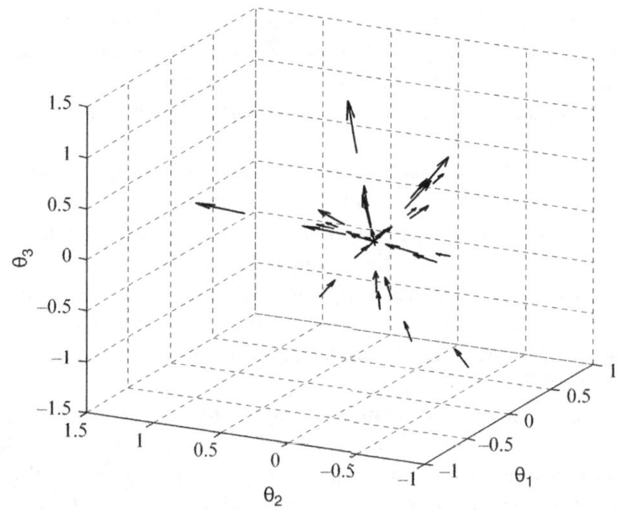

Fig. 7.1 Item arrows in three-dimensional **θ**-space

The two data sets were analyzed with TESTFACT specifying one, two, three, or four dimensions. These data were also analyzed using the unidimensional IRT estimation program, BILOG MG (Zimowski et al. 2003), to determine how the unidimensional estimates of θ corresponded to the multidimensional estimates. The θ-estimates from the BILOG MG analysis of the 3d and 3d1 data sets correlated .9998 and .9996, respectively, with the estimates from TESTFACT when one dimension is extracted. It is clear that BILOG MG is essentially a program to estimate the largest single factor from a set of data.

According to Wang (1985), when a unidimensional model is fit to multidimensional data, the result is an estimate of θs along the reference composite for the test (see Sect. 5.3 of Chap. 5). The direction of the reference composite can be determined by treating the eigenvector corresponding to the largest eigenvalue of the $\mathbf{a}'\mathbf{a}$ matrix as a vector of a-parameters. For the set of items in Table 6.1, the eigenvector corresponding to the reference composite is [.44 .55 .71]. The procedures described in Sect. 8.1.2 of Chap. 8 can be used to rotate the first axes of the $\boldsymbol{\theta}$-space to align with the reference composite. After that is done, the values of θ_1 in the vectors of person parameters are estimates of location along the reference composite. The rotation to align with the reference composite was computed resulting in the following rotation matrix: $\begin{bmatrix} .44 & -.78 & -.44 \\ .55 & .62 & -.55 \\ .71 & 0 & .71 \end{bmatrix}$. The $\boldsymbol{\theta}$-coordinates were transformed using this rotation matrix and the results were correlated with the estimates of θ obtained from the one-dimensional solutions from TESTFACT and BILOG MG. The resulting correlations along with the means and standard deviations for the θ-values are presented

Table 7.1 Correlations of unidimensional θ-estimates, the reference composite, and the generating θs for the 3d data set

	BILOG	TESTFACT 1d	3d reference composite	θ_1	θ_2	θ_3
BILOG	1.0000					
TESTFACT 1d	.9998	1.0000				
3d reference composite	.8637	.8644	1.0000			
θ_1	.4564	.4524	.4423	1.0000		
θ_2	.5071	.5060	.5611	.0172	1.0000	
θ_3	.5518	.5561	.7119	−.0004	.0119	1.0000
Mean	.0000	.0020	.0422	.0157	.0372	.0207
Standard deviation	.8793	.8561	1.0222	1.0055	1.0060	1.0211

in Table 7.1. Note that the standard deviations of the BILOG and TESTFACT estimates have not been scaled to have a standard deviation of 1.0. These programs have a default scaling that has the sum of the error variance and true score variance equal to 1.0. There is also an option in the programs to scale the estimates to have a standard deviation of 1.0.

The results in the correlation matrix show that the estimates from BILOG MG and TESTFACT have almost identical correlations with both the reference composite and the θs used to generate the data. Also, the correlations with the reference composite are as high as is allowed by the error in the estimates from the programs. The estimated reliability of the BILOG MG estimate is .736. The correlation between the BILOG MG estimates and the reference composite is approximately 1.0 when corrected for attenuation.

BILOG MG provides a χ^2 measure of fit for the unidimensional IRT model, in this case the two-parameter logistic model, to the data from each item. Of the 30 test items on this simulated test, the model showed significant deviations from the data for 16 items at the .05 level of significance. This is surprisingly good fit for the data considering the sample size is 5,000, the data were generated using uncorrelated θs, and sets of items were sensitive to differences along each of the coordinate axes. TESTFACT provides a χ^2 test of fit for the full model. In this case, the one factor solution had a χ^2 value of 108686.23 with 4,939 degrees of freedom. This indicates that the one-dimensional model did not do a very good job of representing the relationships in the data file. These fit measures will be discussed in more detail later in this chapter.

The same matrix of item response data was also analyzed using TESTFACT specifying a two-dimensional solution. The item arrows from that two-dimensional solution are presented in Fig. 7.2. The items that are sensitive to differences along the θ_1 and θ_2-axes are clearly evident in the figure. However, the items that are sensitive to differences along the third coordinate axis are projected into the two-dimensional space as item vectors that fall roughly along a 45° line between the other two axes. This gives the appearance that the third set of items is sensitive

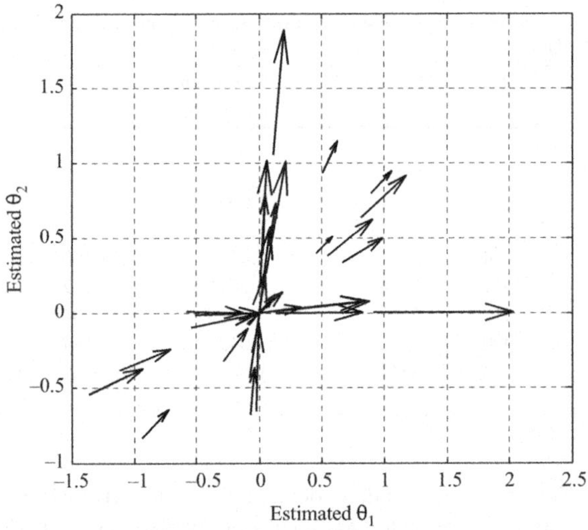

Fig. 7.2 Estimated item vectors in a two-dimensional space

to an equally weighted combination of the other two dimensions when in fact it is sensitive to differences along an axis orthogonal to the other two. The lengths (e.g., multidimensional discrimination) of the item vectors along the 45° line are also shorter because they are projected to a plane that is nearly orthogonal to the direction of differences to which they are most sensitive. The specification of fewer dimensions than is necessary to represent the relationships in the item response data can give quite misleading results.

A more concrete example may help show the types of misinterpretations that can result from underestimating the number of dimensions needed to represent the relationships in the item response data. Suppose that the three clusters of items in Fig. 7.1 represent items that are sensitive to differences in arithmetic problem solving in story problems, the simplification of algebraic expressions, and proof of geometry theorems using graphical methods. These mathematical skills are fairly distinct. If the 30 item test in the example had ten items sensitive to differences in each of these skill areas, the results could very well yield Fig. 7.1. If the item response data from the administration of this test to secondary school students were analyzed specifying two-dimensions, the results might very well yield Fig. 7.2 with θ_1 representing the construct "arithmetic problem solving" and θ_2 representing simplification of algebraic expressions. It would appear that the geometry proof items along the 45° line are a roughly equally weighted combination of arithmetic problem solving and algebraic manipulation when in fact they are measuring a skill that is not strongly related to either of those constructs. To determine that fact, higher dimensional solutions must be considered.

The χ^2 index of fit provided by TESTFACT for the two-dimensional solution was 105915.65 with 4,910 degrees of freedom. This χ^2 value is smaller by 2770.58 than

Table 7.2 Correlations between θs used to generate data and TESTFACT two-dimensional estimates

Generating	TESTFACT	θs
θs	θ_1	θ_2
θ_1	.23	.36
θ_2	.11	.75
θ_3	.80	−.01

the value for the one-dimensional solution with a difference in degrees of freedom of 29. The improvement of the fit of the two-dimensional model over the one-dimensional model is dramatic, but the overall fit of the model is still not good. The overall χ^2 indicates that the observed data is significantly different than that predicted by the two-dimensional MIRT model.

The effect of using too few dimensions to represent the relationships between persons and items can also be seen in the correlations between the elements of the estimated $\boldsymbol{\theta}$-vectors for the two-dimensional solution and the elements of the three-dimensional $\boldsymbol{\theta}$-vectors used to generate the item response data. These correlations are given in Table 7.2. The estimated θs provide fairly good recovery of the θ_2 and θ_3-coordinates from the generating θs, but θ_1 has only a small influence on the estimated θs. The θ that is projected between the other dimensions is difficult to predict. It is likely related to the variance accounted for by the sets of items related to each dimension.

The effect of using too many dimensions can be seen from the analysis of this example data set with TESTFACT specifying four dimensions. The item parameter estimates that result from that analysis are provided in Table 7.3 along with the parameters used to generate the data. The correlations between the estimated θs and the generating θs are given in Table 7.4.

Inspection of Table 7.3 shows the relationships between the estimated item parameters and those used to generate the data. The sets of item parameters and estimates that are most sensitive to differences along each coordinate axis are shown in bold italics. The order of the $\boldsymbol{\theta}$-estimates from TESTFACT is not the same as that for the generating parameters. The TESTFACT order is related to the average a-parameter for each dimension. However, it is easy to see the sets of items that are sensitive to differences along each construct. In fact, the correlations between the corresponding sets of item parameters are uniformly in the high .90s with the correlation between the d-parameter estimates and the generating values close to 1.00. Note that the estimated values and the generating parameters differ by the constant $D = 1.7$ because of differences between the logistic model used to generate the data and the normal ogive model used for estimation. Also, the values of the a_4-parameter estimates are generally low, and there is no relationship between those parameter estimates and those used to generate the data. It is clear that the simulated test items are not distinguishing among θ-points along the unnecessary 4th coordinate axis.

The same pattern is evident in the correlations between the estimated θs from the four-dimensional solution using TESTFACT and the θs used to generate the item response data. The estimated θ-coordinates for dimensions 1, 2, and 3 correlate highly with generating θ-coordinates. The estimated θs for the fourth coordinate

Table 7.3 Generating and TESTFACT estimated item parameters using four dimensions

Item number	Generating item parameters				TESTFACT estimated item parameters				
	a_1	a_2	a_3	d	a_1	a_2	a_3	a_4	d
1	***.75***	.03	.14	.18	.05	.11	***.43***	.02	.13
2	***.46***	.01	.07	−.19	.03	.05	***.29***	.27	−.11
3	***.86***	.01	.40	−.47	.18	.02	***.53***	−.11	−.29
4	***1.01***	.01	.05	−.43	−.08	.08	***.54***	.13	−.29
5	***.55***	.02	.15	−.44	.05	.05	***.34***	.05	−.27
6	***1.35***	.01	.54	−.58	.16	.07	***.81***	.04	−.35
7	***1.38***	.09	.47	−1.04	.16	.11	***.82***	.10	−.57
8	***.85***	.04	.26	.64	.04	.05	***.58***	.07	.40
9	***1.01***	.01	.20	.01	.03	.04	***.63***	−.07	.04
10	***.92***	.01	.30	.09	.12	.06	***.59***	.04	.05
11	.00	.24	***.80***	.81	***.44***	.16	.07	−.16	.52
12	.00	.19	***1.19***	−.19	***.71***	.03	.10	.00	−.10
13	.06	.09	***.71***	.45	***.46***	.01	.08	.04	.27
14	.02	.33	***2.14***	−1.84	***1.22***	.06	.16	.09	−1.10
15	.03	.05	***.86***	.41	***.51***	.03	.11	.13	.26
16	.02	.15	***.93***	.30	***.60***	.10	.06	.10	−.16
17	.03	.29	***1.36***	.18	***.82***	.11	.10	−.04	−.10
18	.00	.22	***.90***	.51	***.55***	.12	.06	−.05	.29
19	.00	.47	***.73***	1.13	***.46***	.21	.04	.01	.68
20	.01	.09	***.64***	.02	***.39***	.05	.11	.01	.02
21	.31	***.97***	.00	.62	−.01	***.56***	.15	−.08	.38
22	.18	***.50***	.00	−.20	.04	***.29***	.07	.09	−.13
23	.41	***1.11***	.20	−.37	.11	***.72***	.25	−.20	−.21
24	.15	***1.73***	.03	−1.76	.13	***.95***	.03	−.01	−.96
25	.15	***.67***	.00	−.24	.04	***.42***	.01	.03	−.16
26	.29	***1.24***	.02	.49	.10	***.71***	.13	.07	.31
27	.13	***1.49***	.00	−.34	.08	***.91***	.02	−.06	−.18
28	.05	***.48***	.00	.29	.04	***.33***	.01	.00	.21
29	.21	***.46***	.01	.01	.01	***.31***	.12	.14	.01
30	.18	***1.12***	.09	.03	.09	***.65***	.13	−.13	.05

Note: The TESTFACT estimates differ from the generating parameters by the constant $D = 1.7$ because of differences between the logistic and normal ogive model

axis, however, do not correlate highly with any of the dimensions and it has a fairly small standard deviation as well. The magnitude of the correlations between estimated and generating θs, approximately .8, is consistent with the amount of error that results from estimating person locations with a 30-item test.

The results from these examples show that using too many dimensions gives a solution that embeds the dimensional structure needed to explain the relationships between item responses in a higher dimensional $\boldsymbol{\theta}$-space. The unneeded dimensions are there, but they do not add to the information about the locations of persons in the space. The results also show that the dimensionality of the solution is limited by the dimensions of variation of the examinee sample. Even if test items are sensitive to differences on several dimensions, unless the examinees also vary along

Table 7.4 Correlations between generating and estimated θs for the four-dimensional solution

	Generating θs			Estimated θs			
	θ_1	θ_2	θ_3	θ_1	θ_2	θ_3	θ_4
Generating θs							
θ_1	1.00						
θ_2	.02	1.00					
θ_3	−.00	.01	1.00				
Estimated θs							
θ_1	−.03	.14	.81	1.00			
θ_2	.14	.80	.00	.07	1.00		
θ_3	.78	.01	.19	.09	.09	1.00	
θ_4	.10	−.11	.04	.03	−.10	.13	1.00
Mean	.02	.04	.02	.01	.01	.00	.00
Standard deviation	1.01	1.01	1.02	.82	.81	.80	.36

the dimensions the dimensionality needed to model the item response matrix will not reflect the characteristics of the test items. The dimensionality needed to model the data is the smaller of the dimensions of variation of the people and the dimensions of sensitivity of the items. This same principle will be demonstrated again in Case 2.

The analysis of the 3d1 data set is also informative about the case when the number of dimensions of variation of the examinees is less than the number of dimensions of sensitivity of the test items. Recall, that for that case, the test items measure along the coordinate axes, but the locations of the examinees are all along a straight line in the $\boldsymbol{\theta}$-space. That means that even though the examinee locations are represented by vectors of three coordinates and there is substantial variation in the values for the coordinates, the coordinates on the different dimensions are correlated 1.00 over the sample of examinees. Thus, the examinee variation is along a single composite of θs that does not correspond to any of the coordinate axes.

When the 3d1 data were analyzed using TESTFACT specifying multiple dimensions, the pattern of discrimination along the three coordinate axes were not recovered. There was a slight tendency for one set of ten test items to have slightly higher a-parameter estimates than the other two sets of items because the line defined by the θ-coordinates was slightly closer to the direction of best measurement for those items. The mean a-parameters for the three sets of items were .33, .49, and .41 for the first, second, and third sets of ten test items. The magnitude of the a-parameter estimates is consistent with those in Table 7.3 because TESTFACT uses the normal ogive model.

In all cases, TESTFACT yielded a first dimension with high positive a-parameters and other dimensions with much lower a-parameter estimates with many around zero. The θ-estimates followed the same pattern. The θ_1 estimates were all correlated with the θs used to generate the data about .87 and about .99 with BILOG estimates of θ for the same data. The θ-estimates for other dimensions had correlations with the θs used to generate the data near 0 and somewhat negative. If the process used to generate the data were not known, the interpretation of the analysis results would likely be that the test items all measured the same construct and that the data could be well fit by a unidimensional IRT model.

These results not only show that the number of dimensions needed to model a set of item response data is dependent on the number of dimensions of variation within the examinee sample, but it also shows that the results of the calibration of the test items is sample specific. The results for the same test items are quite different depending on the covariance structure for the examinee sample.

Case 2: Items Sensitive to Variation along a Single Reference Composite

The example in Case 1 consistently used a set of items that were sensitive to differences in the location of examinees parallel to three distinct coordinate axes. In Case 2, the items are selected to measure best in the same direction in the $\boldsymbol{\theta}$-space. The example used here does not have test items with zero a-parameters related to any dimension. They were selected so that the item arrows point in approximately the same direction in the $\boldsymbol{\theta}$-space. Reckase et al. (1989) demonstrated with both simulated and real item response data that selecting test items in this way would yield item response data that could be well fit by a model with a single person parameter. That person parameter represents a composite of skills and knowledge. As long as all of the test items require the same combination of skills, such as mathematics problems requiring arithmetic, reading, and problem solving skills, the data can be represented using a model with a single person parameter. That parameter represents differences along the composite of skills.

The item parameters used to generate the data for Case 2 are presented in Table 7.5 along with values of their multidimensional discrimination, A, multidimensional difficulty, B, and the angles of the item vectors with the coordinate axes. Figure 7.3 shows the orientation of the item arrows for the simulated test in a three-dimensional $\boldsymbol{\theta}$-space. From the information in Table 7.5, it can be seen that the discrimination parameters are fairly similar in magnitude and the items do not best discriminate along any single axis of the three-dimensional space. This is also reflected in the angles of the item vectors with the coordinate axes. The multidimensional difficulties, B, are spread between -1.68 and 1.25, and the multidimensional discriminations are similar for all the simulated test items.

The item arrows shown in Fig. 7.3 show that all of the items are most discriminating in almost the same direction in the three-dimensional space, although there is some slight variation in direction of maximum discrimination. The items also vary in difficulty and they are not aligned with any of the coordinate axes.

Item response data were generated using these item parameters assuming $\boldsymbol{\theta}$-vectors have a multivariate normal distribution with a mean vector of $\mathbf{0}$ and an identity matrix for the variance/covariance matrix. A sample of 2,000 $\boldsymbol{\theta}$-vectors was obtained from the distribution. Although the simulated examinees have substantial variation on all of the dimensions in the coordinate system, the items are sensitive to only one composite of the dimensions. The generated data were analyzed using TESTFACT specifying one to four dimensions for the solutions.

Table 7.5 Generating item parameters and multidimensional descriptive information

Item number	Generating item parameters				Item descriptive information				
	a_1	a_2	a_3	d	A	B	α_1	α_2	α_3
1	.56	.62	.46	.10	.96	−.10	54	49	61
2	.48	.53	.42	.06	.83	−.08	55	50	59
3	.67	.63	.43	−.38	1.01	.38	49	52	65
4	.57	.69	.51	.46	1.03	−.45	57	48	60
5	.54	.58	.41	.14	.89	−.15	53	49	63
6	.74	.69	.48	.31	1.12	−.28	49	52	64
7	.70	.75	.46	.06	1.12	−.05	51	48	66
8	.59	.63	.50	−1.23	1.00	1.24	54	51	60
9	.63	.64	.51	.47	1.03	−.45	52	52	60
10	.64	.64	.46	1.06	1.02	−1.04	51	51	63
11	.61	.57	.51	−.38	.98	.39	51	54	59
12	.67	.61	.56	.67	1.07	−.63	51	55	58
13	.55	.65	.41	−.03	.94	.03	55	46	64
14	.70	.74	.66	.41	1.22	−.34	55	52	57
15	.53	.67	.50	−.43	.99	.44	58	48	60
16	.57	.64	.54	−.44	1.01	.43	56	51	58
17	.65	.69	.58	.15	1.11	−.13	54	51	59
18	.64	.62	.47	1.63	1.01	−1.62	50	52	62
19	.67	.60	.42	−.11	.99	.11	47	53	65
20	.54	.59	.45	−1.39	.92	1.52	54	50	61
21	.66	.62	.49	−.79	1.03	.77	50	53	62
22	.57	.52	.39	1.46	.87	−1.68	49	53	63
23	.64	.70	.50	.06	1.07	−.05	54	49	62
24	.63	.74	.64	.47	1.16	−.40	57	50	57
25	.59	.57	.44	.88	.93	−.95	50	53	62
26	.67	.70	.48	.91	1.09	−.84	52	50	64
27	.66	.71	.57	−.21	1.13	.18	54	51	60
28	.49	.51	.45	.41	.84	−.49	54	53	57
29	.55	.54	.37	−.05	.86	.06	50	51	64
30	.62	.73	.44	.28	1.06	−.26	54	46	65

Note: A is the multidimensional discrimination, B is the multidimensional difficulty, and the α-values give the angles with the coordinate axes

The TESTFACT analyses of the data resulted in solutions for the one, two, and three-dimensional analyses, but the four-dimensional analysis did not converge to a solution after 100 iterations. In fact, for the four-dimensional analysis, the trend for the parameter estimates for two of the simulated test items was toward unreasonably large values and ten of the response strings did not yield estimates of the $\boldsymbol{\theta}$-vectors. In these cases, the estimates were moving toward infinite values.

The correlations between the θs estimated from each of the analyses and the values used to generate the data give some insight into the results. These correlations are presented in Table 7.6. An interesting result in this table of correlations is that none of the estimated θs is highly correlated with the θs used to generate the data.

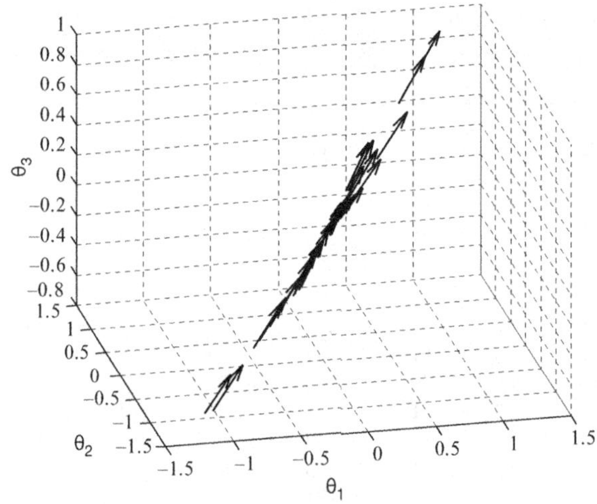

Fig. 7.3 Item arrow plot for items with maximum discrimination in the same direction

Table 7.6 Correlations between estimated and generating θs for the Case 2 data

	1d[a]	2d[a]		3d[a]			Generating θs		
	θ	θ_1	θ_2	θ_1	θ_2	θ_3	θ_{1g}	θ_{2g}	θ_{3g}
θ	1.00								
θ_1	.92	1.00							
θ_2	.81	.51	1.00						
θ_1	.98	.96	.70	1.00					
θ_2	.51	.14	.90	.38	1.00				
θ_3	.40	.35	.35	.30	.18	1.00			
θ_{1g}	.57	.52	.47	.56	.30	.22	1.00		
θ_{2g}	.60	.54	.49	.58	.32	.25	.04	1.00	
θ_{3g}	.44	.40	.36	.43	.22	.21	.00	−.01	1.00
Mean	−.00	−.01	.00	−.00	.00	−.00	.00	.02	−.01
SD	.94	.80	.71	.89	.52	.47	.99	1.01	1.03

Note: [a] indicates the θs estimated by TESTFACT with the number of dimensions specified

All of those correlations tend to range in the .40s to .50s. However, the θs estimated from the one-dimensional solution are highly correlated with the θs from the first dimensions of the two-dimensional solution and the first dimension of the three-dimensional solution. TESTFACT is identifying the same composite of dimensions in each of the analyses as the composite that is consistent with the direction of best measurement for the set of simulated test items.

Other insights into the results of the analyses of these data can be obtained by performing a few other statistical analyses. For example, if the θ-values from the one-dimensional solution are predicted from the θs used to generate the data using linear regression, the resulting equation is

$$\hat{\theta}_{1d} = .52\theta_1 + .54\theta_2 + .40\theta_3 - .01, \tag{7.2}$$

and the multiple-correlation between the generating θs and the one-dimensional θ is .92. This correlation is about as high as can be obtained given the error in estimation for the unidimensional θs. The reliability of the test is estimated as .86. The correlation corrected for attenuation is .999. The reference composite for the set of items has direction cosines with the coordinate axes of [.61.63.48]. Because the generating θs have nearly zero intercorrelations, the beta weights in the regression equation are similar to the direction cosines for the regression line in the multidimensional space. If they are scaled so that their sum of squares is equal to 1.0, a property of the direction cosines, the result is exactly the same as the direction cosines for the reference composite for the test.

A similar analysis can be performed on the two-dimensional estimates of the θ-coordinates except that the analysis uses canonical correlation to compare the two-dimensional vector of $\boldsymbol{\theta}$s with the three-dimensional $\boldsymbol{\theta}$-vector used to generate the data. The correlation of the first canonical variable with the first θ-coordinate is .92, the same value as for the multiple-correlation from the previous analysis. The weights for the first canonical variable are [.60 .62 .47]. When these weights are scaled to so their squares sum to 1.0, they are again identical to the direction cosines for the reference composite. A similar analysis can be performed using the three-dimensional estimates of $\boldsymbol{\theta}$ from the generated data.

This set of analyses indicate that even though the data were generated with three-dimensional $\boldsymbol{\theta}$-vectors, the TESTFACT calibrations are estimating θs along a one-dimensional continuum that is the reference composite for the set of items in the test. That is, the single θ is a weighted composite of the θs used to generate the data with the weights related to the direction cosigns for the reference composite. This relationship is shown by the regression analysis for the one-dimensional solution and the multivariate analyses for the higher-dimensional solutions.

The two cases presented here were designed to demonstrate a number of important points. First, dimensionality is a property of the data matrix, nor the test. Even if the data are generated using multiple θs, or the test items are sensitive to differences along multiple dimensions, the dimensionality of the data matrix may not reflect that level of complexity. The data matrix cannot represent multiple dimensions unless there is variation in the examinee sample along the dimensions of sensitivity of the test items. Restrictions on the variation of the examinee sample will reduce the dimensionality of the data, even though the test items may be sensitive to differences along many dimensions.

Second, even if test items are sensitive to differences on many dimensions, the interaction of examinees with the test items may result in a data set that can be modeled with a unidimensional model if all of the items measure a similar composite of θs. Third, even if test items are sensitive to differences on many dimensions, the data set can be modeled with a unidimensional model if all of the examinees in the sample have locations along a line in a multidimensional space.

The implication of these results is that the dimensionality that is reflected by the analysis of a matrix of responses to test items may not indicate either the dimensions of sensitivity of the test items or the dimensions of variability of the examinee sample. Dimensionality is a sample-specific characteristic of the data matrix. Statements about the dimensionality of a test are generally not very meaningful. The interaction of different examinee samples with the same test may result in quite different judgments of the dimensionality of the resulting data sets.

A realistic example may help make this point. Suppose a mathematics test is designed for use with 12th grade students who have taken a wide variety of mathematics courses. The item response matrix from administering this test to a random sample of 12th grade students might identify five dimensions: arithmetic problem solving, geometry, trigonometry, coordinate geometry, and algebra. But if this same test is administered to 8th grade students, the item response matrix might yield only two dimensions – algebra and arithmetic problem solving – because the amount of variation in the sample of 8th grade students on the other dimensions is very small. If a subset of the test items from this test are selected that are sensitive to differences on the same composite of skills, the item response matrix for this set of test items would likely be well fit by a unidimensional IRT model.

The cases shown here give an empirical demonstration of the complex relationship between the dimensions of variation of the examinee sample and the dimensions of sensitivity for the test items. The next section provides a theoretical explanation for some of the results presented in this section. The theoretical analysis shows that the results from the analysis of the two artificial cases generalize in useful ways.

7.1.2 Theoretical Requirements for Fit by a One-Dimensional Model

The examples provided in the previous section of this chapter were generated using the multidimensional extension of the two-parameter logistic model. This model is one of the class of models labeled as compensatory models. In this section, the results from the previous empirical examples are generalized to a broad class of multidimensional models that includes the compensatory models as a special case. Given the characteristics of this broad class of models, a formal proof is provided that the responses from a set of test items can be well modeled by a unidimensional IRT model, even though the test items are sensitive to differences on multiple dimensions as long as the set of items have certain characteristics. The formal proof was developed by William Stout and the information presented here was presented at a meeting of the Psychometric Society (Reckase and Stout 1995).

The broad class of MIRT models considered here consists of any model for which the probability of correct response increases monotonically with an increase in one or more of the coordinates in the $\boldsymbol{\theta}$-space. All of the models presented in this book are included in this broad class including the partially compensatory model.

Let $\mathbf{U_n}$ represent the vector valued random variable that denotes the dichotomous item scores for the n items on a test. For the general class of MIRT models considered in this book, the following equation gives the probability that a particular vector of item scores will occur.

$$P(\mathbf{U_n} = \mathbf{u}|\boldsymbol{\theta}) = \iint \cdots \int \prod_{i=1}^{n} P_i(\boldsymbol{\theta})^{u_i} Q_i(\boldsymbol{\theta})^{1-u_i} f(\boldsymbol{\theta}) \mathrm{d}\boldsymbol{\theta}, \tag{7.3}$$

for all $\mathbf{u}$ in $\mathbf{U_n}$, where $\mathbf{U_n}$ represents the 2^n possible score vectors for the n-item test. In (7.3), the integration is over all the dimensions in the $\boldsymbol{\theta}$-vector and the u_i are the elements of the vector $\mathbf{u}$. $P_i(\boldsymbol{\theta})$ represents a general MIRT item response function that is assumed to be strictly monotonically increasing in $\boldsymbol{\theta}$ for each item $i = 1, \ldots, n$. Equation (7.3) assumes local independence with respect to $\boldsymbol{\theta} = (\theta_1, \ldots, \theta_m)$. To avoid unnecessary and irrelevant complications, $\boldsymbol{\theta}$ is assumed to range over the entire m-dimensional Euclidean space $\Re^m$ and the random ability vector $\boldsymbol{\theta}$ is assumed to be continuous type with density $f(\boldsymbol{\theta}) > 0$ for all $\boldsymbol{\theta} \in \Re^m$. Thus,

$$\iint \cdots \int f(\boldsymbol{\theta}) \mathrm{d}\boldsymbol{\theta} = 1 \tag{7.4}$$

is assumed. Also, $P_i(\boldsymbol{\theta})$ is assumed to have continuous first-order partial derivatives. That is,

$$\frac{\partial}{\partial \theta_\nu} P_i(\theta_1, \ldots, \theta_m) \tag{7.5}$$

is continuous in θ for each $\nu = 1, \ldots, m$. In short, an m-dimensional, monotone, locally independent, MIRT representation is assumed for the response vector $\mathbf{U_n}$ with certain regularity conditions.

Define an orbit p of the item response function for Item i as

$$O_{pi} = \{\boldsymbol{\theta} | P_i(\boldsymbol{\theta}) = p\}, \tag{7.6}$$

for all p in the range of $P_i(\boldsymbol{\theta})$. That is, the pth orbit for the item response function for Item i is the set of $\boldsymbol{\theta}$-vectors that result in a probability of correct response of p. For example, if $P_i(\boldsymbol{\theta})$ represents the two-dimensional version of the partially compensatory model given in (4.18) with item parameters $c_i = 0, a_{i1} = .7, a_{i2} = 1.1, b_{i1} = -.5$, and $b_{i2} = .5$, Fig. 7.4 shows the orbits[1] for the item from $O_{.1}$ to $O_{.9}$ at .1 intervals. All of the $\boldsymbol{\theta}$-vectors that represent points on the same line have the same probability of correct response. For example, all of the $\boldsymbol{\theta}$-vectors on the line

[1] In Chap. 4, the curves that are labeled orbits here were called equiprobable contours.

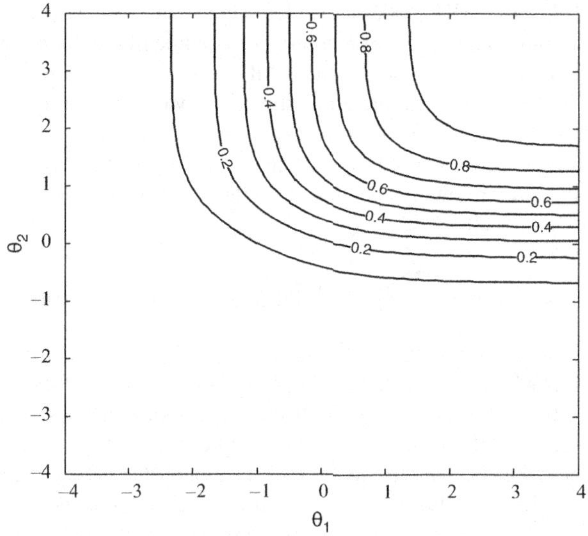

Fig. 7.4 Orbits from $p = .1$ to $.9$ at $.1$ intervals for the partially-compensatory model with $c = 0$, $a_1 = .7, a_2 = 1.1, b_1 = -.5$, and $b_2 = .5$

for $O_{.8}$ meet the requirement that $P_i(\boldsymbol{\theta}) = .8$. Note that $\{O_p, \text{ for all } p\} = O$ forms a set of equivalence classes of the m-dimensional ability space $\Re^m$ in the sense that the intersection of two orbits is the null set and the union of all of the orbits is $\Re^m$. That is $O_p \cap O_{p'} = \emptyset$ for all $p \neq p'$ and $\underset{\text{all p}}{\cup} O_p = \Re^m$.

Definition 1. An item response function $P_k(\boldsymbol{\theta})$ is coherent with respect to the orbits of Item i, O_i, if $P_k(\boldsymbol{\theta})$ is constant on each orbit $O_{ip} \in O_i$.

Note that $P_k(\boldsymbol{\theta})$ coherent to O_i implies that it can be represented by $P_k(\boldsymbol{\theta}) = g(P_i(\boldsymbol{\theta}))$ for some function g of the scalar value of the probability given by the item response function. When Item k is coherent to Item i, the range of $P_k(\boldsymbol{\theta})$ is a function of the unidimensional combination of coordinates given by $p = P_i(\boldsymbol{\theta})$. If coherence holds for items i and k, the probability of correct response on the item whose item response function is $P_k(\boldsymbol{\theta})$ can be predicted knowing only the probability of correct response to Item i. That is, only $p = P_i(\boldsymbol{\theta})$ and $g(p)$ need to be known. It is not necessary to know the specific elements of the $\boldsymbol{\theta}$-vectors. However, for a general set of test items that are modeled in a m-dimensional coordinate system, none of the item response functions may be coherent with respect to the orbits of Item i. Intuitively, if coherence holds for all test items on a test, then even though there are multiple psychological dimensions required to respond correctly to the test items, it seems that the set of test items should result in a matrix of item responses that can be modeled with a unidimensional IRT model.

Theorem 1. *Assume (7.3) holds for the modeling of a matrix of item response data. Suppose that the item response functions for items 1 to* $N-1$ *are coherent with respect the orbits* O_N. *Then the matrix of item response,* $\mathbf{U_N}$, *has a unidimensional, locally independent representation with monotone item response functions. Moreover, the unidimensional latent ability is given by* $p = P_N(\boldsymbol{\theta})$ *or a monotonically increasing function of* p.

Proof. Let $p = P_N(\boldsymbol{\theta})$ define a strictly increasing function of $\boldsymbol{\theta}$. Consider the $\Re^m \to \Re^m$ transformation defined by

$$\boldsymbol{\psi} \equiv h(\boldsymbol{\theta}) = (\theta_1, \cdots, \theta_{m-1}, p). \tag{7.7}$$

Denote the inverse function by $\boldsymbol{\theta} = h^{-1}(\boldsymbol{\psi})$. Because $\boldsymbol{\psi} = h(\boldsymbol{\theta})$ has continuous first-order partial derivatives with positive Jacobian everywhere, it follows from the inverse function theorem (see Apostle 1957, p. 144) that $\boldsymbol{\theta} = h^{-1}(\boldsymbol{\psi})$ is strictly increasing with positive Jacobian which is denoted by $J_{h^{-1}}(\boldsymbol{\psi})$. Define, recalling (7.7),

$$\tilde{f}(p) = \underset{\Re^{m-1}}{\int\int} \cdots \int f\left(h^{-1}(\boldsymbol{\psi})\right) J_{h^{-1}}(\boldsymbol{\psi}) d\psi_1 \ldots \mathrm{d}\psi_{m-1}. \tag{7.8}$$

Define for $1 \leq j \leq N$ and all p

$$\tilde{P}_j(p) = P_j(\boldsymbol{\theta}) \quad \text{for any } \boldsymbol{\theta} \in O_p. \tag{7.9}$$

This results directly from the coherence assumption. By the change of variable theorem for Riemann integration applied to $\boldsymbol{\theta} = h^{-1}(\boldsymbol{\psi})$ and using (7.9) (see Apostle 1957, p. 271) and iterated integration (see Apostle 1957, Sect. 10-6),

$$\begin{aligned} P(\mathbf{U}_n = \mathbf{u}) &= \underset{\Re^m}{\int\int} \cdots \int \prod_{j=1}^{n} \left[P_j(\boldsymbol{\theta})^{u_j}(1-P_j(\boldsymbol{\theta}))^{1-u_j}\right] f(\boldsymbol{\theta})\mathrm{d}\boldsymbol{\theta} \\ &= \underset{\Re^m}{\int\int} \cdots \int \prod_{j=1}^{n} \left[P_j(h^{-1}(\boldsymbol{\psi}))^{u_j}(1-P_j(h^{-1}(\boldsymbol{\psi}))^{1-u_j}\right] \\ &\quad \times f(h^{-1}(\boldsymbol{\psi}))J_{h^{-1}}(\boldsymbol{\psi})\mathrm{d}\psi_1 \ldots \mathrm{d}\psi_m \qquad (7.10) \\ &= \int_{-\infty}^{\infty} \prod_{j=1}^{n} \left[\tilde{P}_j(p)^{u_j}(1-\tilde{P}_j(p))^{1-u_j}\right] \\ &\quad \times \underset{\Re^{m-1}}{\int\int} \cdots \int f(h^{-1}(\boldsymbol{\psi})J_{h^{-1}}(\boldsymbol{\psi})\mathrm{d}\psi_1 \ldots \mathrm{d}\psi_{m-1} \\ &= \int_{-\infty}^{\infty} \prod_{j=1}^{n} \left[\tilde{P}_j(p)^{u_j}(1-\tilde{P}_j(p))^{1-u_j}\right] \tilde{f}(p)\mathrm{d}p \end{aligned}$$

is the desired unidimensional representation. Here, the fact that for constant $p = P_j(\boldsymbol{\theta})$, $P_k(\boldsymbol{\theta}) = P_k(h^{-1}(\boldsymbol{\psi}))$ is constant, holds because of the coherence assumption.

The implication of Theorem 1 is that if a set of test items have orbits that are coherent to each other, then the item-score matrix that results from the interaction between persons and the items can be fit with an unidimensional IRT model and the θ for that model will be related to the p-values associated with each of the orbits. The question still remains of determining the conditions when the coherence property will hold for a set of test items. For the compensatory MIRT models, the coherence property holds when the lines that are defined by the equiprobable contours are coincident for two items. This occurs when two items have the same orientation in the $\boldsymbol{\theta}$-space. That is, they have the same angles with the coordinate axes for their item arrows. A concrete example using a two-dimensional $\boldsymbol{\theta}$-space may help clarify the application of the coherence concept to the compensatory MIRT models.

Suppose two items have the same angles, $\alpha_{i1} = \alpha_{k1} = 25°$ and $\alpha_{i2} = \alpha_{k2} = 65°$, with the coordinate axes for the case when the item/person interaction can be well represented by the multidimensional extension of the two-parameter logistic model in a two-dimensional space. Further, Item 1 has a multidimensional discrimination of $A = .8$ and multidimensional difficulty $D = -.5$. Item 2 has corresponding values of 1.1 and 1.5. From this information, the **a**- and d-parameters can be determined. The item parameters and the other descriptive information about the items are given in Table 7.7. Note that the items do not have the same difficulty or discrimination and the all of the item parameters are different for the two items. The only characteristic shared by the two items is the angles of their item arrows with the coordinate axes. However, the a-parameters are proportional to each other.

Figure 7.5 shows equiprobable contours for the items along with their item arrows. All of the equiprobable contours are parallel to each other. The probabilities are generally not the same at a value of a contour, but the $O_{.9}$ orbit for Item 1 (solid lines) defines almost the same set of points as the $O_{.7}$ orbit for Item 2 (dotted lines). In fact, orbit $O_{.6945}$ for Item 2 contains exactly the same points as $O_{.9}$ for Item 1 and therefore those two orbits are coherent to each other. It is fairly easy to show that for any orbit for Item 1 there is a corresponding orbit for Item 2 that defines the same set of $\boldsymbol{\theta}$-vectors. The reverse is also true. Therefore, if a test is composed of test items that have item arrows pointing in the same direction in the $\boldsymbol{\theta}$-space, Theorem 1 indicates that the resulting item-score matrix can be well fit by a unidimensional IRT model.

This property of the compensatory MIRT model was confirmed empirically by Reckase et al. (1988) using item calibration results from a mathematics test. They showed that when items were selected that had item arrows pointing in approximately the same direction in the multidimensional space, the resulting item response data was well fit by a unidimensional IRT model.

Table 7.7 Item characteristics for the coherence example

	α_1	α_2	A	D	a_1	a_2	d
Item 1	25	65	.8	−.5	.725	.338	.4
Item 2	25	65	1.1	1.5	.997	.465	−1.65

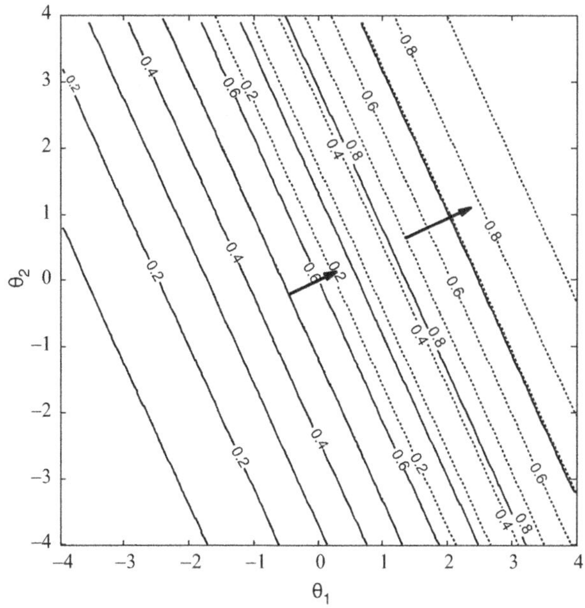

Fig. 7.5 Equiprobable contours and item arrows for the item parameters in Table 7.7

There is an interesting converse to Theorem 1. This theorem indicates that if a matrix of item scores is well represented by a unidimensional IRT model with a scalar parameter θ, and if θ can be shown to be a composite of m coordinates $\boldsymbol{\theta} = (\theta_1, \ldots, \theta_m)$, then a m-dimensional representation should hold for which the item response functions are coherent with respect to the equivalence class of orbits defined by θ.

Theorem 2. *Assume that (7.3) holds for a unidimensional, locally-independent IRT model with respect to a scalar θ with all of the item response functions monotone. Suppose that θ can be represented as a function of m coordinates $\boldsymbol{\theta} = g(\theta_1, \ldots, \theta_m)$ with $g(\boldsymbol{\theta})$ assumed to be strictly increasing in $\boldsymbol{\theta}$ with continuous first-order partial derivatives. Then there exists an m-dimensional IRT representation of the form given in (7.3) for which local independence holds and the item response functions are monotone. Moreover, these item response functions $P_j(\boldsymbol{\theta})$ are all constant on each orbit of $\mathbf{O} = \{O_\theta,$ for all $\theta\}$.*

Proof. Let $\tilde{f}(\theta)$ be the density of θ for the given unidimensional IRT model. Construct $f(\boldsymbol{\theta}) \geq 0$ for all $\boldsymbol{\theta}$ such that

$$\int\int_{O_\theta}\cdots\int f(\boldsymbol{\theta})\,\mathrm{d}\boldsymbol{\theta} = \tilde{f}(\theta) \quad \text{for each } \theta. \tag{7.11}$$

For each θ, the given mass $\tilde{f}(\theta)$ is distributed in a smooth manner over the orbit O_θ and the mass across orbits is distributed in a smooth manner as well.

Define a smooth transformation h from $\Re^m$ to $\Re^m$ by $h(\boldsymbol{\theta}) = (\theta_1, \ldots, \theta_{m-1}, \theta) = \boldsymbol{\psi}$, where $\theta = g(\boldsymbol{\theta})$. As in the proof of Theorem 1, the Jacobian $J_{h^{-1}}(\boldsymbol{\psi})$ of the transformation $\boldsymbol{\theta} = h^{-1}(\boldsymbol{\psi})$ exists and is strictly positive. Then, changing variables with $\boldsymbol{\theta} = h^{-1}(\boldsymbol{\psi})$ for each fixed $\theta^{(0)}$,

$$\int\int_{O_{\theta^{(0)}}}\cdots\int f(\boldsymbol{\theta})\mathrm{d}\boldsymbol{\theta} = \int\int_{\Re^m}\cdots\int f\left(h^{-1}\left(\boldsymbol{\psi}^{(0)}\right)\right) J_{h^{-1}}\left(\boldsymbol{\psi}^{(0)}\right)\mathrm{d}\psi_1, \ldots, \mathrm{d}\psi_{m-1}, \tag{7.12}$$

where $\boldsymbol{\psi}^{(0)} = \left(\psi_1, \ldots, \psi_{m-1}, \theta^{(0)}\right)$. Thus, using (7.11) and (7.12),

$$\begin{aligned}
P(\mathbf{U_N} = \mathbf{u}) &= \int_{-\infty}^{\infty} \prod_{j=1}^{N} P_j(\theta)^{u_j} Q_j(\theta)^{1-u_j} \tilde{f}(\theta)\mathrm{d}\theta \\
&= \int_{-\infty}^{\infty} \prod_{j=1}^{N} P_j(\theta^{(0)})^{u_j} Q_j(\theta^{(0)})^{1-u_j} \left[\iint\cdots\int f(\boldsymbol{\theta})\mathrm{d}\boldsymbol{\theta}\right]\mathrm{d}\theta^{(0)} \\
&= \int_{-\infty}^{\infty} \left[\prod_{j=1}^{N} P_j(\psi_m)^{u_i} Q_j(\psi_m)^{1-u_j}\right] \\
&\quad \times \left\{\iint_{\Re^m}\cdots\int f(h^{-1}(\boldsymbol{\psi}))J_{h^{-1}}(\boldsymbol{\psi})\mathrm{d}\psi_1\ldots\mathrm{d}\psi_{m-1}\right\}\mathrm{d}\psi_m \qquad (7.13) \\
&= \int\int_{\Re^m}\cdots\int \prod_{j=1}^{N} P_j(\psi_m)^{u_j} Q_j(\psi_m)^{1-u_j} f(h^{-1}(\boldsymbol{\psi}))J_{h^{-1}}(\boldsymbol{\psi})\mathrm{d}\boldsymbol{\psi} \\
&= \int\int_{\Re^m}\cdots\int \prod_{j=1}^{N} P_j(g(\boldsymbol{\theta}))^{u_j} Q_j(g(\boldsymbol{\theta}))^{1-u_j} f(\boldsymbol{\theta})\mathrm{d}\boldsymbol{\theta}
\end{aligned}$$

as desired, where the last equality is by change of the variable $\psi = h(\boldsymbol{\theta})$ and uses the fact that $J_{h^{-1}}(h(\boldsymbol{\theta}))J_h(\boldsymbol{\theta}) = 1$ with $J_h(\boldsymbol{\theta})$ denoting the Jacobian of the transformation $\boldsymbol{\psi} = h(\boldsymbol{\theta})$ (see Apostle 1957, p. 140).

The basic premise of Theorem 2 is that if the item score matrix for the items on a test can be well fit by a unidimensional IRT model, that matrix of item scores can be equally well fit by a multidimensional IRT model with coherent item response functions. When that is the case, the unidimensional θs can be represented by $\boldsymbol{\theta}$-vectors with elements that give coordinates along a line in the multidimensional $\boldsymbol{\theta}$-space. The unidimensional θ is then a function of the coordinates for the points on the line in the multidimensional space.

The implications of Theorem 2 are used quite commonly when teaching the mathematical concept of a line. Even though the line is a one-dimensional object, it is often drawn on a chalk board or a piece of paper that are two- dimensional surfaces. The same line can also be represented by a taut string in three-dimensional space. In the two and three-dimensional cases, the points on the line can be represented by pairs or triplets of coordinates, but the locations on the line can be specified as a function of the elements of the pairs or triplets of coordinates.

Theorems 1 and 2 provide the theoretical underpinnings for a procedure in the MIRT literature for determining the number of constructs needed to represent the relationships in the item score matrix. The goal of the procedure is to determine the number of coherent sets of test items there are in the test based on a compensatory MIRT model. Because the criterion of perfect coherence is impossible to meet with real item response data and estimated item parameters, the procedure searches for sets of test items that have item arrows pointing in approximately the same direction in the $\boldsymbol{\theta}$-space. This procedure is described in the Sect. 7.2 of this chapter.

7.2 Procedures for Determining the Required Number of Dimensions

The previous sections of this chapter provide background on the challenges that arise when trying to determine the number of coordinate axes needed to represent the relationships in a matrix of item scores. That matrix is dependent not only on the sensitivity of the test items to differences of the locations of the examinees in the $\boldsymbol{\theta}$-space, but also on the amount of variation that is present in the sample of examinees on the constructs that are the target of the test. Few dimensions are required to model the data if examinees vary on few constructs, or if the items are sensitive to differences in only a few directions in the $\boldsymbol{\theta}$-space. Given the complexities of the causes of relationships in the item score matrix, it is not reasonable to think about the number of dimensions needed to model a test, but only the number of dimensions needed to model the relationships in the data matrix that results from the interaction between a particular sample of examinees and the particular sample if items. That is, the number of required dimensions is sample specific and the results may not generalize to the interaction of another sample of examinees taking the same test.

One way to frame the problem of determining the number of dimensions required to model the data in the item score matrix is that the test items are sensitive to differences in specific directions in a high dimensional $\boldsymbol{\theta}$-space. If the item arrows for the items all point in the same direction, even though multiple cognitive skills are needed to obtain a correct response, the modeling of the data matrix will require only one dimension. This is the result of Theorem 1 in the previous section. For a test containing such a set of test items, the fact that the examinees in the sample vary on a number of different cognitive skills will have little effect on the number of dimensions needed to model the data. However, if the test items, or sets of test items, are sensitive to differences in different directions in the space, possibly as many directions as there are items, then the resulting item score matrix will only require the smaller of the dimensions of sensitivity of the test items and the dimensions of variation on the constructs targeted by the test in the examinee sample to model the data. If examinees do not differ in a particular direction that is the direction of sensitivity for a test item, then the direction of best measurement for that item will not affect the dimensionality needed to model the item-score matrix and the required dimensions needed to model the item-score data is less than that required for a more varied examinee sample.

The goal of this section of the chapter is to review the methods that are currently available to determine the number of dimensions needed to accurately model the relationships in a particular item score matrix. Because of the sample specific nature of the results of these methods, it is useful to determine how much the results generalize to other samples of examinees or other forms of a test constructed to the same specifications. This is particularly important when considering equating test forms.

In a sense, there is no correct answer to the number of dimensions problem. It can be argued that what is required to correctly respond to each test item has components that are uniquely different from those required to correctly respond to every other test item. From this perspective, the item-score matrix from a test requires as many dimensions as test items to totally model all of the relationships in the data. Although this perspective has its merits, the implications are that results should be reported and interpreted at the level of the test item. However, the scores based on individual test items are very unreliable, and it is unwise to put much interpretive weight on item scores. The alternative is to determine how the common information in sets of test items can be combined to define scales that support more reliable reporting of results. This second position is taken here and it leads to statements of the goals for identifying the number of dimensions needed to represent the relationships in a matrix of item scores.

One goal is to determine the number of clusters of items that have directions of measurement that are sufficiently similar to merit defining a scale for reporting the results on the cluster. That is, the desire is to find sets of items that approximate the coherence condition given in Theorem 1. The second goal is to determine the number of orthogonal coordinate axes that are needed to model the locations of persons and the functioning of the test items. These two goals are not the same. Two examples will be used to show the distinction. In later parts of this chapter, data simulated to match these two examples will be used to show the functioning of a number of procedures that are frequently used to determine the number of dimensions needed to model the relationships in an item score matrix.

Example A: Three Item Clusters in Two Dimensions

A teacher working with elementary school children is interested in determining how well students can solve simple arithmetic problems when they are represented either numerically or using words. The teacher is concerned that the level of reading skill of the students might influence the results. A test was designed consisting of three sets of test items. The first set consists of 20 simple arithmetic items of the form $2 + 7 = ?$ or $35/5 = ?$ The second set consists of 20 simple arithmetic items of the form "What does two plus seven equal?" or "What is the result of thirty-five divided by five?" The third set of test items consists of ten simple reading items of the following form:

Select the best word to fill in the blank in the following sentence.
The child on the bicycle was moving very ______.

(a) loud
(b) fast
(c) high
(d) bland
(e) steel

These three clusters of items can be considered to be related in the following way. The knowledge of arithmetic computation in the numerical form is only slightly related to the skill in reading. These types of items may be considered to have item arrows that are almost orthogonal to each other in a two-dimensional $\boldsymbol{\theta}$-space. The arithmetic items in verbal form may be considered to require both of the other skills and may be equally related to the other two skills. The three item sets can be represented in a two-dimensional $\boldsymbol{\theta}$-space using a plot of the item arrows. This plot is shown in Fig. 7.6. The item parameters for these items for a two-dimensional compensatory model are given in Table 7.8.

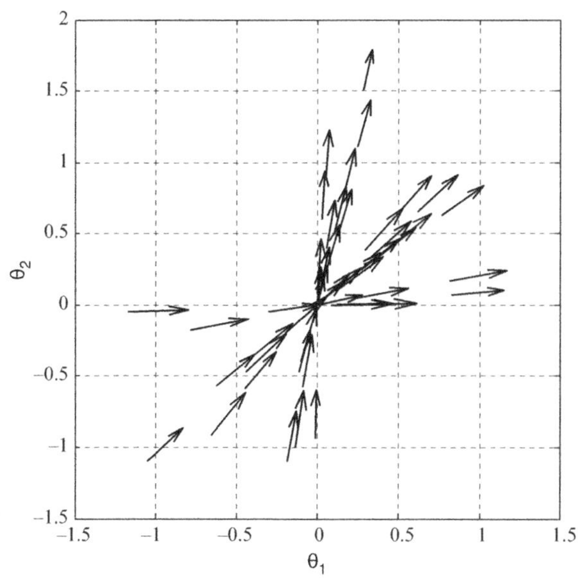

Fig. 7.6 Item arrows for three item clusters in a two-dimensional $\boldsymbol{\theta}$-space

Table 7.8 Item parameters for three item clusters in a two-dimensional $\boldsymbol{\theta}$-space

Item number	a_1	a_2	d
1	0.8887	0.1399	0.2724
2	1.0571	0.0432	1.2335
3	1.0466	0.0160	−0.0918
4	1.1778	0.0231	−0.2372
5	1.0291	0.2347	0.8471
6	0.9295	0.0821	−0.7779
7	1.0124	0.2077	−0.8603
8	0.8730	0.2180	0.0237
9	0.9732	0.1979	−0.2275
10	0.9899	0.0251	−0.1211
11	0.1822	0.9782	0.1300
12	0.2017	0.9426	−0.4898
13	0.2637	1.0781	0.4571
14	0.1535	0.8110	−1.2614
15	0.0956	1.0340	0.0991
16	0.0656	1.0860	−0.0868
17	0.2229	1.0468	−0.7992
18	0.1935	1.0362	−0.0437
19	0.2304	0.9721	0.0669
20	0.1601	1.0525	0.6203
21	0.2511	1.0228	−0.2170
22	0.0090	0.9699	0.9073
23	0.2426	0.9270	−0.4792
24	0.2141	0.9421	−1.0980
25	0.1966	0.8361	0.4159
26	0.0484	0.9709	−0.5838
27	0.0615	1.0050	−0.8838
28	0.1680	1.0129	1.1455
29	0.1508	1.1392	1.1591
30	0.1424	0.9502	−0.3841
31	0.7415	0.7559	0.2964
32	0.6631	0.8494	−0.5205
33	0.8104	0.7333	−0.6240
34	0.6750	0.5972	−0.4491
35	0.7008	0.7361	−0.9179
36	0.7161	0.7249	−0.4769
37	0.5542	0.7089	−0.7501
38	0.6837	0.6217	0.7778
39	0.8004	0.7669	0.0154
40	0.6942	0.6946	0.1077
41	0.6031	0.8405	1.1616
42	0.7347	0.6840	−0.1808
43	0.5646	0.7439	0.6907
44	0.7297	0.5942	−0.9322
45	0.7724	0.6965	0.5861
46	0.6720	0.6063	−0.3350
47	0.8253	0.6898	−0.1651
48	0.7213	0.7673	0.6796
49	0.6335	0.6626	1.3929
50	0.6433	0.7247	0.0401

The arrow plot of the items shows the distinct sets of items. There are 10 test items that measure predominantly along θ_1, 20 test items that measure predominantly along θ_2, and 20 test items that measure an equally weighted combination.

The same pattern can be observed in the set of item parameters. The first 10 test items have larger a_1 parameters than a_2 parameters. The next 20 test items have the reverse pattern, and the last 20 test items have roughly equal a parameters.

The important feature of this set of test items is that there are three distinct clusters of items but the clusters are in a two-dimensional $\boldsymbol{\theta}$-space. The distinction in the sets of test items is that two are fairly pure measures of a particular type of cognitive skill and the third set is a measure of a combination of the two skills.

Example B: Three Item Clusters in Three Dimensions

A teacher working with slightly more advanced school children than those in Example A is also interested in assessing the arithmetic skills of the children. These children have recently been working on arithmetic story problems that require problem solving skill because the steps needed to compute the answer are not specified. The teacher is concerned about the reading level required for the story problems so a test is constructed that consists of three sets of items. The first set is similar to the reading test items in Example A. There are 10 test items in this set. No arithmetic skill is needed for these test items. The second set of test items is similar to the arithmetic computation items in Example A that require no reading. There are 20 test items in this set. A third set of test items consists of the story problem items that require skills in reading, arithmetic computation, and problem solving. There are 20 test items in this set. The item arrow plot for the resulting 50-item test is given in Fig. 7.7. The item parameters for the 50 test items are given in Table 7.9.

Figure 7.7 shows the orientation of the three sets of test items. The set of reading items measures best along the θ_1-axis. The arithmetic computation items measure best along the θ_2-axis. The problem solving dimension is independent of the reading and arithmetic computation dimensions, but the story problems require all three components. As a result, the item arrows for the story problems are not in any of the planes of the $\boldsymbol{\theta}$-space. Rather, they have components from all three axes.

The pattern of relationships between the axes and the test items can also be seen in the item parameters given in Table 7.9. The first 10 test items have a_1 parameters larger than the others. The next 20 items have a_2 parameter larger than the others. The last 20 items have roughly equal a parameters.

This set of test items has a superficial similarity to Example A. Both sets have three fairly distinct clusters of test items, but for Example B the clusters approximate simple structure, while in Example A, one of the clusters does not align with a coordinate axis. The differences in the two example item sets are very important in that Example B requires three dimensions to adequately model the set while Example A requires only two dimensions. The example provides a demonstration of an important concept that the number of test item clusters may be more than the

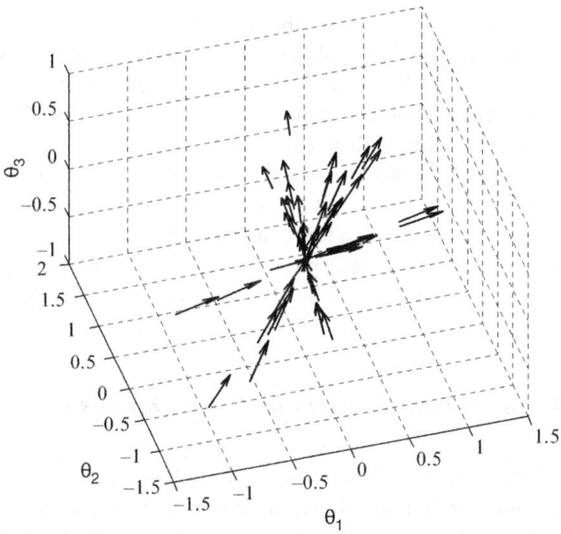

Fig. 7.7 Item arrows for three item clusters in a three-dimensional $\boldsymbol{\theta}$-space

number of dimensions needed to represent the structure of relationships among the test items. A key test of the procedures used to determine the number of dimensions needed to model a matrix of item score data is whether the procedures can accurately distinguish between these two cases. Although it is not the purpose of this chapter to provide a complete evaluation of procedures for estimating the required number of dimensions, these two examples will be used to demonstrate the function of a selected set of procedures for determining the number of dimensions needed to model test data.

There are two distinct types of procedures for determining the number of dimensions needed to accurately model a matrix of item scores – parametric and nonparametric. The nonparametric are based on an analysis of the inter-item covariances for the items in a test. These procedures are not model free because they are based on a statistic that assumes a linear relationship, but they do not assume a mathematical form for the model that is used to analyze the data. In a sense, the nonparametric procedures do not answer the question that is of interest in a book about MIRT models. They do not tell how many dimensions are needed for a particular MIRT model to accurately fit the item score matrix. That number of dimensions needed may be model specific. However, the generality of the nonparametric procedures suggest a logical progression for determining the number of dimensions needed for the analysis of the item score matrix.

One way of approaching the problem of determining the required number of dimensions is to first determine whether more than one dimension is needed. If more than one dimension is needed, then further analyses can be done to determine the number required. It seems logical that the number of dimensions required

Table 7.9 Item parameters for three item clusters in a three-dimensional $\boldsymbol{\theta}$-space

Item number	a_1	a_2	a_3	d
1	0.8952	0.0520	0.0722	0.2724
2	1.0319	0.1323	0.1923	1.2335
3	1.0357	0.1439	0.0482	−0.0918
4	1.1633	0.1303	0.1321	−0.2372
5	1.0224	0.1647	0.2040	0.8471
6	0.9111	0.0874	0.1817	−0.7779
7	1.0187	0.1019	0.1414	−0.8603
8	0.8769	0.0636	0.1914	0.0237
9	0.9753	0.0966	0.1603	−0.2275
10	0.9889	0.0310	0.0419	−0.1211
11	0.0811	0.9707	0.2031	0.1300
12	0.0620	0.9542	0.1221	−0.4898
13	0.0935	1.0852	0.2133	0.4571
14	0.1303	0.8009	0.1509	−1.2614
15	0.1819	1.0216	0.0410	0.0991
16	0.2244	1.0524	0.1609	−0.0868
17	0.1312	1.0613	0.0439	−0.7992
18	0.1727	1.0270	0.1627	−0.0437
19	0.0553	0.9825	0.1724	0.0669
20	0.0543	1.0606	0.0738	0.6203
21	0.0182	1.0448	0.1307	−0.2170
22	0.0763	0.9530	0.1637	0.9073
23	0.1659	0.9380	0.1042	−0.4792
24	0.0098	0.9660	0.0023	−1.0980
25	0.0631	0.8517	0.0912	0.4159
26	0.0404	0.9709	0.0257	−0.5838
27	0.0959	0.9859	0.1805	−0.8838
28	0.0477	1.0221	0.0851	1.1455
29	0.1080	1.1389	0.1085	1.1591
30	0.0205	0.9605	0.0103	−0.3841
31	0.7342	0.6524	0.3956	0.2964
32	0.7266	0.5522	0.5730	−0.5205
33	0.4659	0.6711	0.7261	−0.6240
34	0.3998	0.6282	0.5077	−0.4491
35	0.6808	0.6819	0.3231	−0.9179
36	0.5613	0.5549	0.6444	−0.4769
37	0.5612	0.5577	0.4287	−0.7501
38	0.5889	0.5567	0.4440	0.7778
39	0.7698	0.5713	0.5566	0.0154
40	0.4673	0.6700	0.5451	0.1077
41	0.5526	0.4454	0.7527	1.1616
42	0.6227	0.4916	0.6150	−0.1808
43	0.5537	0.5886	0.4681	0.6907
44	0.6106	0.6144	0.3676	−0.9322
45	0.6775	0.5196	0.5939	0.5861
46	0.5668	0.6377	0.3020	−0.3350
47	0.5287	0.6975	0.6253	−0.1651
48	0.5662	0.5255	0.7158	0.6796
49	0.6173	0.4983	0.4594	1.3929
50	0.4969	0.4985	0.6661	0.0401

is dependent on the model that will be used to represent the data. For that reason, nonparametric procedures are only used for initial checks on dimensionality and parametric procedures are used for making a final determination of the number of dimensions for an analysis. There is also concern about projecting solutions to a space that is smaller than is required and distorting the results through that projection. Therefore, the selection of the number of dimensions will tend to err in the direction of using more dimensions rather than pick the minimum necessary.

7.2.1 DIMTEST

A commonly used procedure for determining whether more than one dimension is needed to accurately model the item-score matrix is implemented in a computer program called DIMTEST (Stout et al. 1999; Stout et al. 2001). The theoretical underpinnings for DIMTEST are described in Stout (1987) and Zhang and Stout (1999a, b). The procedures in DIMTEST are derived assuming that the interaction between persons and test items can be described by a general form of a MIRT model that has the probability of correct response a function of $\mathbf{a}\boldsymbol{\theta}' + d$. The form of the MIRT model assumes that the probability of correct response increases monotonically with an increase in any element of the $\boldsymbol{\theta}$-vector. The compensatory MIRT models described in this book are special cases of this general MIRT model.

The procedures in DIMTEST determine the direction of greatest discrimination for the test as a whole using a generalized version of the concept of a reference composite. The basic statistic used by the procedure is the expected value of the covariances between items conditional on the composite of $\boldsymbol{\theta}$-elements that best measure in the direction of greatest discrimination, $\theta_Y = \mathbf{a}_Y\boldsymbol{\theta}'$, where $\mathbf{a}_Y$ is the vector of $\mathbf{a}$-parameters that define the direction of best measurement:

$$E[\operatorname{cov}(U_i, U_j|\theta_Y)], \quad i \neq j, \tag{7.14}$$

where i and j are the indexes for pairs of items in the test.

Because θ_Y is not directly observable, DIMTEST uses the number correct score, Y, as an approximation for θ_Y. Under the assumption that the matrix of item scores meets the requirements for essential unidimensionality (Stout 1987), Y approaches being a function of θ_Y asymptotically as the test length increases by adding parallel replicates of itself. The actual test statistic used in DIMTEST is the covariance between items conditional on Y

$$E[\operatorname{cov}(U_i, U_j|Y)] = \sum_{k=0}^{n} P(Y = k)\operatorname{cov}(U_i, U_j|Y = k), \tag{7.15}$$

where n is the number of items on the test. The term on the left of (7.15) should converge to the value in (7.14) as n approaches infinite length.

If the item-score matrix can be accurately modeled by a set of item response functions that are coherent as defined in Sect. 7.1.2, then the composite θ_Y is the value of the unidimensional θ that can be used to model the data. Under those conditions, expected covariances conditional on θ_Y should be zero. Thus, DIMTEST tests the null hypothesis of zero conditional covariances against an alternative hypothesis that the observed conditional covariances are not equal to zero indicating that the data cannot be accurately represented with a unidimensional IRT model.

The actual process of applying DIMTEST is somewhat more complex because the covariances conditional on Y were found to be statistically biased for the test lengths that are typically used in practice. Stout et al. (2001) have developed procedures to adjust for the statistical bias. Those procedures are built into the newest version of the DIMTEST software. In addition, to increase the power of the procedure for identifying violations of the assumption that the data can be accurately represented with a unidimensional model, DIMTEST requires that the set of items in the test be partitioned into at least two parts. One set of items is the set that is believed to measure best in the direction specified by the composite θ_Y. This set of items is called the partitioned subtest (PT). The number-correct scores on this subtest are used as the conditioning variable when computing the inter-item covariances. A second partition is composed of the items thought to measure best in a direction that is most different from PT. This set of items is labeled the assessment test (AT). The hypothesis test is based on the inter-item covariances for the items in the AT partition,

$$T = \sum_{i \neq j \in \mathrm{AT}} \sum_{k=0}^{n} \operatorname{cov}\left(U_i, U_j | Y_{\mathrm{PT}} = k\right), \tag{7.16}$$

where Y_{PT} is the number-correct score on the PT partition of the test and n is the number of test items in PT. The T is converted to a z-score by dividing by an estimate of the standard deviation of the sampling distribution under the null hypothesis and then it is compared with a critical value based on the standard normal distribution. The full test statistic is given by

$$T_L = \frac{\sum_{i \neq j \in \mathrm{AT}} \sum_{k=0}^{n} \operatorname{cov}\left(U_i, U_j | Y_{\mathrm{PT}} = k\right)}{\sqrt{\sum_{k=0}^{n} s_k^2}}, \tag{7.17}$$

where

$$s_k^2 = \frac{\left(\hat{\mu}_{4k} - \hat{\sigma}_k^4\right) + \hat{\delta}_{4k}}{J_k}, \tag{7.18}$$

$$\hat{\mu}_{4k} = \frac{1}{J_k} \sum_{j=1}^{J_k} \left(Y_j^{(k)} - \bar{Y}^{(k)}\right)^4, \tag{7.19}$$

$$\sigma_k = \sqrt{\frac{1}{J_k}\sum_{j=1}^{J_k}\left(Y_j^{(k)} - \bar{Y}^{(k)}\right)^2}, \tag{7.20}$$

$$\hat{\delta}_{4k} = \sum \hat{p}_i^{(k)}\left(1-\hat{p}_i^{(k)}\right)\left(1-2\hat{p}_i^{(k)}\right)^2, \tag{7.21}$$

$$\hat{p}_i^{(k)} = \frac{1}{J_k}\sum_{j=1}^{J_k} U_{ij}^{(k)}, \tag{7.22}$$

where J_k is the number of persons in score group k on PT, $Y_j^{(k)}$ is the score on AT for Person j with score k on PT, and $U_{ij}^{(k)}$ is the score on Item i for Person j who has score k on PT.

Because the statistic T_{L} was found to have positive statistical bias in some cases, Stout et al. (2001) devised a correction using replications of simulated data sets that match the observed data, but that are generated using a unidimensional model. When the test statistic in (7.17) is estimated from the generated data, it is labeled T_{G}. To stabilize the correction, N data sets are generated and T_{G} is computed from each one and then averaged. The final test statistic is given by

$$T = \frac{T_{\mathrm{L}} - \overline{T}_{\mathrm{G}}}{\sqrt{1+\frac{1}{N}}}. \tag{7.23}$$

The AT partition of the test can be formed in a number of ways. It can be determined by expert judgment about the set of test items that are most different from those that define the construct for the PT set. It can be determined through a factor analysis procedure. Another alternative is to perform a clustering of the items based on their direction of best measurement in the $\boldsymbol{\theta}$-space. Depending on the method used for identifying the PT and AT sets, the results of DIMTEST will be different. Two researchers analyzing the same set of data could reach different conclusions depending on how those two sets of items were identified. One way to avoid variations in the selection of AT is to allow the DIMTEST software to select the set using the item clustering algorithm. If this option is used, the developers of the software recommend that the sample of test data be divided in half and one part be used to identify AT and then do the statistical test on the other half. This procedure was followed to test whether the application of DIMTEST to Example A and B data sets would lead to the rejection of the null hypothesis that the data can be accurately represented with a unidimensional model.

To determine whether the unidimensionality assumption was supported or rejected for the Example A and B data sets, the data sets were first randomly divided into two samples of 2,500. The first of the two samples in each case was used to determine the PT and AT item sets. Then the second sample was used to compute the test statistic given in (7.23) and determine whether it was beyond the critical value set using the null hypothesis and the estimated sampling distribution. The results of

Table 7.10 DIMTEST statistics with AT and PT item sets

Test Data	T_L	$\overline{T}_G$	T	p	PT Items	AT Items
2 dimensions 3 clusters	30.12	14.42	15.62	.00	1 2 3 4 5 6 7 8 9 10 31 33 34 35 36 37 38 39 40 42 44 45 46 47 48 49 50	11 12 13 14 15 16 17 18 19 20 21 22 23 24 25 26 27 28 29 30 32 41 43
3 dimensions 3 clusters	33.12	11.71	21.31	.00	1 2 3 4 5 6 7 8 9 10 31 32 33 34 35 36 37 38 39 40 41 42 43 44 45 46 47 48 49 50	11 12 13 14 15 16 17 18 19 20 21 22 23 24 25 26 27 28 29 30
6th grade mathematics	13.30	8.78	4.50	.00	1 2 3 4 6 7 8 9 12 15 16 18 19 20 21 22 24 27 28	5 10 11 13 14 17 23 25 26

the analyses are given in Table 7.10. The DIMTEST analysis of a third, real data set is also included. These data are from a 28-item 6th grade mathematics test.

The results from the analyses show that the hypothesis of the adequacy of a unidimensional model is rejected for the two simulated data sets. The T-statistics are quite large and the probability of acceptance of the null hypothesis is close to zero. Because these data were generated using two and three-dimensional compensatory MIRT models, these results are not surprising. The null hypothesis should be rejected. It is interesting, however, that the selection of the test items for the PT and AT sets did not follow the structure used to generate the data. For the two-dimensional data set, items that were modeled as reading items and those that combined both reading and arithmetic were placed in PT. Items that were modeled as requiring only arithmetic were in the AT set. A similar pattern was present for the data generated with a three-dimensional compensatory model. The PT set included items simulated to model reading and problem solving. The AT set included items that were simulated to require both algebra and problem solving skills. The results of the selection of items for the PT and AT sets are possibly a result of the fact that the items are selected to match simple structure. The simulated data did not quite meet the requirements for simple structure.

The real data analysis also results in a rejection of the null hypothesis of good fit to the data with a unidimensional model. However, the magnitude of the statistics is much smaller than those for the simulated data. This mathematics test is fairly complex, covering a number of different content areas including measurement, number sense, algebra, and some geometry. The sets of items in PT and AT do not appear to match any of the specified content structure for the test.

7.2.2 DETECT

DETECT (Zhang and Stout 1999b) is a statistical procedure for determining the number of dimensions needed to represent the relationships in the item-score matrix under an assumption of approximate simple structure. The name of the software for this procedure, DETECT, is an abbreviation for "dimensionality evaluation to enumerate contributing traits." DETECT has the same theoretical basis as DIMTEST. The procedure does not assume any specific form for the item characteristic functions so it is labeled as a nonparametric procedure. Although the desire is to know the number of coordinate dimensions needed to model the data matrix assuming a specific model, DETECT is often used for this purpose so its statistical underpinnings are described here and the method is applied to the two example data sets to demonstrate its use.

The DETECT methodology is based on several assumptions for the characteristics of the probabilistic models that generate the item-score matrix. With one exception, these are the usual assumptions that were made in describing the MIRT models for dichotomously scored items in Chap. 4. They are that the item response functions are monotonically increasing with an increase in any of the θ-coordinates and that local independence holds when determining the probability of a string of item scores conditional on $\boldsymbol{\theta}$ from the probabilities of each item score conditional on $\boldsymbol{\theta}$. The assumption that was not included in Chap. 4 is that the procedure is based on "pairwise local independence" instead of complete local independence. Pairwise local independence specifies that the following conditions hold: $\text{cov}\left(U_i, U_j|\boldsymbol{\Theta} = \boldsymbol{\theta}\right) = 0$ for all $\boldsymbol{\theta}$ and $i \neq j$, where i and j represent item numbers in the test. This definition of local independence is consistent with the estimation used in NOHARM, but TESTFACT uses the full probabilistic definition of local independence.

The basic definition of dimensionality used in the development of DETECT is that an item-score matrix requires a d-dimensional model for accurate representation of the relationships in the matrix if d is the minimum number of elements required in the $\boldsymbol{\theta}$-vector to produce pairwise local independence using a monotonically increasing MIRT model. When the $\boldsymbol{\theta}$-vector results in pairwise local independence, the model is labeled as "complete."

Conceptually, the DETECT method searches for homogeneous clusters of items that best measure in a direction in the multidimensional space that is different than the direction of best measurement for the test as a whole. The direction of best measurement for the test is somewhat similar to the concept of the reference composite described in Chap. 5, but its mathematical definition is not the same. The major distinction is that the reference composite is an estimate of the direction through the origin of the $\boldsymbol{\theta}$-space that corresponds to the weighted composite of coordinates that result from the application of a unidimensional IRT model to the item score matrix. In contrast, the direction of best measurement used in DETECT is the average direction over $\boldsymbol{\theta}$-points that give the greatest change in estimated true score for the set of test items. The derivation of this direction is given in Zhang and Stout (1999a). A short summary is provided here.

The basic concept for the DETECT index is a weighted composite of the θ-coordinates for the complete latent space. The weighted composite is defined as follows

$$\theta_{\text{w}} = \mathbf{w}\boldsymbol{\theta}' = \sum_{k=1}^{m} w_k \theta_k, \tag{7.24}$$

where $\mathbf{w}$ is a vector of weights for the m coordinates in the space and θ_{w} is the value of the composite of the coordinates. The weights are scaled so that the variance of θ_{w} is equal to 1.0.

The DETECT procedure determines the values of the elements of the vector $\mathbf{w}$ that maximize the expected value over the $\boldsymbol{\theta}$-space of the square root of the information function in the direction specified by the composite. $\mathbf{w}^*$ is the vector of weights that provide the maximum expected value. The estimation equation for the elements of $\mathbf{w}^*$ is given by

$$w_\ell^* = c \sum_{i=1}^{k} E \left\{ \frac{\partial P_i(\boldsymbol{\theta})}{\partial \theta_\ell} \left[\sum_{l=1}^{k} P_l(\boldsymbol{\theta}) Q_l(\boldsymbol{\theta}) \right]^{-\frac{1}{2}} \right\} \quad \text{for } \ell = 1, 2, \ldots, m, \tag{7.25}$$

where w_ℓ^* is an element of $\mathbf{w}^*$, c is a scaling constant to result in a variance of 1 for θ_{w}, k is the number of items on the test, $P_i(\boldsymbol{\theta})$ is the item response function for Item i, and m is the number of dimensions needed to model the relationships in the data matrix.

To implement DETECT, the set of items in a test is first partitioned into a series of disjoint sets, $\mathbf{P} = \{A_1, A_2, \ldots, A_q\}$ with the goal of having items in the different sets measuring different constructs. These sets can either be determined by the judgment of the test developer, or DETECT provides an option to find the partition that maximizes the value of the DETECT index. The DETECT index, $D_{\mathrm{w}}(\mathbf{P})$, is given by

$$D_{\mathrm{w}}(\mathbf{P}) = \frac{2}{k(k-1)} \sum_{1 \le i \le j \le k} \delta_{ij}(\mathbf{P}) \, E\left[\mathrm{Cov}\left(U_i, U_j | \theta_{\mathrm{w}}\right)\right], \tag{7.26}$$

where $\mathbf{P}$ is any partition of the items in the test, k is the number of items on the test, i and j are any two items on the test with corresponding scores U_i and U_j, θ_{w} is the composite of interest, and

$$\delta_{ij}(\mathbf{P}) = \begin{cases} 1 & i, j \in A_\ell \\ -1 & \text{otherwise.} \end{cases} \tag{7.27}$$

That is, the δ function assigns 1 if two items are in the same partition of the test and -1 if they are in different partitions. When the composite is based on optimal weights, the index is denoted as $D(\mathbf{P})$ and it is called the theoretical DETECT index for partition $\mathbf{P}$. The partition that maximizes the index is labeled $\mathbf{P}^*$. In the implementation of the DETECT index in the software, the value given by (7.26) is multiplied by 100 (Roussos and Ozbek 2006). The range of values for the index that are typically observed are 0 to positive values less than five. Jang and Roussos (2007) give the following guidelines for interpreting the DETECT index

> "An index value of 1 or more is considered to indicate large multidimensionality (Kim, 1994). Values of .4 to 1 are considered to indicate moderate to large multidimensionality. Values below .4 are considered to indicate moderate to weak multidimensionality, or even unidimensionality for values below .2." (p. 7)

Along with the DETECT index, the software provides two other indicators of the dimensionality of the data. The first is based on a cross-validation of DETECT index. The data matrix is randomly divided into two samples. The partition that maximizes (7.26) is determined for the first sample. The value of $D(\mathbf{P}^*)$ for that sample is labeled $D_{\max}$. The partition that maximizes the second sample is also determined. Then $D(\mathbf{P})$ is computed using the data from the first sample using the partition determined from the second sample. This value is called the reference DETECT index and it is labeled D_{ref}. The ratio of these two values $D_{\text{ref}}/D_{\max}$ is considered as another index of dimensionality. If the value is near 1, it means that the partitions found from the two samples are the same indicating that the solution is stable. If the ratio is small, it means that the partitions are very different. Zhang and Stout (1999b) suggest that small values of the ratio indicate that the partitions are based on "capitalization upon chance" and likely indicate essential unidimensionality.

The other indicator of dimensionality is the proportion of estimated covariances that have signs that follow the pattern that is expected by the partitioning of the test into item sets. The expected pattern is that items within the same partition should have positive covariances, but those in different partitions should have negative covariances. This indicator is called the IDN index. Values close to 1 indicate that the pattern of covariances matches the pattern that is expected if the multidimensional structure of the data is consistent with a simple structure model.

The DETECT analysis was performed on the same data sets as were used with the DIMTEST method – the two simulated data sets and the real data from the mathematics test. For the simulated data, the program was run in two different ways. The first was using the exploratory mode with DETECT identifying the partition of items that maximized the DETECT index. The second was a confirmatory analysis using the partition of test items into clusters according to the way that the data were generated. The results of these analyses are presented in Table 7.11.

The interpretation of the DETECT index suggests that the two- and three-dimensional data sets have moderate to large multidimensionality, as would be expected given how they were generated, but the real data set has weak dimensional

Table 7.11 DETECT results for the three example data sets

Data set	Cross-validated DETECT index	Ratio $D_{\text{ref}}/D_{\max}$	IDN index	Partition 1	Partition 2	Partition 3
2 dimensions 3 clusters	.50	.73	.74	1–10, 32–40, 42, 44–50	11–30, 41, 43	31
3 dimensions 3 clusters	.72	.86	.83	1–10, 31–50	11–30	
6th grade mathematics	.18	.41	.66	1, 2, 15–19	3, 4, 6–9, 12, 20–22, 24, 27, 28	5, 10, 11, 13, 14, 23, 25, 26

structure or support for modeling with a unidimensional model. This is the case for the real data, even though the hypothesis of unidimensionality was rejected by DIMTEST.

The ratios of the DETECT indexes are fairly close to 1 for the simulated data sets indicating stable solutions, but the real data set yielded a smaller ratio of .41 suggesting some instability in the solution. The IDN Index is largest for the three-dimensional data and smallest for the real data set. The results give a clear indication that the real data is more likely to be adequately modeled with a unidimensional model than the other two data sets. This is not a surprising result because the items for the real test were partly selected based on the item-total test correlation. Use of this selection criterion tends to result in a dominant construct for a test, even though there are multiple content areas. In this case, the test is equated using a unidimensional IRT model so the DETECT results support the use of that methodology.

DETECT also gives information on the partitioning of the test items into subsets that maximizes the DETECT Index. In this case, the methodology suggested three clusters of items for the two-dimensional case, but the clusters do not correspond to the structure built into the data. For the three-dimensional case, DETECT suggested two-item clusters rather than the three built into the data. The mismatch between the actual and estimated item clusters is due to the fact that DETECT tends to ignore items that are along the reference composite for the test and it is trying to fit an independent, simple-structure model. For the simulated data, the method combined the item sets that had high a-parameters on a dimension, even though some of the items also had high a-parameters on other dimensions. It is only when the test items with high a-parameters formed disjoint sets with no contribution from other dimensions that the method correctly clusters items.

The partitioning of the test items for the real test is more difficult to interpret because the true underlying structure is not known. There are content classifications for the items, but there is only a partial match between the content classifications and the partitioning of the items from DETECT. For example, the first partition has four items that had content classifications of measurement, but three other items with the same classification were in the other two partitions. There was no strong connection between the content classifications by the test developers and the partitions produced by DETECT.

7.2.3 *Parallel Analysis*

Another approach to determining the number of dimensions is called parallel analysis. The approach has been suggested by Ledesma and Valero-Mora (2007) and others. It has a long history in the factor analysis literature possibly being first suggested by Horn (1965). The procedure has two major steps. First, a dimensional analysis is performed with a program like TESTFACT that provides the first n eigenvalues of the matrix of inter-item correlations. TESTFACT bases its eigenvalues/eigenvector decomposition on tetrachoric correlations that may have been adjusted using the estimate of the lower asymptote for the item characteristic surfaces for the items. The eigenvalues can then be plotted against the number of dimensions extracted to give the traditional scree plot.

The second step is to generate a set of test data that has no relationship among the items, but that has the same proportion correct for each item as the real data and the same sample size. The generated data are then analyzed to get eigenvalues using the same analysis as was applied to the real data. Because the generated data have the same distribution of item difficulties as the real data, the analysis of these data will have the same tendency to have difficulty factors as the real data. The eigenvalues for the generated data are then plotted on the same graph with the corresponding ones from the real data and the number of eigenvalues for the real data that are larger than those for the generated data is determined. That number is the number of dimensions suggested by the analysis. Ledesma and Valero-Mora (2007) suggest replicating the generation of the simulated data that matches the difficulty values for the real data a number of times to get an estimate of the sampling variation of the eigenvalues for the sample size and difficulty distribution from the real data.

To demonstrate the parallel analysis methodology, it was applied to the three data sets described earlier in this chapter – the two simulated data sets and the one real data set. First, TESTFACT was run on each data set to obtain the eigenvalues for each of the dimensions extracted. Next, the proportion correct was computed for each test item from the item-score matrix. The proportion correct was then used as the parameter of a binomial distribution and random binary digits were generated to match that proportion using the binomial random variable generator from MATLAB. The result is a matrix of random $(0, 1)$ data that has the same difficulty distribution as the original data. These random data were then analyzed with TESTFACT to obtain the eigenvalues from the tetrachoric correlation matrix. For the real data, TESTFACT was run with lower asymptote parameters estimated using BILOG-MG.

The results for the two-dimensional simulated data set are shown in Fig. 7.8 and those for the three-dimensional data set are shown in Fig. 7.9. The solid line in each figure is the scree plot for the multidimensional data and the dotted lines are the scree plots for the random data.

The scree plot shows that the first two eigenvalues for the two-dimensional data were larger than the first two eigenvalues for the random data. There was very little variation in the random data so a larger number of replications were not performed. There was one anomaly in the random data. One replication had three of the tetrachoric correlations that did not converge to stable values. Arbitrary values were substituted for those values and they resulted in the two eigenvalues from the random data that were approximately 2. The rule proposed by Ledesma and Valero-Mora (2007) was that the number of dimensions needed to model the data is the number of eigenvalues that are greater than those from the random data. In this case, the rule results in two dimensions. This is the number of dimensions used to generate the data. It is not the number of item clusters used to generate the data, which was three. It is interesting to note that the eigenvalues greater than one rule would result in the retention of over 20 dimensions for this data set. That rule is not very useful for these data.

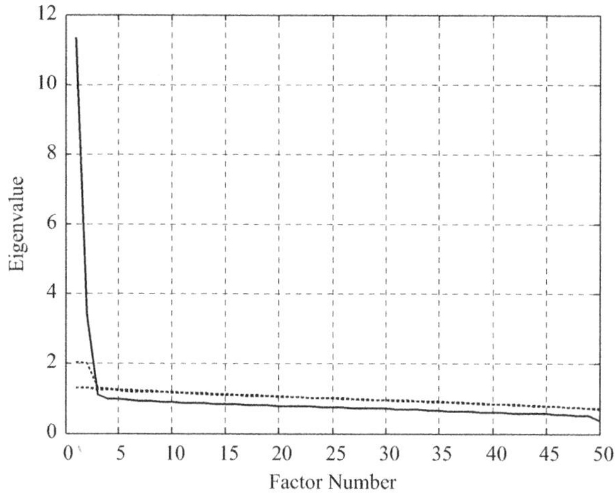

Fig. 7.8 Scree plot for the two-dimensional simulated data and four replications of random data

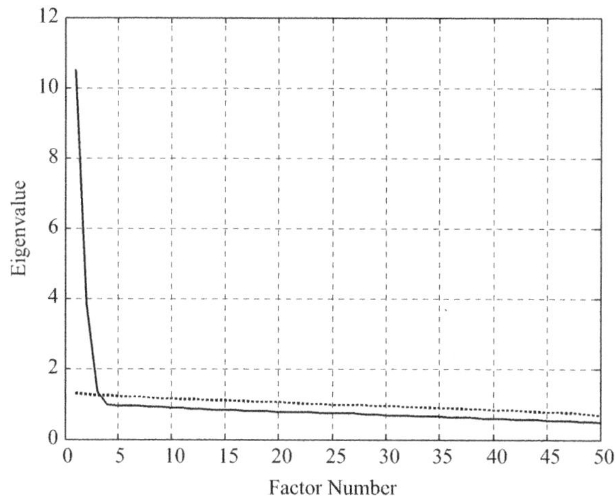

Fig. 7.9 Scree plot for the three-dimensional simulated data and two replications of random data

Figure 7.9 shows the scree plot for the three-dimensional simulated data and Fig. 7.10 shows the plot for the real data set. For the three-dimensional data, the first three eigenvalues from the three-dimensional data exceeded the corresponding eigenvalues from the random data. As for the data generated using two dimensions, the parallel analysis methodology correctly identified the number of dimensions. In this case, only two random data sets were generated to serve as a basis for comparison because the scree plots for those two data sets were nearly identical.

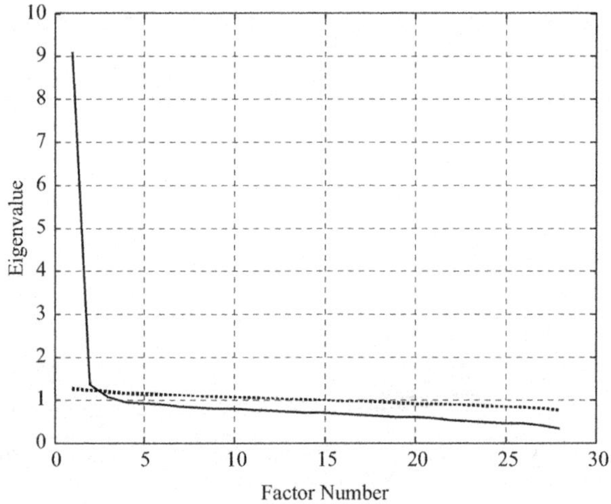

Fig. 7.10 Scree plots for the grade 6 mathematics test data and three replications of random data

The real data consisted of the item score matrix of the response of 6,000 students to 28 multiple-choice test items. The c-parameters for the items were first estimated using BILOG. The c-parameters ranged in value from .09 to .36. The c-parameter estimates were set as fixed values in TESTFACT. The scree plots for the real data set and two randomly generated data sets are shown in Fig. 7.10. The scree plot for the real data is shown with a solid line and those for the simulated data are shown with dotted lines. Only two replications were used for the simulated data because the lines for the replications were indistinguishable indicating there was little variation in the results of the simulation. The first two eigenvalues for the real data were larger than those for the simulated data sets suggesting that modeling the data using a $\boldsymbol{\theta}$-space with two coordinate axes would capture the relationships between the item scores in the data matrix.

7.2.4 Difference Chi-Square

Schilling and Bock (2005) suggest using a χ^2 test of the difference in fit of models with m and $m+1$ dimensions to determine the number of coordinate axes needed to model the relationships in the item response matrix. Tate (2003) selected this χ^2 difference test as one of the methods for evaluation in research on model fit and he generally found that it worked well.

The procedure for implementing the χ^2 difference test is to run TESTFACT on the item response matrix specifying m and then $m+1$ dimensions. For each of the solutions, the χ^2 goodness of fit statistic is computed. There is some question whether this fit statistic really has a χ^2 sampling distribution, but the difference in the fit statistics has been shown to have a χ^2 sampling distribution (Haberman 1977). Therefore, the difference in the χ^2 values for the successive solutions is calculated as well as the difference in the degrees of freedom for the two χ^2 values. The resulting difference in χ^2 statistics is tested as a χ^2 statistic with degrees of freedom equal to the difference in degrees of freedom for the two values. The expression for the difference in χ^2 values as presented in Schilling and Bock (2005) is given in (7.28),

$$\chi^2 = 2\sum_{\ell=1}^{s} r_\ell \log \hat{P}_\ell - 2\sum_{\ell=1}^{s} r_\ell \log \hat{P}'_\ell, \tag{7.28}$$

where χ^2 is the χ^2 difference statistic, s is the number of observed response strings in the observed item score matrix, r_ℓ is the frequency of observing response string ℓ, $\hat{P}_\ell$ is the marginal probability of response string ℓ estimated with m dimensions, and $\hat{P}'_\ell$ is the marginal probability of response string ℓ estimated with $m+1$ dimensions. The degrees of freedom for the difference χ^2 is the number of items in the test, n, minus the number of dimensions, $n - m$.

The χ^2 difference statistic was computed for the simulated and real data used with the previous methods. The results of the statistical test of the null hypothesis that the additional dimension provides no improvement in fit are given in Table 7.12 for the two simulated and one real data set. When the χ^2 difference is statistically significant, it indicates that adding a dimension results in a significant improvement in fit. When the χ^2 value is not significant at the specified level, the additional dimension does not result in significant improvement in fit suggesting that the smaller of the two numbers of dimensions is appropriate for analysis.

For the two simulated data set, following the usual convention of rejecting the null hypothesis when $p < .05$ results in an over estimate in the number of dimensions required to model the data. The two-dimensional data set still has significant

Table 7.12 χ^2 difference test for number of dimensions for the simulated and real data sets

Dimensions tested	Data set			
		2 dimensions 3 clusters	3 dimensions 3 clusters	6th grade mathematics
1 vs. 2	χ^2	4005.86	4926.49	181.05
	d.f.	49	49	27
	Probability	.00	.00	.00
2 vs. 3	χ^2	96.90	399.39	117.19
	d.f.	48	48	26
	Probability	.00	.00	.00
3 vs. 4	χ^2	57.64	85.84	28.31
	d.f.	47	47	25
	Probability	.14	.00	.29
4 vs. 5	χ^2		80.13	
	d.f.		46	
	Probability		.00	

improvement in fit when three dimensions are used. The three-dimensional data set has significant improvement in fit when analyzed using four or even five dimensions. A review of the a-parameter estimates from the solutions with more than enough dimensions indicates that a few items were not well estimated when the true numbers of dimensions were used and these items had improved fit with more dimensions. The added dimensions can be considered as resulting from poor estimation. However, if the kind of "rule of thumb" used in structural equation modeling, such as judging fit as good when the χ^2 divided by the degrees of freedom is less than three were used, the use of the difference χ^2 would recover the number of dimensions used to generate the data.

The analysis of the real data suggested that two dimensions would be needed to model the relationships present in the item score matrix. Even though the χ^2 difference test supports the need for three dimensions, the results from the analyses of simulated data that show a tendency for the difference test to ever-estimate the number of dimensions, the fact that the a-parameters for the third dimension are small, and the difficulty of interpreting the construct for the third coordinate suggest that two dimensions is a better choice. This choice is also consistent with the conclusion drawn from the parallel analysis of the test. The DETECT results lent some support to using only a single dimension for modeling these data. The χ^2 divided by degrees of freedom was still much larger than three for all of the numbers of dimensions considered, so that rule did not seem to be the solution to the number of dimensions problem.

7.3 Clustering Items to Confirm Dimensional Structure

An approach to determining the number of coordinate axes that are needed to model the relationships in the data that is somewhat more subjective than those in the previous section is to perform a cluster analysis of a measure of similarity of the constructs measured by the items. As shown in the two simulated examples in the previous section, the number of clusters does not necessarily indicate the number of coordinate axes needed for the solution. For the two-dimensional simulated data, three item clusters were used to generate the data, but only two coordinates were used to locate the examinees. The number of item clusters is an upper limit on the number of coordinate axes needed, but it may be possible to represent the relationships in the data with fewer coordinates per person than the number of item clusters.

One way to use item clusters to determine the number of dimensions that are needed to model a data set is to compare the results of the cluster analysis for different numbers of dimensions. If the cluster analyses are essentially the same for different numbers of dimensions, the smaller of the number of dimensions used for the analysis is sufficient to model the relationships in the data matrix.

A clustering of items is based on two decisions. The first is the selection of a measure of similarity between items. The second decision is the algorithm for forming clusters. The cluster analysis literature contains a large number of choices for both of these decisions. Within the MIRT literature, there are two major options for each of these. For the similarity measure, one option is the angle between each pair of item arrows (Miller and Hirsch 1992). The other measure is the conditional covariance between the items given in (7.15).

The clustering method that seems to work well when the angle between items is the similarity measure is Ward's method (1963). Kim (2001) evaluated a number of clustering methods and found that Ward's method recovered the underlying structure of the data more accurately than alternatives. The DIMPACK V. 1.0 (2006) software uses the conditional covariances as the similarity measure for identifying item clusters. The software package does not recommend a particular clustering method. Instead, numerous alternatives are provided. However, Roussos et al. (1998) indicate that the unweighted pair-group method of averages (UPGMA) (Sokal and Michener 1958) gave better recovery of clusters in a simulation study than other methods. The remainder of this section describes the procedure for computing the angle between item arrows and the implementation of Ward's method for clustering.

If the item arrow for Item 1 has angles with the coordinate axes in vector $\boldsymbol{\alpha}_1$ and the angles with the coordinate axes for the item arrow for Item 2 are in arrow $\boldsymbol{\alpha}_2$, then the angle between the two item arrows is given by the inverse cosine of the inner product of the cosines of the angles with each the coordinate axes for each item (Harman 1976, p. 60):

$$\alpha_{12} = \arccos\left(\cos\boldsymbol{\alpha}_1'\cos\boldsymbol{\alpha}_2\right). \tag{7.29}$$

Note that α_{12} is a scalar value because the lines formed by extending the item arrows intersect at the origin and two intersecting lines fall within the same plane. Thus, there is only one angle between the two lines extended from the item arrows rather than a vector of angles.

The relationship between the angle between two item arrows and the **a**-parameters for the items can be derived by substituting the expression for the direction cosines for the items (5.8) into (7.29). That is,

$$\cos\alpha_{12} = \frac{\mathbf{a}_1'}{\sqrt{\sum_{\ell=1}^{m} a_{1\ell}^2}} \frac{\mathbf{a}_2}{\sqrt{\sum_{\ell=1}^{m} a_{2\ell}^2}}. \tag{7.30}$$

If the two item arrows are perfectly aligned with each other, the angle between them will be 0°. As the angle between the item arrows increases, the items have their directions of maximum discrimination in different directions in the $\boldsymbol{\theta}$-space. For cognitive test items, the angles between items seldom exceed 90°. Harman (1976, p. 63) shows that the cosine of the angle between two variables, in this case, test items, is the correlation between the two items. The fact that the cosine of 0° is 1 indicates that, when the item arrows are pointing in the same direction, the continuous latent variables assumed to underlie the performance on the items are perfectly correlated. Item arrows pointing at right angles to each other indicate a zero correlation between the underlying latent variables. The input data for the clustering algorithm is the matrix of angles between all possible pairs of test items.

Table 7.13 Angles in degrees between selected test items from Example B for two and three-dimensional analyses

Item number	Item number					
	1	2	11	12	31	32
1		6.0	82.6	81.7	37.9	33.6
2	10.4		76.6	75.7	31.9	27.6
11	81.9	76.1		.9	44.8	49.0
12	79.7	74.5	3.8		43.8	48.1
31	42.1	33.6	44.7	44.0		4.2
32	44.0	34.2	50.1	50.1	9.8	

For the examples used in this chapter, the matrices are too large to fit on a page (50×50 or 30×30) so they are not presented here. A few examples of angles between item pairs are provided in Table 7.13. The item pairs used here are from Example B used earlier in this chapter. For the example, pairs of items have been selected from each set that is best at measuring a different reference composite: items 1 and 2, 11 and 12, and 31 and 32. In Table 7.13, the numbers above the diagonal give the angles between item pairs from a two-dimensional solution for the data and those below the diagonal are from a three-dimensional solution.

The results in Table 7.13 show that the items that have highest discrimination for the same construct have small angles between the item arrows. The largest of these is 10 degrees. The angles between items that are best at measuring different constructs have much large values, for example 82.6° between Items 1 and 11. No values are given in the diagonal of the table because this would be the angle between an item and itself, which is 0. The angles below the diagonal are slightly larger than those above the diagonal. For example, all of the angles with Item 32 in the three-dimensional solution are larger than the corresponding angles with Item 32 in the two-dimensional solution. The differences are not great because this example does not have item arrows that project on top of each other when the lower dimensional solution is used. The small differences suggest that although the clustering of items based on the angle between item vectors is useful for investigating dimensionality, this type of analysis does not give conclusive information about the required number of dimensions. It is only when there is a major difference in the solution that it is clear that it means that the higher number of dimensions is needed.

The cluster analyses dendrograms for the two examples are shown in Fig. 7.11. The upper panel gives the results for the three constructs in two dimensions and the lower panel gives the corresponding results for the three constructs in three dimensions. In both cases, the three sets of items are clearly and accurately identified. This is in contrast to the results from DETECT presented in Sect. 7.2.2 where only two clusters were identified for the case with three constructs in three dimensions.

The vertical axes in Fig. 7.11 are a function of the sum of the squared distance between the items in one cluster and those in another. The values on the axes can not be directly converted into an angle measure. For example, in the lower panel, the average angle between the items with numbers 1 – 10 and those with item numbers

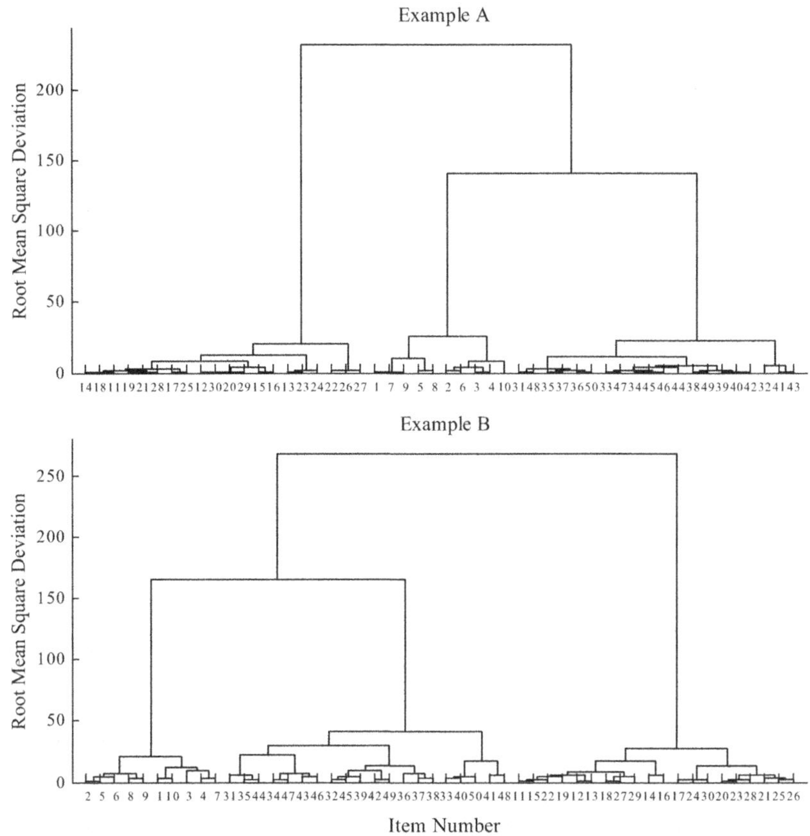

Fig. 7.11 Dendrograms for cluster analyses of Examples A and B

from 31 to 50 is about 40°, but the connecting line between the two item clusters is at 165.4. That value depends on the squared angles and the number of items in the cluster.

The results of a clustering of the angles between test items on a real test cannot be expected to be as precise as those from simulated data. The clusters from the two-dimensional solution of the grade 6 mathematics test are given in Fig. 7.12.

The results in Fig. 7.12 show that there is a fairly clear clustering of the items in the test, but that the clustering does not match well with the subjective classification of test items by content. With the exception of the items labeled "D", Data Analysis and Probability, the single content areas do not fall within a distinct cluster. The other content areas are "M", Measurement, "G", Geometry and Spatial Sense, "N", Number Sense and Numeration, and "P", Patterning and Algebra. A detailed analysis of the content of the items might give a better explanation for the clustering. Better yet would be information from the students about how they approached each

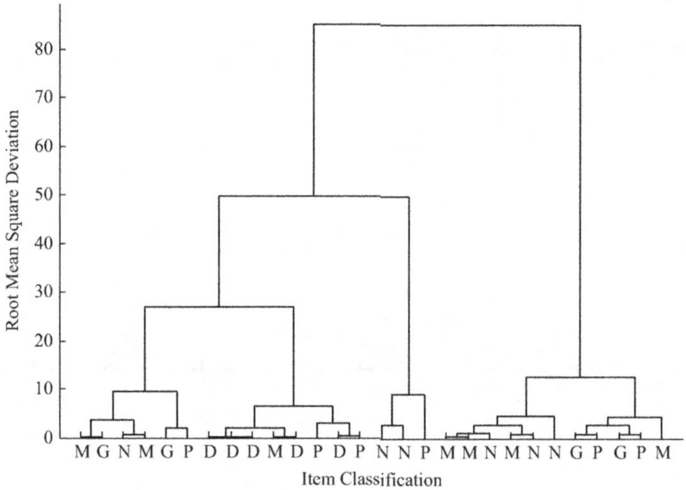

Fig. 7.12 Dendrogram for clustering of grade 6 mathematics test items

test item. This clustering is based on the similarity of the way in which students responded to the items. The way that students approach the items might not be the same as the way that the persons writing the items intended.

The angles between the items in the two major clusters tend to be about 30° to 50° apart. This amount of separation corresponds to correlations between reference composites of .6 or .7. This level of correlation is not surprising for the content within a mathematics test. It would be expected that students would learn all of the content together as part of the classroom instruction. Within the clusters, the angles between items are much smaller, usually varying from almost perfect alignment in direction to a few degrees between the item vectors. The results support reporting three or four subcontent areas within the test, but they do not seem to match up with the content classifications supplied by the writers of the test items.

7.4 Confirmatory Analysis to Check Dimensionality

The analysis procedures described in previous sections were exploratory in the sense that directions of best measurement of test items were not specified in advance of doing the analysis. The DIMTEST and DETECT procedures do allow prespecification of test items to clusters yielding a check on how well the data in the item-score matrix conform to the hypothesized structure. Other programs such as NOHARM and ConQuest provide options for either fixing parameters at specified values or indicating which a-parameters should be set to zero. These confirmatory procedures are often used to check hypotheses of a dimensional structure when a test has been designed to measure specific constructs. The simulated test in Example A of Sect. 7.2 is used here to demonstrate the confirmatory approach using the NOHARM software. Recall that this simulated test had three clusters of test items, but the clusters can be represented in a two-dimensional coordinate system.

Because there are three specific item types in the test, an initial confirmatory analysis might be to specify each of the item sets as defining a construct and hypothesizing a three-dimensional orthogonal coordinate system with each item set aligned with one of the coordinate axes. That means that the confirmatory analysis will set two of the a-parameters for each item to 0 and allow one to be nonzero. The correlation between the coordinates for the persons would also be set to zero and the units for the dimensions would be fixed by setting the standard deviations of each of the coordinates to 1.0.

The results of that analysis resulted in a sum of squared (SS) residuals of .06 and a root mean square of residuals (RMSE) of .0211. These measures of fit might seem small, but they are averages over 1225 values in the lower diagonal of product moment matrix and the averaging may hide some clusters of relatively high residuals. As a formal hypothesis test of whether the residuals are from a MIRT model that fits the data, Gessaroli et al. (1996) developed an approximate χ^2 test of fit. Their procedure converts the residual matrix from the NOHARM output into estimated residual correlations and then converts those correlations to z-scores using the Fisher r to z transformation. Finally, these z-scores are squared and summed over the lower diagonal matrix. The result is a χ^2 distributed fit measure with degrees of freedom equal to $^1/_2 \quad I\,(I-1)-t$, where I is the number if test items in the analysis and t is the number of independent parameters being estimated. In the current example, the number of test items is 50 and the number of parameters being estimated is one a-parameter per item and one d-parameter per item, so $t = 100$. The total degrees of freedom is $1,225 - 100 = 1,125$.

The χ^2 value for this initial confirmatory analysis of the data was very large (see Table 7.14) so it seems logical to free some parameters to improve the fit. The clusters of items might not be orthogonal to each other so allowing nonzero correlations among the coordinates seems to be a good next step in the confirmatory analysis. The results for the solution with correlated coordinates are a substantial improvement over the orthogonal solution. The SS residuals and RMSE are much

Table 7.14 Fit measures for successive models of the two-dimensional, three-cluster simulated data

	Analysis model			
	3d orthogonal	3d oblique	2d orthogonal	2d oblique
χ^2	55,697	1410	4056	1264
df	1125	1122	1105	1104
p	.00	.00	.00	.00
χ^2/df	49.51	1.26	3.67	1.15
SS	.06	.02	.04	.01
RMSE	.021	.004	.006	.003

smaller than the three-dimensional orthogonal solution and the χ^2 value is much smaller as well. The significance level for the χ^2 statistics still indicates that the residuals are significantly larger than those for a perfectly fitting model, but the χ^2 divided by the degrees of freedom is 1.26, a value that would be considered as good fit in the structural equation model literature. Overall, this three dimensional solution might be considered as doing a good job of representing the relationships in the data and this solution might be accepted. The only part of the result that might raise some further questions about the appropriateness of the three dimensional model is the high intercorrelations between the coordinates on the third dimension and those from the other two dimensions. The correlations between the coordinates are given in the correlation matrix $\begin{bmatrix} 1 & .30 & .78 \\ .30 & 1 & .82 \\ .78 & .82 & 1 \end{bmatrix}$.

Because the correlations of the coordinates for the third dimension were so high with the other two dimensions, the items assumed to measure that dimension were allowed to have nonzero a-parameters on the other two dimensions. First, this was tried with the constraint that the coordinates were uncorrelated. This is the "2d orthogonal" column of the table. These results were worse fitting than the "3d oblique" solution but better than the "3d orthogonal" solution. Because relaxing the constraint on the correlation between coordinates improved fit when specifying three dimensions, the same approach was taken for two-dimensions. These results are given in the last column of the table and the give slightly better fit than the "3d oblique" solution.

The fit of the two cases with correlated coordinates is so close that either could be considered as acceptable models for the data. Because the data were generated assuming two-dimensions, this demonstrates a point made in an earlier chapter that data that are well modeled in m dimensions can always be well modeled in $m + 1$ dimensions.

Confirmatory analyses seldom have the luxury of knowing the correct solution as a means of judging the quality of the result. A more realistic example of the confirmatory approach is shown here using the data from the sixth grade mathematics test that was analyzed using cluster analysis earlier in this chapter (see Sect. 7.3 and Fig. 7.12). This test was constructed to cover material from five content domains. Therefore, a logical first confirmatory analysis might be to hypothesize that each of the five content domains measure orthogonal components. For the analysis, each item was constrained to have a nonzero a-parameter on one coordinate dimension and zero values on all others. The correlations between the coordinates for the locations of the examinees were also fixed at zero. The results for the NOHARM analysis using this set of constraints are given in Table 7.15. The results show poor fit using all criteria.

A logical next step might be to remove the constraints on the correlations. It seems unlikely that a test of mathematics would have zero correlations between numerical computation skill and a data analysis skill, for example. This analysis allowing correlated coordinates dramatically improves the fit of the model to the

Table 7.15 Fit measures for successive models of the two-dimensional, three-cluster simulated data

	Analysis model				
	5d orthogonal	5d oblique	4d oblique	3d oblique	4d clusters
χ^2	48,298	735.92	735.84	759.55	616.04
df	322	312	316	319	316
p	0	0	0	0	0
χ^2/df	150.00	2.35	2.33	2.39	1.95
SS	.405	.0057	.0057	.0059	.0049
RMSE	.0327	.0039	.0039	.0039	.0036

data. The results of this analysis are presented in the second data column of Table 7.15. Although the fit is very good for this confirmatory analysis, the estimated correlations between coordinates were very high and one estimate between the first and third coordinate was 1.002. A conclusion form these results might be that the first two content domains were measuring essentially the same set of skills even thought they were labeled "Measurement" and "Number Sense and Numeration." To check this hypothesis, another confirmatory analysis was run with the items from these two content categories coded to be measuring the same dimension yielding a four dimensional model. Correlations between the coordinates remained unconstrained.

The results for the four dimensional solution are also given in Table 7.15. The fit of this model is essentially the same as that for the five-dimensional model indicating that there was no reduction in the recovery of the relationships in the data. The correlations between the coordinates for the four-dimensional model were also very high, but none reached the level of 1.00. The correlation matrix is $\begin{bmatrix} 1 & .93 & .88 & .92 \\ .93 & 1 & .90 & .96 \\ .88 & .90 & 1 & .93 \\ .92 & .96 & .93 & 1 \end{bmatrix}$. To check if an even simpler model might be appropriate, the test items for the second and forth dimensions were combined into a single set to produce a three-dimensional confirmatory solution. This model had slightly worse fit than the four-dimensional model. This supports a conclusion that the four-dimensional model is the best of those considered.

There is always a concern when doing confirmatory analyses of matrices of item response data that the results are dependent on the subjective judgments of those doing the classification of items into content categories. Those classifications are based on the expert judgments of content experts and those individuals might not approach the test items in the same way as a 6th grade student. As a basis for comparison, the confirmatory analysis was repeated using the results of the cluster analysis for the data shown in Fig. 7.12. The items were classified into four clusters based on the diagram. These fit statistics for this model are shown in the last column of Table 7.15. The fit of the confirmatory model based on the cluster analysis is notably better than that for the four-dimensional solution based on the subjective classifications of items into clusters. This is not a surprising result because the clusters were based on the same set of data that was used for judging fit. It does raise some concerns about the judgmental classification of test items into content categories. It is wise to look for support for the validity of the classifications using some exploratory analyses or other sources of evidence.

7.5 Concluding Remarks

This chapter presents a conceptual framework for considering the problem of deciding on the number of dimensions needed when analyzing the matrix of item responses. The number of dimensions is considered to be the same as the number of orthogonal coordinate axes and not the number of constructs assessed by a test. The number of constructs is the number of reference composites defined by meaningful clusters of test items in a test. These clusters of test items should have characteristics that result in close approximations to the requirements for coherence. From a practical perspective, the number of coherent sets of test items also indicates the number of meaningful subscores that can be provided for the test. Of course, for subscores to be useful, the locations of persons along the continua defined by the corresponding reference composites must be determined with a sufficient degree of accuracy or reliability. Generally, the number of coordinate axes needed to describe the structure of the data from the interaction of persons with the test items is less than or equal to the number of coherent item sets in the test. The number of coordinate axes is less then the number of coherent item sets when the directions for the reference composites based on some test item sets fall within the same plane.

Along with providing a conceptual framework, this chapter describes a number of methods for deciding on the number of coordinate axes needed to represent the relationships in the data matrix. The recommended approach is to first determine if the hypothesis that the data can be modeled with a unidimensional item response theory model is rejected. DIMTEST is a good procedure for testing this hypothesis. If the hypothesis is rejected, then there are a number of procedures for determining the number of coordinate axes (e.g., the number of θs to estimate) for further analysis. In general, it is somewhat better to slightly overestimate the number of coordinate axes rather than underestimate them because of the danger of projecting item sets and person locations into the same location when in reality they differ in important ways. The price for overestimating the number of coordinate axes is an increase in the amount of estimation error.

The final section of the chapter describes a method for identifying the coherent sets of items using cluster analysis. Research on clustering procedures has been promising, but much more needs to be done in this area. There are many clustering methods and there are even more measures of the similarity of items. It is likely that these methods will be refined in the future. However, use of the methods described in this chapter should give fairly good information about the functioning of the items on a test.

7.6 Exercises

1. Fifty sets of random data were simulated to have the same proportion correct for each test item as a real data set. Then each data set was analyzed using principal components and the eigenvalues were obtained. The mean and standard deviation of the first through fifth eigenvalues for the simulated data were computed. The eigenvalues for the real data set were also obtained using principal components analysis. The results are presented in the table below. Given this information, how many dimensions should be used to calibrate the test items using a multidimensional item response theory procedure? Explain your answer.

Component number	Eigenvalues from the real data	Mean Eigenvalues from the simulated data	Standard deviation of Eigenvalues from the simulated data
1	9.1	1.25	.07
2	2.3	1.20	.06
3	1.5	1.15	.05
4	1.1	1.10	.06
5	.9	1.05	.05

2. A group of individuals are distributed exactly along a line in three-dimensional space. The line has the following angles in degrees with the coordinate axes: 65.91, 54.74, 45. The line runs through the origin of the three-dimensional space and the distribution of the individuals along that line is normal with mean 0 and standard deviation 1. What are the distributions of the coordinates of the individuals for each of the coordinate axes? What is the correlation between the three coordinates for the individuals? Show the correlation matrix for the three coordinates.

3. A psychometrician is interested in determining whether the matrix of item response that was obtained from administering a test to 5,000 individuals can be adequately fit by a unidimensional IRT model. The psychometrician used the DIMTEST program to check for significant violations of the unidimensionality assumption. The T_L statistic for the matrix of responses was 30.1. The test statistic was also computed for 100 matrices of simulated data of the same size. The mean value of those 100 replications was 14.4. What is the final test statistic for checking whether the unidimensionality assumption has been violated? What does this statistic say about the assumption of unidimensionality for the analyses of this data matrix?

4. All of the test items in a test require capabilities on three distinct, but correlated constructs to answer them correctly. The item-score matrix from the test was analyzed with a unidimensional IRT model and three of the examinees' $\boldsymbol{\theta}$-estimates are: 2.58, −.87 and −1.54. The reference composite for this test has angles with the coordinate axes of 67.6, 52.1, and 46.3 respectively. If all three of these examinees fall exactly on the reference composite, what are there coordinates in the three dimensional coordinate system?

5. What is the logical progression that is suggested for determining the number of coordinate dimensions needed to model the relationships in a matrix of item scores? What is the difference between non-parametric and parametric procedures used to decide of the number of coordinate dimensions for an analysis?

6. What is the required first step when using the DETECT procedure for determining the number of coordinate axes to use in an analysis? Suppose that you plan to analyze the data from a 30-item test of knowledge of world geography. How would you implement this first step?

7. Develop your own example of a case where the number of item clusters is greater than the number of coordinate axes needed to model the data accurately. Explain why fewer coordinate axes than item clusters is adequate for this case.

8. Consider the following variance/covariance matrix: $\begin{bmatrix} .1670 & .2362 & .2892 \\ .2362 & .3340 & .4091 \\ .2892 & .4091 & .5010 \end{bmatrix}$. Determine the correlation matrix that corresponds to this variance/covariance matrix. What can you infer about the number of coordinate axes needed to uniquely identify the locations of individuals whose coordinate vectors were used to generate this matrix?

9. Table 7.6 shows the correlations between θs used to generate data based on three coordinates for each examinee and the estimated θs in three dimensions. Note that the correlations among the θs used to generate the data are all near 0 and correlations computed from the estimates are moderately high. Explain why this is the case. Does the difference in correlations indicate that the TESTFACT analysis does not adequately fit the data? Explain your answer.

10. Explain the meaning of Theorem 2 in a way that would make sense to a person who has taken only one course in educational testing. What implication does the theorem have for relating test results from one grade level to the next grade level when the content of the tests changes somewhat?

11. The set of test items shown in Fig. 7.7 requires three coordinate axes to adequately model the relationships among them. Give an example of a situation when the administration of these test items would result in a matrix of item scores that could be well modeled by a unidimensional IRT model. Explain why your example would lead to that result.

12. Under what circumstances does DETECT tend to underestimate the number of item clusters suggested by a matrix of item scores? Describe the characteristics of a set of test items that you believe would result in not identifying a set of test items as belonging to a cluster.

13. Specify a model and two sets of item parameters that are not equal to each other that will make the two sets of items coherent. Show some of the orbits for the two items that demonstrate the property of coherence.

Chapter 8
Transforming Parameter Estimates to a Specified Coordinate System

All measurement systems have some arbitrariness to them. When length is measured, the size of the unit used is arbitrary. Length units can be chosen from feet, meters, miles, light years, etc. The origin of the length measurements is usually set at true 0 and measurements using different units are typically linear transformations of each other.[1] A common exception is astronomical measurements of distance that are taken from some arbitrary origin such as the Sun or the center of the Milky Way Galaxy. Although measurements of length are much easier to understand than the measurements that result from the applications of IRT models, some of the same concepts can be used for both types of measurements. For example, the concepts of invariance and indeterminacy that are often discussed in the IRT literature also apply to length measurement. The unit of the measurement for length is indeterminate but the length itself is invariant. The length being measured does not change because different units of measurement are used, but there is nothing in the measurement of length that indicates that one unit of measurement is more "correct" than any other unit of measurement. Some units might be more convenient than others such as using Angstroms when measuring things at the atomic level instead of miles, but that does not make them more correct.

MIRT models have the same problems of indeterminacy as other measurement systems. Because of the multidimensional nature of these models, the analogy to physical measurement is more appropriate to the way that stars are located in the night sky than to simple length measurement. At least for relatively short time spans, stars are assumed to have invariant locations and star guides give information about how to locate individual stars. This is complicated by the fact that our viewing platform, the Earth, is moving so stars seem to have different locations at different times of the year. The viewer's location on the Earth is also important because some stars can only be seen from the Northern Hemisphere and others only from the Southern Hemisphere. Despite all of these complexities, stars can be located using a relatively simple coordinate system. The coordinates from a particular location at a particular time of year are the distance above the horizon in a specified direction. This is the coordinate system used with success by amateur star gazers.

[1] When objects are extremely different in length, they are sometimes measured on a logarithmic scale and there are some special cases when negative lengths make sense. Those special cases are not considered here.

M.D. Reckase, *Multidimensional Item Response Theory*, Statistics for Social and Behavioral Sciences, DOI 10.1007/978-0-387-89976-3_8,

© Springer Science+Business Media, LLC 2009

Professional astronomers use multiple systems for indicating the locations of stars. They can be located relative to a reference plane that is the equator of the Earth, or a reference plane that is the plane of the Solar System, or a reference plane that is the plane of the Milky Way Galaxy, or other options. The coordinate system that is used to locate points in space is arbitrary and more a matter of convenience than a specific characteristic of the points being located. At this time, coordinate systems for locating stars are standardized so astronomers can easily communicate locations of objects with each other. However, if different researchers use different coordinate systems, it is important that it be possible to translate among them so that results can be compared.

For MIRT, there is no standard coordinate system. As was mentioned in Chap. 6, persons developing estimation programs select their own system of convenience for setting up a coordinate system. One typical method is to set the origin of the solution space to have a mean $\boldsymbol{\theta}$-vector as the $\mathbf{0}$-vector. This is roughly equivalent to considering the Earth as the center of the coordinate system for locating objects in the Solar System during the Middle Ages. This same approach is also used for many unidimensional IRT calibration programs when the mean θ-estimate is set to 0.

Another common choice in the development of MIRT estimation programs is to use the standard deviation of coordinates along a coordinate axis as the unit of measurement for that axis. This parallels what is often done in unidimensional IRT calibration programs. This choice of unit keeps the measurements along an axis within a reasonable range of numbers, typically -3 to 3. The selection of unit of measurement in this way is similar to using miles for local distance measurements, but using parsecs for measurements of distance in the Solar System and light years for distances between stars. These selections of units make the numerical values reasonable in size. There are no generally accepted units for the axes of an MIRT solution so different estimation programs can set them in different ways.

A third arbitrary decision that is commonly made in estimation programs is that the correlations between coordinates be fixed at zero. This is done for the convenience of the statistical estimation procedures – it makes estimation simpler. Using the constraint on the correlations places the axes of the coordinate system in a particular orientation. This is similar to choosing the plane of the Earth's equator, or the Solar System, or the galaxy to set several of the axes for star locations. The original coordinate system obtained using the constraint on correlations can be rotated to yield coordinates that better represent the constructs being assessed. These rotations do not change the locations of the people in the space, but they may simplify interpretations of the results of MIRT analyses. There is no unidimensional IRT parallel to selecting an orientation for the coordinate axes in MIRT because there is only a single scale. There is no rotational indeterminacy for unidimensional IRT models.

The purpose of this chapter is to consider what is invariant and what is arbitrary in defining a coordinate system for representing the person locations and item characteristics based on MIRT models. These locations and characteristics are given by the parameters of the models. The approach taken in this chapter is to first show how the parameters of the MIRT models change with changes in the coordinate system selected for the solution. Then, methods for converting parameter estimates to a specified coordinate system are considered. These methods will be important in Chap. 9 where putting calibration information from different tests into the same multidimensional coordinate system is considered. That chapter also discusses how to select an appropriate coordinate system. The methods in this chapter are important for test equating and creating item pools for computerized adaptive testing.

8.1 Converting Parameters from One Coordinate System to Another

To show the consequences of selecting different coordinate systems on the parameters from an MIRT model, a series of examples will be presented related to each type of indeterminacy that is present in an MIRT model – placement of the origin, selection of units of measurement along axes, and orientation of the axes. In all cases, the location of the persons and the characteristics of the items will be assumed to be invariant. That is, proficiencies and other characteristics of the persons will remain constant and the sensitivity of items to differences in persons' characteristics will be the same. The result is that the item–person interaction is invariant resulting in the same probability of response for the person to the test item. The invariance property of the MIRT models means that the probabilities of the selected response do not change with change in the coordinate system. The indeterminacies of the MIRT models mean that results in different coordinate systems are equally good and it is up to the user to determine what origin, units, and orientation of axes are most convenient for a particular application.

Two sets of parameters will be used for all of the examples in this section of the chapter. One set of parameters is based on the assumption that differences in persons can be accurately represented in a two-dimensional space. This set consists of the locations of ten persons in the space and the characteristics of two test items that are sensitive to differences among the ten persons. For the examples, the multidimensional extension of the two-parameter logistic model is assumed to accurately represent the item–person interactions. The person locations in a space that has a multivariate normal distribution for the full population of examinees with a mean vector of $\mathbf{0}$ and an identity matrix for the variance–covariance matrix are given in Table 8.1. Note that even though the persons were sampled from a population with a standard normal distribution, the means are not exactly 0, the standard deviations are not exactly 1.0, and the correlation is not 0. This is the result of sampling variation when ten examinees are sampled from a much larger population. The item parameters for the two items are given in Table 8.2.

The locations of each of the ten persons and the item vectors for the two items are shown in Fig. 8.1. Item 1 is represented by the arrow that shows better differentiation among persons along the θ_2-axis. Item 2 distinguishes persons in a direction that is between the two axes. The persons are randomly scattered over the $\boldsymbol{\theta}$-plane.

The invariant part of the model is the probability of correct response of each person to each item. These probabilities for these ten simulated persons and the

Table 8.1 Person locations in the two-dimensional space

Person	θ_1	θ_2
1	−.43	−.36
2	−1.67	−1.89
3	.13	.49
4	.29	.70
5	−1.15	−.29
6	1.19	−.59
7	1.19	−1.23
8	−.04	3.02
9	.33	1.61
10	.17	.10
Mean	.00	.16
Standard deviation	.90	1.41
Correlation	.19	

Table 8.2 Item parameters for two items in the two-dimensional space

Item	a_1	a_2	d	A	B	α_x	α_x
1	.26	.97	−.5	1	.5	75	15
2	.92	.77	.6	1.2	−.5	40	50

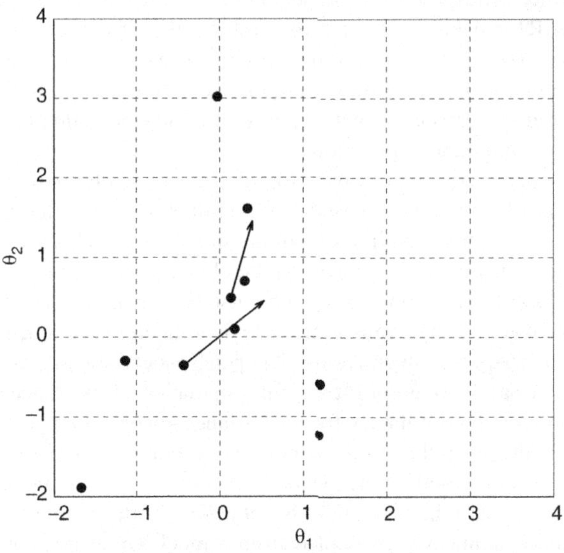

Fig. 8.1 Locations of persons and items in initial coordinate system

two items are given in Table 8.3. These probabilities show that Item 2 is generally easier than Item 1 (the B-parameter is −.5) and Person 2, who is low on both θ-coordinates, has low probabilities of correct responses on both items. With transformations of the parameters of the models, these probabilities should remain the

Table 8.3 Probabilities of correct response for each person for each item

Person	Item 1	Item 2
1	.28	.48
2	.06	.08
3	.50	.75
4	.56	.80
5	.25	.34
6	.32	.78
7	.20	.68
8	.92	.95
9	.76	.89
10	.41	.70

Table 8.4 Person locations in a five-dimensional space

Person	θ_1	θ_2	θ_3	θ_4	θ_5
1	−.43	−.36	1.30	.12	−1.24
2	−1.67	−1.89	.27	−.43	−.22
3	.13	.49	−.16	−.07	−.21
4	.29	.70	.03	.44	.08
5	−1.15	−.29	.99	.37	−.11
6	1.19	−.59	−1.36	2.25	−.11
7	1.19	−1.23	.98	.72	.90
8	−.04	3.02	−.89	.24	.76
9	.33	1.61	−.36	.32	.16
10	.17	0.10	−.14	1.86	−.20
Mean	.00	.16	.07	.58	−.02
Standard deviation	.90	1.41	.85	.84	.59
			Correlations between coordinates		
θ_1	1.00				
θ_2	.19	1.00			
θ_3	−.40	−.47	1.00		
θ_4	.63	−.07	−.45	1.00	
θ_5	.41	.32	−.31	.07	1.00

same. Comparing the probabilities of item responses before and after transformations of the coordinate system is a good way to check whether the transformations have been done properly.

The second set of parameters is based on the assumption that differences in persons need a five-dimensional space to be accurately represented. Ten $\boldsymbol{\theta}$-vectors are used as examples along with five test items that are sensitive to differences in the persons. The $\boldsymbol{\theta}$-vectors for the ten persons are presented in Table 8.4 along with descriptive statistics for this sample of vectors. Note that the descriptive statistics are sometimes quite different than the population values with mean values of 0, standard deviations of 1 and intercorrelations of 0. These differences are simply the result of sampling variation.

Table 8.5 Item parameters for five items in the five-dimensional space

Item	a_1	a_2	a_3	a_4	a_5	d	A	B	α_1	α_2	α_3	α_4	α_5
1	.78	.53	.24	.01	.35	.31	1.04	−.30	41	59	76	90	71
2	.70	.22	.36	.24	.60	1.21	1.04	−1.17	48	77	70	77	55
3	.29	.36	.29	.03	.58	−.07	.79	.09	69	62	69	88	43
4	.32	.33	.17	.17	.69	−.17	.87	.20	68	68	78	78	37
5	.51	.23	.34	.07	.51	.67	.83	−.80	52	74	65	85	53

Table 8.6 Probabilities of correct response for each person and item

Person	Item 1	Item 2	Item 3	Item 4	Item 5
1	.42	.64	.34	.26	.55
2	.12	.38	.21	.18	.34
3	.64	.77	.49	.46	.66
4	.72	.85	.58	.57	.74
5	.37	.67	.43	.38	.58
6	.64	.87	.42	.52	.69
7	.76	.94	.66	.67	.86
8	.87	.88	.77	.77	.81
9	.80	.86	.65	.64	.77
10	.60	.84	.48	.52	.68

The parameters for the five items that are used as examples along with these $\boldsymbol{\theta}$-vectors are given in Table 8.5. Along with the standard item parameters, the angles with the coordinate axes are provided. Note that none of the items have angles with the coordinate axes near 0 indicating that none is sensitive to differences along a single dimension. Some of the items are not very sensitive to differences along a particular axis. For example, Item 1 has a very small a-parameter for Dimension 4. This results in a 90° angle for the item vector for that item with the θ_4 coordinate axis. The item arrow falls in the hyperplane that is orthogonal to the θ_4-axis.

As with the two-dimensional example, the only thing that is invariant about the model is the probability of correct response for each person to each item. The probabilities for the ten example persons and the five example items are given in Table 8.6. Item 2 is the easiest overall for the sample of examinees. That is consistent with the B value for that item of −1.17. Person 2 has difficulty correctly responding to all test items. That person had low θ-values on two of the dimensions.

These two sets of item- and person-parameters will be used to demonstrate the results of various transformations of the $\boldsymbol{\theta}$-space that result in invariant solutions in terms of the probabilities of item responses. Although these examples are based on the compensatory multidimensional extension of the two-parameter logistic model, the same results would be achieved with any of the models that yield linear equi-probable contours for the response probabilities.

8.1.1 Translation of the Origin of the θ-Space

The simplest conversion of parameters that maintains the invariance of the probability of item responses is the translation of the origin of the $\boldsymbol{\theta}$-space to a new location. This translation does not involve rotation of coordinate axes or change of units along the axes. The translation of the origin of the $\boldsymbol{\theta}$-space occurs quite often in the process of calibrating sets of test items and estimating the person parameters. Suppose that the persons with the parameters in Table 8.1 are included in two different calibration samples. One sample has a mean vector of $\mathbf{0}$ and an identity matrix for the variance–covariance matrix. The second sample has the same variance–covariance matrix, but the mean vector is $[2 - 1]$. That is, the second sample has a higher mean on θ_1 and a lower mean on θ_2. Suppose further that the two samples were administered the same test. If the data are analyzed with a program like TESTFACT, the estimated means for the two calibrations will both be set to the $\mathbf{0}$-vector. This way of dealing with the indeterminacy of the solution results in the translation of the results for the second sample to a set off coordinates that is not the same as the first. This will be shown by differences in the person parameter estimates for the ten persons in the example and for the item parameter estimates in the test. The effect of translation and how to convert from one set of coordinate axes will be presented through a number of examples using the parameters given earlier.

For the two-dimensional case, person locations and item vectors are presented in Fig. 8.1. What would the item- and person-parameters be if the origin of the space were moved from $(0, 0)$ to $(2, -1)$? Figure 8.2 shows the original coordinate axes with dark lines and the new coordinate axes with dotted lines. One of the points representing a person's location in the space is marked with an "X." In the original coordinate system, this person had $\boldsymbol{\theta}$ coordinates $(1.19, -.59)$. In the new coordinate system, the location of this person is given by $(-.81, .41)$. It is important to note that the person has not changed location – there is only one point representing that person in Fig. 8.1. What has changed is the location of the coordinate axes. The origin was moved two units higher on the horizontal axis. Because the person locations remain fixed, their coordinates relative to the new axis are decreased by two units. The opposite is the case for the vertical axis. The origin was moved one unit lower so the coordinates of person locations increase by one unit on the vertical axis. In general, conversion of the person location coordinates from the first set of axes to the second set of axes is given by

$$\boldsymbol{\nu}_j = \boldsymbol{\theta}_j - \boldsymbol{\delta}, \tag{8.1}$$

where $\boldsymbol{\nu}_j$ is the vector of coordinates for Person j in the new coordinate system, $\boldsymbol{\theta}_j$ is the vector of coordinates for Person j in the old coordinate system, and $\boldsymbol{\delta}$ is the vector representing the location of the new origin using the old coordinate system.

In this example, $\boldsymbol{\delta}$ is the vector $[2 - 1]$ and $\boldsymbol{\theta}$ is a 10×2 matrix of coordinates for all ten persons. The matrix equation for converting the coordinates of the person locations from the old coordinate system to the new coordinate system is

$$\boldsymbol{\nu} = \boldsymbol{\theta} - \mathbf{1}\boldsymbol{\delta}, \tag{8.2}$$

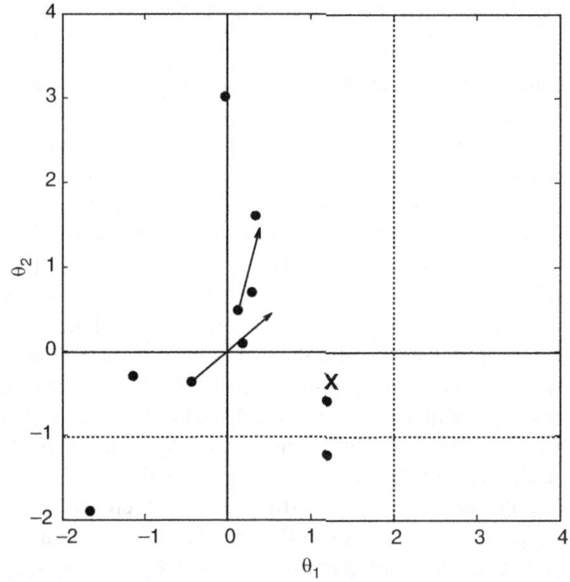

Fig. 8.2 Shift of origin of coordinate axes to (2, −1)

Table 8.7 Person locations in the two-dimensional space with the new origin

Person	θ_1		θ_2
1	−2.43		.64
2	−3.67		−.89
3	−1.87		1.49
4	−1.71		1.70
5	−3.15		.71
6	−.81		.41
7	−.81		−.23
8	−2.04		4.02
9	−1.67		2.61
10	−1.83		1.10
Mean	−2.00		1.16
Standard deviation	.90		1.41
Correlation		.19	

where **1** is a 10 × 1 vector of 1s. The results of the conversion of the coordinates in Table 8.1 are given in Table 8.7. Note that even though the mean values for each coordinate change, the standard deviations and correlation do not change. This is because there is constant shift in each axis. Also note that the change in the means is exactly equal to $\boldsymbol{\delta}$. This gives a way for determining the amount of shift in the origin of the coordinate system.

$$\bar{\boldsymbol{\theta}} - \bar{\boldsymbol{\nu}} = \bar{\boldsymbol{\theta}} - \left(\bar{\boldsymbol{\theta}} - \bar{\boldsymbol{\delta}}\right) = \bar{\boldsymbol{\delta}} = \boldsymbol{\delta}. \tag{8.3}$$

The difference in the mean values is equal to the vector of change in coordinates for the origin. Note that the mean of $\boldsymbol{\delta}$ is $\boldsymbol{\delta}$ because it is a constant.

When calibration programs like TESTFACT are run on different data sets, the amount of shift in origin is typically unknown because the programs automatically set the origin of the solution space to the $\mathbf{0}$-vector. As a result, when the locations of persons are plotted on the same set of axes from the two calibrations, it looks like the persons have shifted location rather than the origin shifting. But, if the persons are assumed to be unchanged, (8.3) can be used to determine the shift in origin. The person locations for this example for the two coordinate systems are plotted in Fig. 8.3.

Equation (8.2) can be used with any number of dimensions. For example, if the ten persons represented in Table 8.4 were calibrated with a sample that had mean values of [.2 .5 0 .1 .3] in the original coordinate system, the calibration program would set those mean values to the $\mathbf{0}$-vector and the coordinates of the same ten people in this new coordinate system would be the values given in Table 8.8.

The conversion of the item parameters to the coordinate system with the new origin is only slightly more complicated than the process for converting the person parameters. Figure 8.4 shows the person locations on the initial coordinate system along with the item vectors and the .5 equiprobable line for Item 1 in Table 8.2. The base of the item vector is on that line and it is perpendicular to it. That line shows the places in the coordinate space that have a .5 probability of correct response for the item. After conversion to the coordinate system with an origin at [2 − 1] in the

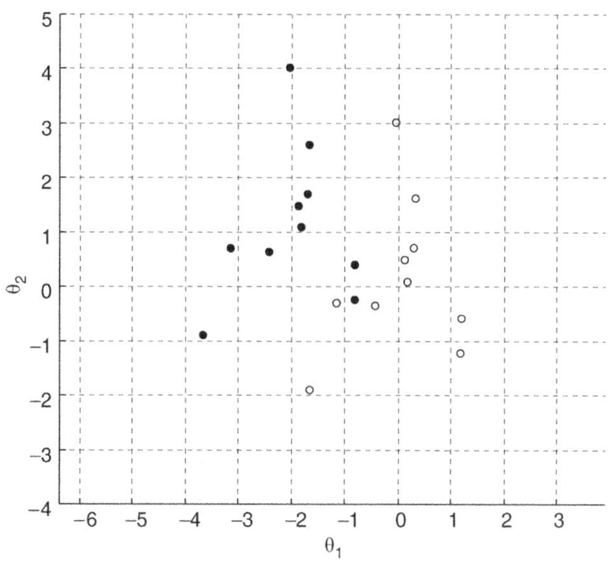

Fig. 8.3 Shift in location of person locations because of shift in origin to (2, −1). *Open circles* give original locations and *solid circles* give converted locations

Table 8.8 Five-dimensional person location after conversion to new origin

Person	θ_1	θ_2	θ_3	θ_4	θ_5
1	−.63	−.86	1.30	.02	−1.54
2	−1.87	−2.39	.27	−.53	−.52
3	−.07	−.01	−.16	−.17	−.51
4	.09	.20	.03	.34	−.22
5	−1.35	−.79	.99	.27	−.41
6	.99	−1.09	−1.36	2.15	−.41
7	.99	−1.73	.98	.62	.60
8	−.24	2.52	−.89	.14	.46
9	.13	1.11	−.36	.21	−.14
10	−.03	−.40	−.14	1.76	−.50

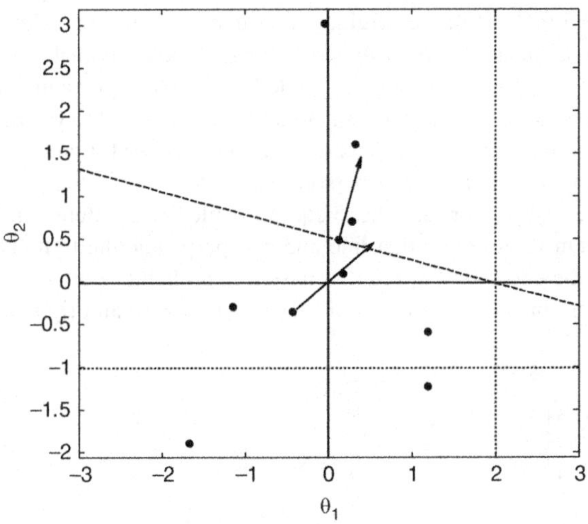

Fig. 8.4 .5 equiprobable contour for Item 1 with the original coordinate axes (*dark lines*) and coordinate axes with origin at $(2, -1)$ (*dotted lines*)

initial coordinate system, these points in the coordinate space should still have the same probability of a correct response. This is the invariance property of the MIRT model. In the initial coordinate system the equation for the line is given by

$$a_{11}\theta_1 + a_{12}\theta_2 + d = 0. \tag{8.4}$$

To yield the same results in the new coordinate system, the following substitution is made into the equation, $\theta_v = \mathbf{v}_v + \boldsymbol{\delta}_v$, where v is the index for the dimension.

$$a_{11}(v_1 + \delta_1) + a_{12}(v_2 + \delta_2) + d = a_{11}v_1 + a_{12}v_2 + d + a_{11}\delta_1 + a_{12}\delta_2. \tag{8.5}$$

Equation (8.5) shows that the change in origin requires a change in the d-parameter to maintain the invariance property of the MIRT model. The change in d-parameter is the addition of a term that is the shift in origin weighted by the a-parameter corresponding to the coordinate axis. In matrix terms, the d-parameter vector $\mathbf{d}$ converted to the new set of axes, denoted by $\tilde{\mathbf{d}}$, is shown in (8.6).

$$\tilde{\mathbf{d}} = \mathbf{d} + \mathbf{a}\boldsymbol{\delta}'. \tag{8.6}$$

The invariance property of the MIRT model indicates that as long as the parameters of the model are from the same coordinate system, the probabilities of response will remain the same. After the shift in origin, the **a**-parameters are unchanged, but the person parameters and the **d**-parameters need to be converted to the new coordinate system. The expressions in the exponent of the model, $\mathbf{a}\boldsymbol{\theta}' + \mathbf{1d}$ and $\mathbf{a}\boldsymbol{\nu}' + \mathbf{1}\tilde{\mathbf{d}}$ result in exactly the same response probabilities for all persons and items.

The original and transformed **d**-parameters and the multidimensional difficulty values are presented in Table 8.9. The shift in origin for the two-dimensional case was more along θ_1 than θ_2 so there is more effect on the d-parameter and B statistic for the item that is more sensitive to differences on the first dimension, that is, Item 2. Item 2 is notably easier in the new coordinate system. Of course, the person parameters had been reduced by two points along that dimension as a result of the conversion. These conversions of the person parameters and the item parameters balance out to result in invariance in the probability of correct response. For the five-dimensional case, the shift in difficulty parameters is fairly large, even though the shift in the location of the origin along each dimension is fairly small. It is the cumulative effect of the shift in all of the dimensions that results in the change in the difficulty parameters.

The conversion of parameter estimates from one coordinate system to another is an important activity in the application of MIRT models to practical testing problems. Test equating and the development of item banks for computerized adaptive tests are examples of such applications. If the person parameters for the same persons are available from the two coordinate systems, the shift in origin between the two coordinate systems can be determined from (8.3). Often, persons' locations from two calibrations are not available, but the item parameter estimates for the same test items from calibrations using two different coordinate systems are

Table 8.9 Original **d**-parameter vector and multidimensional difficult, **B**, for the 2- and 5- dimensional examples and values converted to the new coordinate systems

Item	2d Example				5d Example			
	d	$\tilde{d}$	B	Δ	d	$\tilde{d}$	B	Δ
1	−.5	−.97	.5	.95	.31	.84	−.30	−.81
2	.6	1.67	−.5	−1.39	1.21	1.66	−.17	−1.60
3					−.07	.35	.09	−.44
4					−.17	.28	.20	−.32
5					.67	1.05	−.80	−1.25

Note: Δ is used to represent the converted value of the B parameter.

available. It is useful to be able to determine the shift in origin of the coordinate system from the two sets of item parameter estimates. If the **a**-parameters for the item calibrations from two samples are the same, such as when ConQuest is used to analyze item response data with a specified matrix of **a**-parameters, then (8.6) can be solved for $\boldsymbol{\delta}$. The result is given in (8.7).

$$\left(\mathbf{a}'\mathbf{a}\right)^{-1}\mathbf{a}'\left(\tilde{\mathbf{d}}-\mathbf{d}\right)=\boldsymbol{\delta}'. \tag{8.7}$$

The value of $\boldsymbol{\delta}$ obtained from this equation can be used to convert item parameters for test items not in the common item set and person parameters to values in a common coordinate system.

8.1.2 Rotating the Coordinate Axes of the θ-Space

A second type of indeterminacy that is present in the compensatory MIRT models is that of the orientation of the coordinate axes. There is no correct orientation of the axes; there are only orientations for the axes that are more mathematically convenient or easier to interpret from a substantive perspective. There is a large factor analytic literature on rotations of axes to meet a variety of criteria (see, e.g., Harman 1976) and no attempt will be made to summarize all of that literature here. Rather, a general presentation will be made of orthogonal methods for rotation of axes. These methods maintain the distance and relative location of the points in the $\boldsymbol{\theta}$-space. Issues related to nonorthogonal rotations will be discussed later in this chapter.

Consider again the representation of person locations and test item characteristics in Fig. 8.1. Distances along the coordinate axes of this initial coordinate system do not have any inherent meaning related to the content of the two test items. An alternative set of axes could be defined that have a stronger connection to the content of the test items. For example, Item 2 has a direction of greatest increase of slope that is 40° from the current θ_1-axis. If the axes were rotated 40° counter-clockwise, then the new θ_1-axis would be perfectly aligned with the direction of best measurement for Item 2. Distances along the rotated axis would then be a direct measure of the composite of skills and knowledge assessed by Item 2.

Conversion of coordinates in a space to a different set of rotated coordinate axes is done by multiplication of the initial coordinates by a rotation matrix. For the two-dimensional case, the rotation matrix is given by

$$\mathbf{Rot}=\begin{bmatrix}\cos\alpha & \sin\alpha\\ -\sin\alpha & \cos\alpha\end{bmatrix}, \tag{8.8}$$

where α is the number of degrees of rotation in the clockwise direction. To rotate in the counter-clockwise direction, negative values of α are used.

The rotation to line the θ_1-axis with the direction of the item arrow for Item 2 is $-40°$ and the rotation matrix is

$$\begin{bmatrix} .7660 & -.6428 \\ .6428 & .7660 \end{bmatrix}.$$

Both the $n \times m$ matrix of $\boldsymbol{\theta}$ coordinates and the $i \times m$ matrix of **a**-parameters are postmultiplied by this rotation matrix. It is important to note that the orthogonal transformation matrix has its transpose as its inverse. Therefore, $\mathbf{Rot'Rot} = \mathbf{RotRot'} = \mathbf{I}$, the identity matrix. As a result, the exponent of the model before and after rotation has identical values after the rotation is applied to the discrimination and person parameters:

$$\mathbf{aRot}\,(\boldsymbol{\theta}\mathbf{Rot})' + \mathbf{1d} = \mathbf{aRotRot'}\boldsymbol{\theta}' + \mathbf{1d} = \mathbf{a}\boldsymbol{\theta}' + \mathbf{1d}. \tag{8.9}$$

Note that the **d**-parameter is not changed because distances from the origin are unchanged by an orthogonal rotation.

The result of the application of the rotation matrix given earlier to the coordinates and items in the two-dimensional example is shown in Fig. 8.5. Note that when the axes are rotated counter-clockwise, the person locations and item vectors are rotated clockwise relative to the axes.

Table 8.10 contains the coordinates of the ten person-locations after the rotation of the axes along with the means, standard deviations, and correlations of the coordinates. An important result of this rigid rotation is that the descriptive statistics for the coordinates do not remain the same as those in Table 8.1. The shift of origin

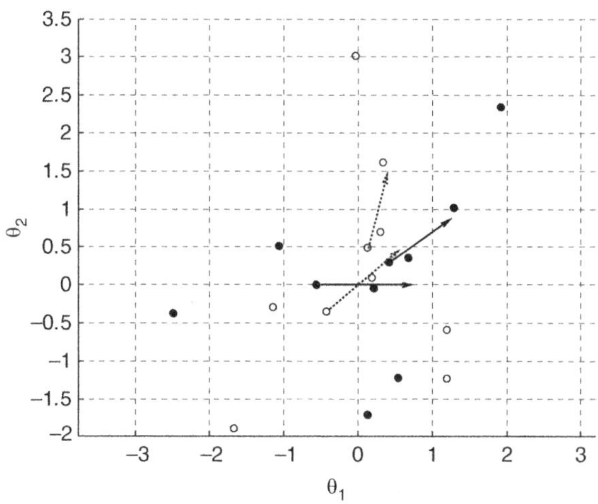

Fig. 8.5 Rotation to align Item 2 with θ_1-axis (Original locations – *open circles and dotted arrows*; New locations – *solid circles and solid arrows*)

Table 8.10 Coordinates of person locations in the two-dimensional space after rotating axes 40° in a counter-clockwise direction.

Person	θ_1	θ_2
1	−.56	.01
2	−2.49	−.38
3	.41	.30
4	.67	.35
5	−1.07	.51
6	.54	−1.22
7	.12	−1.70
8	1.91	2.34
9	1.29	1.02
10	.19	−0.04
Mean	.10	.12
Standard deviation	1.24	1.12
Correlation	.44	

shown in Table 8.7 changed only the mean values of the coordinates while leaving the standard deviations and correlations unchanged. The rotation around the same origin changes all three descriptive statistics even though the distances between the person locations do not change.

The reason for this result can be determined from the relationship between the variance–covariance matrix before and after the rotation. The variance–covariance matrix after rotation is given by $\mathbf{Rot}'\boldsymbol{\Sigma}\,\mathbf{Rot}$ (Timm 1975, p. 111). In this case, the original variance–covariance matrix for the values in Table 8.1 is

$$\begin{bmatrix} .816 & .242 \\ .242 & 1.983 \end{bmatrix}.$$

After applying the −40° rotation given earlier, the transformed variance/covariance matrix is

$$\begin{bmatrix} 1.536 & .617 \\ .617 & 1.263 \end{bmatrix}.$$

The square roots of the diagonal elements give the standard deviations in Table 8.10 and converting the covariance into a correlation gives the value of .44 given in the table. Note that the population covariance matrix was the identity matrix. When the variance–covariance matrix is diagonal with equal variances in the diagonal, the rotation results in the same variance–covariance matrix. Therefore, the population variance–covariance matrix remains unchanged in this case because the data were sampled from a standard bivariate normal distribution with $\rho = 0$.

Table 8.11 contains the discrimination parameters after rotation and the multidimensional IRT statistics for the items. The d-parameter does not change with the rotation, nor do the values of A and B. The angles with the coordinate axes are quite different. Item 2 is now aligned with the θ_1-axis so the angle with that axis is 0°. Because the axes are at right angles to each other, the angle with the θ_2-axis is 90° for that item. The angles with the coordinate axes for Item 1 have also changed.

Table 8.11 Item parameters for two items in the two-dimensional space after rotation

Item	a_1	a_2	d	A	B	α_1	α_1
1	.82	.57	−.5	1.00	.50	35	55
2	1.2	0	.6	1.2	−.5	0	90

Because Item 2 is aligned with the θ_1-axis, the a_1 value is equal to A. The maximum discriminating power for the item is the same as its discriminating power along θ_1 after the rotation. An important result from this rotation is that the coordinates on θ_1 now give a direct measure of the persons on the construct measured by Item 2.

Determining angles of rotation in a higher dimensional space is much more challenging. One way to simplify the process of computing the rotation matrix is to separate a particular rotation into a series of rotations around each of the orthogonal coordinate axes. The full rotation is then the product of each of the separate rotation matrices. For an example of the development of a rotation matrix in a higher dimensional space, suppose that it is desirable to rotate the axes of the five-dimensional space containing the items in Table 8.5 so that the θ_1-axis is aligned with the item vector for Item 1.

The first step in developing the rotation matrix is to determine the angle of rotation needed in each of the planes that contain the θ_1-axis. These are the planes defined by the θ_1-axis and each of the other axes. The angle of rotation needed in each of the planes is determined by projecting the item arrow onto each of the planes, or hyperplanes if the number of dimensions is greater than three. The way the full rotation is developed is cumulative because the angles in different (hyper) planes are dependent on the results of the rotation within the previous plane.

The order of working with pairs of axes or planes is not unique as long as all the possible orthogonal components are included. For convenience, the example will assume that the goal is to rotate the set of axes so that the θ_1-axis is aligned with the direction specified by a particular test item. However, the same procedure works to rotate the axes to match up with a direction given by a vector of direction cosigns. The process will work with the axes in numerical order so it is easy to keep track of the angles, but this is not a mathematical requirement.

The first rotation is in the θ_1, θ_2-plane. To determine the angle of rotation the angle between the projection of the item arrow onto the plane and the θ_1-axis is needed. The cosine of that angle can be computed as the ratio of the θ_1-coordinate for the base of the item arrow over the distance of the projection of the base of the arrow onto the plane. This distance is given by $\sqrt{\theta_1^2 + \theta_2^2}$. The θ-coordinates for the base of the item arrow are given by $\theta_v = B \cos \alpha_v$, where v specifies the particular coordinate axis. Therefore, the angle between θ_1 and the projection of the item arrow onto the θ_1, θ_2-plane, γ_{12}, can be computed using the following equation:

$$\gamma_{12} = \text{arc cos} \frac{B \cos \alpha_1}{\sqrt{(B \cos \alpha_1)^2 + (B \cos \alpha_2)^2}} = \text{arc cos} \frac{\cos \alpha_1}{\sqrt{\cos^2 \alpha_1 + \cos^2 \alpha_2}}. \tag{8.10}$$

Note that the Bs cancel in the expression. Further, because $\cos\alpha_v = a_v \Big/ \sqrt{\sum a_i^2}$, where the summation is over all of the a-parameters for the item, (8.11) gives another useful expression for the angle. Substituting the expression for $\cos\alpha_v$ into (8.10), the result is

$$\gamma_{12} = \operatorname{arc\,cos}\left[\frac{\dfrac{a_1}{\sqrt{\sum\limits_{i=1}^{m} a_i^2}}}{\sqrt{\dfrac{a_1^2}{\sum\limits_{i=1}^{m} a_i^2} + \dfrac{a_2^2}{\sum\limits_{i=1}^{m} a_i^2}}}\right] = \operatorname{arc\,cos}\left[\frac{a_1}{\sqrt{a_1^2 + a_2^2}}\right]. \tag{8.11}$$

The expression in the brackets on the right is not the expression for the cosine between the item arrow and the θ_1-axes because the denominator does not contain all of the elements of the **a**-vector. It is the angle between the line projected into the θ_1, θ_2-plane and the θ_1-axis.

In general, the angle of rotation needed in each of the θ_1,θ_v-planes is given by

$$\gamma_{1v} = \operatorname{arc\,cos}\left[\frac{\sqrt{\sum\limits_{i=1}^{v-1} \cos^2\alpha_i}}{\sqrt{\sum\limits_{i=1}^{v} \cos^2\alpha_i}}\right] = \operatorname{arc\,cos}\left[\frac{\sqrt{\sum\limits_{i=1}^{v-1} a_i^2}}{\sqrt{\sum\limits_{i=1}^{v} a_i^2}}\right], \qquad \text{for } v = 2,\ldots,m. \tag{8.12}$$

Equation (8.12) results in $m - 1$ angles of rotation; one in each of the planes defined by pairing the θ_1-axis with each of the other axes. Note that while the form of (8.12) is the same for each coordinate axis, v, the number of terms in the summations changes as the angle with each axis is computed. This indicates that the order of applications of the rotations is important. The second angle is the amount of rotation after the first rotation has been completed. For example, if the goal is to rotate the θ_1-axis to coincide with the item arrow for Item 1 in Table 8.5 with **a**-vector [.78 .53 .24 .01 .35], then the angles of rotation computed using (8.12) are 34°, 14°, .59°, and 20° and they need to be applied in that order.

The rotation matrix for the rotation in each plane is similar to (8.8). The matrix is an $m \times m$ identity matrix with four cells replaced by the following values: cell 11 by $\cos -\gamma_{1v}$, cell $1v$ by $\sin -\gamma_{1v}$, cell $v1$ by $-\sin -\gamma_{1v}$, and cell vv by $\cos -\gamma_{1v}$. The negative angles are used to determine the rotation matrices because the axes are rotated to align with the item rather than rotating the item to align with the axes. It seems more logical to consider the locations of persons and items to be fixed in the space and the orientation of the axes to be arbitrary than to consider the items and persons moving each time parameters are estimated.

The four rotation matrices for this example are

$$\begin{bmatrix} .83 & -.56 & 0 & 0 & 0 \\ .56 & .83 & 0 & 0 & 0 \\ 0 & 0 & 1 & 0 & 0 \\ 0 & 0 & 0 & 1 & 0 \\ 0 & 0 & 0 & 0 & 1 \end{bmatrix}, \begin{bmatrix} .97 & 0 & -.25 & 0 & 0 \\ 0 & 1 & 0 & 0 & 0 \\ .25 & 0 & .97 & 0 & 0 \\ 0 & 0 & 0 & 1 & 0 \\ 0 & 0 & 0 & 0 & 1 \end{bmatrix}, \begin{bmatrix} .9999 & 0 & 0 & -.01 & 0 \\ 0 & 1 & 0 & 0 & 0 \\ 0 & 0 & 1 & 0 & 0 \\ .01 & 0 & 0 & .9999 & 0 \\ 0 & 0 & 0 & 0 & 1 \end{bmatrix},$$

and

$$\begin{bmatrix} .94 & 0 & 0 & 0 & -.34 \\ 0 & 1 & 0 & 0 & 0 \\ 0 & 0 & 1 & 0 & 0 \\ 0 & 0 & 0 & 1 & 0 \\ .34 & 0 & 0 & 0 & .94 \end{bmatrix}.$$

These matrices can be applied individually in the sequence shown to perform the rotation on the item parameters and the $\boldsymbol{\theta}$-vectors, or they can be multiplied together using matrix multiplication to obtain a single rotation matrix,

$$\mathbf{Rot} = \prod_{i=2}^{v} \mathbf{Rot}_{1i}, \tag{8.13}$$

where $\mathbf{Rot}_{1i}$ is the rotation matrix within the plane of θ_1 and θ_i. The order of the multiplication is important. Multiplying the rotations together in a different order will not give the desired result. For this example, the full rotation matrix is

$$\begin{bmatrix} .75 & -.56 & -.20 & -.01 & -.27 \\ .51 & .83 & -.14 & -.01 & -.18 \\ .23 & 0 & .97 & -.00 & -.08 \\ .01 & 0 & 0 & 1.00 & -.00 \\ .34 & 0 & 0 & 0 & .94 \end{bmatrix}.$$

The item and person parameters after rotation are obtained by postmultiplying the **a** and $\boldsymbol{\theta}$ matrices by the rotation matrix, **a Rot** and $\boldsymbol{\theta}$**Rot**. The results of the application of the rotation to the **a**-matrix are given in Table 8.12 and the results for the $\boldsymbol{\theta}$-matrix are given in Table 8.13.

Table 8.12 Discrimination parameters after rotating to align θ_1-axis with the most discriminating direction for Item 1

Item number	a_1	a_2	a_3	a_4	a_5
1	1.04	−.00	−.00	.00	−.00
2	.92	−.21	.17	.23	.31
3	.66	.14	.17	.03	.38
4	.68	.09	.06	.17	.49
5	.76	−.10	.19	.07	.27

Table 8.13 $\boldsymbol{\theta}$-vectors after rotating the θ_1-axis to align with the most discriminating direction for Item 1

Person	θ_1	θ_2	θ_3	θ_4	θ_5
1	−.61	−.05	1.40	.12	−1.09
2	−2.24	−.64	.87	−.41	.56
3	.24	.34	−.24	−.07	−.30
4	.61	.42	−.12	.44	−.13
5	−.82	.40	1.24	.38	.17
6	.26	−1.15	−1.48	2.25	−.21
7	.81	−1.68	.87	.72	.67
8	1.56	2.52	−1.27	.23	.26
9	1.04	1.15	−.64	.31	−.19
10	.09	−.02	−.19	1.86	−.25
Mean	.10	.13	.04	.58	−.05
Standard deviation	1.09	1.18	1.02	.84	.50
			Correlation		
θ_1	1.00				
θ_2	.42	1.00			
θ_3	−.64	−.37	1.00		
θ_4	.28	−.35	−.46	1.00	
θ_5	−.04	−.14	.01	−.13	1.00

A number of important results can be noted about the a-parameters after rotation. First, Item 1 has only one nonzero a-parameter. This is a result of rotating the θ_1-axis to align with the most discriminating direction for that item. A second result is that the first a-parameter for Item 1 is now equal to the multidimensional discrimination for the item, A, because the discrimination along θ_1 is the most discriminating direction. A third result is that some of the a-parameters now have negative values. That means that the probability of correct response decreases with an increase in the corresponding θ-coordinate. The rotation has resulted in a violation of the monotonically increasing assumption for the MIRT model. Although some small negative a-parameters can be tolerated in a solution, care should be taken when rotating solutions if there is an assumption of monotonically increasing functions. Although there are negative values, the values of A and B are unchanged by the rotation. The discriminating power and difficulty of the items stay the same after an orthogonal rotation of the axes.

The $\boldsymbol{\theta}$-vectors after rotation also have some interesting features. First, the means and standard deviations have changed somewhat from the values given in Table 8.4. The mean and standard deviations for θ_1 have increased and the corresponding values for some of the other θs have decreased. θ_4 is the exception. Because the a_4 parameter is near 0, the direction for Item 1 is nearly orthogonal to the θ_4-axis. As a result, the rotation in the θ_1, θ_4-plane is very close to an identity matrix so the θ_4 values are only slightly changed. Note that because θ_1 is now aligned with the most discrimination direction for Item 1, the values of θ_1 are now a direct measure of proficiency on the composite of skills and knowledge measured by that test item. These θ-values are a projection onto the line defined by the direction of best measurement for that item.

The correlations between the θ-coordinates have also changed even though an orthogonal rotation was used. For example, the correlation between θ_2 and θ_5 is now $-.14$. The coordinates from the previous orientation of the axes had a correlation of .32. The orthogonal rotation does not maintain any of these properties of the θ-coordinates. Although the values of both the a- and θ-parameters have both changed, the matrix product, $\mathbf{a}\boldsymbol{\theta}'$, has not changed. The probabilities of correct response predicted by the model are unchanged when rotated parameters are used in the model.

When MIRT calibration programs such as TESTFACT are used to obtain estimates of the item- and person-parameters, the orientation of the axes is fixed by constraints and optimization procedures built into the programs. This means that different calibration programs will probably result in coordinate systems that are not the same. Even the application of the same program to different samples of item response data from the same test may lead to different orientations for the coordinate axes. Therefore, it is important to consider how to determine the rotation needed to place axes in the same orientation. The examples given here used orthogonal rotations to change the orientation of the coordinate axes because those rotations maintain the same relative location of the person locations in the $\boldsymbol{\theta}$-space. If constant distances between person locations can be assumed for two set of axes, then it is reasonable to determine the rotation between two solutions assuming orthogonality.

A useful procedure for determining the rotation is the Procrustes methodology. This methodology is named after a Greek mythological figure who purportedly would cut off limbs that were too long, or stretch people to make them exactly fit a bed (Bulfinch 1855, p. 124). The Procrustes methodology requires the specification of a target matrix (the bed) and then determines the rotation that minimizes the squared distance between the rotated points and those in the target. The mathematical details of the Procrustes methodology are described in such texts as Gower and Dijksterhuis (2004).

The orthogonal Procrustes rotation from one matrix to a target matrix is obtained from the singular value decomposition of the matrix product of the two matrices. If the target matrix is the matrix of person location coordinates, $\boldsymbol{\theta}$, and the alternate matrix is the rotated set of coordinates, $\boldsymbol{\upsilon}$, then the singular value decomposition of the product is given by

$$\operatorname{svd}\left(\boldsymbol{\theta}'\boldsymbol{\upsilon}\right) = \mathbf{USV}', \tag{8.14}$$

where $\mathbf{S}$ is a $m \times m$ diagonal matrix with positive values in the diagonal, and $\mathbf{U}$ and $\mathbf{V}$ are $m \times m$ orthogonal matrices.

The orthogonal Procrustes rotation, $\mathbf{R}_\mathrm{P}$, to transform the values in $\boldsymbol{\upsilon}$ to values of $\boldsymbol{\theta}$ is given by

$$\mathbf{R}_\mathrm{P} = \mathbf{VU}'. \tag{8.15}$$

Because exactly the same rotation matrix was used to transform both the $\boldsymbol{\theta}$-matrix of person locations and the **a**-matrix of discrimination parameters, the singular value decomposition of the product of a target **a**-matrix and a rotated **a**-matrix can be used to compute exactly the same rotation matrix. If the target matrix of discrimination parameters is **a** and the other matrix of discrimination parameters is **å**, then parallel equations to (8.14) and (8.15) can be specified.

$$\text{svd}\left(\mathbf{a}'\mathbf{\mathring{a}}\right) = \mathbf{USV}' \quad \text{and} \quad \mathbf{R}_\text{P} = \mathbf{VU}'. \tag{8.16}$$

Under the conditions for the examples given here that do not include estimation error, the rotation matrix $\mathbf{R}_\text{P}$ will be identical when obtained from the location and discrimination matrices.

For the two-dimensional example given previously, the computation of the rotation matrix to convert the values in Tables 8.10 and 8.11 back into the values in Tables 8.1 and 8.2, respectively, can be done through the following steps:

1. $\text{svd}\left(\mathbf{a}'\mathbf{\mathring{a}}\right) = \text{svd}\left(\begin{bmatrix} .26 & .97 \\ .92 & .77 \end{bmatrix}' \begin{bmatrix} .82 & .57 \\ 1.2 & 0 \end{bmatrix}\right) = \text{svd}\left(\begin{bmatrix} 1.32 & .15 \\ 1.72 & .55 \end{bmatrix}\right).$

2. $\text{svd}\left(\mathbf{a}'\mathbf{\mathring{a}}\right) = \text{USV}' = \begin{bmatrix} -.59 & -.81 \\ -.81 & .59 \end{bmatrix} \begin{bmatrix} 2.22 & 0 \\ 0 & .21 \end{bmatrix} \begin{bmatrix} -.97 & -.24 \\ -.24 & .97 \end{bmatrix}'.$

3. $\mathbf{R}_\text{P} = \mathbf{VU}' = \begin{bmatrix} -.97 & -.24 \\ -.24 & .97 \end{bmatrix} \begin{bmatrix} -.59 & -.81 \\ -.81 & .59 \end{bmatrix}' = \begin{bmatrix} .77 & .64 \\ -.64 & .77 \end{bmatrix}.$

Note that the matrix $\mathbf{R}_\text{P}$ is the inverse of the matrix given following (8.8) that was used to perform the rotation of the axes to the new orientation. The results would be exactly the same if the location coordinates for persons had been used. The same process can be used for the five-dimensional example.

8.1.3 Changing the Units of the Coordinate Axes

Two sources of indeterminacy in the MIRT solutions for the compensatory model have been presented in the previous two sections – location of the origin of the $\boldsymbol{\theta}$-space and the orientation of the coordinate axes in that space. In both cases, the aspects of the solutions can be changed without violating the principle of invariance. The probabilities of correct response to the test items remain the same if both the item- and person-parameters are transformed in a consistent way.

There is a third type of indeterminacy in the compensatory MIRT models. That indeterminacy is the unit of measurement used along each coordinate axis. This unit of measurement is typically set by either specifying the size of the a-parameter in a program like ConQuest, or by setting the standard deviation of the location coordinates to a particular value – usually 1.0 – in programs like TESTFACT. This means that the results of different calibrations of the same set of item response data may result in different size units for the coordinate axes. For example, if the same test were administered to two different groups of examinees, one with high variance on θ_1 and the other with low variance on θ_1, a calibration program might set the θ_1-scale for both calibrations to have a standard deviation of 1 for the estimated θ_1-values. The result would be that the unit of measurement on the θ_1-axis would be larger for the first group than the second. This change in unit would result in quite different values for the item- and person-parameters estimated from the analysis of the two data sets. The same result can occur when different programs are used. The defaults for setting the units for the scales on the coordinate axes might be different resulting in estimates that appear to be quite different.

In this section, the item- and person-parameters used in the previous sections are used to show the impact of changing the units for the coordinate axes in the form of a solution. The results are shown while keeping the origin in the same location and the orientation of the axes the same so that the specific impact of changing units can be noted. In the next section, the effects of combinations of shifts in origin, rotations, and change in units are considered.

Suppose that the person location coordinates given in Table 8.1 were from a calibration of a long test to a large, well selected group of examinees. The program used to estimate the parameters of the MIRT model sets the standard deviations of the estimated values for each dimension to 1.0, thus setting the units for the coordinate axes. Later the response strings for the same ten examinees shown in Table 8.1 were used in a second analysis on a subsample of the first examinee sample, but this subsample has a restricted range on θ_1 resulting in a standard deviation that was .8 as much as the full sample, and an expansion of the range on θ_2 because of the inclusion of some extreme examinees. θ_2 had a standard deviation that is 1.4 as large as that for the full sample. How would the solution from the first sample compare to that from the second sample?

Because the calibration program sets the unit for the coordinate scale as one standard deviation, a person who had a θ_1-coordinate of .8 in the first analysis would have a coordinate of 1.00 in the second. Because the standard deviation was smaller, the units are smaller, but the numerical value of the coordinate is bigger. This is the same result as measuring height in feet or inches, or meters or centimeters. If a person is 6 ft tall, changing to the smaller inch unit results in 72 in. – a much larger number. In this case, all of the θ_1-coordinates from the first analysis would be multiplied by $1/.8 = 1.25$ to get the coordinate value from the second analysis. This is an example of *dilation* of the coordinate values.

The θ_2-coordinates for the second analysis show the opposite effect. Because the standard deviation is larger, the units on the scale will be larger. A person with a coordinate of 1.4 from the first analysis would have a coordinate of 1 in the second analysis. The coordinates in the second analysis could be obtained from the first by multiplying them by $1/1.4 = .714$. This is an example of *contraction* of the scale.

Converting the coordinates using one set of units to those using another set of units is done by multiplying by a constant. This can be done in matrix algebra by multiplying the θ-matrix by a diagonal matrix with the conversion constants in the diagonal. For the case described earlier, the scaling constant matrix is

$$C = \begin{bmatrix} 1.25 & 0 \\ 0 & .714 \end{bmatrix}$$

and the matrix equation for the transformation of units is

$$\boldsymbol{\nu} = \boldsymbol{\theta}\mathbf{C}, \tag{8.17}$$

where $\boldsymbol{\nu}$ is the matrix of coordinates after transforming the units of the coordinate scales, $\boldsymbol{\theta}$ is the matrix of original coordinates, and $\mathbf{C}$ is the diagonal matrix of scaling constants.

Table 8.14 gives the coordinates of the locations of the ten examinees from Table 8.1 after changing the units on the coordinate axes as described earlier. The means, standard deviations, and correlation for the coordinates are also provided for comparison. The means and standard deviations for the coordinates change slightly, they are both multiplied by the constant, but the correlation is unaffected by the change of scale.

It is well known that when all of the values of a variable are multiplied by a constant, the mean and standard deviations of the new values are the original means and standard deviations multiplied by the constant. This gives a method for determining the scaling values for each of the coordinate axes. The ratio of the new mean or standard deviation to the original mean or standard deviation should recover the scaling constant. That is

$$\frac{\overline{\nu}_w}{\overline{\theta}_w} = \frac{s_{\nu_w}}{s_{\theta_w}} = c_w, \tag{8.18}$$

where c_w is the diagonal element of the scaling matrix corresponding to dimension w. Either the means or the standard deviations can be used to determine the

Table 8.14 Person locations in the two-dimensional space after changing units for the coordinate axes

Person	θ_1	θ_2
1	−.54	−.25
2	−2.08	−1.35
3	.16	.35
4	.36	.50
5	−1.43	−.21
6	1.49	−0.42
7	1.49	−.88
8	−.05	2.16
9	.41	1.15
10	.22	.07
Mean	.00	.11
Standard deviation	1.13	1.01
Correlation	.19	

scaling constants, but sometimes it is more useful to use one of the statistics than the other. For example, if the coordinate values have originally been scaled to have a mean of 0, then multiplying that mean by a constant results in a 0 for the mean of the coordinates with the new units. The ratio 0/0 is not defined. In that case, using the standard deviations to determine the scaling constants will be more useful.

Determining the scaling constants using the values of the means and standard deviations from Tables 8.1 and 8.14 identify an important problem with the level of accuracy used to report the statistics. The values in the tables are rounded to two decimal places. If they are used to determine the scaling constants, values of .6875 and 1.255 might be obtained instead of .7143 and 1.25, respectively. These differences are due solely to rounding error. If the means and standard deviations were computed to more decimal places (e.g., 15), the scaling constants would be recovered with high precision.

To maintain the invariance property of the MIRT model, the item parameters must be converted after the change in unit for the coordinate axes. To determine the appropriate conversion for the item parameters, the linear exponent of the compensatory MIRT model is considered. The numerical value of that exponent must remain the same after the change in scale for the probability of response from the model to remain the same. In the case of change in units on the coordinate scales, the new scale values are given by $\boldsymbol{\nu}_{jw} = c_w \theta_{jw}$, were j is the index for person and w is the index for dimension. Then, $\theta_{jw} = \nu_{jw}/c_w$. This expression can be substituted for the θ-variables in the expression for the exponent of the model. In the simple two-dimensional case, this yields

$$a_1\theta_1 + a_2\theta_2 + d = a_1\frac{\nu_1}{c_1} + a_2\frac{\nu_2}{c_2} + d = \frac{a_1}{c_1}\nu_1 + \frac{a_2}{c_2}\nu_2 + d. \tag{8.19}$$

In this expression, the person index, j, is not included to simplify the notation. Equation (8.19) shows that, to maintain the same value of the exponent, the discrimination parameters, a_w, are divided by the corresponding scaling constant. The d-parameter is not changed. In matrix algebra terms, the **a**-parameters in the $\boldsymbol{\theta}$-space with the new units for the coordinate axes can be obtained by multiplying the original **a**-parameters by the inverse of the matrix of the scaling constants, $\mathbf{aC}^{-1}$.

The item parameters for the coordinate space with the new units on the coordinate axes are given in Table 8.15 along with the other descriptive statistics for the test items. Note that the multidimensional discrimination, A, the multidimensional difficulty, B, and the angles with the coordinate axes are all different than the values in Table 8.2. This is a very important observation because it implies that changes in

Table 8.15 Item parameters for two items in the two-dimensional space after a change in units on the coordinate axes

Item	a_1	a_2	d	A	B	α_1	α_1
1	.21	1.35	−.5	1.37	.37	81	9
2	.74	1.08	.6	1.31	−.46	56	34

the units on the scales of the coordinate axes are the equivalent of a nonorthogonal rotation of the axes. The original and new $\boldsymbol{\theta}$-locations and item vectors are shown in Fig. 8.6 to help clarify this point.

The scaling constants can be estimated from the original and converted sets of **a**-parameters just as they were from the two-sets of $\boldsymbol{\theta}$-coordinates. In theory, the scaling constants can be computed from the two sets of parameters for one item, but for estimated item parameters, the estimates of the scaling constants will be more stable based on the means of the a-parameters,

$$c_w = \frac{\bar{a}_{ow}}{\bar{a}_{nw}}, \tag{8.20}$$

where c_w is the scaling constant for coordinate axis w, a_{ow} is the original set of a-parameters for dimension w, and a_{nw} is the set of a-parameters for dimension w after change of scale.

A number of the results of the change of scale for the coordinate axes can be observed in Fig. 8.6. First, the person locations are further from the origin on the horizontal scale. That is, the variance of the $\boldsymbol{\theta}_1$-coordinates is larger as a result of the transformation. This is the dilation of the locations because of the use of a smaller unit on the θ_1-axis. Correspondingly, the locations are shifted toward the origin on the vertical scale. The variance of the θ_2-coordinates is smaller as a result of the transformation. This is the contraction of the locations because of the use of larger units on the θ_2-axis.

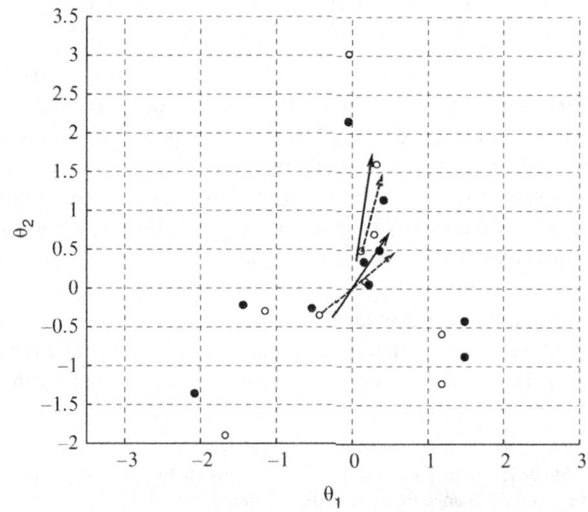

Fig. 8.6 Person locations and item arrows before and after change of scale of coordinate axes (initial locations – *circles*; new locations – *dots*: initial item arrows – *dashed lines*; new item arrows – *solid lines*)

A second result is the shift of the item arrows. The item arrow for Item 1 has shifted to be closer to the θ_2-axis and its length has increased indicating a higher level of discrimination in the direction of best measurement. The increased length reflects the increase in value of A after the change in units. Because this item is more sensitive to changes along θ_2 than θ_1, the use of larger units along θ_2 means that the test item is sensitive to smaller changes in numerical values of location along that axis. This is represented by an increase in the maximum slope for the surface for that test item. Item 1 has a slight decrease in maximum slope for the opposite reason, the use of smaller units for the θ_1-axis. Of course, the locations of the persons and the characteristics of the items have not changed. The change in the descriptive statistics for the test items is solely the result of the change in units for the coordinate axes.

The change in units for the coordinate axes is accomplished in exactly the same way for the five-dimensional case. The constants for converting from the original set of units to the new set of units are placed in the cells of a diagonal matrix that correspond to the appropriate axis. New vectors of $\boldsymbol{\theta}$-coordinates are obtained by postmultiplying the $\boldsymbol{\theta}$-matrix by the diagonal scaling matrix, **C**. The **a**-parameter matrix is postmultiplied by the inverse of the **C**-matrix.

8.1.4 Converting Parameters Using Translation, Rotation, and Change of Units

The previous three sections have discussed the three types of indeterminacy that are present in the linear compensatory MIRT models. Each was considered as a separate type of change to a coordinate system while keeping the other two types unchanged. This section considers changes to the coordinate system that use all three kinds of transformations – shift in origin, rotation of axes, and change in units on the coordinate axes. In all cases, however, four important assumptions are made.

1. The relative locations of the persons in the space defined by the MIRT model are unchanged. The only thing that is changing is the coordinate system used to describe the locations of the persons.
2. The capabilities of the test items for distinguishing among person locations remain unchanged. The statistical descriptions of the items may change because of changes in the coordinate system, but these are only different ways of describing the same characteristics.
3. As a result of 1. and 2., the predicted probability of the observed response for each person to each test item remains unchanged. This is the invariance property of the MIRT model.
4. The coordinate axes in all cases are orthogonal to each other. Only orthogonal rotations have been used to change coordinate systems.

When deciding to change the coordinate system for a solution, a decision must be made on the order that the various conversions are used. If a change in the units for the coordinate axes is made first, then a shift in the origin is made in the new units. Making the same numerical shift in the coordinates of the origin first uses the original units for the coordinate axes and a subsequent change in units, even using the same multiplicative constants, will give a different result for coordinates of points in the $\boldsymbol{\theta}$-space. Rotations of the coordinate axes are always made using the origin of the $\boldsymbol{\theta}$-space as the center of rotation. As a result, a rotation performed before a shift in the origin will result in a different solution than a rotation after a shift in the origin. If there are fixed matrices for rotation of a solution and scaling the units of the coordinate axes and a fixed vector of distances for a shift in the origin of the space, there are six possible expressions for transforming the $\boldsymbol{\theta}$-space. Each of the expressions yields a different set of numerical values for the coordinates representing the location of the same person. Although there are six representations for that location, the location itself has not changed – only the orientation of the coordinate axes and the units on the axes have changes.

The expressions for the six possible transformations are given in (8.21a) through (8.21f) with $\boldsymbol{\upsilon}$ representing the matrix of coordinates in the transformed system and $\boldsymbol{\theta}$ representing the matrix of original coordinates. The **Rot** and **C** matrices and the $\boldsymbol{\delta}$-vector have the same definitions as was used when describing the shift in the coordinate axes. The "1" in the expression is a $n \times 1$ vector of 1s used to produce a matrix with identical rows of shift values for the origin of the coordinate system.

$$\boldsymbol{\upsilon} = (\boldsymbol{\theta} - \mathbf{1}\boldsymbol{\delta})\mathbf{Rot}\mathbf{C}, \tag{8.21a}$$

$$\boldsymbol{\upsilon} = (\boldsymbol{\theta} - \mathbf{1}\boldsymbol{\delta})\mathbf{C}\,\mathbf{Rot}, \tag{8.21b}$$

$$\boldsymbol{\upsilon} = (\boldsymbol{\theta}\mathbf{Rot} - \mathbf{1}\boldsymbol{\delta})\mathbf{C}, \tag{8.21c}$$

$$\boldsymbol{\upsilon} = (\boldsymbol{\theta}\mathbf{C} - \mathbf{1}\boldsymbol{\delta})\mathbf{Rot}, \tag{8.21d}$$

$$\boldsymbol{\upsilon} = \boldsymbol{\theta}\mathbf{Rot}\,\mathbf{C} - \mathbf{1}\boldsymbol{\delta}, \tag{8.21e}$$

$$\boldsymbol{\upsilon} = \boldsymbol{\theta}\mathbf{C}\,\mathbf{Rot} - \mathbf{1}\boldsymbol{\delta}. \tag{8.21f}$$

To show the effect of each of these transformations, they have been applied to the $\boldsymbol{\theta}$-matrix given in Table 8.1. The translation, rotation, and scaling transformations are the same as were used in the two-dimensional examples in this chapter. The coordinates for each of the transformations along with the means, standard deviations, and correlations of the coordinates are given in Table 8.16.

There are a number of important results shown in Table 8.16. First, none of the transformed coordinates have the same means and standard deviations. Second, each of the six transformations yields a different set of θ-coordinates. Each of the transformations gives a uniquely different result. A third important result is the difference in correlations for the different transformations. The original correlation was .19. After the transformations, the correlations are either .44 or −.08. It is clear that quite different correlations can result from different transformations of the coordinate system.

However, there are similarities among various coordinate sets that highlight some of the features of the transformations. Transformations (a), (c), and (e) have the

Table 8.16 Coordinates before and after six different transformations in (8.21)

Person	Original		8.21a		8.21b		8.21c		8.21d		8.21e		8.21f	
1	−.43	−.36	−1.81	1.47	−2.03	2.31	−3.20	.72	−1.47	2.20	−2.70	1.00	−2.58	1.15
2	−1.67	−1.89	−4.23	1.19	−3.92	2.46	−5.62	.44	−3.35	2.35	−5.12	.73	−4.46	1.30
3	.13	.49	−.60	1.68	−1.11	2.32	−1.99	.93	−.54	2.22	−1.49	1.21	−1.65	1.17
4	.29	.70	−.27	1.72	−.86	2.31	−1.66	.97	−.29	2.20	−1.16	1.25	−1.40	1.15
5	−1.15	−.29	−2.45	1.83	−2.69	2.91	−3.83	1.08	−2.12	2.81	−3.33	1.37	−3.23	1.76
6	1.19	−.59	−.44	0.60	−.59	.88	−1.83	−.15	−.02	0.77	−1.33	.13	−1.13	−.28
7	1.19	−1.23	−.96	0.25	−.88	.53	−2.35	−.50	−.31	0.42	−1.85	−.22	−1.42	−.63
8	−.04	3.02	1.28	3.13	−.11	3.84	−.11	2.38	.46	3.73	.39	2.67	−.65	2.68
9	.33	1.61	.49	2.20	−.40	2.77	−.89	1.44	.16	2.67	−.39	1.73	−.95	1.62
10	.17	.10	−.87	1.44	−1.24	2.07	−2.26	.69	−.68	1.96	−1.76	.97	−1.79	.91
Mean	.00	.16	−.98	1.55	−1.38	2.24	−2.37	.80	−.82	2.14	−1.87	1.08	−1.93	1.08
Standard deviation	.90	1.41	1.55	.80	1.17	.95	1.55	.80	1.17	.95	1.55	.80	1.17	.95
Correlation	.19		.44		−.08		.44		−.08		.44		−.08	

same value for the correlations as do transformations (b), (d), and (f). The first three transformations use **RotC** as the multiplier of $\boldsymbol{\theta}$ while the second set use **CRot**. Within those same sets of transformations the standard deviations of the coordinates are the same as well, while different across the two sets. The reason for the different results is that the rotations are applied to results on different scales. The **RotC** transformation performs the rotation on the original $\boldsymbol{\theta}$ coordinates and then transforms the units for the coordinate axes of the results, while **CRot** transforms the units of the coordinate axes first and then does the rotation on the transformed coordinates. The different transformations of units of the coordinate axes cause the differences in the standard deviations and correlations.

To maintain the invariance properties of the MIRT model, each of these transformations of $\boldsymbol{\theta}$-coordinates must also be accompanied by a transformation of item parameters. One way to determine the transformation of the item parameters is to solve each of the equations in (8.21a) to (8.21f) for $\boldsymbol{\theta}$ and then substitute the result into the general expression in the exponent of the MIRT model, $\mathbf{a}\boldsymbol{\theta}' + \mathbf{d1}$ After the substitution, the multiplier of $\boldsymbol{\nu}$ is the transformed matrix of **a**-parameters and the summative term contains the transformed **d**-parameters. The equations in (8.22a) to (8.22f) are the exponents after the substitution for each of the equations in (8.21a) to (8.21f). Brackets have been placed around the terms that are the converted **a**- and **d**-parameters. The expressions are in pairs with the main difference in each pair being a reversal in the order of the product of **R** and **C**. The other difference in the expressions is the multiplier of **a** in the intercept term. That multiplier is dependent on whether the shift in the origin of the space occurs before, (8.22a) and (8.22b), or after a rotation or change in unit. To be consistent with the expressions in (8.21), the **1** is a $n \times 1$ vector of 1s so the transpose is a $1 \times n$ vector of 1s.

$$\left[\mathbf{a}(\mathbf{RotC})^{-1'}\right]\boldsymbol{\nu}' + \left[\mathbf{a}\boldsymbol{\delta}' + \mathbf{d}\right]\mathbf{1}', \tag{8.22a}$$

$$\left[\mathbf{a}(\mathbf{CRot})^{-1'}\right]\boldsymbol{\nu}' + \left[\mathbf{a}\boldsymbol{\delta}' + \mathbf{d}\right]\mathbf{1}', \tag{8.22b}$$

$$\left[\mathbf{a}(\mathbf{RotC})^{-1'}\right]\boldsymbol{\nu}' + \left[\mathbf{a}(\boldsymbol{\delta}\mathbf{Rot}^{-1})' + \mathbf{d}\right]\mathbf{1}', \tag{8.22c}$$

$$\left[\mathbf{a}(\mathbf{CRot})^{-1'}\right]\boldsymbol{\nu}' + \left[\mathbf{a}(\boldsymbol{\delta}\mathbf{C}^{-1})' + \mathbf{d}\right]\mathbf{1}', \tag{8.22d}$$

$$\left[\mathbf{a}(\mathbf{RotC})^{-1'}\right]\boldsymbol{\nu}' + \left[\mathbf{a}(\boldsymbol{\delta}(\mathbf{RotC})^{-1})' + \mathbf{d}\right]\mathbf{1}', \tag{8.22e}$$

$$\left[\mathbf{a}(\mathbf{CRot})^{-1'}\right]\boldsymbol{\nu}' + \left[\mathbf{a}(\boldsymbol{\delta}(\mathbf{CRot})^{-1})' + \mathbf{d}\right]\mathbf{1}'. \tag{8.22f}$$

Table 8.17 shows the original item parameters and descriptive statistics for the items from the two-dimensional item set and the transformed item parameters corresponding to each of (8.22a) to (8.22f). The transformations of the item parameters have a similar pattern to the transformation of the $\boldsymbol{\theta}$-vectors. The **d**-parameters are

Table 8.17 Initial and transformed item parameters for items in the two-dimensional space

Item	a_1	a_2	d	A	B	α_1	α_1
1	.26	.97	−.5	1	.5	75	15
2	.92	.77	.6	1.2	−.5	40	50
8.22a	.66	.80	−.95	1.04	.91	51	39
	.96	0	1.67	.96	−1.74	0	90
8.22b	1.03	.90	−.95	1.37	.69	41	49
	1.26	.35	1.67	1.31	−1.28	16	74
8.22c	.66	.80	.56	1.04	−.54	51	39
	.96	0	3.00	.96	−3.12	0	90
8.22d	1.03	.90	−1.44	1.37	1.05	41	49
	1.26	.35	.99	1.31	−.76	16	74
8.22e	.66	.80	.01	1.04	−.01	51	39
	.96	0	2.52	.96	−2.63	0	90
8.22f	1.03	.90	.65	1.37	−.48	41	49
	1.26	.35	2.76	1.31	−2.11	16	74

different in every case. There are only two different sets of **a**-parameters. These depend on the order of the product of **R** and **C**. The values of A and α follow the pattern of the **a**-parameters and B follows the pattern of the **d**-parameters.

8.2 Recovering Transformations from Item- and Person-Parameters

There are many situations when it is desirable to convert from one coordinate system to another, but the form of transformation from one set of person- or item-parameters is unknown. Perhaps the most important case when determining the form of the transformation needed is in linking of multiple calibrations to get the values of the parameter estimates in the same $\boldsymbol{\theta}$-space, or for the equating of test forms. These cases will be discussed in detail in Chap. 9. Other cases are when the recovery of parameters using various calibration programs is being investigated, or when the solutions from different calibrations programs are being compared. These areas of research require that the item- and person-parameter estimates be placed in the same $\boldsymbol{\theta}$-space before they can be compared.

Two cases will be considered in this section. The first is when two sets of $\boldsymbol{\theta}$-vectors are available for the same people. This case holds when two programs that estimate the $\boldsymbol{\theta}$-vectors are applied to the same item-score matrix, or when there are $\boldsymbol{\theta}$s used to generate data and $\boldsymbol{\theta}$-estimates are available from a program. The second case is when two sets of item-parameters are available for the same test items. This occurs when there are common items in two test forms that are separately calibrated or when an item parameter recovery study is performed.

8.2.1 Recovering Transformations from θ-vectors

Suppose that a group of individuals have been administered a very long and high quality test that allows the accurate estimation of their locations in a five-dimensional proficiency space. Because the test is long and of high quality, and the calibration program is very good, the estimates of $\boldsymbol{\theta}$-vectors are assumed to have so little error that the amount of error can be ignored. The $\boldsymbol{\theta}$-vectors are treated as error free estimates of location. However, the group of individuals has been included in two separate convenience samples that are used for calibration. Therefore, because of the way that the calibration program deals with the indeterminacy in the model, the location of the origin, orientation of the axes, and units of measurement might not be the same. The question of interest is whether the $\boldsymbol{\theta}$-vectors obtained from the two calibrations represent the same locations in the $\boldsymbol{\theta}$-space.

The first ten of the $\boldsymbol{\theta}$-vectors from the first calibration are given in Table 8.18 along with the means, standard deviations, and correlations for the coordinate estimates for each axis. The descriptive statistics are for this sample of ten observations. Because of the small sample, the correlations are not significantly different than 0 at the .05 level. This set of $\boldsymbol{\theta}$-vectors is arbitrarily selected as the base set and is labeled $\boldsymbol{\theta}_\mathbf{b}$. The goal will be to determine if the second set of $\boldsymbol{\theta}$-vectors can be transformed to be the same as the base set.

The second set of $\boldsymbol{\theta}$-vectors and their descriptive statistics are given in Table 8.19. This alternate set of $\boldsymbol{\theta}$-vectors is represented as the matrix $\boldsymbol{\theta}_\mathbf{a}$. The descriptive

Table 8.18 $\boldsymbol{\theta}$-vectors for the Base Set

Person	θ_{b1}	θ_{b2}	θ_{b3}	θ_{b4}	θ_{b5}
1	−.43	−.36	1.30	.12	−1.24
2	−1.67	−1.89	.27	−.43	−.22
3	.13	.49	−.16	−.07	−.21
4	.29	.70	.03	.44	.08
5	−1.15	−.29	.99	.37	−.11
6	1.19	−.59	−1.36	2.25	−.11
7	1.19	−1.23	.98	.72	.90
8	−.04	3.02	−.89	.24	.76
9	.33	1.61	−.36	.32	.16
10	.17	.10	−.14	1.86	−.20
Means	.00	.16	.07	.58	−.02
Standard deviations	.90	1.41	.85	.84	.59
			Correlations		
θ_{b1}	1.00				
θ_{b2}	.19	1.00			
θ_{b3}	−.40	−.47	1.00		
θ_{b4}	.63	−.07	−.45	1.00	
θ_{b5}	.41	.32	−.31	.07	1.00

Table 8.19 $\boldsymbol{\theta}$-vectors for the alternate set

Person	θ_{a1}	θ_{a2}	θ_{a3}	θ_{a4}	θ_{a5}
1	−.22	−.28	1.12	.26	−1.25
2	−1.36	−.92	.69	−.38	.24
3	.38	.15	−.20	.03	−.54
4	.64	.24	−.10	.65	−.39
5	−.36	.22	.99	.57	−.11
6	.39	−1.49	−1.19	2.82	−.46
7	.77	−2.07	.70	.98	.33
8	1.30	2.56	−1.02	.40	−.04
9	.94	1.05	−.51	.49	−.44
10	.28	−.24	−.15	2.35	−.49
Means	.28	−.08	.03	.82	−.32
Standard deviations	.76	1.30	.81	1.01	.45
			Correlations		
θ_{a1}	1.00				
θ_{a2}	.42	1.00			
θ_{a3}	−.64	−.37	1.00		
θ_{a4}	.28	−.35	−.46	1.00	
θ_{a5}	−.04	−.14	.01	−.13	1.00

statistics for the coordinates of this set of $\boldsymbol{\theta}$-vectors are quite different than those for the base set. Some of the correlations are notably different. The means and standard deviations are also different.

The question to be addressed is whether the two sets of $\boldsymbol{\theta}$-coordinates represent the same locations in a $\boldsymbol{\theta}$-space. Do they only differ in appearance because of changes in origin, rotation and units of the coordinate axes, or do they represent different locations? If they do represent the same points in the $\boldsymbol{\theta}$-space, then the goal is to recover the rotation and scaling matrices and the shift in origin.

If all of the expressions in (8.21) are expanded to remove the parentheses, all of the equations are of the form $\boldsymbol{\nu} = \boldsymbol{\theta}\mathbf{M} + \mathbf{K}$. If $\boldsymbol{\theta}$ represents the coordinates for the base set, $\boldsymbol{\theta}_{\mathbf{b}}$, and $\boldsymbol{\nu}$ represents the coordinates for the alternative set, $\boldsymbol{\theta}_{\mathbf{a}}$, the goal is to determine the multiplier of the $\boldsymbol{\theta}$-matrix and the intercept term in (8.21). To simplify the estimation of the various terms in the equation, it is useful to subtract the mean vector from each of the coordinates.

$$\boldsymbol{\nu} - \bar{\boldsymbol{\nu}} = \boldsymbol{\theta}\mathbf{M} + \mathbf{K} - (\bar{\boldsymbol{\theta}}\mathbf{M} + \mathbf{K}) = (\boldsymbol{\theta} - \bar{\boldsymbol{\theta}})\mathbf{M}. \tag{8.23}$$

In (8.23), the matrices $\mathbf{M}$ and $\mathbf{K}$ are constants. The result of subtracting the mean vector is that the intercept term is not included in the right side of (8.23) so it can be solved for the matrix, $\mathbf{M}$. Because $\boldsymbol{\theta}$ is considered the base test, the goal is to determine the matrix $\mathbf{M}^{-1}$, the matrix used to convert $\boldsymbol{\nu}$ to $\boldsymbol{\theta}$. This matrix consists of the product of the rotation and scaling matrices.

Although all of the transformations of the $\boldsymbol{\theta}$-space were done assuming an orthogonal coordinate system, performing different changes of scale for the different coordinate axes can result in a change in the angles between item vectors and a change in the correlation between coordinate axes. As a result, the rotation from $\boldsymbol{\nu}$ to $\boldsymbol{\theta}$ is determined using the nonorthogonal Procrustes solution (e.g., Gower and Dijksterhuis 2004). In this case, the rotation is given by

$$\mathbf{M}^{-1} = \left((\boldsymbol{\nu} - \overline{\boldsymbol{\nu}})' (\boldsymbol{\nu} - \overline{\boldsymbol{\nu}})\right)^{-1} (\boldsymbol{\nu} - \overline{\boldsymbol{\nu}})' \left(\boldsymbol{\theta} - \overline{\boldsymbol{\theta}}\right). \tag{8.24}$$

The matrix $\mathbf{M}^{-1}$ is the product of the rotation matrix $\mathbf{Rot}^{-1}$ and the scaling matrix $\mathbf{C}^{-1}$ and the order of the product is important because matrix multiplication does not have the commutative property, $\mathbf{AB} \neq \mathbf{BA}$. A different $\mathbf{M}^{-1}$ results from the two possible orders for the product. For the coordinates presented in Tables 8.18 and 8.19, the matrix $\mathbf{M}^{-1}$ is given by

$$\begin{bmatrix} 1.08 & .73 & .34 & .01 & .48 \\ -.51 & .75 & .00 & .00 & -.00 \\ -.26 & -.17 & 1.21 & .00 & .00 \\ -.01 & -.00 & -.00 & .83 & -.00 \\ -.30 & -.20 & -.09 & -.00 & 1.05 \end{bmatrix}.$$

When this matrix is postmultiplied times the matrix of deviations from the coordinate means for the alternate coordinate values, $\boldsymbol{\nu} = \boldsymbol{\theta}_{\mathbf{a}}$, the result is exactly the values of the deviations from the coordinate means for the base coordinate values, $\boldsymbol{\theta}_{\mathbf{b}}$. The inverse of this matrix can be used as part of the transformation from $\boldsymbol{\theta}_{\mathbf{b}}$ to $\boldsymbol{\theta}_{\mathbf{a}}$. The inverse of matrix, $\mathbf{M}^{-1}$, $\left(\mathbf{M}^{-1}\right)^{-1} = \mathbf{M}$ is

$$\begin{bmatrix} .53 & -.62 & -.17 & -.01 & -.24 \\ .36 & .91 & -.11 & -.01 & -.16 \\ .16 & .00 & .77 & -.00 & -.07 \\ .01 & -.00 & -.00 & 1.2 & -.00 \\ .23 & -.00 & .00 & -.00 & .85 \end{bmatrix}.$$

The matrix $\mathbf{M}$ can also be determined directly by determining the nonorthogonal Procrustes rotation for transforming $\boldsymbol{\theta}$ to $\boldsymbol{\nu}$. This transformation is obtained by substituting $\boldsymbol{\theta}$ for $\boldsymbol{\nu}$ and $\boldsymbol{\nu}$ for $\boldsymbol{\theta}$ in (8.24).

According to the way that the transformation of the base coordinate system to the alternate coordinate system was conducted, it is known that $\mathbf{M}$ is the product of an orthogonal rotation matrix and a diagonal matrix of positive values for converting the units on the coordinate axes. A singular value decomposition (e.g., Gentile 1998) factors matrices into component parts that have these properties so it can be used to recover **Rot** and **C**. The result of a singular value decomposition is a set of three matrices – $\mathbf{U}$, $\boldsymbol{\Sigma}$, and $\mathbf{V}$ – where $\mathbf{U}$ and $\mathbf{V}$ are orthogonal matrices and $\boldsymbol{\Sigma}$ is a diagonal matrix with positive values such that $\mathbf{M} = \mathbf{U}\boldsymbol{\Sigma}\mathbf{V}'$. The decomposition of the $\mathbf{M}$-matrix given earlier yields

$$\mathbf{U} = \begin{bmatrix} .01 & -.56 & -.27 & .21 & -.76 \\ .00 & .83 & -.18 & .14 & -.51 \\ .00 & .00 & -.08 & -.97 & -.23 \\ -1 & 0 & -.00 & -.00 & -.01 \\ .00 & .00 & .94 & -.00 & -.33 \end{bmatrix}, \mathbf{\Sigma} = \begin{bmatrix} 1.2 & 0 & 0 & 0 & 0 \\ 0 & 1.1 & 0 & 0 & 0 \\ 0 & 0 & .9 & 0 & 0 \\ 0 & 0 & 0 & .8 & 0 \\ 0 & 0 & 0 & 0 & .7 \end{bmatrix}, \text{ and}$$

$$\mathbf{V} = \begin{bmatrix} 0 & 0 & 0 & 0 & -1 \\ .00 & 1 & -.00 & .00 & 0 \\ .00 & .00 & -.00 & -1 & 0 \\ -1 & 0 & -.00 & .00 & 0 \\ -.00 & .00 & 1 & .00 & 0 \end{bmatrix}.$$

These matrices have interesting properties. Either one of the **U** or **V** matrices might be composed of 0s and +1 s or −1 s. In this case it is matrix **V**. The matrix with this form has the function of rearranging the rows, columns, and signs of values in the transformation matrix so that the coordinates match on direction of increasing values and the appropriate axes match each other. The **Σ**-matrix contains the scaling factors used to change the units on the axes, but for the MATLAB (2007) solution reported here, these have been ordered from large to small. That order is not necessarily the order in the original scaling of the axes. The original ordering can be determined multiplying the absolute value of the rearrangement matrix, in this case **V**, times a column vector with the diagonal values of **Σ**. In this case, the result is the ordering of scaling factors of $[.7\ 1.1\ .8\ 1.2\ .9]'$. Thus, the original scaling matrix, **C**, is a matrix with these values in the diagonal.

The original rotation matrix, **Rot**, can be obtained by UV'. The matrix that is the rearrangement matrix indicates the order of the initial product of **Rot** and **C** providing the initial transformation from $\boldsymbol{\theta}$ to $\boldsymbol{\nu}$. If **V** is the rearrangement matrix, the order was **RotC**. If **U** is the rearrangement matrix, the order is **CRot**. For the example given here the recovered matrix

$$\mathbf{Rot} = \begin{bmatrix} .75 & -.56 & -.21 & -.01 & -.27 \\ .51 & .83 & -.14 & -.00 & -.18 \\ .23 & -.00 & .97 & -.00 & -.08 \\ .01 & -.00 & -.00 & 1.00 & -.00 \\ .33 & -.00 & -.00 & -.00 & .94 \end{bmatrix}.$$

This is the matrix used to rotate the θ_1-axe to align with the direction of greatest discrimination for the first item in the example item set.

The transformation from the alternate set of coordinates to the base set of coordinates requires another term to account for the shift in origin, **K**. Solving the general equation for the conversion from one set of coordinates to another for **K**, $\boldsymbol{\nu} = \boldsymbol{\theta}\text{M} + \mathbf{K}$, for **K** yields $\mathbf{K} = \boldsymbol{\nu} - \boldsymbol{\theta}\mathbf{M}$. But, the rows of **K** are constant since the shift in origin is the same for all $\boldsymbol{\theta}$-points. Therefore, the means of the columns of

K give the same shift in origin as the individual rows. Thus, a vector of translation of origin values can be obtained from

$$\overline{\mathbf{K}} = \overline{\mathbf{v}} - \overline{\boldsymbol{\theta}}\mathbf{M}. \tag{8.25}$$

Solving $\mathbf{v} = \boldsymbol{\theta}\mathbf{M} + \mathbf{K}$, for $\boldsymbol{\theta}$ and substituting for $\mathbf{K}$ yields

$$\boldsymbol{\theta} = \mathbf{v}\mathbf{M}^{-1} - \mathbf{K}\mathbf{M}^{-1} = \mathbf{v}\mathbf{M}^{-1} - \mathbf{1}'\left(\overline{\mathbf{v}} - \overline{\boldsymbol{\theta}}\mathbf{M}\right)\mathbf{M}^{-1} = \mathbf{v}\mathbf{M}^{-1} + \mathbf{1}'\left(\overline{\boldsymbol{\theta}} - \overline{\mathbf{v}}\mathbf{M}^{-1}\right). \tag{8.26}$$

where $\mathbf{1}'$ is a 1 x n vector of 1s. The last term on the right gives the term that accounts for the shift in origin. This term is given the variable name, **k**, resulting in the final expression for the conversion of the alternate set of coordinates to the base set as

$$\boldsymbol{\theta} = \mathbf{v}\mathbf{M}^{-1} + \mathbf{1}'\mathbf{k}. \tag{8.27}$$

For the example, $\mathbf{k} = [-.42\ -.04\ -.10\ -.10\ .18]$. This is not the set of translation values for the initial transformation of the $\boldsymbol{\theta}$-coordinates. The transformation used to produce the alternate $\boldsymbol{\theta}$-coordinates for this example was that given in (8.21c). If that equation is solved for $\boldsymbol{\theta}$ in terms of $\mathbf{v}$, the **k** term in (8.27) is found to be equal to $\boldsymbol{\delta}\mathbf{Rot}^{-1}$. Therefore, multiplying **k** by **Rot** will recover the original vector of values used to translate the origin $[-.3\ .20 - .1\ .3]$. However, there is no way to determine the terms that are multiplied together to form the **k**-term in the equation. That term might be $\boldsymbol{\delta}$, or $\boldsymbol{\delta}$ multiplied by the inverse of **Rot** or **C** or both.

8.2.2 Recovering Transformations Using Item Parameters

The perspective taken in this chapter has been that the space of interest in MIRT analysis is the space defined by the location of persons. These locations are indicated by vectors of θ-coordinates. The origin of the space, the rotation of the axes, and the units used on the coordinate axes are arbitrary decisions of the person performing the analysis, or the person writing the estimation program used to obtain estimates of the model parameters. Previous sections of this chapter have shown how the $\boldsymbol{\theta}$-space can be transformed and how the item parameters need to be transformed to maintain the invariance property of the MIRT model. The last section showed how the relationship between representations of the same $\boldsymbol{\theta}$-space can be determined using the original and alternate sets of $\boldsymbol{\theta}$-coordinates. In many applications of MIRT, two sets of coordinate representations are not available for the same persons. However, item parameter estimates may be available for the same items in the two coordinate systems. This section shows how to determine the relationship between two coordinate systems that represent the same $\boldsymbol{\theta}$-space using item parameters that result in invariant probabilities of response from the two coordinate systems.

8.2.2.1 Recovery of the Rotation and Scaling Matrices

The transformation of the θ-coordinates shown in (8.22a) is used here to provide an example of the logic behind the recovery of the rotation matrix, **Rot**, and the scaling matrix, **C**. It is assumed that the item parameters for the multidimensional extension of the two-parameter logistic model were transformed to be consistent with the transformation of the θ-coordinates so that the invariance property of the MIRT model holds. This means that the expressions for the exponents of the model for the same person and items should yield identical values. That is,

$$\boldsymbol{\upsilon}\boldsymbol{\nu}' + \boldsymbol{\zeta}\mathbf{1} = \mathbf{a}\boldsymbol{\theta}' + \mathbf{d}\mathbf{1}, \tag{8.28}$$

where $\boldsymbol{\upsilon}$ is the matrix of discrimination parameters for the transformed space, $\boldsymbol{\nu}$ is the matrix or person parameters after transformation, and $\boldsymbol{\zeta}$ is the intercept parameter after transformation. The other parameters are as defined previously.

The relationship between the item parameters before transformation to those after transformation can be determined by substituting the expression for the transformation of $\boldsymbol{\theta}$ to obtain $\boldsymbol{\nu}$ in place of $\boldsymbol{\nu}$ in (8.28). The result is given in (8.29).

$$\begin{aligned}\boldsymbol{\upsilon}\left(\boldsymbol{\theta}\mathbf{RotC} - \mathbf{1}\boldsymbol{\delta}'\mathbf{RotC}\right)' + \boldsymbol{\zeta}\mathbf{1} &= \boldsymbol{\upsilon}\left(\boldsymbol{\theta}\mathbf{RotC}\right)' - \left(\mathbf{1}\boldsymbol{\delta}'\mathbf{RotC}\right)' + \boldsymbol{\zeta}\mathbf{1} \\ &= \boldsymbol{\upsilon}\mathbf{C}'\mathbf{Rot}'\boldsymbol{\theta}' - \left(\mathbf{1}\boldsymbol{\delta}'\mathbf{RotC}\right)' + \boldsymbol{\zeta}\mathbf{1}.\end{aligned} \tag{8.29}$$

Comparison of the second line of (8.29) with the right side of (8.28) shows that the multiplier of $\boldsymbol{\theta}'$ in (8.29) is the equivalent of **a** in (8.28).

$$\mathbf{a} = \boldsymbol{\upsilon}\mathbf{C}'\mathbf{Rot}'. \tag{8.30}$$

Because **a** and $\boldsymbol{\upsilon}$ are known, the equation in (8.30) can be solved for $\mathbf{C}'\mathbf{Rot}'$. In this case, the same nonorthogonal Procrustes procedure is used as was used to determine the rotation and scaling of the $\boldsymbol{\theta}$-coordinates. That is, the **a**-matrix is used as the target matrix and the nonorthogonal Procrustes rotation is used to determine the transformation from $\boldsymbol{\upsilon}$ to **a**.

To demonstrate the recovery of the rotation matrix and the scaling matrix, the a-parameters given in Table 8.5 were transformed to be consistent with the transformation of the coordinate system in (8.21a). The transformed discrimination parameters are given in Table 8.20. The original parameters in Table 8.5 are used as the target for the Procrustes rotation procedure and the transformation matrix was determined for rotating and scaling the parameters in Table 8.20 to match the original set. That is,

$$\mathbf{C}'\mathbf{Rot}' = \left(\boldsymbol{\upsilon}'\boldsymbol{\upsilon}\right)^{-1}\boldsymbol{\upsilon}'\mathbf{a}. \tag{8.31}$$

Table 8.20 Discrimination parameters after rotating to align θ_1-axis with the most discriminating direction for Item 1 and changing the units on the coordinate axes

Item number	ν_1	ν_2	ν_3	ν_4	ν_5
1	1.48	.00	−.00	.00	−.00
2	1.32	−.19	.22	.19	.34
3	.94	.13	.21	.02	.42
4	.98	.08	.07	.14	.55
5	1.08	−.09	.24	.06	.30

For the item parameters in the example, the result is

$$\mathbf{C}'\mathbf{Rot}' = \begin{bmatrix} .53 & .36 & .16 & .01 & .23 \\ -.62 & .91 & -.00 & -.00 & -.00 \\ -.17 & -.11 & .77 & .00 & -.00 \\ -.01 & -.01 & -.00 & 1.20 & -.00 \\ -.24 & -.16 & -.07 & -.00 & .85 \end{bmatrix}.$$

Note that this matrix is the transpose of the matrix, **M**, used to transform the coordinate axes (see (8.23)). It can be decomposed into the rotation and scaling matrices using the singular value decomposition in the same way that was done for **M**. Postmultiplying $\boldsymbol{\nu}$ by the matrix given earlier will exactly recover the original a-parameters because in this case all of the values are true parameters without estimation error.

8.2.2.2 Recovery of the Translation of Origin

The recovery of the translation of the origin of the $\boldsymbol{\theta}$-space from the differences in the item parameters is surprisingly difficult. The reason for the difficulty is that the item parameters do not give information about whether the translation of origin occurred on the original $\boldsymbol{\theta}$-space before rotation and scaling, or after one or both of the rotation and scaling transformations. It is possible to determine the multiplier of the **a**-matrix in the right hand terms of (8.22a) to (8.22f). In some cases, this multiplier is the $\boldsymbol{\delta}$-vector of values used to translate the origin of the $\boldsymbol{\theta}$-space, but in other cases, the $\boldsymbol{\delta}$-vector is multiplied by functions of the rotation and scaling matrices.

The terms on the right side of (8.22a) to (8.22f) are the possible definitions of the intercept term of the model after transformation of the θ-space. These transformed intercept terms maintain the invariance property of the model. In every case they are in the form of the **a**-matrix multiplied times a term plus **d**. The general symbol used for the multiplier of **a** is $\boldsymbol{\Omega}$. Using this notation, the transformed value of the intercept term is given by

$$\tilde{\mathbf{d}} = \mathbf{a}\boldsymbol{\Omega} + \mathbf{d}. \tag{8.32}$$

The solution for **d** is simply

$$\tilde{\mathbf{d}} - \mathbf{a}\boldsymbol{\Omega} = \mathbf{d}, \tag{8.33}$$

but the value of $\boldsymbol{\Omega}$ is needed to transform the intercept parameter from the alternate θ-space back to the initial $\boldsymbol{\theta}$-space. Solving for $\boldsymbol{\Omega}$ is complicated slightly by the fact that $\mathbf{a}$ is typically not a square matrix so the equation cannot be solved with the simple inverse of $\mathbf{a}$. However, with a little matrix manipulation, the following equation can be used to solve for $\boldsymbol{\Omega}$.

$$\boldsymbol{\Omega} = \left(\mathbf{a}'\mathbf{a}\right)^{-1} \mathbf{a}' \left(\tilde{\mathbf{d}}-\mathbf{d}\right). \tag{8.34}$$

The matrix that is the result of (8.34) can substituted into (8.33) to recover $\mathbf{d}$ from $\tilde{\mathbf{d}}$. This may seem like a tautology because (8.34) requires the knowledge of $\mathbf{d}$. However, this equation is often used when $\boldsymbol{\Omega}$ is determined from a subset of all of the items that have the intercept terms from both representations of the $\boldsymbol{\theta}$-space and then it can be applied to the items that are not contained in that subset. This application of the procedure will be described in more detail in Chap. 9. The same result that is shown here was derived in a different way by Joseph Martineau and that derivation is present in Reckase and Martineau (2004).

It seems that it should be possible to determine the translation of origin of the person space from the item parameters that yield invariant probabilities. At this point in time, the procedure for doing this has not been determined. It is left to the next generation of psychometricians to work out the finer details about how to recover the translation of origin from the two sets of item parameters.

The relationships presented in this part of the chapter have been developed assuming the multidimensional generalization of the two-parameter logistic model. They generalize directly to the multidimensional normal ogive model and to other logistic models including those for polytomous items. The same relationships also hold for the multidimensional generalization of the three-parameter logistic model when there is a single c-parameter for each item. That is, there is a single lower asymptote for the item response surface. It is left to the reader to confirm the generalizations.

8.3 Transforming the $\boldsymbol{\theta}$-space for the Partially Compensatory Model

The transformation of the proficiency space has quite different effects on the item parameters for the partially compensatory model than it does on the item parameters for the compensatory model. Although it is possible to consider the same transformations to the $\boldsymbol{\theta}$-space as those given in Sect. 8.1, the rotation of axes is not allowed by the model. Because the equiprobable contours for the partially compensatory model have asymptotes that are parallel to the coordinate axes, rotating the axes, but keeping the location of the item response surface constant would result in a model that is mathematically unwieldy. Estimation of the item parameters for this model fixes the orientation of the coordinate axes. There is still indeterminacy in the model concerning the origin of the space and the units on the coordinate axes.

The partially compensatory model that was presented in (4.18) is repeated here for convenience:

$$P(U_{ij} = 1|\boldsymbol{\theta}_j, \mathbf{a}_i, \mathbf{b}_i, c_i) = c_i + (1 - c_i)\left(\prod_{\ell=1}^{m} \frac{e^{1.7a_{i\ell}(\theta_{j\ell}-b_{i\ell})}}{1 + e^{1.7a_{i\ell}(\theta_{j\ell}-b_{i\ell})}}\right). \tag{8.35}$$

Suppose that the original $\boldsymbol{\theta}$-space is transformed to have a different origin as was done in (8.1). That is, the new coordinates for the locations of persons are determined by subtracting shift constants from the coordinates on each axis. The amount of shift need not be the same – $\boldsymbol{\nu} = \boldsymbol{\theta} - \boldsymbol{\delta}$. To maintain the invariance property of the MIRT model, it is only necessary to add the same shift constant to the difficulty parameters for each dimension. That is, the difficulty parameters in the new person space are $\mathbf{b} - \boldsymbol{\delta}$. Substituting the two sets of translated values into (8.35) results in exactly the same probabilities of responses as the original set of parameters.

Similarly, if the units of the coordinate axes are changed by multiplying each by a constant and the constants are collected into the diagonal of a diagonal matrix $\mathbf{C}$, the coordinates of the locations of persons are multiplied by this matrix, that is $\boldsymbol{\theta}\mathbf{C}$. Then the invariance property of the MIRT model is maintained if the same scaling is performed on $\mathbf{b}$, $\mathbf{bC}$, and the inverse scaling is performed on $\mathbf{a}$, $\mathbf{aC}^{-1}$. These transformations are conceptually the same as those that result in invariance of probabilities for the unidimensional IRT models.

If coordinates for the same persons are available from the original person space and the transformed one, the details of the transformations can be determined in the same way as described in Sect. 8.2. If the item parameters are available for the same items as represented in two different coordinate systems, the functions used to translate from one to the other can be determined by considering each coordinate dimension separately. If the θ on a dimension is transformed to a new coordinate system by the equation $\theta' = c\theta + \delta$, then the difficulty parameter for that dimension, b, is transformed in the same way – $b' = cb + \delta$. If both b and b' are available for a set of items, the linear function that relates them can be determined. If the difficulty parameters are the true model parameters, the correlation between the pairs of difficulty parameters should be 1.0, and all the (b, b')-points should fall exactly on the line defined by the linear function. From that line, the slope and intercept terms can be determined. Similarly, the plot of the a-parameters should fall along a straight line with slope $1/c$. The fitting of the linear function is done separately for each dimension in the coordinate space.

The transformations used for each dimension are exactly the same as those used to transform the parameters of the unidimensional IRT models. Further discussion of this type of transformation of scale can be found in one of the standard texts on IRT.

8.4 Exercises

1. Four persons have $\boldsymbol{\theta}$-coordinates in a two-dimensional space of (−.6, .9), (.3, 1.1), (−1.4, 0), and (.7, −2). Plot the locations of these four persons on a Cartesian coordinate system. The origin of the coordinate system is shifted to (.5, −.7). List the coordinates of each person's location in the coordinate system after converting to the coordinates system with the new origin. Plot the new coordinates and tell how they have changed compared to the original set of coordinates.

2. Suppose the four persons listed in #1 earlier are administered an item that is fit well by the multidimensional extension of the two-parameter logistic model. The parameters of the item in the original coordinate system are $a_1 = .8$, $a_2 = 1.4$, and $d = .3$. Compute the probability of correct response for the item for each person (include $D = 1.7$ in the model). What do the parameters for the item have to be after the shift in the origin of the space to maintain the same probabilities of correct response? Describe how you determined the parameters for the transformed $\boldsymbol{\theta}$-space.

3. What would the coordinates of the points in #1 be if the coordinate system were transformed to have mean coordinates on each dimension equal to 0? Describe how you determined the new set of coordinates.

4. The units of the coordinate axes from #1 are changed so that units for Axis 1 are 1.5 times as large and those for Axis 2 are half as large. What are the coordinates of the four examinees in the coordinate system after the change of units? Show the process of conversion using matrix multiplication. Give the matrices used in the computation.

5. Define a coordinate system for locating persons at a particular point in time in your classroom. What are the coordinate axes? What do you choose as the units for measuring along the coordinate axes? Where is the origin of your coordinate system? What is the rationale for these choices? Provide the location of four persons using this coordinate system. How does your coordinate system relate to other existing coordinate systems such as latitude and longitude or street addresses? What are the advantages and disadvantages of the different systems?

6. IRT models are said to have an "invariance" property but at the same time the scales of the IRT models have "indeterminacies." Explain how something can be invariant and indeterminate at the same time.

7. The table below contains the coordinates for the same persons in a two-dimensional space before and after a change of units on the coordinate axes. Determine the scaling constants for the change in units. Explain how you determined the values.

Person	Original 1	Original 2	Rescaled 1	Rescaled 2
1	−0.4326	−1.1465	−0.3461	−1.4904
2	−1.6656	1.1909	−1.3325	1.5482
3	0.1253	1.1892	0.1003	1.5459
4	0.2877	−0.0376	0.2301	−0.0489

8. Matrix **O** below gives the original coordinates for four persons in a three-dimensional $\boldsymbol{\theta}$-space. Matrix **A** gives the coordinates for the same four persons after a transformation of the coordinate system. Determine the rotation matrix and the scaling matrix that converts the values in **O** into the values of **A**.

$$\mathbf{O} = \begin{bmatrix} 0.3273 & -0.5883 & 1.0668 \\ 0.1746 & 2.1832 & 0.0593 \\ -0.1867 & -0.1364 & -0.0956 \\ 0.7258 & 0.1139 & -0.8323 \end{bmatrix},$$

$$\mathbf{A} = \begin{bmatrix} 0.4858 & -0.3187 & 1.4612 \\ 0.5585 & 1.0584 & -0.1327 \\ -0.2258 & -0.0504 & -0.0577 \\ 0.4937 & -0.0089 & -1.4914 \end{bmatrix}.$$

9. The elements of the pairs of coordinates of a population of examinees in a two-dimensional space have a correlation of .2. The coordinate axes are rotated using an orthogonal rotation and a new set of coordinates are obtained for the same set of examinees. The distances between all of the locations of the examinees remain exactly the same. What are the possible values of the correlation between the pairs of coordinates after rotation? Explain the reasons for your answer.

10. The origin of a coordinate system is shifted from (0, 0) to (1, 1). No other changes are made to the coordinate system. How will this translation of origin affect the **a**-parameters for items that have been specified in the first system of coordinates? Explain why this is the case.

11. The **a**-parameter matrix for a set of four items in a three-dimensional coordinate space is given below. The same four items also have **a**-parameters in another coordinate space where the first item is constrained to measure best along the first coordinate axis. This **a**-matrix is labeled $\mathbf{a}^*$ below. Find the rotation matrix and scaling matrix that will convert the elements of the $\mathbf{a}^*$-matrix into the elements of the **a**-matrix.

$$\mathbf{a} = \begin{bmatrix} 1.1 & 0.2 & 0.3 \\ 0.3 & 0.9 & 0.2 \\ 0.1 & 0.1 & 0.8 \\ 0.7 & 0.8 & 0.6 \end{bmatrix} \quad \mathbf{a}^* = \begin{bmatrix} 1.6537 & 0.0000 & -0.0000 \\ 0.7034 & 0.6932 & 0.0833 \\ 0.4566 & 0.0671 & 0.8250 \\ 1.3698 & 0.5516 & 0.4044 \end{bmatrix}.$$

12. For what type of transformation of the $\boldsymbol{\theta}$-space will the correlation between the $\boldsymbol{\theta}$-coordinates remain the same before and after the transformation? Explain your answer.

Chapter 9
Linking and Scaling

If the application of MIRT were only to single forms of fixed length, there would be no need to consider the issues of linking and scaling. The item-score matrix from the administration of the single test form to a large and representative set of examinees could be analyzed using one of the MIRT calibration programs and the results could be interpreted using the methods described in the previous chapters of this book. But many situations are more complex than this simple case. It is sometimes important to develop large sets of test items with item parameters in the same coordinate system. Such sets of items are needed for computerized adaptive tests (CATs), a methodology that is described in Chap. 10. The number of test items needed for a CAT, usually called an item pool, is much greater than the number that can be administered to examinees in one sitting. Therefore, to get the item parameters into the same coordinate system requires methodology called "linking." Large sets of test items, also called item banks, are also used to create multiple forms of a test for a testing program. For example, new forms of college admissions tests are produced each year. Items are selected from the item bank to produce multiple, parallel test forms with the goal of developing test forms that will give reported scores that can be used interchangeably.

There are also situations when it is desirable to use the same coordinate system for reporting results from test forms that are not strictly parallel. A common case is test forms that are designed for use with different grade levels within a school. Policy makers would like to know how much students have changed as a result of a year of instruction. In the MIRT context, they want to know the difference in location of a student's points in the coordinate system defined by the tests at two or more times. Determining the amount of change in location requires putting the item- and person-parameter estimates from the two tests into the same coordinate system. This situation also exits when there is a change in the specifications for a test, but the goal is to report results using the same score reporting system as previous forms of the test. Even though the tests are somewhat different, it is desirable to use the same coordinate system for reporting.

The position taken in this chapter is consistent with that given in Holland (2007) that all of these situations fall under then general category of procedures called *linking*. However, Holland defines linking as only referring to scores. "The term *linking* refers to the general class of transformations between scores from one test and those of another" (p. 6). Here the term will be used to refer to transformations used to put

M.D. Reckase, *Multidimensional Item Response Theory*, Statistics for Social and Behavioral Sciences, DOI 10.1007/978-0-387-89976-3_9,
© Springer Science+Business Media, LLC 2009

both item parameters and person locations into the same coordinate system. *Equating* is a term given to a special case of linking that has a set of properties given by Holland (2007, p. 23). These include that the reported scores represent the same constructs, that they are measured with equivalent accuracy across different test forms, that the transformation from one coordinate system to the other is symmetric, that the examinee is indifferent to the test form that is taken, and that the transformation is population invariant.

This chapter presents a number of methods for linking the calibration results from two or more tests. It covers two general cases. Linking when the test forms are designed to be equivalent and to be used with the same examinee population, and linking when the test forms do not have the same content and/or statistical specifications and the examinees are not from the same population. The first case corresponds to the case of test equating. The goal is to report information about the locations of examinees in the multidimensional space that can be used interchangeably independent of test form. The second case includes the multidimensional extension of vertical scaling and reporting results in the same coordinate system when test specifications change. The development of large item pools and item banks also may require the linking of calibrations from nonparallel test forms.

Once the results from different test forms are placed into the same coordinate system, the information about the locations of examinees in that coordinate system can be reported in a number of different ways. The most commonly reported result is the vector of coordinates for the location of each person. In the terminology of factor analysis, these are called factor scores. These scores depend on the orientation of the coordinate axes in the multidimensional space defined by the analyses of the item-score matrices. The information in the estimates of locations can also be reported by projecting the locations onto lines defined by the directions of best measurement of sets of test items. In previous chapters, these are called reference composites. Methods for reporting the locations of examinees will be covered in the second part of this chapter.

As in all linking and equating methodology, there are two parts – a data collection design and a statistical methodology for determining the transformation from one space to the other. No attempt will be made in this chapter to cover all possible combinations of data collection designs and statistical linking methods. There are already very good books on linking and equating (e.g., Kolen and Brennan 2004; Dorans, Pommerich and Holland 2007) and the designs given in those sources can be generalized to the multidimensional case. This chapter covers the major features of the linking problem. The application to specific designs and situations is left to others.

9.1 Specifying the Common Multidimensional Space

The first step in any application of linking methodology is specifying the base coordinate system. The goal is to transform all calibration results into this coordinate system. This is true for the unidimensional case as well as the multidimensional case. In the unidimensional case, there is the need to specify the location of the origin of the unidimensional scale and the size of units on the scale. Unidimensional IRT calibration programs do this in two different ways. One way is to set the mean of the estimates of the person locations to 0.0 and the standard deviation of those locations to 1.0. A common alternative is to set the mean of the difficulty parameter estimates of the items to 0.0 and the a-parameters of the items to 1.0. Because the a-parameter is related to the slope of the item characteristic curve of the items, setting it to a fixed value is the same as setting a unit for the scale because the slope is the change in probability over a fixed distance on the scale.

The scales set by calibration programs are arbitrarily determined by the sample of individuals that is tested or the set of items that is calibrated. Unidimensional scales are often transformed to have origin and units that are related to consciously selected aspects of the testing program. For example, the origin might be fixed at a cut score on the scale that is used to determine a pass/fail decision. The unit of measurement might be set to give a convenient number of score points between two performance levels on the scale. The important point is that the base coordinate system should be thoughtfully considered rather than selecting the default output of a calibration program.

Selecting the base coordinate system for the multidimensional case is more complex than for the unidimensional case because not only is there the necessity of deciding the location for the origin of the space, but there is also the need to set units of measurement on each of the coordinate axes. Further, the orientation of the coordinate axes needs to be determined as well. Of course, the number of coordinate axes needs to be determined using the methods described in Chap. 7. It is always possible to select the default solution from a calibration program to set the base coordinate system. However, as for the unidimensional case, it might be better to relate the coordinate system to features of the testing program. There is no single correct base coordinate system for a testing program, but the following artificial example sets out some of the possible choices.

Suppose that a new testing program is being developed to measure the English language competency of persons learning English as a new language. A competency test is developed to measure three related constructs – reading, conversation, and vocabulary. The reading component uses traditional, reading comprehension test items with a reading passage and a series of questions. The conversation component asks the examinee to take part in a conversation with an examiner and the response to each part of a script is rated as being either adequate or inadequate. The vocabulary component is a traditional multiple-choice test of vocabulary knowledge. The conversation component of the test does not require any reading, but it does require knowledge of vocabulary as does the reading test.

This hypothetical test is administered to a large, representative sample of examinees from the target population of English language learners who want to have their competence certified through the use of the test. The initial form of this test was very carefully constructed and it will be used to define the base coordinate system for the testing program. The results from all future test administrations with test forms constructed to be parallel to the initial form of the test will be transformed back to this base coordinate system. The designers of the testing program would like to report an overall measure of competency and scores on each of the constructs – reading, conversation, and vocabulary. How should the origin, units of measurement, and orientation of the coordinate axes for the base coordinate system be defined?

The results of the calibration of the test items for this hypothetical test are given in Table 9.1. The first 30 test items are intended to measure the reading construct, the next 20 test items the vocabulary construct, and the last 30 test items the speaking construct. Note that for the first 30 items, the a_1-parameter estimates are three or four times larger than the a_2-parameter estimates. The next 20 items have a_1- and a_2-estimates that are more similar in magnitude, but the a_1-estimates are somewhat larger than the a_2 estimates. Test items 51 to 80 have the a_2-parameter estimates larger than the a_1-parameter estimates.

The d-parameter estimates for the test items indicate that there are difficulty trends among the items related to the three constructs. The d-parameter estimates for the first 30 test items are moderately positive indicating that these test items have a slightly greater than a .5 proportion correct. The next 20 test items have slightly large d-parameter estimates indicating that they are slightly easier for this examinee sample than the first 30 items. The d-parameter estimates for the last 30 items all have negative signs indicating that the proportion correct for these items are all less than .5 for this examinee sample. They are more difficult than the test items associated with the other constructs.

The item arrow plot for these test items is given in Fig. 9.1. The plot shows the vocabulary items at the lower left, the reading items as a cluster above and to the right, and the conversation items best discriminating along the θ_2-axis. However, none of the test item sets are aligned along the coordinate axes and they are not at right angles to each other indicating that the constructs that they best measure are correlated.

A cluster analysis using the angles between the item vectors was also performed using the item parameter estimates. The result of the cluster analysis is given in Fig. 9.2. The cluster analysis clearly shows the test items associated with the three constructs that are targets for the test. The cluster to the far right contains most of the vocabulary items. The middle cluster contains the reading items and a few vocabulary items. All of the conversation items are in the cluster at the left of the dendrogram.

If these results had been obtained from the first operational administration of an actual test, the evidence from the calibration would show that the test developers had been successful at producing a test with a structure that is consistent with their design. The results given here, however, are based on the default settings in the TESTFACT program. Those default settings resulted in $\boldsymbol{\theta}$-vectors with elements correlated .08 with a mean vector of $[-.02\ .01]$ and standard deviations of .96 and .94, respectively. Because of the indeterminacies in the origin of the space, the units of measurement along each coordinate axis, and the orientation of the axes, the space will be the base for all future test form calibrations and for score reporting can be changed to be more convenient as long as it is done in such a way as to maintain the invariance property of the MIRT model. That means that if the item parameters are transformed in some way, the inverse transformation must be applied to the $\boldsymbol{\theta}$-estimates.

Table 9.1 TESTFACT item parameter estimates for the simulated English Language Test

Item number	a_1	a_2	d	Item number	a_1	a_2	d
1	.81	.17	.53	41	.61	.39	1.10
2	.78	.23	.79	42	.69	.40	.80
3	.84	.12	.43	43	.52	.30	.86
4	.64	.18	.26	44	.56	.38	.48
5	.74	.26	.64	45	.60	.39	.87
6	.80	.08	.15	46	.48	.32	.56
7	.63	.09	.16	47	.49	.33	.60
8	.60	.20	.32	48	.69	.38	1.06
9	.83	.16	.38	49	.56	.42	1.17
10	.69	.21	.32	50	.54	.37	.72
11	.78	.12	.46	51	.34	.77	−.20
12	.71	.20	.27	52	.11	.71	−.48
13	.66	.22	.47	53	.20	.61	−.44
14	.63	.21	−.02	54	.33	.79	−.83
15	.78	.26	.45	55	.15	.77	−.53
16	.61	.19	.37	56	.21	.88	−.30
17	.80	.26	.22	57	.23	.77	−.52
18	.82	.14	.44	58	.24	.64	−.19
19	.67	.12	.42	59	.14	.56	−.31
20	.71	.15	.54	60	.26	.68	−.37
21	.57	.12	.29	61	.18	.68	−.36
22	.50	.09	.45	62	.25	.61	−.28
23	.83	.23	.29	63	.27	.73	−.63
24	.70	.13	.11	64	.17	.87	−.05
25	.80	.09	.58	65	.22	.70	−.41
26	.79	.19	.19	66	.17	.60	−.46
27	.75	.15	.14	67	.21	.68	−.49
28	.63	.15	.59	68	.18	.79	−.55
29	.63	.24	.56	69	.17	.63	−.32
30	.70	.06	.28	70	.21	.58	−.41
31	.52	.36	.71	71	.10	.68	−.48
32	.57	.25	.57	72	.27	.71	−.32
33	.80	.44	.77	73	.37	.77	−.36
34	.68	.29	.67	74	.16	.69	−.31
35	.53	.34	.39	75	.21	.71	−.08
36	.59	.42	.66	76	.18	.68	−.34
37	.53	.24	.46	77	.18	.74	−.42
38	.48	.34	.80	78	.29	.88	−.55
39	.63	.36	.74	79	.20	.61	−.57
40	.72	.42	.93	80	.14	.60	−.24

Suppose that the designers of this testing program have decided that it would be very useful if the values of the $\boldsymbol{\theta}$-coordinates corresponded to the reading and conversation constructs. The θ_1-value could be a direct measure of the reading construct

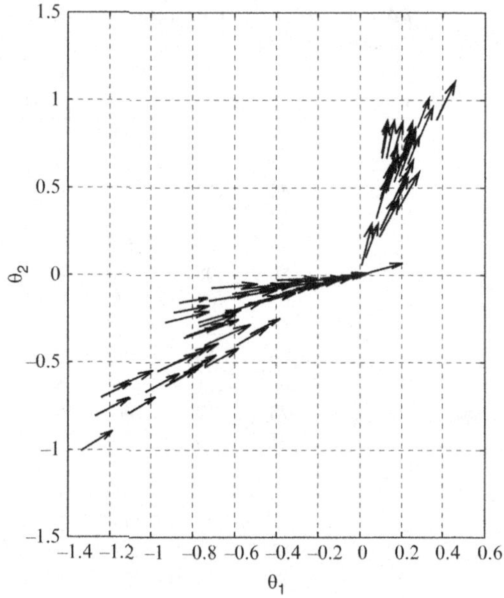

Fig. 9.1 Item arrows for the simulated English Language Test

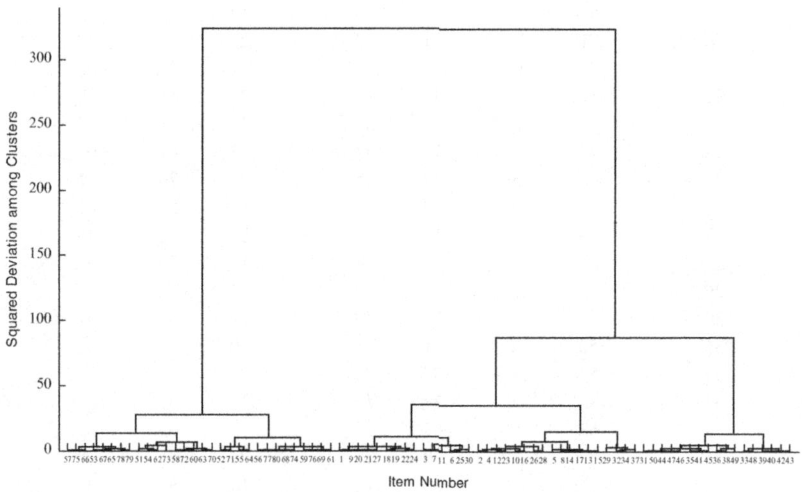

Fig. 9.2 Cluster analysis dendrogram for the simulated English Language Test

and the θ_2-value a direct value of the conversation construct. Note that the solution is only in two dimensions so it is not possible to align three different constructs with coordinate axes. The estimate of the vocabulary construct will have to be produced in a different way. Methods for estimating each person's location on the vocabulary construct will be described in Sect. 9.3 of this chapter.

One way to align the reading and conversation constructs of the test along the coordinate axes is to determine the reference composites for the sets of test items related to each construct and then determine the nonorthogonal Procrustes rotation that will align the reference composites with the axes. The inverse rotation must be applied to the $\boldsymbol{\theta}$-vectors to maintain the invariance properties of the MIRT model.

The reference composite for the reading construct was determined by computing the eigenvector that corresponds to the largest eigenvalues of the $\mathbf{a}'\mathbf{a}$-matrix for the reading comprehension items. For this example, the eigenvalues are 16.41 and .10, and the eigenvector corresponding to the largest eigenvalue is [.9741 .2262]. The MATLAB routine for eigenvalue/eigenvector decomposition gives a result that scales the elements of the eigenvector so that their squares sum to 1.0. This means that they have the characteristics of direction cosines. For the reading construct, the angles with the coordinate axes of the reference composite are 13° and 77° respectively for θ_1 and θ_2. The same procedure results in eigenvalues of 16.43 and .10 for the $\mathbf{a}'\mathbf{a}$-matrix for the conversation items with an eigenvector of [.2898 .9571]. The angles of this reference composite with the coordinate axes are 73° and 17°, respectively.

The elements of the eigenvectors also serve as $\mathbf{a}$-parameters for the reference composites. That is, if items had $\mathbf{a}$-parameters equal to the elements of the eigenvectors, the item vectors would perfectly align with the reference composites. Therefore, a matrix can be constructed from the eigenvectors with reference composites as rows. That matrix in this case is given by

$$\begin{bmatrix} .9741 & .2262 \\ .2898 & .9571 \end{bmatrix}.$$

If the reference composites were perfectly aligned with the coordinate axes, this matrix would be

$$\begin{bmatrix} 1 & 0 \\ 0 & 1 \end{bmatrix}$$

so this is the target matrix for determining the rotation. Using the nonorthogonal Procrustes procedure described in Chap. 8, the rotation matrix needed to transform the observed matrix for the reference composites to the target matrix is

$$\begin{bmatrix} 1.1043 & -.2610 \\ -.3344 & 1.1239 \end{bmatrix}.$$

This is the $(\mathbf{Rot}')^{-1}$ matix defined in Chap. 8. All of the $\mathbf{a}$-parameter vectors for the items can be postmultiplied by this matrix to put them into a coordinate system that is consistent with the reference composites aligned with the coordinate axes. However, to maintain the invariance property of the MIRT model, the $\boldsymbol{\theta}$-vectors for each person must be multiplied by the transpose of the inverse of the matrix. This is given by

$$\begin{bmatrix} .9741 & .2898 \\ .2262 & .9571 \end{bmatrix},$$

the **Rot** matrix. In this case, the inverse of the rotation matrix is the matrix of eigenvectors for the reference composites. This special case occurs because the target matrix for the nonorthogonal Procrustes rotation is the identity matrix.

The results from applying the rotation to the **a**-parameter matrix are presented in Table 9.2. The item arrows for this solution are given in Fig. 9.3. It is useful to compare the item arrows in Fig. 9.1 to those in Fig. 9.3 to see the change in the configuration of item arrows. The rotated **a**-parameters show that the items related to the reference composites used as the targets for the rotation have elements near zero for the coordinate axis that was not the target. Some of these values are slightly negative because the reference composite is aligned to the coordinate axis, not specific items. The a-values along the coordinate axis increase slightly in value. The d-parameters are unchanged by the rotation.

The item arrows in Fig. 9.3 show the expected results. The item arrows associated with the reference composites that are the target of the rotation are now clustered along the coordinate axes with some item arrows on either side of the axis. The item arrows for the third construct in the test point in a direction between the other two.

Transforming the $\boldsymbol{\theta}$-coordinates for each person using the transpose of the inverse of the rotation matrix for items results in a change in the correlation between the $\boldsymbol{\theta}$-coordinates. The initial set of coordinates had a correlation of .08. After applying the rotation, the correlation is .56. This change in correlation illustrates an important point about MIRT modeling of the item-score matrix. The item-score matrix contains certain relationships. Those relationships can be modeled either through similarity of direction of best measurement for test items, or through correlations between $\boldsymbol{\theta}$-coordinates for examinees. If a change is made in the relationships between the directions of best measurement for the test items, a compensating change must be made in the relationships between the θs, if the invariance property of the MIRT model is to be maintained. The user of the MIRT model has the choice of how to represent the relationships in the data. In this case, to have the convenience of coordinates representing scores on two of the constructs, the reading and conversation constructs, the two sets of item vectors have been nonorthogonally rotated to align with the orthogonal coordinate axes, but to maintain the relationships in the item-score matrix, the coordinates for the locations of the examinees must have a corresponding rotation that gives them a correlation of .56.

If it is more important to keep the θ-coordinates uncorrelated than to have the values of the coordinates represent levels on the constructs, the scores on the constructs can be obtained by projecting the $\boldsymbol{\theta}$-points for each individual in a coordinate space with 0 intercorrelations onto each reference composites for the constructs. The values of the projections onto the reference composites will have the correlation observed here, but the θ-coordinates themselves will be uncorrelated. Because of the indeterminacies in the model specification, there is flexibility in the way that relationships in the data can be portrayed. This is a source of confusion, but it is also a powerful feature of the MIRT models.

For this example, the initial calibration of this test is now reoriented so that the coordinate axes are related to two of the constructs assessed by the test, but the

Table 9.2 Item parameter estimates for the simulated English Language Test after rotation

Item number	a_1	a_2	d	Item number	a_1	a_2	d
1	.84	−.02	.53	41	.55	.28	1.10
2	.79	.05	.79	42	.63	.27	.80
3	.89	−.09	.43	43	.48	.20	.86
4	.65	.04	.26	44	.49	.28	.48
5	.73	.10	.64	45	.53	.28	.87
6	.86	−.12	.15	46	.42	.23	.56
7	.67	−.06	.16	47	.43	.24	.60
8	.60	.07	.32	48	.64	.25	1.06
9	.87	−.03	.38	49	.48	.33	1.17
10	.69	.05	.32	50	.48	.28	.72
11	.82	−.07	.46	51	.12	.77	−.20
12	.71	.04	.27	52	−.11	.77	−.48
13	.65	.07	.47	53	.01	.63	−.44
14	.63	.07	−.02	54	.10	.81	−.83
15	.77	.09	.45	55	−.10	.83	−.53
16	.61	.05	.37	56	−.06	.93	−.30
17	.80	.08	.22	57	−.00	.81	−.52
18	.85	−.05	.44	58	.05	.66	−.19
19	.70	−.04	.42	59	−.03	.59	−.31
20	.74	−.02	.54	60	.07	.69	−.37
21	.59	−.02	.29	61	−.02	.72	−.36
22	.52	−.03	.45	62	.08	.62	−.28
23	.85	.04	.29	63	.05	.75	−.63
24	.73	−.03	.11	64	.10	.93	−.05
25	.86	−.11	.58	65	.00	.73	−.41
26	.81	.01	.19	66	−.01	.63	−.46
27	.77	−.02	.14	67	.01	.71	−.49
28	.64	.01	.59	68	−.06	.84	−.55
29	.62	.11	.56	69	−.02	.66	−.32
30	.76	−.11	.28	70	.04	.60	−.41
31	.46	.27	.71	71	−.12	.74	−.48
32	.55	.23	.57	72	.06	.73	−.32
33	.74	.28	.77	73	.16	.77	−.36
34	.66	.15	.67	74	−.05	.73	−.31
35	.47	.25	.39	75	−.00	.74	−.08
36	.51	.32	.66	76	−.03	.71	−.34
37	.51	.13	.46	77	−.05	.78	−.42
38	.42	.26	.80	78	.03	.92	−.55
39	.57	.24	.74	79	.02	.64	−.57
40	.66	.28	.93	80	−.04	.63	−.24

origin of the proficiency space and the units of measurement along the coordinate axes are still those set by defaults in the TESTFACT program. These could be left at those default values (e.g., set the origin at the means of the coordinates and the

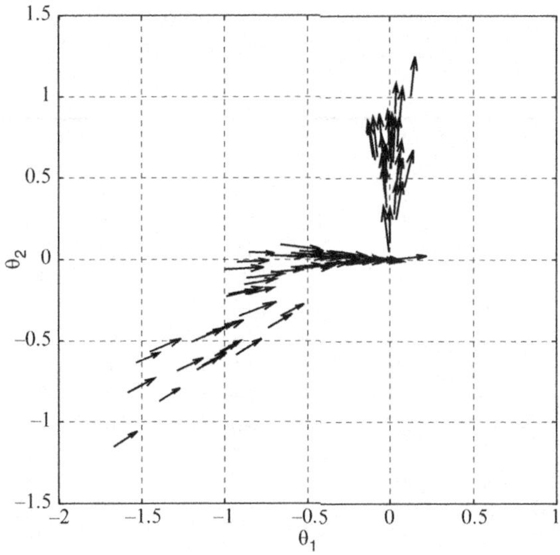

Fig. 9.3 Item arrows for the simulated English test after rotation

units to the standard deviations of the coordinates) or they can be changed to more meaningful values for the base calibration of this testing program.

Deciding on an origin and the units for the coordinates is a nontrivial problem that generally requires extended discussions by interested parties. For this example, it is assumed that the interested parties have decided that it would be useful to have the 0-points for the coordinate axes be related to standards for proficiency on the constructs. Those standards might have been determined by using standard setting methodology on the item sets related to the constructs. Suppose that the agreed upon standard is a coordinate of −.5 on the θ_1-coordinate axis after rotation (reading) and .7 on the θ_2-coordinate axis (conversation). The new origin for the space can be shifted to that point using (8.2) with $\boldsymbol{\delta} = [-.5\ .7]$.

The users of the test have also decided that they would like somewhat finer grained scoring on the reading construct than on the conversation construct. The latter is more difficult to score and it might not be as reliably measured. Therefore, the units for the reading construct are made slightly smaller (.8 in the original metric is now one unit) meaning that an original coordinate of 1.0 is now 1.25. That is, all θ_1 coordinates are multiplied by 1.25. For the conversation construct, the units are made larger so that 1.6 on the original θ_2-coordinate axis is now equal to 1. That is, all θ_2 coordinates are multiplied by .625. The conversion to the new units on the coordinate axes are made using (8.17) with

$$\mathbf{C} = \begin{bmatrix} 1.25 & 0 \\ 0 & .625 \end{bmatrix}.$$

All of these decisions can be implemented by using the transformations of scale and origin given in Chap. 8, Sect. 8.1.4. In this case, because the rotation was performed first and the shift of origin is done before changing the units on the scale, the transformation to the new framework is given by (8.21c). The "**Rot**" in that equation is the transpose of the inverse of the rotation obtained when aligning the two reference composites with the coordinate axes. The full transformation of the $\boldsymbol{\theta}$-vectors from the initial calibration of the test data is given by

$$\begin{aligned}\boldsymbol{\nu} &= (\boldsymbol{\theta}\mathbf{Rot} - \mathbf{1}\boldsymbol{\delta})\mathbf{C} = \boldsymbol{\theta}\mathbf{RotC} - \mathbf{1}\boldsymbol{\delta}\mathbf{C} \\ &= \boldsymbol{\theta}\begin{bmatrix} .9741 & .2898 \\ .2262 & .9571 \end{bmatrix}\begin{bmatrix} 1.25 & 0 \\ 0 & .625 \end{bmatrix} - \mathbf{1}\begin{bmatrix} -.5 & .7 \end{bmatrix}\begin{bmatrix} 1.25 & 0 \\ 0 & .625 \end{bmatrix} \\ &= \boldsymbol{\theta}\begin{bmatrix} 1.2176 & .1811 \\ .2828 & .5982 \end{bmatrix} - \mathbf{1}\begin{bmatrix} -.625 & .4375 \end{bmatrix}.\end{aligned} \tag{9.1}$$

where the $\mathbf{1}$ is a $n \times 1$ vector of 1s that makes the matrix subtraction conform so that the same scaling constants are applied to each location vector in $\boldsymbol{\theta}$.

The results of the translation, rotation, and scaling can be seen in the summary statistics in Table 9.3. After the rotation, the coordinates are correlated .56 instead of the .08 before the transformation. The means of the coordinates are no longer approximately 0 because of the shift in origin. They are not exactly equal to the shift in origin because the units for the coordinate axes were changed after the shift in origin. The standard deviations after the transformation reflect the change in units for the coordinate axes.

In order for the invariance properties of the MIRT model to hold, the item parameters need to be transformed to be consistent with the $\boldsymbol{\theta}$ transformation. The transformation of item parameters that corresponds to that used on the $\boldsymbol{\theta}$s is given in (8.22c). The transformation of the **a**-matrix is in the left bracket and the transformation of the **d**-vector is given in the right bracket.

$$\begin{aligned}\mathbf{a}\left((\mathbf{RotC})^{-1}\right)' &= \mathbf{a}\left(\left(\begin{bmatrix} .9741 & .2898 \\ .2262 & .9571 \end{bmatrix}\begin{bmatrix} 1.25 & 0 \\ 0 & .625 \end{bmatrix}\right)^{-1}\right)' \\ &= \mathbf{a}\begin{bmatrix} .8834 & -.4177 \\ -.2675 & 1.7982 \end{bmatrix},\end{aligned} \tag{9.2}$$

Table 9.3 Means, standard deviations and correlations for the initial and transformed coordinates

	θ_1	θ_2	ν_1	ν_2
θ_1	1.00			
θ_2	.08	1.00		
ν_1	.98	.30	1.00	
ν_2	.36	.96	.56	1.00
Means	−.02	.01	.61	−.44
Standard deviations	.96	.94	1.21	.60

$$\mathbf{a}\left(8\mathbf{Rot}^{-1}\right)' + \mathbf{d} = \mathbf{a}\left(\begin{bmatrix}-.5 & .7\end{bmatrix}\begin{bmatrix}.9741 & .2898\\ .2262 & .9571\end{bmatrix}^{-1}\right)' + \mathbf{d}$$

$$= \mathbf{a}\begin{bmatrix}-.7349\\ .9539\end{bmatrix} + \mathbf{d}. \tag{9.3}$$

The item parameters after transformation are given in Table 9.4. A comparison of the parameters in Table 9.4 to those in Table 9.1 will show that they are quite different. The a_2-parameters for the last 20 items are substantially larger than the original set while many of the a_1-parameters are smaller. This is a result of the change in units on the coordinate axes. The d-parameters are generally more positive. This change is due mostly to the shift in the origin of the space, but there is also some effect of the change in units.

Even though the item parameters after the transformation to the new $\boldsymbol{\theta}$-space are quite different, when used in the model with the transformed $\boldsymbol{\theta}$-vectors, they result in exactly the same probability of correct response for each test items as the original item parameters and $\boldsymbol{\theta}$s. The item vectors based on the transformed item parameters are given in Fig. 9.4. The plot of the arrows clearly shows the shift of the item arrows as a result of the shift in the origin of the $\boldsymbol{\theta}$-space. In other respects, the plot of the arrows is similar to the result after rotation shown in Fig. 9.3.

The transformed $\boldsymbol{\theta}$-space and the set of item parameter estimates given in Table 9.4 are used as the base for the examples of equating and linking given in the following sections of this chapter. The sets of items related to the three constructs in the test are used in the last section of this chapter to demonstrate computing subscores on the reference composites for these item sets.

9.2 Relating Results from Different Test Forms

Many operational testing programs use more than one form of a test. Multiple test forms are usually necessary to maintain test security or to control for memory of previous responses in pretest and posttest experimental designs. In most cases, the different forms of the tests are constructed using the same test specifications and they are intended to be equivalent forms of the test. In that case, putting the results from the different test forms into the same coordinate system is called *equating*.

Sometimes the test forms are not constructed according to the same test specifications but there is still a desire to report the results using the same coordinate system. A common example is a state testing program that has modified the tests to match a change in the state curriculum. In such cases, the statistical processes for putting results into a common coordinate system are the same as are used for equating, but the result is called *linking* or *scaling for comparability* because the resulting estimates of constructs do not have the same level of accuracy and may have slightly different meaning. There are extensive books on equating and linking of calibrations (e.g., Dorans, Pommerich and Holland 2007; Kolen and Brennan 2004) so there is no attempt to give full coverage to these issues here. Instead, three basic

Table 9.4 Item parameter estimates for the simulated English Language Test after rotation, translation, and scaling

Item number	a_1	a_2	d	Item number	a_1	a_2	d
1	.67	−.03	.09	41	.44	.45	1.02
2	.63	.08	.43	42	.50	.43	.67
3	.71	−.14	−.08	43	.38	.32	.76
4	.52	.06	−.04	44	.39	.45	.43
5	.58	.16	.34	45	.42	.45	.81
6	.69	−.19	−.36	46	.34	.37	.52
7	.54	−.10	−.21	47	.34	.39	.55
8	.48	.10	.07	48	.51	.40	.92
9	.69	−.05	−.08	49	.38	.53	1.17
10	.55	.08	.01	50	.38	.44	.67
11	.66	−.12	−.01	51	.09	1.24	.29
12	.57	.06	−.06	52	−.09	1.23	.11
13	.52	.12	.20	53	.01	1.01	−.00
14	.50	.11	−.29	54	.08	1.29	−.31
15	.62	.14	.12	55	−.08	1.33	.10
16	.49	.08	.10	56	−.05	1.49	.38
17	.64	.14	−.12	57	−.00	1.29	.05
18	.68	−.09	−.02	58	.04	1.05	.24
19	.56	−.07	.04	59	−.02	.94	.12
20	.59	−.03	.15	60	.05	1.11	.08
21	.47	−.03	−.02	61	−.02	1.15	.16
22	.42	−.04	.17	62	.06	1.00	.12
23	.68	.06	−.11	63	.04	1.20	−.13
24	.58	−.05	−.28	64	−.08	1.49	.66
25	.69	−.18	.07	65	.00	1.17	.10
26	.65	.02	−.20	66	−.01	1.00	−.02
27	.62	−.04	−.27	67	.01	1.13	.00
28	.51	.02	.28	68	−.05	1.34	.07
29	.49	.17	.32	69	−.02	1.06	.16
30	.61	−.19	−.18	70	.03	.95	−.02
31	.37	.43	.67	71	−.09	1.18	.09
32	.44	.21	.39	72	.05	1.17	.16
33	.59	.45	.60	73	.13	1.23	.10
34	.52	.23	.44	74	−.05	1.17	.23
35	.37	.39	.33	75	−.00	1.19	.45
36	.41	.51	.63	76	−.03	1.14	.18
37	.41	.20	.30	77	−.04	1.26	.15
38	.33	.42	.78	78	.02	1.46	.07
39	.46	.38	.62	79	.02	1.02	−.14
40	.53	.45	.80	80	−.03	1.01	.22

designs are considered and demonstrations are given of the transformations to the same coordinate systems for these designs. The distinction between equating and linking is mentioned only when it adds to the understanding of the procedures.

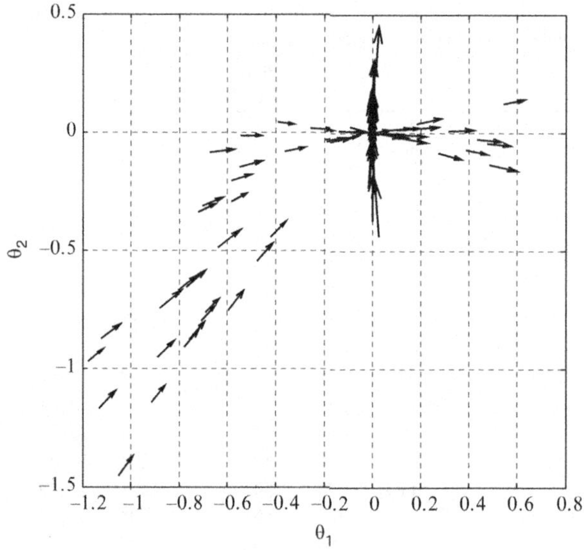

Fig. 9.4 Item arrows for the simulated English test after rotation, translation, and scaling

The three designs that are considered here are: the common-person design; the common-item, nonequivalent-groups design (also called the nonequivalent group anchor test (NEAT) design); and the randomly equivalent-groups design. The common-person design develops the transformation to the same coordinate system from the responses from a set of persons who take both test forms. No test items are in common between the test forms. The common-item nonequivalent-groups design develops the transformation to the same coordinate system from the calibration of the same set of items in both test forms. The randomly equivalent-groups design uses common reference composites for the tests and the assumption that the origin of the space is in the same location because the groups of examinees are randomly equivalent.

9.2.1 Common-Person Design

Suppose that a testing program has two forms of a test and would like to report the results of the tests within the same multidimensional framework. The goal is to put the $\boldsymbol{\theta}$-estimates from the two tests into the same coordinate system. One approach to doing this is to administer both test forms to a sample of examinees under conditions where it can be assumed that no change has occurred to the examinees between the administrations of test forms. The two test forms may be administered in counterbalanced order to control for fatigue or familiarity effects.

Because the examinees are assumed to be unchanged for the two test administrations, their relative locations in the $\boldsymbol{\theta}$-space should be the same. Any observed differences in location should be because of the arbitrary setting of origin, rotation of axes, and units on the coordinate axes. If a transformation can be identified that converts the locations of the examinees from the calibration of one test into the location from the calibration of another test, then that same transformation can be used to place the $\boldsymbol{\theta}$-points for all examinees taking the second test into the $\boldsymbol{\theta}$-space defined by the first test. Functions of the transformation of the $\boldsymbol{\theta}$s can also be used to put the item parameters into the same framework as the initial test.

For the example given here, the $\boldsymbol{\theta}$-space defined at the end of Sect. 9.1 will be considered as the results from the base form and the goal will be to transform the results from a second test form built to the same test specifications to this coordinate system. A random sample of 200 examinees from the calibration population for the first test form is administered the second test form along with the regular calibration sample for that form of 6,000. The sample of 6,000 may not be from the same population as the sample used to calibrate the first test form. Overall, the calibration sample for the second test is 6,200. This sample size should give item parameters that are well estimated, but the coordinate system defined by the second calibration is not expected to be equivalent to that defined by the calibration of the first test form. The results of the calibration of the items for the second test form are given in Table 9.5. The arrow plot based on the item parameter estimates is given in Fig. 9.5. A comparison of the item parameter estimates and the arrow plot for Form 2 to those from the initial form show that they have a very similar pattern, but they are not exactly the same. The results shown here are similar to those that would be obtained from careful construction of test forms to the same table of specifications.

The sample size of 200 used in the example was chosen for convenience. This should not be taken as a recommendation for the sample size for a common-person design. There is no research at this time that has investigated the size of sample needed for a common-person design. If the locations of the examinees were estimated without error, only a small number of examinees would be needed to determine the transformation. However, TESTFACT reports that the standard errors for the estimates of the coordinates for the examinee locations are in the range from .3 to .5 so a reasonably large sample size is needed to compensate for error in estimation when determining the transformation. A sample size of 200 was selected in this case because that number results in fairly good estimates of correlations.

Once the $\boldsymbol{\theta}$-estimates are obtained for the common examinees, the procedures described in Chap. 8 are used to determine the transformation that will minimize the squared difference in the locations of the individuals. The first step is to subtract the vector of the means of the coordinates from each of the coordinate vectors for the common examinees. Then a nonorthogonal Procrustes rotation is determined for rotating the estimates of the common persons' locations from the second test to match the same persons' locations in the base coordinate system (i.e., the coordinate system after aligning the reference composites to the axes and changing the origin and units). This methodology was described in Sect. 8.2.1.

Table 9.5 TESTFACT item parameter estimates for the simulated English Language Test Form 2

Item number	a_1	a_2	d	Item number	a_1	a_2	d
1	.60	.21	.21	41	.55	.25	.53
2	.64	.22	.30	42	.50	.37	.98
3	.77	.20	.44	43	.67	.28	.85
4	.67	.20	.20	44	.63	.46	.69
5	.71	.13	.50	45	.67	.36	.91
6	.67	.11	.50	46	.79	.53	.83
7	.42	.08	.19	47	.47	.36	.44
8	.63	.24	.29	48	.71	.32	.88
9	.88	.25	.37	49	.46	.37	.69
10	.83	.09	.57	50	.83	.41	1.35
11	.78	.17	.78	51	.28	.63	−.29
12	.62	.07	.28	52	.23	.60	−.58
13	.92	.13	.79	53	.23	.66	−.42
14	.79	.24	.04	54	.13	.58	−.53
15	.57	.17	.32	55	.21	.72	−.53
16	.61	.10	.34	56	.24	.76	−.39
17	.56	.14	.37	57	.29	.78	−.04
18	.85	.19	.23	58	.30	.82	.11
19	.74	.17	.25	59	.25	.50	−.11
20	.91	.28	.36	60	.18	.96	−.47
21	.84	.31	.50	61	.10	.57	−.15
22	.73	.15	.59	62	.22	.62	−.41
23	.83	.21	.46	63	.18	.81	−.47
24	.73	.18	.49	64	.29	.70	−.41
25	.59	.17	.45	65	.23	.82	−.01
26	.86	.34	.74	66	.12	.54	−.25
27	.79	.19	.58	67	.12	.72	−.46
28	.90	.25	.51	68	.26	.64	−.54
29	.91	.11	.34	69	.22	.65	−.45
30	.68	.19	.50	70	.21	.58	−.40
31	.64	.40	.85	71	.21	.74	−.48
32	.55	.42	.96	72	.20	.55	−.23
33	.64	.47	.82	73	.20	.60	−.28
34	.66	.34	.88	74	.20	.69	−.51
35	.65	.43	.53	75	.10	.56	−.30
36	.68	.33	.42	76	.29	.80	−.42
37	.67	.34	.75	77	.17	.57	−.27
38	.72	.35	.94	78	.13	.73	−.46
39	.59	.37	.91	79	.28	.73	−.64
40	.55	.41	.77	80	.18	.71	−.30

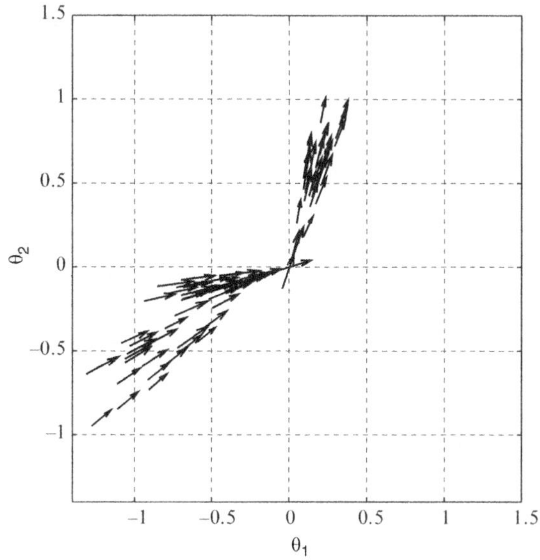

Fig. 9.5 Item arrows for the simulated English Language Test Form 2

In this case, the transformation matrix, labeled $\mathbf{M}^{-1}$ in (8.24), is

$$\begin{bmatrix} 1.0992 & .2089 \\ .2722 & .5530 \end{bmatrix}.$$

This matrix is the equivalent of **RotC** in (9.1). It is a fairly close match to that term, but it is not exactly the same. The differences are because of a combination of estimation error in the locations of the 200 common persons and differences between the first and second test forms.

The transformation matrix given earlier only accounts for the difference in the orientation of the coordinates axes between the TESTFACT calibration results and the base coordinate system that was developed earlier in this chapter. There is also a need to shift the origin from the results of the TESTFACT calibration to the origin of the base coordinate system. The expression for the shift in origin is given in (8.26). For the data used in this example, the value of **k** is given by

$$\begin{aligned} \mathbf{k} &= \bar{\boldsymbol{\theta}}_{\text{base}} - \bar{\boldsymbol{\theta}}_{\text{Form2}}\,\mathbf{M}^{-1} \\ &= \begin{bmatrix} .5385 & -.4301 \end{bmatrix} - \begin{bmatrix} -.0411 & .0125 \end{bmatrix} \begin{bmatrix} 1.0992 & .2089 \\ .2722 & .5530 \end{bmatrix} \\ &= \begin{bmatrix} .5802 & -.4285 \end{bmatrix}. \end{aligned} \tag{9.4}$$

The vector obtained here can be compared to the shift in origin from the original transformation to the base coordinate system given in (9.1). Note that the signs are different because in (9.1) the vector is subtracted while in determining **k** the terms are summed. The complete transformation for the **θ**-estimates from the second test is given by

$$\hat{\boldsymbol{\theta}}_{\text{base}} = \hat{\boldsymbol{\theta}}_{\text{Test}} \begin{bmatrix} 1.0992 & .2089 \\ .2772 & .5530 \end{bmatrix} + [.5802 \quad -.4285]. \tag{9.5}$$

As with the original transformation to the base coordinate system, the item parameters from the second test need to be transformed to the base coordinate system to maintain the invariance properties of the MIRT model. The **a**-parameter vectors must be multiplied by the transpose of the inverse of the multiplier of the **θ**-estimates from the second test. That is,

$$\hat{\mathbf{a}}_{\text{base}} = \hat{\mathbf{a}}_{\text{Test2}} \left(\mathbf{M}^{-1}\right)^{-1'} = \hat{\mathbf{a}}_{\text{Test2}} \mathbf{M}' = \hat{\mathbf{a}}_{\text{Test2}} \begin{bmatrix} 1.0036 & -.4940 \\ -.3792 & 1.9950 \end{bmatrix}. \tag{9.6}$$

Similarly, the d-parameter for each item needs to be transformed to the base coordinate system. This transformation is given by

$$\hat{\mathbf{d}}_{\text{base}} = \hat{\mathbf{d}}_{\text{Test2}} - \hat{\mathbf{a}}_{\text{Test2}} \mathbf{M}'\mathbf{k}'. \tag{9.7}$$

The results of the transformation of the item parameter estimates from the calibration of test Form 2 to the base coordinate system are given in Table 9.6 and Fig. 9.6. These results can be compared to those from the conversion of the calibration of the initial form to the base coordinate system. As with the initial conversion of Form 1 to the base coordinate system, the a_2-parameter estimates for the first 30 test items are now near zero with some negative. Similarly, for the last 30 test items, the a_1-parameter estimates are near zero. The item arrows in Fig. 9.6 show the orientation of the two item sets along the coordinate axes. This plot can be compared to Fig. 9.4 to determine the similarity of the solutions after they have been transferred to the base coordinate system.

9.2.2 Common-Item Design

Although the common-person design is conceptually straight forward, it is not used very often for operational linking and equating. There is usually some concern that the examinees will not be equally motivated when responding to the two test forms and counterbalancing the administration of the test forms may not be sufficient to balance differences in motivation. There may also be other types of carry-over effects, such as experience taking the test or fatigue effects, that may affect the comparability of performance on the two test forms. There may also be difficulties recruiting a sufficient size examinee sample to take both test forms. For these reasons other equating designs are more often implemented.

Table 9.6 TESTFACT item parameter estimates for the simulated English Language Test Form 2 after rotation, translation, and scaling to the base coordinate system using the common-person approach

Item number	a_1	a_2	d	Item number	a_1	a_2	d
1	.52	.13	−.03	41	.46	.23	.37
2	.56	.13	.03	42	.36	.49	.98
3	.70	.02	.04	43	.56	.23	.62
4	.59	.08	−.11	44	.46	.60	.68
5	.67	−.10	.07	45	.54	.39	.77
6	.63	−.10	.09	46	.59	.67	.77
7	.39	−.05	−.06	47	.34	.48	.45
8	.54	.17	.05	48	.59	.29	.67
9	.79	.06	−.07	49	.32	.52	.73
10	.79	−.22	.02	50	.68	.40	1.12
11	.73	−.05	.33	51	.04	1.13	.17
12	.59	−.16	−.13	52	.00	1.08	−.12
13	.87	−.20	.20	53	−.02	1.20	.11
14	.70	.10	−.32	54	−.09	1.10	−.01
15	.51	.05	.05	55	−.06	1.34	.08
16	.57	−.09	−.03	56	−.05	1.40	.24
17	.51	−.00	.07	57	−.01	1.41	.56
18	.78	−.04	−.24	58	−.01	1.48	.76
19	.68	−.03	−.16	59	.06	.87	.22
20	.81	.12	−.06	60	−.18	1.83	.42
21	.72	.21	.17	61	−.11	1.08	.37
22	.68	−.07	.17	62	−.02	1.14	.09
23	.75	.00	.03	63	−.12	1.52	.26
24	.67	−.00	.10	64	.02	1.26	.12
25	.53	.04	.16	65	−.08	1.52	.69
26	.74	.25	.41	66	−.08	1.01	.23
27	.72	−.01	.15	67	−.15	1.38	.22
28	.80	.06	.07	68	.02	1.14	−.06
29	.88	−.23	−.22	69	−.02	1.19	.07
30	.61	.05	.17	70	−.01	1.06	.06
31	.49	.48	.77	71	−.07	1.38	.16
32	.39	.57	.98	72	−.01	1.00	.21
33	.47	.62	.80	73	−.02	1.09	.20
34	.53	.35	.73	74	−.06	1.27	.07
35	.49	.54	.47	75	−.11	1.06	.22
36	.56	.33	.24	76	−.01	1.46	.21
37	.54	.35	.58	77	−.04	1.05	.21
38	.59	.35	.75	78	−.14	1.39	.22
39	.45	.45	.84	79	.01	1.31	−.09
40	.40	.54	.77	80	−.09	1.32	.32

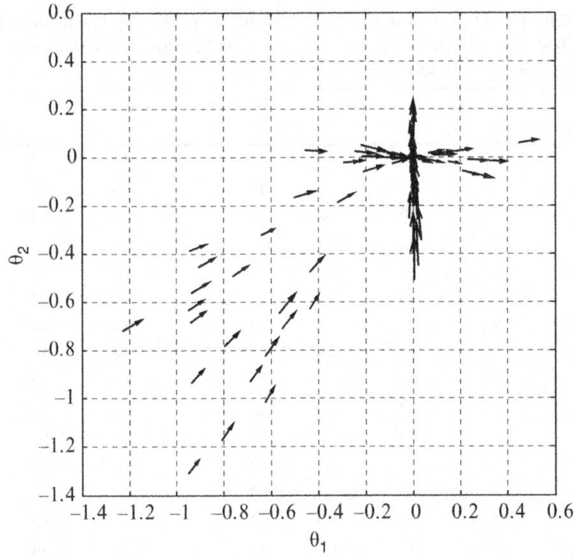

Fig. 9.6 Item arrows for Form 2 of the simulated English test after rotation, translation, and scaling

A frequently used equating design is the common-item design. Under this design, both test forms contain a subset of items that are identical across the forms. The size of the subset in common is usually 20% to 25% of the total test length. This set of items is typically selected to span the content of the test as a whole and to be as parallel as possible to the full test. Recent research (Sinharay and Holland 2007) has suggested that the common-item set does not need to have the same variation in difficulty as the full form, but it is not clear if that research will generalize to the MIRT case.

When a common-item design is used for linking calibrations or equating the reported scores from test forms, there is an assumption that the common test items will function in the same way in the two test forms. That means that the same relationship exists between the locations of the examinees in the $\boldsymbol{\theta}$-space and the probability of correct response for the test items. Any differences in the numerical values of item parameters from the calibration of the common items in the two test forms are assumed to be because of differences in the way that indeterminacies in the MIRT model are resolved by the calibration program. That is, if the item parameter estimates were represented in the same coordinate system, then the values should be the same because the items are identical across test forms.

A number of methods have been developed for determining the transformation needed to place the item parameter estimates from a common-item design onto the same scale. Some of these are summarized in Oshima, Davey, and Lee (2000). These methods are generalizations of the methods used for linking unidimensional

IRT calibrations. Among them are generalizations of the Stocking and Lord (1983) and the Haebara (1980) methods. Oshima, Davey, and Lee (2000) evaluated these different methods, but only considered a two-dimensional case. It is not clear that the results would generalize to item response data modeled using more than two dimensions. It is clear that more research is needed to investigate the functioning of methods for putting calibrations into the same coordinate system when the common-item design is used.

To demonstrate the use of the common-item design in this section, the two test forms from the previous section are used. As before, the initial test form is used to set the base coordinate system for the testing program. Sixteen test items are randomly selected from the 80 in the test form to produce the common-item link between the two calibrations. Six test items were selected from the first 30 items, four test items from the next 20 items, and six test items from the last 30 items. This stratified selection process insured that the common-item set would represent the three constructs that were the focus of the test.

The second test form is modified for this demonstration by replacing the corresponding items in that form with the common items selected from the first form. The item parameter estimates from the first form after transformation to the base coordinate system are the target for the transformation. The goal of the linking/equating is to find the transformation that will convert the item parameter estimates from the second test form to be as close as possible to those in the base coordinate system. Table 9.7 lists the item numbers for the common items, the item parameter estimates in the base coordinate system and the item parameter estimates from the calibration of Form 2 based on a sample of 6,000 examinees.

Table 9.7 Item parameter estimates for the common items from the base coordinate system and from the initial calibration of Form 2

Item	Base calibration			Form 2 calibration		
number	a_1	a_2	d	a_1	a_2	d
3	.71	−.14	−.08	.82	.17	.40
6	.69	−.19	−.36	.74	.74	.18
8	.48	.10	.07	.66	.17	.38
16	.49	.08	.10	.59	.20	.33
18	.68	−.09	−.02	.77	.15	.45
21	.47	−.03	−.02	.58	.13	.29
37	.41	.20	.30	.54	.26	.47
44	.39	.45	.43	.55	.38	.48
45	.42	.45	.81	.55	.42	.86
49	.38	.53	1.17	.54	.45	1.17
63	.04	1.20	−.13	.26	.72	−.63
70	.03	.95	−.02	.16	.62	−.42
71	−.09	1.18	.09	.12	.74	−.50
72	.05	1.17	.16	.29	.72	−.33
77	−.04	1.26	.15	.18	.70	−.39
79	.01	1.02	−.14	.20	.64	−.56

The transformation from the Test 2 item parameter estimates for the common items to the item parameter estimates on the base coordinate system can be determined from the equations given in Chap. 8. The rotation and scaling of the **a**-parameters is given by (8.31). The matrix determined by this equation is the nonorthogonal Procrustes rotation of the Test 2 **a**-parameter estimates to the base coordinate system **a**-parameters. For the common items given in Table 9.7, the transformation matrix for the **a**-parameters is

$$\begin{bmatrix} .9140 & -.4705 \\ -.2674 & 1.7781 \end{bmatrix}.$$

The matrix of **a**-parameters from Test 2 is postmultiplied by this matrix to put the parameters onto the scale of the base coordinate system. The transpose of the inverse of this matrix can be used to transform the $\boldsymbol{\theta}$-estimates after they have been translated to have a mean of 0. The matrix given earlier is comparable to the result of (9.6) for the common-person method of linking calibrations. These matrices are not the same because the two methods are minimizing different errors. The common-person method is minimizing differences in person locations. The common-item method is minimizing errors in item parameters.

The conversion of the **d**-parameters from the common items to the base coordinate system is done using (8.33). The **a**-parameters in that equation are those in the base coordinate system. The value of $\boldsymbol{\Omega}$ is determined from (8.34) using the item parameter estimates from the items that are common to the two test forms. For the item parameter estimates given in Table 9.7, $\boldsymbol{\Omega}$ is

$$\begin{bmatrix} .6285 \\ -.4363 \end{bmatrix}.$$

Once these two conversion equations have been determined, the full set of item parameters from Test 2 can be converted to the base coordinate system. There is one complication in the use of (8.33). Test Form 2 does not have **a**-parameters for the noncommon items from the base coordinate system. Therefore, the **a**-parameters for the full Form 2 must first be converted to the base coordinate system as described earlier, and then the converted **a**-parameters are used in (8.33). The result of the application of (8.33) to the **d**-parameters is given in Table 9.8.

The results of the transformation of the item parameters from the Test 2 calibration to the base coordinate system can be checked by comparing the item parameter estimates from the common items after transformation with the values from the calibration in the base coordinate system. For example, the parameter estimates for Item 49 in the base coordinate system were [.38 .53 1.17]. The results from the Test 2 calibration after transformation are [.37 .54 1.17], an extremely close match. Not all of the pairs of parameter estimates were this close, but the overall match in this example is very good.

Table 9.8 Test 2 item parameter estimates for the simulated English Language Test Form 2 after rotation, translation, and scaling to the base coordinate system using the common-item approach

Item number	a_1	a_2	d	Item number	a_1	a_2	d
1	.49	.03	−.04	41	.44	.28	.36
2	.56	.03	−.03	42	.38	.49	1.00
3	.70	−.08	−.08	43	.51	.22	.58
4	.60	−.05	−.17	44	.41	.41	.40
5	.62	−.12	.09	45	.39	.49	.82
6	.65	−.14	−.29	46	.55	.59	.72
7	.37	−.10	−.07	47	.34	.44	.44
8	.56	−.00	.03	48	.53	.31	.67
9	.75	−.06	−.12	49	.37	.54	1.17
10	.65	−.14	.13	50	.62	.31	1.08
11	.64	−.09	.32	51	.08	.91	.05
12	.49	−.08	−.04	52	.06	.91	−.22
13	.76	−.21	.22	53	.03	1.11	.06
14	.69	−.01	−.39	54	−.02	1.07	−.04
15	.47	.02	.04	55	.03	1.16	−.00
16	.48	.08	.06	56	.02	1.24	.12
17	.47	−.03	.06	57	.04	1.25	.45
18	.65	−.09	−.00	58	.02	1.39	.70
19	.57	−.07	−.13	59	.04	.82	.17
20	.69	.10	−.01	60	−.04	1.48	.25
21	.49	−.04	−.04	61	−.04	.91	.27
22	.60	−.06	.15	62	.02	1.14	.05
23	.67	−.02	.00	63	.05	1.15	−.15
24	.57	−.03	.14	64	.08	1.12	.04
25	.52	−.05	.09	65	−.05	1.43	.65
26	.65	.14	.35	66	−.02	.92	.18
27	.64	−.08	.09	67	−.06	1.09	.07
28	.80	−.08	−.02	68	.03	1.09	−.10
29	.77	−.13	−.12	69	.05	1.00	−.04
30	.59	−.04	.14	70	−.02	1.03	.05
31	.44	.41	.72	71	−.08	1.26	.10
32	.42	.46	.89	72	.07	1.14	.12
33	.47	.59	.81	73	−.00	.99	.19
34	.49	.30	.72	74	−.03	1.21	.04
35	.49	.52	.45	75	−.06	.97	.12
36	.50	.26	.20	76	−.00	1.32	.12
37	.42	.21	.30	77	−.03	1.17	.13
38	.53	.39	.81	78	−.12	1.31	.18
39	.44	.35	.80	79	.02	1.04	−.12
40	.39	.44	.72	80	−.02	1.10	.26

After the item parameter estimates from the test have been converted to the base coordinate system, the transformation of the $\boldsymbol{\theta}$-vectors can be determined. The transformation is derived by noting that the values of the exponents of the model for the items must remain the same for the invariance property of the MIRT model to hold. Using the notation that $\mathbf{a_b}$ represents the item discrimination parameters after transformation to the base coordinate system, $\mathbf{a}_2$ represents the item discrimination parameters for the same items from the initial calibration of Test 2, $\mathbf{d_b}$ and $\mathbf{d_2}$ are the corresponding intercept terms, $\boldsymbol{\theta}$ is the matrix of coordinates in the base coordinate system for the examinees used in the calibration, and $\boldsymbol{\nu}$ is the matrix of coordinates for the calibration sample from the Test 2 calibration, the transformation of the Test 2 person parameters, $\boldsymbol{\nu}$, to the base coordinate system is given in (9.8).

$$\begin{aligned}
\mathbf{a}_b\boldsymbol{\theta}' + \mathbf{d}_b\mathbf{1} &= \mathbf{a}_2\boldsymbol{\nu}' + \mathbf{d}_2\mathbf{1}, \\
\mathbf{a}_b\boldsymbol{\theta}' &= \mathbf{a}_2\boldsymbol{\nu}' + \mathbf{d}_2\mathbf{1} - \mathrm{d}_b\mathbf{1}, \\
\mathbf{a}_b'\mathbf{a}_b\boldsymbol{\theta}' &= \mathbf{a}_b'\left[\mathbf{a}_2\boldsymbol{\nu}' + (\mathbf{d}_2 - \mathrm{d}_b)\,\mathbf{1}\right], \\
\left(\mathbf{a}_b'\mathbf{a}_b\right)^{-1}\mathbf{a}_b'\mathbf{a}_b\boldsymbol{\theta}' &= \left(\mathbf{a}_b'\mathbf{a}_b\right)^{-1}\mathbf{a}_b'\left[\mathbf{a}_2\boldsymbol{\nu}' + (\mathbf{d}_2 - \mathbf{d}_b)\,\mathbf{1}\right], \\
\boldsymbol{\theta}' &= \left(\mathbf{a}_b'\mathbf{a}_b\right)^{-1}\mathbf{a}_b'\mathbf{a}_2\boldsymbol{\nu}' + \left(\mathbf{a}_b'\mathbf{a}_b\right)^{-1}\mathbf{a}_b'(\mathbf{d}_2 - \mathbf{d}_b)\,\mathbf{1}.
\end{aligned} \tag{9.8}$$

The last line of (9.8) has the nonorthogonal Procrustes rotation to a target of $\mathbf{a}_2$ as the multiplier of $\boldsymbol{\nu}$. This is the opposite of the rotation of the $\mathbf{a}_2$-parameters that has a target of the rotation of $\mathbf{a_b}$. The term on the right of the last line is the same as (8.34). The equation in the last line of (9.8) can only be used after the item parameter estimates have been transformed from the Test 2 calibration to the base coordinate system. At that time, all of the values needed in the equation are available and the estimates of location in the space defined by the calibration of Test 2 can be transformed to locations in the base coordinate system.

9.2.3 Randomly Equivalent-Groups Design

The randomly equivalent-groups design is used with some frequency for equating when tests are assumed to be sensitive to differences in examinee performance on a single composite of skills. The examinee sample is randomly divided into two or more subsamples with the number of samples equal to the number of test forms to be equated. The assumption is that the distribution of performance on the composite of skills being assessed should be the same across samples because of the random assignment of forms to samples and any differences in distributions are because of slight differences in the characteristics of the tests. Transforming the scores from the different forms of the tests to a common scale involves determining the transformation that will yield distributions with the same features for all test forms. Linear transformations and the equipercentile method are often used with the randomly equivalent-groups design (see Kolen and Brennan 2004).

The randomly equivalent-groups design is effective because carefully constructed test forms can be assumed to result in score scales that have the same conceptual meaning. That is, the construct that is represented by the test scores is the same across all forms. Also, the distributions of performance are assumed to be the same because of the random assignment to groups. With sufficient sample size, there is statistical justification for the assumption of a common distribution.

The use of the randomly equivalent-groups design for the multidimensional case has an additional complication over the unidimensional application because the orientation of the coordinate axes might not be the same for the calibration of two test forms even when the examinee groups are random samples from the same population. Also, there are no common test items that can be used to determine the rotation needed to align the coordinate axes. The use of randomly equivalent groups in the multidimensional case requires developing a criterion for rotating the coordinate axes to a common orientation.

Future work in MIRT will no doubt come up with other ways of solving this problem, but here the solution is determined from the reference composites for the constructs assessed by the tests. As with the unidimensional case, it is assumed that the test forms were constructed to be parallel, or at least be measuring common constructs. If those constructs can be identified for both test forms, then the coordinate axes can be transformed to a common orientation by finding the rotation that will align the reference composites from the tests.

This approach to equating or linking MIRT calibrations has the following steps:

1. For a test with parameters in the base coordinate system, determine the sets of test items that best measure each of the reference composites. A transformation to the base coordinate system should already be available for this test form.
2. Administer the base test, Test 1, and the new test, Test 2, to randomly eqivalent groups of examinees.
3. Calibrate Test 1 using this sample and determine the directions of the reference composites in the coordinate space. The direction cosines of the reference composites are used as the **a**-parameters for the reference composites. They are collected together into a matrix that will be used as the target to determine the rotation for the calibration results from Test 2.
4. Calibrate Test 2 using a sample of examinees that is randomly equivalent to the sample for the base test.
5. Using procedures like the cluster analysis described in Sect. 8.3, determine the sets of items that correspond to the reference composites from Test 1.
6. Determine the directions of the reference composites for Test 2 and compute the reference composite **a**-matrix for Test 2.
7. Determine the nonorthogonal procrustes rotation that will convert the directions of the reference composites in Test 2 to the directions of the reference composites for Test 1.
8. The rotation matix can be used to convert all of the **a**-parameters on Test 2 to the coordinate system for Test 1. The inverse rotation can be used to convert the location parameters from Test 2.

After the rotation of the item and person parameters to the Test 1 coordinate system, they can be transformed to the base coordinate system using the same transformation that was used on Test 1. Because the groups are randomly equivalent, there should be no need to change the origin and units of measurement, but if necessary, the same methods used in Sect. 9.2.1 can be applied.

This method of linking calibrations can be demonstrated using the two test forms with item parameter estimates given in Tables 9.1 and 9.5. These two sets of parameters were estimated from data generated assuming the same underlying distribution of $\boldsymbol{\theta}$. Therefore, they are equivalent to results from tests calibrated using the randomly equivalent-groups design.

Because this is a simulated example, the clusters of test items related to constructs are known. For real tests, the test items are intended to measure specific sets of content and skills, but it is important to verify that test items measuring the same constructs cluster together. This can be part of the evidence for the content validity of the test.

For the simulated tests used here, the reference composites for the clusters of items were determined for the two test forms. The eigenvectors corresponding to the largest eigenvalues for each construct are given in Table 9.9. After obtaining the eigenvectors for the reference composites for the two test forms, the nonorthogonal Procrustes rotation was determined for rotating the Test 2 reference composites to align with the Test 1 reference composites. In this case, the two test forms were very parallel in construction so the rotation was close to the identity matrix

$$\begin{bmatrix} 1.0036 & -.0115 \\ -.0056 & 1.0080 \end{bmatrix}.$$

The matrix of eigenvectors from Test 2 is then postmultiplied by this rotation matrix to transform them to the same coordinate system as Test 1. This same rotation matrix would also be applied to the **a**-parameter matrix from Test 2 to put the **a**-parameters into the Test 1 coordinate system. After this adjustment, the same transformation that was applied to Test 1 in Sect. 9.1 can be applied to the results for Test 2 to put them onto the base coordinate system for the testing program.

The results presented here are much better than those obtained for operational tests. In actual testing situations, it is difficult to identify the sets of items that are best at measuring each reference composite and the construction of the tests will not

Table 9.9 Eigenvectors for the reference composites for Test 1, Test 2, and Test 2 after nonorthogonal Procrustes rotation to match Test 1.

Construct	Eigenvectors					
	Test 1		Test 2		Rotated Test 2	
	1	2	1	2	1	2
Reading	.9741	.2262	.9700	.2429	.9722	.2337
Vocabulary	.8568	.5157	.8590	.5120	.8592	.5062
Conversation	.2898	.9571	.2933	.9560	.2890	.9603

likely be as parallel as this example. The quality of the linkage of the calibrations will depend on how well items can be connected to constructs and how well forms have been constructed.

9.3 Estimating Scores on Constructs

Many tests of cognitive abilities are purposely constructed to assess many different types of skills and content knowledge. For example, the Mathematics Test of the ACT college admissions test battery (ACT, Inc. 2007) includes test items that are designed to assess prealgebra, elementary algebra, intermediate algebra, coordinate geometry, plane geometry, and trigonometry. When tests are constructed to cover a wide variety of skills and content, there is often a desire to report results on the performance on the full set of test items and on the constructs defined by the subsets of items. The common approach to reporting results on the separate constructs in the test design is to create shorter tests from the separate sets of items related to each construct and develop proficiency estimates from each test item set. This approach can sometimes lead to inaccurate results when the number of test items related to a construct is small. But even in those cases, there are often pressures from users of the tests to report those inaccurate results.

The approach to the reporting of scores on separate constructs taken in this section avoids the problem of using small sets of test items by not estimating proficiency on those sets of items in isolation. Rather, the full set of test items is used to estimate the location of an individual in the multidimensional space defined by the matrix of item response data and the MIRT model. The subsets of test items that are of interest for reporting results are used to define reference composites in the same multidimensional space. Then, the reporting of results on these item sets is accomplished by mapping the estimated location of the person onto each of the reference composites. Two methods for accomplishing this mapping are presented here: rotation and projection. These methods are mathematically closely related, but they are somewhat different from a conceptual viewpoint so they will be described separately. To make the description of the methods concrete, the first example from this chapter will be used to demonstrate the methods.

Suppose the test described at the beginning of this chapter was administered to a large sample of examinees and the resulting item-score matrix was calibrated yielding the results given in Table 9.1. The constructs assessed by the test were described in the test specifications and were confirmed using cluster analysis of the angular differences yielding the result in Figs. 9.1 and 9.2. The goal is to report four measures of performance on this test, a measure of overall performance and a measure on each of the three constructs described in the test specifications – reading, vocabulary, and conversation.

The $\boldsymbol{\theta}$-vectors estimated from each person obtained from the original calibration of the item response data do not provide any of the desired measures. The $\boldsymbol{\theta}$-vectors do provide estimates of the locations of the individuals in the coordinate system

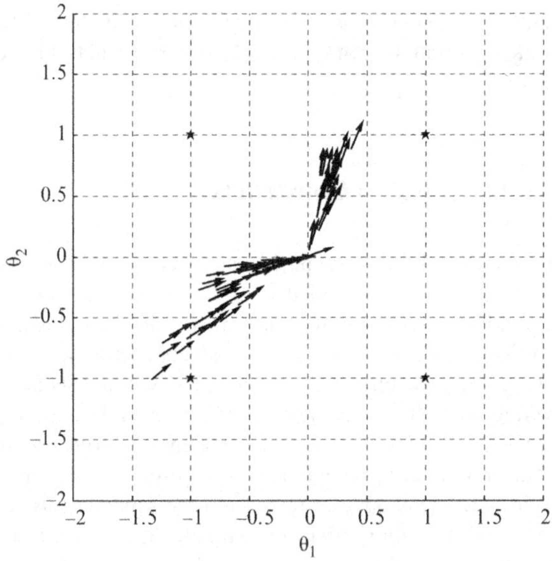

Fig. 9.7 $\boldsymbol{\theta}$-points (*stars*) and item arrows from the initial calibration

initially defined by the TESTFACT calibration. The demonstration given here will use four hypothetical individuals out of the initial calibration sample to show how to derive the reported proficiency estimates. Suppose these four individuals have initial $\boldsymbol{\theta}$-vectors of (1, 1), (1, −1), (−1, 1), and (−1, −1). Each of these $\boldsymbol{\theta}$-vectors from the initial calibration will be used to determine the levels of proficiency on each of the desired reporting constructs. The locations of these points are given in Fig. 9.7 along with the item vectors for the test.

9.3.1 Construct Estimates Using Rotation

When determining the base coordinate system in Sect. 9.1 of this chapter, the reference composites for the reading and conversation constructs were rotated to align with the coordinate axes. The result is that if the $\boldsymbol{\theta}$-vectors are transformed using the corresponding rotations and translations, the new coordinates for the person locations yield the estimates on two of the constructs that were targets of measurement for this test. Part of the work of getting the estimates of proficiency can be done by transforming the four $\boldsymbol{\theta}$-vectors to the new base coordinate system using the transformations given in (9.1). After this transformation, the θ_1 values are the estimates of the reading construct and the θ_2 values are the estimates of the conversation construct. The location of the points for the four hypothetical individuals and the item arrows after transformation to the base scale is shown in Fig. 9.8.

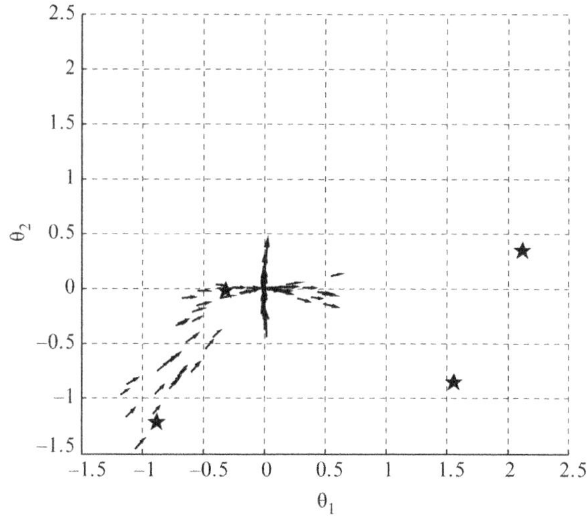

Fig. 9.8 Locations of points (*stars*) and item arrows after transformation

Although the rotation of the initial calibration to align two of the constructs along the coordinate axes solves part of the problem, there is still the need to determine the estimates for the vocabulary construct and the test as a whole. To do that, the reference composites for the total test and the vocabulary items are needed for the final reporting coordinate system. These can be determined using the final **a**-parameters shown in Table 9.4. The eigenvector for the reference composite of the vocabulary items is [.73 .68]. This is a direction that is 43° from the θ_1-axis. If the axes are rotated around the origin 43° in a counterclockwise direction, the θ_1-axis will be aligned with the reference composite for the vocabulary items. Then the coordinates of the person locations on the θ_1-axis will give estimates of the proficiency on the vocabulary component of the test.

The rotation required to align the θ_1-axis with the vocabulary reference composite can be determined using (9.8) in this case because the solution is in two dimensions. The rotation matrix to align the vocabulary reference composite with the θ_1-axis is

$$\begin{bmatrix} .73 & -.68 \\ .68 & .73 \end{bmatrix}.$$

Postmultiplying the locations of persons in the space with this same matrix results in their locations in the rotated coordinate system. The item vector plot and the locations of the four reference points after the rotation are shown in Fig. 9.9. After this rotation, the vocabulary proficiency can be determined from the projections of the locations on the θ_1-axis.

The same process can be followed to determine the level of performance on the reference composite for the entire test. The eigenvector for the reference composite for the full test is [.100 .995]. This corresponds to a reference compose that is at

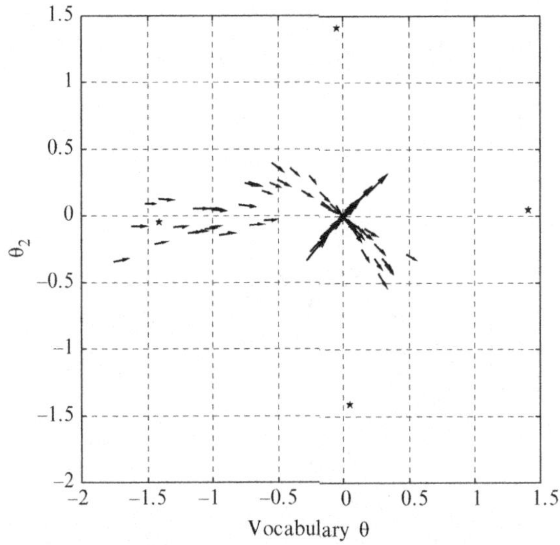

Fig. 9.9 Item arrows and locations (*stars*) after aligning θ_1 with the vocabulary reference composite

84° with the θ_1-axis. This reference composite is closely aligned with the directions of best measurement for the speaking items because of the rescaling that was done that resulted in higher a-parameters for the θ_2-coordinate axis. Under this scaling, the total test score estimates will be highly related to the speaking construct. The transformation of scale resulted in a higher weighting in the reference composite of the speaking construct. The rotation to align the full test reference composite with the θ_1-axis is

$$\begin{bmatrix} .100 & -.995 \\ .995 & .100 \end{bmatrix}.$$

The results of the rotation are shown in Fig. 9.10. As with the previous result, the coordinates of the locations shown by the stars on the θ_1-axis are now a measure of the proficiency of the persons on the full reference composite for the test.

9.3.2 *Construct Estimates Using Projection*

Another approach to obtaining estimates of the location of examinees on the constructs defined by sets of test items is to project the locations of the examinees in the $\boldsymbol{\theta}$-space orthogonally onto the lines for each of the reference composites for the sets of items. Using the example from the previous section, consider the locations of the four example points in the $\boldsymbol{\theta}$-space and four reference composites for the

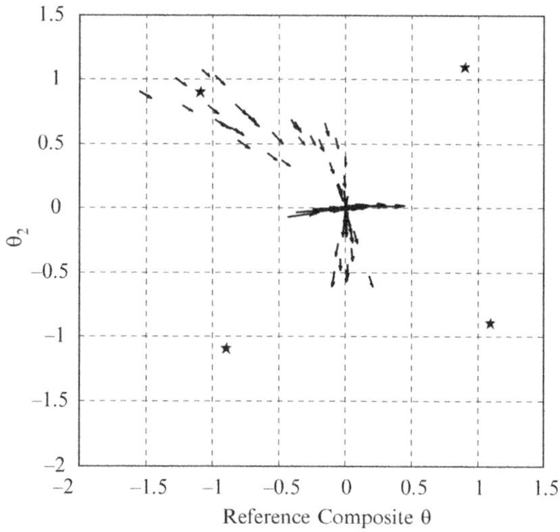

Fig. 9.10 Rotation to align the θ_1-axis with the reference composite of the test

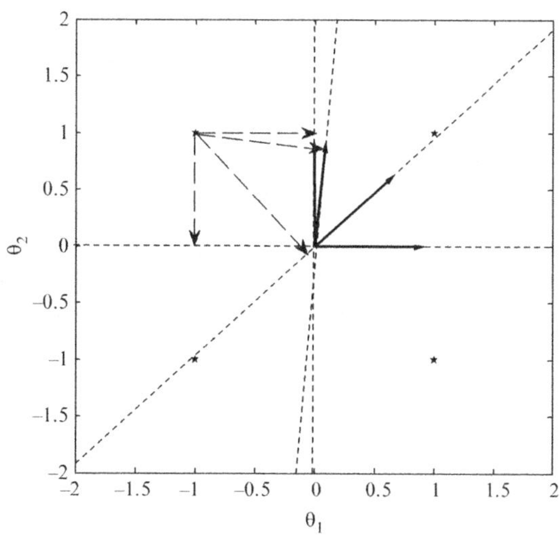

Fig. 9.11 Reference composites (*solid arrows*) with four points in the $\boldsymbol{\theta}$-space (*stars*) with projections from one point to each of the reference composites (*broken line arrows*).

test – the reference composites for each of vocabulary, reading, conversation, and the total test. The four points and the four reference composites are shown the base coordinate system in Fig. 9.11.

Figure 9.11 shows each reference composite as an arrow and the dotted lines show the extensions of the reference composites to the full space. The arrows drawn with broken lines in the figure show the orthogonal projections from the (−1, 1)

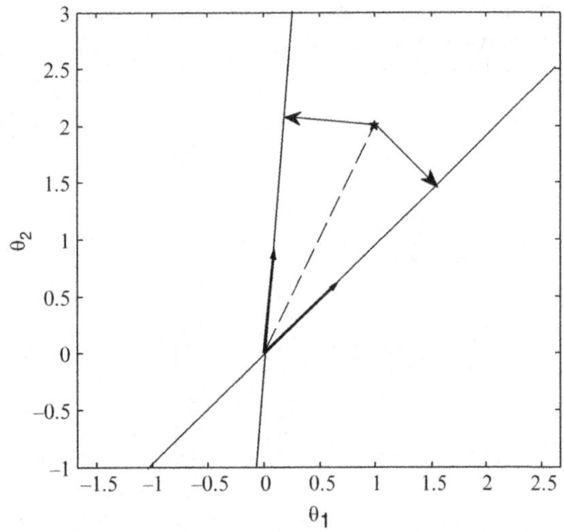

Fig. 9.12 Reference composites for the test and the set of vocabulary items (*dark arrows*) and projections from a $\boldsymbol{\theta}$-point (*star*) to the reference composites (shown by *light arrows*)

$\boldsymbol{\theta}$-point to each of the reference composites. The remainder of this section will show how to determine the values of the projections of the points in the $\boldsymbol{\theta}$-space onto any line specified in the $\boldsymbol{\theta}$-space. To simplify the presentation, a two-dimensional example will be used to show the development of the projections, but all of the methods work equally well for projections in higher dimensions.

Reference composites are specified by vectors of direction cosines related to the angles between the coordinate axes and the line indicating the reference composite. Figure 9.12 shows the reference composites for the total test and the vocabulary items and one $\boldsymbol{\theta}$-point at $(1,2)$ in the $\boldsymbol{\theta}$-space. There is also a line in the figure from the origin of the space to the $\boldsymbol{\theta}$-point. This line also has angles with the coordinate axes and corresponding direction cosines. The length of the line from the origin to the point is given by

$$L = \sqrt{\sum_{\ell=1}^{m} \theta_\ell^2}, \tag{9.9}$$

and the direction cosines for the line are given by

$$\cos\alpha_\ell = \frac{\theta_\ell}{L}, \quad \ell = 1 \ldots m, \tag{9.10}$$

where α_ℓ is the angle between axis ℓ and the line to the $\boldsymbol{\theta}$-point. For this example, the direction cosines with the two axes are .4472 and .8944. These correspond to angles of 63° and 27° with the coordinate axes.

The direction cosines for the vocabulary reference composite are .7305 and .6829 with corresponding angles of 43° and 47° with the coordinate axes. Thus, the angle between the line to the $\boldsymbol{\theta}$-point and the vocabulary reference composite is 20°. The line from the origin to the $\boldsymbol{\theta}$-point, the arrow from the $\boldsymbol{\theta}$-point to the vocabulary reference composite, and the line segment of the reference composite from the origin to the projection for the $\boldsymbol{\theta}$-point form a right triangle. The right triangle properties can be used to determine the projection of the $\boldsymbol{\theta}$-point onto the reference composite. The distance from the projection of the $\boldsymbol{\theta}$-point on the vocabulary reference composite to the origin is simply $\cos 20^\circ \sqrt{1^2 + 2^2} = 2.1$. A similar approach can be taken for the reference composite for the full test. The difference in angles is 21° and the distance of the projection on that reference composite from the origin is also about 2.1.

This process of projection onto a reference composite for $\boldsymbol{\theta}$-points can be done in matrix terms for all of the estimated $\boldsymbol{\theta}$s in a sample. The vector of distances of the $\boldsymbol{\theta}$-points from the origin, $\mathbf{L}$, is given by

$$\mathbf{L} = \sqrt{\operatorname{diag}\left(\boldsymbol{\theta}\boldsymbol{\theta}'\right)}, \tag{9.11}$$

and the direction cosines for each point are determined by dividing each set of coordinates, $\boldsymbol{\theta}_j$ by the corresponding element of $\mathbf{L}$, L_j.

$$\cos \boldsymbol{\alpha}_{\mathrm{j}} = \frac{\boldsymbol{\alpha}_{\mathrm{j}}}{L_j}. \tag{9.12}$$

The cosine of the angle between the line from the origin to the $\boldsymbol{\theta}$-point and the direction of the reference composite can be found by the inner product of the direction cosines from (9.12) and those for the reference composite, $\cos\, \boldsymbol{\alpha}_{\mathrm{rc}}$. If $\mathbf{A}$ is the full matrix of angles between the lines from the origin to each $\boldsymbol{\theta}$-point, then the direction cosines for the angles between these lines and the line for each reference composite, $\mathbf{A}_{\theta\mathrm{rc}}$, is given by (see (7.30) in Chap. 7)

$$\cos\, \mathbf{A}_{\theta\mathrm{rc}} = \cos\, \mathbf{A} \cos\, \boldsymbol{\alpha}_{\mathrm{rc}}'. \tag{9.13}$$

The projection of each $\boldsymbol{\theta}$-point onto each reference composite is then given by

$$RC_j = L_j \cos\, \alpha_{j,\theta rc} \tag{9.14}$$

where RC_j is the projection on the reference composite for person j and $\cos\, \alpha_{j,\theta rc}$ is the jth element of $\cos\, \mathbf{A}_{\theta\mathrm{rc}}$.

The projections onto each of the reference composites from the simulated language test were determined for each of the four example $\boldsymbol{\theta}$-points used in the previous section. The results are presented in Table 9.10. These projections give the same results as the rotation method used in the previous section.

While the projection and rotation methods for determining estimates on the reference composites yield the same results, the projection method is much more convenient. A number of reference composites can be specified as rows in a matrix of direction cosines and a matrix of $\boldsymbol{\theta}$-values can be projected on each of the reference composites in one operation. The concept of reference composite and the

Table 9.10 Projections of the four $\boldsymbol{\theta}$-points onto each of the reference composites

θ_1	θ_2	Reference composite			
		Total	Reading	Vocabulary	Speaking
1	1	1.09	.99	1.41	1.00
1	−1	−.90	1.01	.05	−1.00
−1	1	.90	−1.01	−.05	1.00
−1	−1	−1.09	−.99	−1.41	−1.00

projection method provide a practical way for computing subscores from an MIRT analysis. Meaningful subscores can be identified by finding sets of items that best measure in approximately the same direction in the multidimensional space. Reference composites can be determined for these sets of items. Then, each $\boldsymbol{\theta}$-point can be projected onto as many reference composites as have been identified. The goal for the testing enterprise is to accurately estimate the location of the person in the $\boldsymbol{\theta}$-space. With an accurate estimate of $\boldsymbol{\theta}$, results on specific composites of coordinates can easily be determined.

9.4 Summary and Discussion

This chapter provides a set of tools for reporting the results of MIRT analyses of the item-score matrices from tests. First, methods are provided for configuring a $\boldsymbol{\theta}$-space for reporting results. This $\boldsymbol{\theta}$-space need not be the one that is the default given by a calibration program. The initial calibration can be rotated, translated, and scaled to give a more useful solution. In the example provided in the Sect. 9.1 , the solution was rotated so that the coordinate axes aligned with two of the constructs being measured by the test. The result of that rotation is that the values of the coordinates for $\boldsymbol{\theta}$-points correspond to measures of the selected constructs. The calibrations were also scaled to yield the size of units desired for each coordinate axis.

The second section of this chapter, Sect. 9.2, shows how to link the results of calibrations from different tests. This is a necessary step if the results of the tests are to be reported in a way that has common meaning. Linking calibrations is also needed when large sets of test items are needed with comparable item parameter estimates. This is the case for banking test items for use in later test construction and for the development of item pools for CATs. A number of methods for linking calibrations are provided, but the common-item item design is the most commonly used. As MIRT applications become more common, it is likely that additional linking methods will be developed.

The procedures for linking calibrations and equating tests are essentially the same, but equating places much stronger requirements on the process. For estimates of persons' locations from different test forms that have had item parameter estimates transformed to the same $\boldsymbol{\theta}$ coordinate system to be considered equated, the estimates must have the same error in every direction in the space. This places very strong requirements on creating parallel test forms. While it is theoretically possible to perform multidimensional equating using MIRT models, there has been little research that shows that the results meet the theoretical requirements for equating. This is an interesting area for future research.

Section 9.3 showed how to determine estimates of proficiency on composites of the coordinate axes. These composites are typically specified by selecting subsets of test items and determining the direction of best measurement for the set. This direction is called the reference composite for the set. The methodology for getting estimates on the composite is very general, however. Users can specify any direction in the space and get estimates of performance on the composite that corresponds to that direction by either rotating a coordinate axis to align with that direction, or projecting onto a line in that direction. These methods provide very powerful tools for subscore reporting. The methods shown here are different than those that fit a unidimensional IRT model to the subsets of test items in that information from all test items are used to estimate $\boldsymbol{\theta}$. All of that information is used to estimate the location on the reference composite rather than only the information from the limited set of items.

MIRT procedures for linking calibrations, equating test forms, and reporting examinee scores are still very much in development. It will be interesting to track how these methods are refined through future research.

9.5 Exercises

1. The randomly equivalent-groups method of linking MIRT calibrations and person locations is based on some strong assumptions about the examinee samples and the characteristics of the test forms. List the assumptions and indicate how the results of the linking will likely be affected if the assumptions do not hold.

2. Specify your own desired orientation for the item calibration results given in Table 9.1. Develop a rotation matrix, translation constants, and scaling constants and apply them to the item parameters. Also, transform two or three $\boldsymbol{\theta}$ vectors. Show that the probability of correct response to one of the test items stays the same before and after the transformation.

3. After the calibration of a set of test items in a two-dimensional $\boldsymbol{\theta}$-space, the angle between the reference composites for two sets of test items is 45°. The correlation between the coordinates for the $\boldsymbol{\theta}$-points for this calibration is 0.0. The results were then rotated to align the two reference composites with the coordinate axes so that the angle between them is 90°. What will be the correlation between the $\boldsymbol{\theta}$-coordinates if they are transformed to maintain the invariance properties of the model?

4. Discuss the results presented in Figs. 9.1 and 9.2. Identify the clusters that correspond to the sets of item vectors. Explain how the horizontal lines in the dendrogram relate to the orientation of the item vectors in Fig. 9.1.

5. The vocabulary projection in Table 9.10 yields a larger value for the $\boldsymbol{\theta}$-point $(1,1)$ than for the projections on the other reference composites. Explain why that is the case. Can this result be interpreted that the person at $(1,1)$ is more proficient in vocabulary than on the other reference composites? Explain why you think your answer is correct.

6. A reference composite for one of the constructs measured by the items on a test has direction cosines [.53 .59 .08 .60]. The estimated location in the $\boldsymbol{\theta}$-space for an examinee is $[-.4\ \ -1.7\ \ .1\ \ .3]$. What is the estimated location on the line defined by the reference composite for this examinee?

7. For the point at $(-1,-1)$ in Fig. 9.11, draw the projection arrows to each of the reference composites for the example test. What is the estimate on each of the reference composites for a person located at this point?

8. List the assumptions required by the use of the randomly equivalent-groups design for linking MIRT calibrations and putting $\boldsymbol{\theta}$-estimates into a common $\boldsymbol{\theta}$-space. Suppose one test form does not include any test items sensitive to differences on a construct that is well measured by the items on the other test form. Discuss the problems that are likely to occur if an attempt is made to link the calibrations from these two tests.

9. An examinee has a $\boldsymbol{\theta}$-estimate of $(-1.1, 1.2)$ on Form 2 of the test used in Sect. 9.2.2. What is the $\boldsymbol{\theta}$-estimate on the base form for this examinee?

10. The $\boldsymbol{\theta}$-space defined by one test form is transformed to align with the $\boldsymbol{\theta}$-space for another test form using the common-person, nonequivalent-groups design. When this design is used, the $\boldsymbol{\theta}$-estimates after transformation for the two test forms are usually not exactly the same. Explain why that is the case. Suggest a statistic that would be useful for indicating the level of similarity of the locations of persons after the transformation to a common coordinate system.

11. Refer to the item parameter estimates given in Table 9.5. Assuming that the examinee population has a standard bivariate normal distribution of $\boldsymbol{\theta}$ with mean vector $\mathbf{0}$ and the identity matrix for the variance–covariance matrix, what is the item number for the easiest item on the test? Explain how you identified this test item. What test item is most sensitive to differences on the vocabulary construct? Again, explain how you identified that test item.

Chapter 10
Computerized Adaptive Testing Using MIRT

Computerized adaptive testing (CAT) is a methodology for constructing a test, administering it to an examinee, and scoring the test using interactive computer technology. This methodology has a history that is as long as that of interactive computing. An early summary of CAT methods is given in Weiss (1974). A detailed description of the development of an operational application for the Armed Services Vocational Aptitude Battery is given in (Sands 1997). There are also several books available that describe the basic components of CAT procedures (Wainer, Dorans, Flaugher, Green, Mislevy, Steinberg and Thissen 1990; Parshall, Spray and Davey 2002; van der Linden and Glas 2000) so the basic details of the methodology are not presented here. A review of that literature will show that most of the current CAT methodology is based on the assumption that a unidimensional IRT model accurately represents the interaction between persons and test items. In this chapter, the generalization of the CAT methodology to the multidimensional case is considered. To provide a framework for this material, a brief summary of the conceptual basis for CAT is provided.

10.1 Component Parts of a CAT Procedure

In the most general case, a computerized adaptive test (also abbreviated as CAT) has a small number of component parts and procedures. The first is a set of test items that are available for use on the test. These are either a preexisting set of test items that have been calibrated using an IRT model and that have calibrations in the same coordinate system, or a set of test items generated by computer software to have specific item parameters based on an IRT model. The former of these two options is the most commonly used so it will be the approach assumed in this chapter. The collection of test items stored in computer media with their item parameters is usually called an item bank or item pool, but creative psychometricians have also used terms such as "item vat" to indicate very large collections of test items. Because it is necessary to keep the computer storage of the test items secure and because the CAT methodology will withdraw the items from the computer storage for use, the term "item bank" is used in this chapter.

M.D. Reckase, *Multidimensional Item Response Theory*, Statistics for Social and Behavioral Sciences, DOI 10.1007/978-0-387-89976-3_10,

© Springer Science+Business Media, LLC 2009

Most CAT procedures have the goal of selecting a set of test items for administration to an examinee that will give information that can be used to accurately locate the examinee within a $\boldsymbol{\theta}$-coordinate system. Thus, a major component of CAT procedures is the method for selecting a test item from the item bank for administration to the examinee. This methodology is usually applied in real time based on the information known about the examinee up to that point in time. A CAT procedure typically uses all of the information from the previously administered test items to estimate relevant characteristics of the person and uses the estimate to select the next test item for administration. The process for deciding the next test item for administration to an examinee is called the *item selection rule*. Item selection rules generally are based on either maximizing information about the location of the examinee on the $\boldsymbol{\theta}$-coordinate system or minimizing the error in the estimate of location.

Most item selection rules are designed to select the next item for administration to an examinee based on the current estimate of location for the examinee. Other options are also available such as selecting items to maximize decision accuracy, or selecting sets of related items for administration. The methodology for the MIRT version of CAT has not reached that level of development so only the case of selecting the next test items to administer to an examinee is included in this chapter. A fruitful area for future research may be to develop MIRT procedures that are generalizations of some of the more elaborate item selection rules.

The typical CAT procedure administers the test item selected by the item selection rule to the examinee on a computer screen and it accepts the response to the test item from some computer input device such as the keyboard or mouse. After the response is obtained, the estimate of the location of the examinee in the $\boldsymbol{\theta}$-coordinate system is updated for use by the item selection rule for the selection of the next test item to be administered. The estimate of location typically uses the responses to all of the test items that have been administered to that point in time. This part of the CAT methodology is called the *ability estimation procedure*. The term "ability" is somewhat inaccurate because the CAT methodology can be used for measuring achievement or personality as well as ability. Here, the term "location estimation procedure" will be used to emphasize that the estimates are of the location of the examinee in the $\boldsymbol{\theta}$-coordinate system.

CAT methods usually follow a simple cycle: (1) get an estimate of location, (2) select a test item from the item bank that maximizes or minimizes a criterion related to the measurement of location, (3) administer the test item to the examinee and collect a response, (4) score the response and update the estimate of location. Then the cycle begins again. In theory, this cycle could continue forever, but for pragmatic reasons, the procedure stops when the estimation of location is sufficiently accurate for the purpose of test. The method for determining when to stop the cyclic procedure is called the "stopping rule." The stopping rule can be when a specified number of test items have been administered, when the estimate of location has reached the desired level of accuracy, or when a decision has been made with the desired level of confidence. Other criteria for stopping the CAT are likely to be developed in the future as well.

Operation implementations of CAT also include procedures for minimizing the test items in common between the test for one examinee and the next. These procedures are used to reduce the likelihood that an examinee will gain an unfair advantage on the test by getting prior information about the test items from other examinees. These procedures fall under the general category of *exposure control*. Most of the exposure control procedures from unidimensional CAT can be used with MIRT CAT so they are not included in this chapter.

CAT methods that focus on estimating the location of an examinee in a $\boldsymbol{\theta}$-coordinate system are among the purest applications of IRT. It is clear that the goal is not to determine the number of test items a person answered correctly. It is also clear that the CAT operates one person at a time and the performance of other individuals does not enter into the test construction and scoring for the person taking the CAT. Group data is only needed to obtain calibration information for the item bank. The basic idea is that there is a level on a construct to be estimated and items should be selected for use that gives information about an examinee's location on the construct. As more information is gained about the location of an examinee, a more refined selection of test items can be made to further hone the estimate of location. The decision about when to stop administering test items is directly related to the accuracy of the estimate of the examinee's location.

The generalization of the concept of selecting test items that will give good information about an examinees location can be generalized in a straight forward way to the multidimensional case. An item bank is needed that has item calibration information based on the selected MIRT model. The goal of the test is to determine the location of the examinee in the coordinate system for the $\boldsymbol{\theta}$-space. Test items are selected that best further the goal of estimating the location. The test is stopped when the estimate is of sufficient accuracy for the purpose of the test. While the generalization to the multidimensional case is conceptually straightforward, the practical implementation of MIRT CAT has a number of technical challenges. It is the practical implementation of MIRT CAT that is the focus of this chapter.

10.2 Generalization of CAT to the Multidimensional Case

When considering how to generalize the conceptual framework for a CAT to the multidimensional case, four basic components must be addressed: (1) the development of an item bank, (2) the implementation of an item selection rule, (3) the selection of a method for estimating the location of the examinee, and (4) determining when to stop administering test items. It would seem logical to describe each of these components in the order listed, but in fact, the desired characteristics of the item bank are dependent on the other three and sometimes the stopping rule depends on the accuracy of the estimate of location. For these reasons, the procedures for estimating the location of the examinee in the $\boldsymbol{\theta}$-space will be presented first, followed by the item selection and stopping rules. The development of the item bank will be considered last.

When this book was being written, MIRT CAT was not being used for any operational testing programs so there is little information about the operational functioning of this methodology. There are operation CAT programs that measure multiple constructs, but they typically estimate locations on each construct sequentially, obtaining the estimate of one construct before going on to the next construct. The item banks for the different constructs are kept separate. As MIRT methods become more widely known and tested, it is likely that MIRT CAT methodology will become more refined and operational examples will become available.

10.2.1 Estimating the Location of an Examinee

The ultimate goal for most CAT procedures is estimating the location of the examinee in the multidimensional space defined by the coordinate system used to calibrate the items in the item bank. The development of an item bank and the desired characteristics of the item bank are discussed in Sect. 10.2.4. In this section, it is assumed that the decisions about the number of coordinate axes required to model the interaction of the examinees with the target test constructs have been made and that test items have been calibrated within that coordinate system.

The typical CAT methodology begins by assuming an initial estimate of the location of the examinee in the $\boldsymbol{\theta}$-space, $\boldsymbol{\theta}_0$, and then selecting a test item that is optimal according to a criterion such as those described in Sect. 10.2.2 and administering that test item to the examinee. The response to the test item is then scored and the estimate of location is updated with the information from the response. This section describes methods that are currently used to update the estimate of location.

The methods that are used are basically the same as those described in Chap. 6: maximum likelihood and Bayesian estimation procedures. The complication to those methods that is added by their application to CAT is that the methods need to be used when the number of items administered is still small, beginning with a one-item test. Two general classes of methods are typically used with MIRT CAT procedures: maximum likelihood (see, e.g., Lee, Ip and Fuh 2008) and Bayesian. The implementation of a maximum likelihood procedure is described first.

10.2.1.1 Maximum Likelihood Estimation

The basic estimation equation (6.1) for the maximum likelihood method is described in Sect. 6.1.1. The estimation method searches the $\boldsymbol{\theta}$-space for the $\boldsymbol{\theta}$-point that yields a maximum value for the equation given the item parameters and item scores for the administered test items. In practice, methods often search for the $\boldsymbol{\theta}$-point that minimizes the negative log likelihood rather than the likelihood itself. This is done for computational reasons because the magnitude of the likelihood becomes very small as the number of test items administered increases. Use of the likelihood directly can result in error because of the capabilities of computers for storing very small numbers.

A problem that is immediately confronted when using maximum likelihood estimation is that the estimates of location are not finite when the number of test items is small. This problem is discussed in some detail in Chap. 6. The lack of finite estimates is not limited to the multidimensional case, it also occurs in unidimensional implementations of maximum likelihood estimation to CAT. Two solutions have been implemented in the unidimensional case to address the problem: updating the estimates of location using a fixed increment when infinite estimates are encountered or using Bayesian methods until the maximum likelihood estimates are finite. The former approach is described here. The fixed increment approach has not been described previously for multidimensional CAT, but it is used here because it is somewhat simpler than alternative methods. It is shown latter in this chapter that this method yields comparable results to other methods. The mix of Bayesian and maximum likelihood is described at the end of Sect. 10.2.1.2.

Suppose that an MIRT CAT is designed to function in a three-dimensional coordinate system and the CAT procedure begins the process of the estimation of location of an examinee with a starting estimate of [0 0 0]. A first item is selected for administration with **a**-parameters [.5774 .5774 .5774][1] and $d = 0$. This test item provides some information about the location of the examinee relative to each coordinate axis. The examinee provides a correct response to this test item and an attempt is made to get a maximum likelihood estimate of the location of the examinee. For a correct response to this single item, the maximum likelihood estimate goes to positive infinity for all of the coordinate axes. This result indicates that the true location of the examinee is likely further out on each coordinate axis than [0 0 0] so a fixed step of .7 is added to each coordinate value resulting in a new estimate of location of [.7 .7 .7]. If the estimates had gone to negative infinity, the .7 would have been subtracted from the initial estimate. The information in all increasing directions in the $\boldsymbol{\theta}$-space is then computed and the direction with the least information is determined. Then an item is selected that has the most information in that direction and it is administered to the examinee.

The second item administered had parameters $\mathbf{a} = [1\ 0\ 0]$ and $d = -7$. This is an item that has a .5 probability of correct response at the current estimate of location. The response to the second item was incorrect and the estimate of θ_1 went to negative infinity while the estimates of the other two coordinates were still at positive infinity. Continuing to use the fixed step-size procedure resulted in a new estimate of location of [0 1.4 1.4]. The process continued as before. The information at this new location was computed in all directions (actually directions at 10° intervals between 0° and 90°) for the two-item tests and the direction with the least information was determined. Then an item was selected that had the most information in that direction. In this case, it was $\mathbf{a} = [0\ 1\ 0]$ and $d = -1.4$. For this example, the fixed step-size process was used to update the estimates until five items were administered. At that point in the CAT, finite estimates were obtained for the maximum likelihood procedure.

---

[1] This **a**-parameter vector has multidimensional discrimination of 1 and best measurement in a direction with equal angles with all three coordinate axes.

This maximum likelihood estimation procedure was applied to a simulated adaptive test assuming that the true location of the examinee was at [1 1 1] in the three-dimensional $\boldsymbol{\theta}$-space. The simulation had the following characteristics. First, all test items had MDISC values of 1. Second, test items were always available that met the selection criteria that the item had maximum information in the direction determined to have the least information. Finally, the d-parameter for each test item that was administered resulted in a .5-probability of correct response at the current estimate of location. This means that $d = -\mathbf{a}\boldsymbol{\theta}'$, where $\boldsymbol{\theta}$ is the current estimate of location. Table 10.1 shows the successive estimates of the location, the item parameters for the test items administered, and the responses to the test items for a 60-item simulated test.

The columns labeled θ_1 to θ_3 in the table show the successive estimates of the location of the simulated examinee. The first row has the starting location set by the MIRT CAT, [0 0 0]. Each row shows the item parameters for the test item that was selected for administration based on the criterion of maximizing the information at the current estimate in the direction with least information. The last column shows the item score for the item that was administered. The row following each item shows how the location was changed based on the item score and the item parameters.

There are a number of interesting results in Table 10.1. First, except for the first item that was set in the program to have equal values in the **a**-vector, all of the other test items have **a**-parameter vectors that contain a single 1 and the rest 0s. That is, all of the selected items were best at measuring along one coordinate axis. The set of parameters for the administered test item was the result of the item selection rule that selected the test item that gave the most information in the direction with the least cumulative information at that point in the MIRT CAT. For every test item selection, the direction of least information was along a coordinate axis. The end result was that the MIRT CAT essentially administered three unidimensional CATs.

A second observation from the table is that the $\boldsymbol{\theta}$-coordinates change the most after an item has been administered with a 1 for the corresponding a-parameter. This is the expected result because those items are providing the most information about that $\boldsymbol{\theta}$-coordinate. It can also be observed that the $\boldsymbol{\theta}$-coordinates are reduced in value after an incorrect response and increase after a correct response, but only on the dimension that corresponds to the a-parameter of 1.

Another important observation is that finite maximum likelihood estimates were not obtained for all three coordinates until after the administration of the sixth test item. Prior to that point in the test, the estimates of location were updated using the fixed step-size method. The number of test items that need to be administered before all estimates of coordinates are finite varies depending on the test items selected by the procedure and the responses by the examinee. The minimum number of test items needed to get finite estimates of coordinates for the examinees location for three dimensions is three, but the number actually required to get finite estimates can be somewhat larger than that.

Overall, the procedure converges toward the true location of the examinee of [1 1 1]. The final estimate from the MIRT CAT is not exactly equal to the true

Table 10.1 Results from the simulation of a multidimensional CAT using maximum likelihood estimation

Items administered	θ_1	θ_2	θ_3	a_1	a_2	a_3	d	Response
0	0	0	0	0.58	0.58	0.58	0	1
1	0.70	0.70	0.70	1.00	0	0	−0.70	0
2	0	1.40	1.40	0	1.00	0	−1.40	1
3	−0.70	2.10	2.10	0	0	1.00	−2.10	0
4	−1.40	2.80	1.40	1.00	0	0	1.40	1
5	−0.35	3.50	0.70	0	1.00	0	−3.50	0
6	−0.25	2.55	0.27	0	0	1.00	−0.27	1
7	−0.30	2.50	1.23	1.00	0	0	0.30	1
8	0.29	2.48	1.21	0	1.00	0	−2.48	0
9	0.30	1.88	1.23	0	0	1.00	−1.23	0
10	0.32	1.90	0.68	1.00	0	0	−0.32	0
11	−0.08	1.91	0.69	0	1.00	0	−1.91	0
12	−0.07	1.50	0.72	0	0	1.00	−0.71	1
13	−0.08	1.48	1.09	0	1.00	0	−1.48	0
14	−0.07	1.13	1.10	1.00	0	0	0.07	1
15	0.23	1.12	1.09	0	1.00	0	−1.12	0
16	0.24	0.80	1.10	0	0	1.00	−1.10	0
17	0.25	0.81	0.82	0	1.00	0	−0.81	0
18	0.26	0.51	0.83	0	1.00	0	−0.51	0
19	0.27	0.22	0.84	0	1.00	0	−0.22	1
20	0.26	0.45	0.83	1.00	0	0	−0.26	1
21	0.51	0.45	0.82	0	0	1.00	−0.82	1
22	0.50	0.44	1.05	1.00	0	0	−0.50	0
23	0.30	0.45	1.06	0	0	1.00	−1.06	1
24	0.29	0.44	1.25	0	1.00	0	−0.44	1
25	0.29	0.62	1.25	1.00	0	0	−0.29	1
26	0.46	0.62	1.24	0	0	1.00	−1.24	0
27	0.46	0.62	1.07	0	1.00	0	−0.62	1
28	0.46	0.77	1.07	1.00	0	0	−0.46	1
29	0.62	0.77	1.07	0	0	1.00	−1.07	0
30	0.62	0.77	0.92	1.00	0	0	−0.62	1
31	0.77	0.77	0.92	1.00	0	0	−0.77	1
32	0.91	0.77	0.92	0	1.00	0	−0.77	0
33	0.91	0.64	0.92	0	0	1.00	−0.92	1
34	0.91	0.63	1.05	1.00	0	0	−0.91	1
35	1.04	0.63	1.05	1.00	0	0	−1.04	0
36	0.92	0.63	1.05	0	1.00	0	−0.63	1
37	0.92	0.76	1.05	0	0	1.00	−1.05	0
38	0.92	0.76	0.93	0	1.00	0	−0.76	0
39	0.92	0.65	0.93	1.00	0	0	−0.92	1
40	1.03	0.65	0.93	0	0	1.00	−0.93	0
41	1.03	0.65	0.83	1.00	0	0	−1.03	0
42	0.93	0.65	0.83	0	1.00	0	−0.65	1
43	0.93	0.75	0.83	0	0	1.00	−0.83	0

(continued)

Table 10.1 (continued)

Items administered	θ_1	θ_2	θ_3	a_1	a_2	a_3	d	Response
44	0.93	0.75	0.73	0	0	1.00	−0.73	1
45	0.93	0.75	0.82	0	1.00	0	−0.75	1
46	0.93	0.84	0.82	1.00	0	0	−0.93	1
47	1.02	0.84	0.82	1.00	0	0	−1.02	1
48	1.11	0.84	0.82	0	1.00	0	−0.84	1
49	1.11	0.92	0.82	0	0	1.00	−0.82	1
50	1.11	0.92	0.90	1.00	0	0	−1.11	1
51	1.20	0.92	0.90	1.00	0	0	−1.20	0
52	1.12	0.92	0.90	0	1.00	0	−0.92	1
53	1.12	1.00	0.90	0	0	1.00	−0.90	0
54	1.12	1.00	0.82	0	1.00	0	−1.00	0
55	1.12	0.93	0.82	1.00	0	0	−1.12	1
56	1.19	0.93	0.82	0	0	1.00	−0.82	1
57	1.19	0.93	0.90	1.00	0	0	−1.19	1
58	1.27	0.93	0.90	1.00	0	0	−1.27	1
59	1.34	0.93	0.90	0	1.00	0	−0.93	0
60	1.34	0.86	0.90					

location, but the results are in line with what is expected given the error in estimation from the maximum likelihood approach. The information along each coordinate axis at the last estimate of location is in the range from 10 to 12, so the standard error of the estimate is approximately .3 for each coordinate. The obtained location estimates are consistent with that amount of estimation error.

The d-parameters for the items are approximately -1 toward the end of the test. This is the parameter value that will give a probability of correct response of about .5 for $\boldsymbol{\theta}$-locations around [1 1 1] when the test items are most sensitive along one of the coordinate axes.

A different sense of the functioning of this implementation of an MIRT CAT is a plot of successive estimates of the locations as the test progresses. This plot is shown in Fig. 10.1. In the figure, the true location is represented by a star and the line starting at [0 0 0] shows the path of successive estimates of $\boldsymbol{\theta}$. The location of the estimates is quite unstable when the number of items administered is small, but after about 30 test items have been administered, the estimates of location are in the proximity of the true value and further item responses are used to refine the estimates. Figure 10.1 shows that the adjustments to the estimates of location are fairly small after that point. Note that the changes in estimates of location are usually at right angles to each other. This is a result of the selection of test items to be measuring along the coordinate axes. A plot of this type for real item banks would not have these sharp angles because the items would probably not follow exact simple structure.

One way to evaluate the functioning of an MIRT CAT design is to simulate the estimation of location a number of times for the same true $\boldsymbol{\theta}$ and then determine

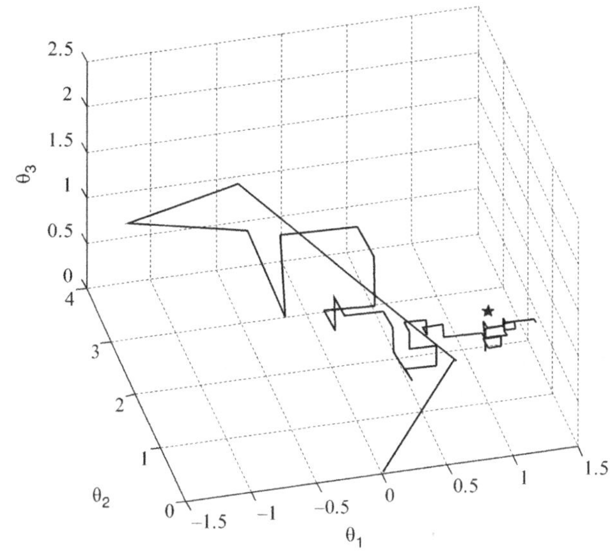

Fig. 10.1 Successive **θ**-estimates for an MIRT CAT with true **θ** (*star*) [1 1 1] using maximum likelihood estimation

Table 10.2 Means and standard deviations of 20 replications of the estimation of location with an MIRT CAT for true $\boldsymbol{\theta} = [1\ 1\ 1]$ using maximum likelihood estimation

	θ_1	θ_2	θ_3
Mean	1.02	.94	.90
Standard deviation	.35	.22	.29

how well the procedure recovers the true coordinates. Comparison of the mean of the estimates to the true value gives an indication of estimation bias. The standard deviation of the estimates gives a measure of the standard error. Table 10.2 shows the means and standard deviations of the three coordinates for 20 replications of the MIRT CAT procedure described earlier for true $\boldsymbol{\theta}$ of [1 1 1].

The mean estimates of the coordinates are all within two standard errors of the mean from the true values indicating that the estimates at least appear unbiased. In theory, maximum likelihood estimates are unbiased and these results support the theory for this implementation. The standard deviations of the estimates of the coordinates are the order of magnitude that is predicted by the MIRT model. The information from the items that were administered ranges from 10 to 12 in the direction along the coordinate axes at the location of the final estimates. Because the standard error of the estimates should be asymptotically equal to the reciprocal of the square root of the information, the standard deviations should fall in the range from .28 to .32. The values in Table 10.2 are close approximations to the predicted values.

Operational MIRT CATs that are based on maximum likelihood estimation will probably not give results that are as close to the predicted values as this simulation because they use estimated rather than true item parameters and the item bank will probably not include all of the items that are requested by the item selection algorithm. Instead, test items that are closest to those with the desired characteristics are administered. The use of estimates rather than true item parameters and the best available test items will likely degrade the accuracy of the estimates of location.

10.2.1.2 Bayesian Estimation

Maximum likelihood estimation has the problem that finite estimates of coordinates may not exist when the number of items that has been administered is small. The example in the previous section gives one demonstration of the problem with that approach to estimation. To overcome the problem of nonfinite estimates and to stabilize the estimation of location, a Bayesian estimation procedure has been proposed by Segall (1996). The procedure used by Segall (1996) is essentially a practical implementation in an MIRT CAT environment of the estimation method discussed in Chap. 6 and given in (6.3). Only a summary of Segall's method is provided here because the details are available in the original article.

The basic equation for the Bayesian estimation of the location in the multidimensional space is the expression for the posterior probability. Equation (10.1) is the same expression given in (6.3) of Chap. 6.

$$h(\boldsymbol{\theta}|\mathbf{U}_j) = \frac{L(\mathbf{U}_j|\boldsymbol{\theta})f(\boldsymbol{\theta})}{\int\limits_{\theta} L(\mathbf{U}_j|\boldsymbol{\theta})f(\boldsymbol{\theta})\mathrm{d}\boldsymbol{\theta}}, \tag{10.1}$$

where $f(\boldsymbol{\theta})$ is the prior probability density function for $\boldsymbol{\theta}$, $\mathbf{U}_j$ is the item score string for Examinee j, $L(\mathbf{U}_j|\boldsymbol{\theta})$ is the probability of the item score string given $\boldsymbol{\theta}$, and $h(\boldsymbol{\theta}|\mathbf{U}_j)$ is the posterior probability density of $\boldsymbol{\theta}$ given the item score string.

This is the same expression used by Segall (1996) except that he represents the denominator as $f(\mathbf{U})$ to indicate the marginal density of the observed string of item scores for the test items administered by the MIRT CAT to the examinee at that point in the test.

Segall (1996) assumes that the prior probability for $\boldsymbol{\theta}$ is the multivariate normal with mean vector $\boldsymbol{\mu}$ and variance–covariance matrix $\boldsymbol{\Phi}$. The expression for the multivariate normal density is given by

$$f(\boldsymbol{\theta}) = (2\pi)^{-\frac{m}{2}} |\boldsymbol{\Phi}|^{-\frac{1}{2}} \mathrm{e}^{-\frac{1}{2}(\boldsymbol{\theta}-\boldsymbol{\mu})'\boldsymbol{\Phi}^{-1}(\boldsymbol{\theta}-\boldsymbol{\mu})}, \tag{10.2}$$

where m is the number of dimensions and $|\boldsymbol{\Phi}|$ is the determinant of the variance–covariance matrix. All other symbols have been previously defined. Using (10.2) as the definition of the prior density in (10.1) gives the expression for the posterior density. Segall (1996) used the mode of the posterior density as the estimate of location because determining the mode required less computation than finding the mean vector for the posterior density.

An important aspect of Segall's development is that he did not assume that the prior distribution had uncorrelated θ elements. In the example in his article, he uses information about the observed correlation between the constructs that are the focus of the test to set the covariances in the prior. He points out that this is a major advantage of the Bayesian estimation procedure because information about the intercorrelations of the coordinates can be used to increase the efficiency of the estimates of $\boldsymbol{\theta}$.

Just as with the maximum likelihood procedure where the log likelihood was maximized rather than direct maximization of the likelihood, Segall maximized the log of the posterior density to estimate the location of the examinee. The expression he used is

$$\ln h(\boldsymbol{\theta}|\mathbf{U}) = \ln L(\mathbf{U}|\boldsymbol{\theta}) - \frac{1}{2}(\boldsymbol{\theta} - \boldsymbol{\mu})\,\boldsymbol{\Phi}^{-1}\,(\boldsymbol{\theta} - \boldsymbol{\mu})' + C, \tag{10.3}$$

where ln is the natural logarithm of the function and C is a constant. Because C is a constant it does not enter into determining the maximum of the function. Note that $\boldsymbol{\theta}$ and $\boldsymbol{\mu}$ are row vectors.

To show the effect of the use of the Bayesian modal estimation method on the MIRT CAT, the same case used for the maximum likelihood example was simulated. That is, a 60-item CAT was simulated with true $\boldsymbol{\theta} = [1\ 1\ 1]$. In this case, the multivariate normal with mean vector [0 0 0] and variance–covariance matrix equal to the identity matrix was used as the prior. The results from the simulated test are presented in Table 10.3.

Comparing the results in Table 10.3 to those in Table 10.1 shows the stabilizing effect of the Bayesian modal estimation procedure. Even after the administration of only one test item, the estimates of the $\boldsymbol{\theta}$-coordinates are finite and near the origin. The estimates then successively move out from the origin and with a 60 item test the influence of the prior is relatively minimal. The plot of successive estimates of the $\boldsymbol{\theta}$ location is given in Fig. 10.2. The axes have been scaled to be the same length and have the same orientation as Fig. 10.1 to facilitate comparisons with the maximum likelihood estimation procedure.

A comparison of the two plots shows the substantial reduction in the variation of the estimates of location early in the adaptive test. The lack of finite estimates early in the CAT for the maximum likelihood estimation procedure and the use of the fixed step-size procedure for early estimates result in erratic movement of the estimates of location over the $\boldsymbol{\theta}$-space. The Bayesian estimation procedure stabilizes the early estimates of location.

To further check the functioning of the Bayesian estimation procedure, an MIRT CAT with true $\boldsymbol{\theta}$ of [1 1 1] was simulated 20 times and the estimates of location from each simulation were recorded. Table 10.4 presents the means and standard deviations of the estimates of coordinates for the simulations. A comparison between the results in Tables 10.4 and 10.2 shows that the Bayesian modal estimates are slightly

Table 10.3 Results from the simulation of a multidimensional CAT using Bayesian modal estimation

Items administered	θ_1	θ_2	θ_3	a_1	a_2	a_3	d	Response
0	0	0	0	0.58	0.58	0.58	0	1
1	0.29	0.29	0.29	1.00	0	0	−0.29	0
2	−0.17	0.36	0.36	0	1.00	0	−0.36	1
3	−0.22	0.82	0.29	0	0	1.00	−0.29	1
4	−0.26	0.78	0.75	1.00	0	0	0.26	0
5	−0.62	0.81	0.78	0	0	1.00	−0.78	1
6	−0.65	0.78	1.14	0	1.00	0	−0.78	1
7	−0.67	1.13	1.12	1.00	0	0	0.67	1
8	−0.38	1.12	1.10	0	0	1.00	−1.10	0
9	−0.37	1.13	0.83	0	1.00	0	−1.13	0
10	−0.36	0.86	0.84	1.00	0	0	0.36	1
11	−0.14	0.85	0.83	0	0	1.00	−0.83	1
12	−0.14	0.84	1.05	0	1.00	0	−0.84	1
13	−0.15	1.06	1.04	0	0	1.00	−1.04	0
14	−0.14	1.07	0.86	0	1.00	0	−1.07	0
15	−0.14	0.88	0.86	1.00	0	0	0.14	1
16	0.05	0.87	0.86	1.00	0	0	−0.05	0
17	−0.11	0.88	0.86	0	0	1.00	−0.86	1
18	−0.12	0.87	1.02	0	1.00	0	−0.87	0
19	−0.11	0.71	1.03	0	0	1.00	−1.03	1
20	−0.12	0.71	1.17	1.00	0	0	0.12	1
21	0.03	0.71	1.17	0	1.00	0	−0.71	0
22	0.03	0.56	1.17	0	0	1.00	−1.17	0
23	0.04	0.56	1.04	0	1.00	0	−0.56	1
24	0.03	0.69	1.04	1.00	0	0	−0.03	0
25	−0.10	0.70	1.04	0	0	1.00	−1.04	1
26	−0.10	0.69	1.16	1.00	0	0	0.10	1
27	0.02	0.69	1.16	0	1.00	0	−0.69	0
28	0.02	0.57	1.16	0	0	1.00	−1.16	1
29	0.02	0.57	1.27	0	1.00	0	−0.57	1
30	0.02	0.68	1.27	1.00	0	0	−0.02	1
31	0.12	0.68	1.27	0	0	1.00	−1.27	1
32	0.12	0.68	1.37	1.00	0	0	−0.12	1
33	0.22	0.68	1.37	0	0	1.00	−1.37	0
34	0.23	0.68	1.27	0	1.00	0	−0.68	1
35	0.22	0.77	1.27	1.00	0	0	−0.22	1
36	0.32	0.77	1.27	1.00	0	0	−0.32	1
37	0.41	0.77	1.27	0	1.00	0	−0.77	1
38	0.41	0.86	1.27	1.00	0	0	−0.41	1
39	0.50	0.86	1.27	0	0	1.00	−1.27	0
40	0.50	0.86	1.18	1.00	0	0	−0.50	1
41	0.59	0.86	1.18	0	1.00	0	−0.86	1
42	0.59	0.95	1.18	1.00	0	0	−0.59	1
43	0.67	0.94	1.18	1.00	0	0	−0.67	1

(continued)

Table 10.3 (continued)

Items administered	θ_1	θ_2	θ_3	a_1	a_2	a_3	d	Response
44	0.76	0.94	1.18	0	0	1.00	−1.18	1
45	0.76	0.94	1.26	1.00	0	0	−0.76	1
46	0.84	0.94	1.26	0	1.00	0	−0.94	1
47	0.84	1.02	1.26	1.00	0	0	−0.84	1
48	0.92	1.02	1.26	1.00	0	0	−0.92	0
49	0.84	1.02	1.26	0	0	1.00	−1.26	1
50	0.84	1.02	1.34	0	1.00	0	−1.02	1
51	0.84	1.10	1.34	0	0	1.00	−1.34	0
52	0.84	1.10	1.27	0	1.00	0	−1.10	1
53	0.84	1.17	1.27	0	1.00	0	−1.17	0
54	0.84	1.10	1.27	1.00	0	0	−0.84	1
55	0.91	1.10	1.27	1.00	0	0	−0.91	1
56	0.98	1.10	1.27	0	0	1.00	−1.27	1
57	0.98	1.10	1.33	1.00	0	0	−0.98	0
58	0.92	1.10	1.33	0	1.00	0	−1.10	0
59	0.92	1.04	1.33	0	0	1.00	−1.33	0
60	0.92	1.04	1.27					

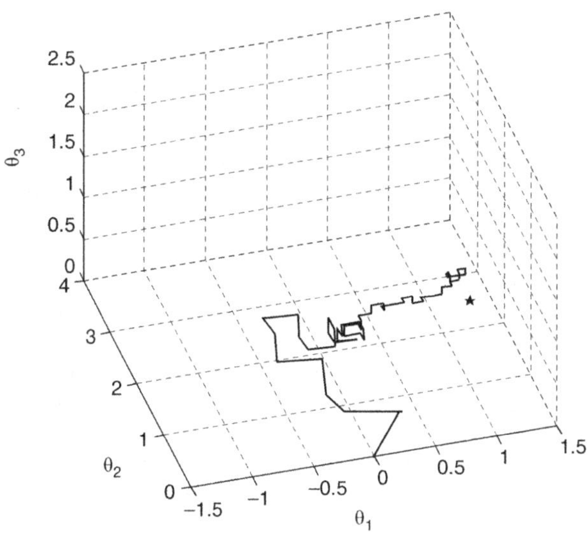

Fig. 10.2 Successive **θ**-estimates for an MIRT CAT with true **θ** (*star*) [1 1 1] using Bayesian modal estimation

smaller than those from the maximum likelihood procedure. This is the expected result because Bayesian estimates tend to be statistically biased toward the mean of the prior. They also tend to have smaller standard errors of estimation. In this

Table 10.4 Means and standard deviations of 20 replications of the estimation of location with an MIRT CAT for true $\boldsymbol{\theta} = [1\ 1\ 1]$ using Bayesian modal estimation

	θ_1	θ_2	θ_3
Mean	.92	.99	.85
Standard deviation	.21	.31	.33

small sample of 20 simulated values, the reduction in standard errors is not obvious. With an MIRT CAT of 60 items, there seems to be enough information to overcome the influence of the prior distribution so the bias seems minimal. More research is needed to determine the influence of the prior distribution for Bayesian estimation in MIRT CAT.

One more example may be helpful for understanding the issues related to the selection of the maximum likelihood or Bayesian approaches to estimate the location of an examinee within the MIRT CAT framework. The previous example used a true $\boldsymbol{\theta}$ that was along a line that is consistent with highly correlated $\boldsymbol{\theta}$-coordinates. The values on each coordinate axis were similar. If a Bayesian prior had been used with a variance–covariance matrix with high covariances, it would have facilitated the estimation of the location of this examinee. However, if the true location of the examinee is counter to the characteristics of the prior, there may be an opposite effect. Poorer quality estimates of location might be obtained.

To check for the existence of effects of the prior on the estimation of such points, the simulation procedures were run using a true $\boldsymbol{\theta} = [1.6\ .8\ -1.1]$. This point was selected because it was in the range of what could reasonably be expected when $\boldsymbol{\theta}$-coordinates are correlated about .5, but that it was at the extremes of those expectations. This $\boldsymbol{\theta}$-point was used to simulate 50 MIRT CAT tests using three different estimation procedures: maximum likelihood, Bayesian modal with an identity matrix for the variance–covariance matrix, and Bayesian modal with off diagonal values of .5 in the variance–covariance matrix and 1s in the diagonal. This last estimation procedure uses a prior that assumes correlated coordinates.

The results from the three estimation procedures are summarized in Table 10.5. The results show a clear trend over methods. The means of the maximum likelihood estimates are fairly close to the true values, but they also tend to have the largest standard deviations – estimates of the standard error of the estimation procedure. The Bayesian method with the identity matrix for the variance–covariance matrix also recovers the true $\boldsymbol{\theta}$ fairly well, but all means of the estimates are closer to the prior mean vector than those from the maximum likelihood procedure. The Bayesian method assuming a prior correlations of the θs of .5 had estimates that are regressed more toward the mean vector of [0 0 0] than the other two procedures. Both Bayesian methods tend to have smaller standard deviations than the maximum likelihood method.

These results are generally consistent with what would be expected for a comparison of maximum likelihood and Bayesian estimators. The use of the Bayesian prior results in statistical bias toward the mean of the prior. This statistical bias diminishes

Table 10.5 Means and standard deviations of 50 replications of simulated MIRT CATs for true $\boldsymbol{\theta} = [1.6\ .8\ -1.1]$ for three estimation procedures

Estimation method		θ_1	θ_2	θ_3
Maximum likelihood	Mean	1.62	.84	−1.15
	SD	.26	.28	.31
Bayesian modal identity matrix	Mean	1.53	.80	−.97
	SD	.24	.24	.21
Bayesian modal .5 correlation	Mean	1.35	.64	−.93
	SD	.28	.21	.23

in magnitude as the test length increases. However, the amount of statistical bias is also dependent on the strength of the prior. In this case, using a prior distribution with nonzero covariances seems to result in more statistical bias for this case where the true $\boldsymbol{\theta}$ is not consistent with the prior. The maximum likelihood estimates should be asymptotically unbiased, but they will tend to have higher standard errors than the Bayesian methods.

There are few direct comparisons of these methods in the research literature so it is difficult to draw any general conclusions about the selection of methods. Tam (1992) compared a number of methods including maximum likelihood and his own versions of Bayesian procedures, but only for the two-dimensional case and at a time when there was more limited computing power than is common today. He noted the same instabilities in the maximum likelihood procedure noted here and found that an expected a posteriori (EAP) method and a weighted likelihood method tended to perform well.

More recent studies are based on a single method of $\boldsymbol{\theta}$ estimation rather than comparing methods because they focus on other aspects of CAT. For example, Li, Ip and Fuh (2008) investigated the control of exposure of test items with an MIRT CAT using a maximum likelihood estimation procedure. Wang and Chen (2005) compared the results of an MIRT CAT using Bayesian estimation with those from a number of individual tests scored using the unidimensional Rasch model. At this time, it seems that maximum likelihood and Bayesian methods are both common in research studies on MIRT CAT.

10.2.1.3 Other $\boldsymbol{\theta}$ estimation procedures

The two approaches to the estimation of the $\boldsymbol{\theta}$-coordinates for a person described in the previous two sections are not the only estimation methods that have been implemented in an MIRT CAT context. One of the first methods investigated for MIRT CAT was a multivariate generalization of the approximation to the Bayesian approach developed by Owen (1975). This approach was developed and studied by Bloxom and Vale (1987). The method uses a standard normal distribution as an approximation to the posterior density function from the Bayesian updating procedure. The estimate of $\boldsymbol{\theta}$ is the centroid (mean vector) of the posterior distribution.

Bloxom and Vale (1987) evaluated the method and concluded that the estimates did converge toward the true $\boldsymbol{\theta}$ as the test length increased. However, they also found that the characteristics of the estimates depended on characteristics of the item bank and that poor estimates were sometimes obtained. It was difficult to determine what caused the procedure to perform poorly.

The only other implementation of the Bloxom and Vale (1987) procedure was found in the doctoral dissertation by Tam (1992). Tam found that the procedure worked well, but there were other methods that worked better. These included one that was developed for use in the dissertation including a combination of the approach developed by Bloxom and Vale (1987) and a number theory approach to computing the EAP estimator. The weighted likelihood method developed by Warm (1989) was also found to work well. These methods are not described here because no further research was found using these methods. The reader is referred to the Tam (1992) dissertation to get the details of these methods.

A more recent variation on the Bloxom and Vale (1987) estimation method was described by Veldkamp and van der Linden (2002). Rather than use a normal approximation to the posterior distribution, they used the actual posterior and estimated each $\boldsymbol{\theta}$-coordinate as the expected value of the marginal posterior distribution of each $\boldsymbol{\theta}$. They provide an example of the application of this method to real test data assuming a two-dimensional $\boldsymbol{\theta}$-space.

It is clear that many different estimation methods could be used in the context of MIRT CAT. These methods can also be combined. For example, a CAT could use the Bayesian modal procedure proposed by Segall (1996) for the early part of the test and then switch to maximum likelihood once the problem of nonfinite estimates is under control. At least one operational CAT procedure uses this approach for the unidimensional case. Other combinations of procedures could also be developed.

While it appears that some of these methods function well, thorough comparative studies were not in the research literature at the time that this chapter was written. With the exception of Tam (1992), there were no studies that compared multiple methods. Also, most studies considered the two-dimensional case so it is difficult to generalize the results to higher dimensions. Persons interested in developing an MIRT CAT should check the recent research literature to determine if comparative studies of $\boldsymbol{\theta}$ estimation in an MIRT CAT context have been conducted. Lacking those studies, it would be best to select two or three promising methods and perform studies that are customized to the characteristics of the test design such as number of dimensions, length of test, and number of scores to be reported. The results of such studies should be shared with the research community so that we can begin to develop a better understanding of the estimation process within MIRT CAT.

10.2.2 Selecting the Test Item from the Item Bank

Even the best $\boldsymbol{\theta}$ estimation method will not function well unless appropriate items are administered to the examinee. If items that are too hard, or too easy, or that provide little information are selected for use, the adaptive test will not function well. Therefore, the rule for selecting test items from the item bank for presentation to the examinee is a critical component of the MIRT CAT.

All test item selection rules are based on maximizing or minimizing some criterion value at the most recent estimate of $\boldsymbol{\theta}$. The feature that differs across test item selection rules is the definition of the criterion. This section of the chapter describes a number of the test item selection rules that appear in the research literature, but it starts with one that was created for this chapter. As with the $\boldsymbol{\theta}$-estimation methods, there are many different test item selection rules and each rule can be combined with an estimation method resulting in many possible MIRT CAT procedures. The first method described here has not been used on any operational testing program, but it is a generalization of commonly used maximum information methods for unidimensional CAT.

10.2.2.1 Maximize Information in Direction with Minimum Information

As described in Chap. 5, the amount of information provided by a set of test items differs depending on the direction of interest from a point in the $\boldsymbol{\theta}$-space. If the test characteristic surface has a zero slope along the line connecting two points, the information in the direction along that line is zero, even though the test characteristic surface may be very steep in other directions from the points. If one of the points being considered is the most recent estimate of $\boldsymbol{\theta}$ from the MIRT CAT, and if the information from the test administered up to that time is computed in all directions from the $\boldsymbol{\theta}$-point, it is likely that some directions have less accumulated information than others. In those directions from $\boldsymbol{\theta}$, the test discriminates less well than other directions. The logic of this test item selection method is to determine the direction from $\boldsymbol{\theta}$ with the least information and select the item that provides the most information in that direction.

An example may help clarify the functioning of this item selection method. Suppose that the 60-item MIRT CAT described in Sect. 10.2.1.1 is being used to estimate the location of a person in a three-dimensional space. Suppose also that 30 test items have been administered. The first step in selecting test item 31 is to determine the number of directions to be checked for the amount of information provided by the first 30 test items. In theory, it might be best to consider all possible directions. In practice the amount of information provided in directions that are very close is not very different. Therefore, only a finite number of directions are considered. Further, it is expected that the test items in the item bank will have positive a-parameters. This means that they will have the most information in directions in the portion of the $\boldsymbol{\theta}$-space with angles with the axes between 0° and 90°. For this example, the directions were equally spaced at 10° intervals from the θ_1-axis and the θ_2-axis. The angle from the θ_3-axis was determined by using the property that the sum of the squared cosines of the angles must equal 1. The set of angles used for the procedure used in Sect. 10.2.1.1 is given in Table 10.6 along with the amount of information in each direction after 30 test items were administered. The amount

Table 10.6 Directions and information at [.56 .75 −1.01] after 30 test items

Direction from axis i			Information in specified direction
α_1	α_2	α_3	
0	90	90	5.78
10	80	90	5.84
10	90	80	5.84
20	70	90	5.85
20	80	73	5.94
20	90	70	5.86
30	60	90	5.82
30	70	69	5.97
30	80	62	5.92
30	90	60	5.82
40	50	90	5.74
40	60	66	5.94
40	70	57	5.92
40	80	52	5.85
40	90	50	5.75
50	40	90	5.63
50	50	65	5.85
50	60	54	5.87
50	70	47	5.83
50	80	42	5.74
50	90	40	5.64
60	30	90	5.50
60	40	66	5.72
60	50	55	5.76
60	60	45	5.75
60	70	37	5.70
60	80	32	5.61
60	90	30	5.50
70	20	90	5.36
70	30	69	5.56
70	40	57	5.62
70	50	47	5.63
70	60	37	5.61
70	70	29	5.55
70	80	23	5.47
70	90	20	5.37
80	10	90	5.24
80	20	73	5.39
80	30	62	5.46
80	40	52	5.49
80	50	42	5.50
80	60	32	5.47
80	70	23	5.41
80	80	14	5.33
80	90	10	5.24

(continued)

Table 10.6 (continued)

Direction from axis i			Information in specified direction
α_1	α_2	α_3	
90	0	90	**5.14**
90	10	80	5.22
90	20	70	5.29
90	30	60	5.34
90	40	50	5.37
90	50	40	5.37
90	60	30	5.34
90	70	20	5.29
90	80	10	5.22
90	90	0	**5.14**

of information for each test item was computed using (5.16) and it was summed over items to get the information after 30 test items. The estimate of $\boldsymbol{\theta}$ after the 30 test items is [.56 .75 − 1.01]. The configuration of angles has 55 possible combinations and they are roughly equally spaced in the octant of increasing values of $\boldsymbol{\theta}$ in the $\boldsymbol{\theta}$-space.

Reviewing the amount of information provided by the previous 30 test items shows that information does not vary different with change in direction. The lowest information is 5.1354 and the largest is 5.9658. This fact indicates that the test item selection procedure was successful at estimating the examinee's location in all of the directions that were considered. The lowest information corresponds to a direction with the successive coordinate axes of 90°, 0°, and 90°. That is, the direction with the least information is parallel to the θ_2-axis. Using this test item selection rule would require searching the item bank for the test item with the greatest amount of information at the $\boldsymbol{\theta}$-estimate in a direction parallel to the θ_2 axis. For each test item in the item bank, the information in the specified direction would be computed using (5.16) and the item with the largest value would be selected. In this simulation where all possible items are available, it would be an item with a high a_2-parameter relative to the magnitude of the other a-parameters. The d-parameter for the item would be equal to $-\mathbf{a}\boldsymbol{\theta}'$. This d-parameter would result in a probability of .5 for a correct response to the test item for a person at the $\boldsymbol{\theta}$-estimate if the test item has a zero c-parameter.

An interesting result of the simulated MIRT CAT shown in Sect. 10.2.1 is that the test items selected by this rule always measured best in a direction parallel to a coordinate axis. The reason for this is that the information provided by a test item diminishes as the angle from the direction of measurement increases. For items with positive a-parameters, the information along the coordinate axes will always be less than in the direction of best measurement. The only exception is if the test item has its direction of best measurement along one of the coordinate axes. In that case, the information parallel to the other coordinate axes will be zero.

10.2.2.2 Maximize the Determinant of the Fisher Information Matrix

Segall (1996) suggested a method for selecting the next item in a CAT that is based on properties of the maximum likelihood estimator of $\boldsymbol{\theta}$. He notes that conditional distribution of $\boldsymbol{\theta}$-estimates given the true value of $\boldsymbol{\theta}$ is asymptotically multivariate normal with variance–covariance matrix related to the Fisher information matrix given by

$$I_{ij}\left(\boldsymbol{\theta},\hat{\boldsymbol{\theta}}\right) = -E\left[\frac{\partial^2 \ln L}{\partial\theta_i \partial\theta_j}\right], \tag{10.4}$$

where $\boldsymbol{\theta}$ is the true location of the examinee, $\hat{\boldsymbol{\theta}}$ is the maximum likelihood estimate of location, θ_i and θ_j are the ith and jth elements of the $\boldsymbol{\theta}$-vector, and L is the likelihood function for the set of responses up to that point in the MIRT CAT.

Specifically, the variance–covariance matrix for the estimate after the kth test item in the adaptive test, Σ_k, is approximated by the inverse of the information matrix,

$$\Sigma_k = \left\{I\left(\boldsymbol{\theta},\hat{\boldsymbol{\theta}}_k\right)\right\}^{-1}, \tag{10.5}$$

where $\hat{\boldsymbol{\theta}}_k$ is the estimate of the location of the examinee after k test items.

When estimating locations in the $\boldsymbol{\theta}$-space using MIRT models, the information matrix is given by

$$I_{ii}\left(\boldsymbol{\theta},\hat{\boldsymbol{\theta}}_k\right) = \sum_{\ell=1}^{k}\frac{\left[\frac{\partial P_\ell(\boldsymbol{\theta})}{\partial\theta_i}\right]^2}{P_\ell(\boldsymbol{\theta})\,Q_\ell(\boldsymbol{\theta})}, \tag{10.6}$$

for the diagonal elements of the matrix, and

$$I_{ij}\left(\boldsymbol{\theta},\hat{\boldsymbol{\theta}}_k\right) = \sum_{\ell=1}^{k}\frac{\frac{\partial P_\ell(\boldsymbol{\theta})}{\partial\theta_i}\frac{\partial P_\ell(\boldsymbol{\theta})}{\partial\theta_j}}{P_\ell(\boldsymbol{\theta})\,Q_\ell(\boldsymbol{\theta})}, \tag{10.7}$$

for the off diagonal elements. All of the symbols are used as previously defined. The terms within the summations are the terms in the information matrix for single test items. The test information matrix for the estimates of $\boldsymbol{\theta}$ is the sum of the information matrices for the single items. It is also interesting to note that the diagonal elements of the information matrix are the same as the unidimensional information functions along a single axis of the coordinate system.

The test item selection criterion suggested by Segall (1996) is based on a relationship between the Fisher information matrix and the confidence region around the estimates of $\boldsymbol{\theta}$ specified by Anderson (1984). Anderson showed that the equivalent of a confidence interval around the estimate of $\boldsymbol{\theta}$ is an ellipsoid in the multivariate space. The volume of this ellipsoid is a function of Σ_k. Segall (1996) showed that when the following expression is maximized, the volume of the confidence ellipsoid around the $\boldsymbol{\theta}$-estimate is minimized.

$$\left|I\left(\boldsymbol{\theta},\hat{\boldsymbol{\theta}}_k\right) + I\left(\boldsymbol{\theta},u_{k+1}\right)\right|. \tag{10.8}$$

In the expression in (10.8), the vertical bars indicate the determinant of the matrix, the term on the left is the information matrix for the test already administered with k test items, and the expression on the right is the item information matrix for the item to be administered next. The process for selecting the next item to administer is to identify the item that has an item information matrix that, when added to the current test information matrix, will result in the largest value for the determinant of the sum.

While it is not immediately obvious from the expression in (10.8), this criterion for test item selection seems to yield the same result as the method described in Sect. 10.2.2.1, the selection of a test item with maximum information in the direction that has the least test information at that point in the MIRT CAT. There was no discussion of the relationship between these two methods in the research literature at the time this book was written and there is no known formal proof, but the two methods select the same items for the few cases that have been checked. For example, suppose that 30 test items have been administered and the information in each of the directions listed in Table 10.6 is computed for the true $\boldsymbol{\theta}$-vector of $[.56 \ \ .75 \ \ -1.01]$. The minimum information criterion would select an item with the most information in the direction with minimum information. In this case, that would be the direction parallel to θ_1 with information in that direction of 5.28. The Fisher information matrix after the 30 test items is

$$\begin{bmatrix} 5.28 & .23 & .54 \\ .23 & 5.47 & .23 \\ .54 & .23 & 5.33 \end{bmatrix}.$$

Note that the diagonal entry in the $(1, 1)$ cell of the matrix is equal to the information parallel to θ_1 and it is the smallest of the values. If the information matrix for items in each direction listed in Table 10.6, all with multidimensional discrimination values equal to 1.0, are added to the current information matrix and the determinant is computed, the largest value of the determinate is for the item measuring parallel to θ_1. The same test item would be selected as the next item using both criteria.

A plot of the information in each direction from the current $\boldsymbol{\theta}$-estimate and the value of the determinant of the Fisher information matrix for each possible test item is given in Figure 10.3. The plot shows that the minimum information criterion and the maximum determinant criterion are highly correlated ($r = -.998$). The slight deviations from a straight line are likely because of differences in rounding error for the two sets of computations.

10.2.2.3 Largest Decrement in the Volume of the Bayesian Credibility Ellipsoid

Segall (1996) suggested another method for selecting the next test item for a multidimensional CAT that was consistent with the Bayesian approach to estimating the location of the examinee. This method determines which of the available test items

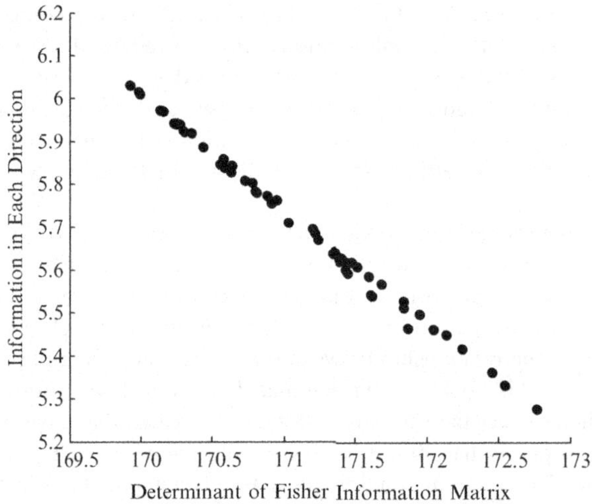

Fig. 10.3 Plot of test information in each direction and determinant of the Fisher information criteria for items selected to measure in each direction at [1.74 −.32 −1.75]

will result in the largest decrease in the volume of the Bayesian credibility ellipsoid for the estimate of the location of the person. This method assumes that there is prior information about the distribution of coordinates for the examinee population and that the variance–covariance matrix for this prior distribution can be specified in advance. Segall (1996) assumed that the prior distribution for the $\boldsymbol{\theta}$-coordinates was multivariate normal with variance–covariance matrix $\boldsymbol{\Phi}$. He then showed that the volume of the Bayesian credibility ellipsoid for the estimate of $\boldsymbol{\theta}$ is related to the following expression:

$$\left| I\left(\boldsymbol{\theta}, \hat{\boldsymbol{\theta}}_k\right) + I\left(\boldsymbol{\theta}, u_{k+1}\right) + \boldsymbol{\Phi}^{-1} \right|. \tag{10.9}$$

When this expression is maximized, the volume of the credibility ellipsoid is minimized. The expression in (10.9) differs from that in (10.8) by the addition of the inverse of the prior variance–covariance matrix term. If the variance–covariance matrix is the identity matrix, it will have no effect on the test item selection process.

To show the influence of the prior distribution on the test item selection process, an adaptive test in three dimensions was simulated using prior variance–covariance matrices of

$$\mathbf{C}_1 = \begin{bmatrix} 1 & .5 & .5 \\ .5 & 1 & .5 \\ .5 & .5 & 1 \end{bmatrix} \quad \text{and} \quad \mathbf{C}_2 = \begin{bmatrix} 1 & .9 & .55 \\ .9 & 1 & .15 \\ .55 & .15 & 1 \end{bmatrix}.$$

Table 10.7 The item parameters for the first 15 items of a Bayesian CAT using two different prior variance–covariance matrices

Item number	$\mathbf{C}_1$				$\mathbf{C}_2$			
	a_1	a_2	a_3	d	a_1	a_2	a_3	d
1	.58	.58	.58	0	.58	.58	.58	0
2	.64	.50	.58	−.43	.64	.77	.00	−.52
3	.17	.87	.47	−.12	.50	.17	.85	−.40
4	1.00	0	0	−.01	.64	.77	.00	−.87
5	0	0	1.00	.08	.34	0	.94	−.67
6	0	1.00	0	.16	.64	.77	.00	−1.13
7	1.00	0	0	−.32	.64	.77	.00	−1.19
8	0	0	1.00	.40	.34	0	.94	−.22
9	0	1.00	0	−.09	.17	0	.98	−.84
10	1.00	0	0	−.56	.64	.77	.00	−.82
11	0	0	1.00	.18	.17	0	.98	−.90
12	0	1.00	0	−.30	.17	0	.98	−.88
13	.98	0	.17	−.78	.64	.77	.00	−.87
14	0	0	1.00	−.05	.17	0	.98	−.93
15	.50	.87	0	−.51	.64	.77	.00	−.92
Estimate of $\boldsymbol{\theta}$	1.47	.83	−.60		.85	1.61	−1.89	

The first variance–covariance matrix is relatively uninformative in that the correlations between the coordinates are all of moderate size and they are equal. The second variance–covariance matrix is fairly extreme with high and low correlations. Table 10.7 shows the item parameters for the selected test items for the first 15 test items for the two different priors for the same true $\boldsymbol{\theta}$-vector of $[1.6 \;\; .8 \;\; -1.1]$. The last line of the table shows the estimated $\boldsymbol{\theta}$-vector for each case after a 60-item CAT using Bayesian estimation and item selection.

The results in Table 10.7 show the effect of the selection of the prior distribution on the item selection and $\boldsymbol{\theta}$-estimation. For the $\mathbf{C}_1$-case, except for the first few test items, the test items selected follow the same pattern as for the procedures described in Sect. 10.2.2.1 and 10.2.2.2. That is, the test items selected tend to alternate being most sensitive to differences parallel to each of the coordinate axes. For the $\mathbf{C}_2$-case, however, the test items are selected to measure best for a composite of the highly correlated dimensions. For this example, the highest correlation is between θ_1 and θ_2. Occasionally, a test item is selected to be sensitive to differences mainly along θ_3.

The estimation of $\boldsymbol{\theta}$ is also different for the two different selections of prior distributions. The $\mathbf{C}_1$-case gives $\boldsymbol{\theta}$-estimates that have the correct order of magnitude, although the θ_3-estimate is quite different from the value used to generate the responses to the test items. Case $\mathbf{C}_2$ yields quite a different result for the estimates of $\boldsymbol{\theta}$. The estimates for all three dimensions show large differences from the values used to generate the responses. These results are likely a function of the large difference in correlations used in the prior multivariate distribution. While these correlations are quite different and the correlations are relatively large, they are consistent with the correlations in the example given by Segall (1996). The results from the example suggest that using a prior distribution with large correlations may result in inaccurate estimates of $\boldsymbol{\theta}$. Little research is present in the literature about the functioning of these item selection and estimation methods. More evaluative work needs to be done on these methods before they can be used with confidence.

10.2.2.4 Maximize Kullback–Leibler Information

Another approach to selecting test items for a multidimensional CAT was proposed by Veldkamp and van der Linden (2002). This method uses a different measure of the sensitivity of test items to differences in persons' locations in the $\boldsymbol{\theta}$-space called Kullback–Leibler information (Kullback 1968). This approach was proposed by Chang and Ying (1996) for a unidimensional CAT to solve the problem of identifying appropriate test items when estimates of θ were poor early in the CAT. Lehmann and Casella (1998, p. 259) indicate that this information statistic indicates the amount of information for discriminating between two density functions. For this application, the likelihood functions for two possible $\boldsymbol{\theta}$-locations are used as the density functions.

Suppose that the true location of an examinee is indicated by $\boldsymbol{\theta}_0$ and that there is another possible location denoted by $\boldsymbol{\theta}$. Then, for item response u_i to a test item, the Kullback–Leibler information is given by

$$K_i(\boldsymbol{\theta}, \boldsymbol{\theta}_0) = E\left[\ln \frac{L(\boldsymbol{\theta}_0|u_i)}{L(\boldsymbol{\theta}|u_i)}\right], \tag{10.10}$$

where ln is the natural logarithm and the likelihood function L is defined as

$$L(\boldsymbol{\theta}|u_i) = P_i(\boldsymbol{\theta})^{u_i} Q_i(\boldsymbol{\theta})^{(1-u_i)}. \tag{10.11}$$

When only one test item is considered, the Kullback–Liebler information is given by

$$K_i(\boldsymbol{\theta}, \boldsymbol{\theta}_0) = P_i(\boldsymbol{\theta}_0) \ln\left[\frac{P_i(\boldsymbol{\theta}_0)}{P_i(\boldsymbol{\theta})}\right] + [1 - P_i(\boldsymbol{\theta}_0)] \ln\left[\frac{Q_i(\boldsymbol{\theta}_0)}{Q_i(\boldsymbol{\theta})}\right]. \tag{10.12}$$

For the case when the probability of correct response at $\boldsymbol{\theta}_0$ is .5 and the probability of correct response at $\boldsymbol{\theta}$ is .7, $K = .087$. As the likelihoods become more different, the value for K increases. For example, if the probability of a correct response to the item at $\boldsymbol{\theta}$ is .9, then $K = .51$. Veldkamp and van der Linden (2002) show that the Kullback–Liebler information for n items is equal to the sum of the information for the individual items if the assumption of local independence holds,

$$K_n(\boldsymbol{\theta}, \boldsymbol{\theta}_0) = \sum_{i=1}^{n} K_i(\boldsymbol{\theta}, \boldsymbol{\theta}_0). \tag{10.13}$$

The item selection rule suggested by Veldkamp and van der Linden is to select the item that maximizes the posterior expected Kullback–Leibler information. This is the information weighted by the posterior density function for the $\boldsymbol{\theta}$ estimate. The expression for the expected information is given by

$$K_i^{\mathrm{B}}\left(\hat{\boldsymbol{\theta}}^{k-1}\right) = \int\limits_{\boldsymbol{\theta}} K_i\left(\boldsymbol{\theta}, \hat{\boldsymbol{\theta}}^{k-1}\right) f(\boldsymbol{\theta}|u_1, \cdots, u_{k-1})\partial\boldsymbol{\theta}, \tag{10.14}$$

where K_i^{B} is the Bayesian posterior expected information, $\hat{\boldsymbol{\theta}}^{k-1}$ is the estimate of location after $k-1$ test items, and $f(\boldsymbol{\theta}|u_1, \cdots, u_{k-1})$ is the posterior density after $k-1$ items.

Veldkamp and van der Linden (2002) used Gauss–Hermite quadrature to evaluate the integral in (10.14), but other quadrature methods can be used as well. The key feature of this method is that early in the MIRT CAT test items are selected that are good at differentiating the current estimate of $\boldsymbol{\theta}$ from other possible $\boldsymbol{\theta}$-vectors over a significant portion of the $\boldsymbol{\theta}$-space. As the estimates of $\boldsymbol{\theta}$ improve, the selection of the test items becomes more focused.

The implementation of the item selection based on the Kullback–Leibler information is somewhat complex because it requires the evaluation of two integrals, one for estimating the posterior density function for the $\boldsymbol{\theta}$-estimate given the response string and the item parameters, and the second for evaluating the expectation given in (10.14). My own attempts at implementing this item selection methodology in three dimensions was very computationally slow using the triple integral quadrature procedure from MATLAB. For that reason, no examples of the item selection results are provided here. This should not be taken as a strong negative factor for this method because it is likely that more efficient programming methods are possible. However, as the number of dimensions for the $\boldsymbol{\theta}$-space increases, the evaluation of the integrals will no doubt increase the computer processing time. With fast computers and efficient programming, that may not be a problem.

10.2.3 Stopping Rules

The stopping rules for a CAT fall into two general categories – fixed length and variable length. The fixed length stopping rule is very simple. The total number of test items to be administered to an examinee is determined in advance of implementing the testing procedure, and when that number of test items is reached, the final ability estimate is computed. The number of test items selected for the fixed length stopping rule might be based on practical considerations of testing time, or on an evaluation of the desired size for the error ellipse or posterior credibility region for the test. Another alternative is to determine the desired accuracy for a decision to be made for the test. The average test length needed for that decision accuracy could be selected as the fixed test length. The research studies referenced in this chapter used fixed length multidimensional adaptive tests.

Variable length adaptive tests select a statistical criterion to control the length of the test. For example, a specified volume of the posterior credibility ellipsoid could be used to determine when to stop the test. After each test item is administered, the volume of the credibility ellipsoid is computed, and if it is less than the specified volume, the test is terminated and a final estimate of the examinees location is computed. Information or decision criteria could also be used for determining when to stop administering test items. As the label suggests, variable length adaptive tests administer different numbers of test items to different examinees. The number will depend on where the examinee is located in the $\boldsymbol{\theta}$-space, the consistency of the examinee's responses to the test items, and the amount of information provided by the item pool in the region near the examinee's location. Little research was found in the literature on the features of variable length multidimensional CATs. This is an important area for future research.

10.2.4 Item Pool

CATs are very sophisticated methodological procedures with substantial theoretical underpinnings. It is clear from the work that has been done so far that CATs work well and that MIRT-CATs have strong potential. However, the best of the CAT procedures will not work well if the items available for selection are not appropriate for the examinees in the examinee population. Therefore, the design and development of the item pool for a CAT is critical for its proper functioning.

No research could be found that specifically addressed the design of item pools for MIRT-CAT procedures. Those studies of MIRT-CAT that do appear in the research literature use either simulated item pools or real item pools created from existing paper-and-pencil tests. For example, Veldkamp and van der Linden (2002) used a 176-item pool from the paper-and-pencil ACT Assessment Program. Lee, Ip and Fuh (2008) used a 480-item simulated item pool with items divided into four levels of discrimination. The results of these studies are dependent on the quality of the item pool that is used.

In earlier sections of this chapter, demonstrations were presented of MIRT-CATs using a variety of $\boldsymbol{\theta}$-estimation and item selection procedures. For these demonstrations, all items were assumed to have multidimensional discrimination values of 1.0 and the directions of best measurement and the multidimensional difficulty were determined to optimize the selection criterion. Ideal item sets were identified for the examples. The item sets shown in Tables 10.1 and 10.3 suggest that an optimal item pool for an MIRT-CAT would have an equal number of test items with directions of best measurement parallel to the coordinate axes, and a roughly uniform distribution of multidimensional difficulty over the range of $\boldsymbol{\theta}$s that is of interest. Real item pools are not likely to meet these strict requirements. A good target for an item pool would be items with directions of best measurement that are within 15° of the coordinate axes and a good spread of difficulty along each axis.

When there is a strong Bayesian prior with relatively high covariances, the item pool needs different specifications. The $\mathbf{C}_2$-case in Table 10.7 shows that many of the items that were selected had directions of best measurement that were for combinations of θs. An ideal pool for this case would require items that measured composites of θs rather than measuring parallel to the coordinate axes. There would also need to be a spread of difficulties so that the range of $\boldsymbol{\theta}$-vectors in the population of examinees would be accurately estimated.

The lack of work on item pool design for MIRT-CAT shows that this is an area that is ripe for future research. Questions such as "How large an item pool is needed?" and "How does the size of the needed item pool change with the number of dimensions?" need to be addressed.

10.3 Future Directions for MIRT-CAT

Although development of MIRT began many years ago, practical applications of the methodology are fairly recent. MIRT-CAT is even younger as an area of research and application so practical applications are likely years in the future. However, progress is being made on practical issues for MIRT-CAT. Lee, Ip and Fuh (2008) investigated exposure control for MIRT-CAT using the a-stratified methodology. Veldkamp and van der Linden (2002) considered content balancing within the MIRT-CAT framework using the shadow test approach. It is likely that much more research will be done on MIRT-CAT with the goal of bringing this methodology to the point that it can be used for operational testing programs.

Some obvious areas for future research are easy to identify. Most of the published research is for the special case of two-coordinate axes. It seems unrealistic to assume that most practical applications will fit within this simple framework. Work needs to be done to determine how well methods work when three or more coordinates are used to specify the location of individuals in the $\boldsymbol{\theta}$-space. Most of the current research also uses fixed length tests. It will be useful to investigate the number of items needed to converge to within a specified distance from the true $\boldsymbol{\theta}$-location. This research may not lead to the implementation of variable length MIRT-CAT, but it would at least provide information on what is the appropriate length for a fixed length CAT.

Developing guidelines for item pools for MIRT-CAT is another obvious area for future research. Of course, this needs to be connected to work on the practical development of test items to match the specifications for such item pools. If item pool specifications indicated that test items are needed that measure an equally weighted composite of two constructs, will it be possible to construct the required test items?

MIRT-CAT is an exciting area for new development. It will be interesting to watch the research literature and presentations at professional meetings to note the directions (probably multiple directions) that these developments take.

10.4 Exercises

1. Suppose that an MIRT-CAT procedure is designed to function in a $\boldsymbol{\theta}$-space with four coordinate axes. It was determined that the first item to be administered should have a direction of best measurement that has equal angles with all of the coordinate axes. If the multidimensional discrimination for this item is 1.0, what is the **a**-parameter vector for this item and what is the angle for the item vector for this item with each coordinate axis?

2. The third sentence below (10.9) indicates that if the prior variance–covariance matrix is the identity matrix, then selecting a test item to minimize the volume of the credibility ellipsoid will give the same result as maximizing the determinant of Fisher information matrix. Explain why this is the case.

3. Consider the results given in Table 10.7. How do the second items in the tests using the different prior distributions differ in what they best measure? Explain why different items were selected when both tests had the same first item and the same response from the examinee.

4. Draw a diagram that shows the processes that need to be performed in a CAT and the connections between the processes. Clearly label each of the parts of the diagram and show the flow of the testing process with arrows connecting the processes.

5. How do the diagonal entries of the Fisher information matrix relate to unidimensional estimates of information? Also, how does the information in different directions in the $\boldsymbol{\theta}$-space relate to the Fisher information matrix?

6. In Table 10.6, which direction of measurement has the greatest amount of information at the current estimate of $\boldsymbol{\theta}$? How much does the information in the direction of most information differ from that with the least information? What does this difference indicate about the success or failure of the MIRT-CAT process after the administration of 30 test items? Would it be desirable to have a larger difference in the amount of information in the different directions from the current estimate?

7. When using maximum likelihood estimation for an MIRT-CAT, why is it appropriate to minimize the negative log likelihood rather than maximize the likelihood? Provide an example to support your argument.

8. Compare the results after two items have been administered in Tables 10.1 and 10.2. How do the items selected to be administered third in the test differ? How do the $\boldsymbol{\theta}$-estimates after two items have been administered differ? Explain why the estimates are different.

9. Does (10.7) indicate that the Fisher information matrix is a symmetric matrix? Explain your reasoning.

10. Select a test battery that contains a number of tests. Suppose that you would like to create an MIRT-CAT to estimate an examinee's performance on all of the tests at the same time using a Bayesian estimation and test item selection method. What variance–covariance matrix would you specify for the prior distribution for this MIRT-CAT? Explain how you arrived at this prior distribution and defend your selection.

References

Abrahamowicz M, Ramsay JO (1992) Multicategorical spline model for item response theory. Psychometrika 57:5–27

Ackerman TA (1992) A didactic explanation of item bias, item impact, and item validity from a multidimensional perspective. Journal of Educational Measurement 29:67–91

Ackerman TA (1996) Graphical representation of multidimensional item response theory analyses. Applied Psychological Measurement 20:311–329

Ackerman TA, Gierl MJ, Walker CM (2003) Using multidimensional item response theory to evaluate educational and psychological tests. Educational Measurement: Issues and Practice 22:37–51

ACT, Inc. (2007) The ACT technical manual. ACT, Inc., Iowa City, IA

Adams RJ, Wilson M, Wang W (1997) The multidimensional random coefficients multinomial logit model. Applied Psychological Measurement 21:1–24

Anderson TW (1984) An introduction to multivariate statistical analysis (2nd ed.). John Wiley, New York

Andrich D (2004) Controversy and the Rasch model: A characteristic of incompatible paradigms? Medical Care 42:I-7–I-16

Apostle TM (1957) Mathematical analysis. Addison-Wesley, Reading, MA

Asimov I (1972) Asimov's new guide to science. Basic Books, New York

Bai J, Ng S (2002) Determining the number of factors in approximate factor models. Econometrica 70:191–221

Baker FB, Kim S-H (2004) Item response theory: Parameter estimation techniques (2nd edition, revised and expanded). Marcel Dekker, New York

Bayes, T (1793) An essay towards solving a problem in the doctoring of chances. Philosophical Transactions of the Royal Society of London 53:370–418

Béguin AA, Glas CAW (2001) MCMC estimation and some model-fit analysis of multidimensional IRT models. Psychometrika 66:541–561

Bejar II (1977) An application of the continuous response level model to personality measurement. Applied Psychological Measurement 1:509–521

Binet A, Simon T (1913) A method of measuring the development of intelligence in children (Translated from the French by CH Town). Chicago Medical Book Company, Chicago

Birnbaum A (1968) Some latent trait models and their use in infering an examinee's ability. In FM Lord MR Novick (eds.) Statistical theories of mental test scores. Addison-Wesley, Reading, MA

Bloxom B Vale CD (1987) Multidimensional adaptive testing: an approximate procedure for updating. Paper presented at the annual meeting of the Psychometric Society, Montreal

Bock RD, Aitkin M (1981) Marginal maximum likelihood estimation of item parameters: Applications of an EM algorithm. Psychometrika 46:443–459

Bock RD, Gibbons R, Muraki E (1988) Full information item factor analysis. Applied Psychological Measurement 12:261–280

Bock RD, Schilling SG (2003) IRT based item factor analysis. In M du Toit (ed) IRT from SSI: BILOG-MG, MULTILOG, PARSCALE, TESTFACT (pp. 584–591). Scientific Software International, Lincolnwood, IL

Bolt DM, Lall VF (2003) Estimation of compensatory and noncompensatory multidimensional item response models using Markov chain Monte Carlo. Applied Psychological Measurement 27:395–414

Bulfinch T (1855) The age of fable. Reprinted in Bulfinch's mythology. The Modern Library, New York

Burgess MA (1921) The measurement of silent reading. Russell Sage Foundation, New York

Camilli G (1994) Origin of the scaling constant d = 1.7 in item response theory. Journal of Educational and Behavioral Statistics 19:293–295

Camilli G, Wang M, Fesq J (1995) The effects of dimensionality on equating the Law School Admissions Test. Journal of Educational Measurement 32:79–96

Carroll JB (1945) The effect of difficulty and chance success on correlations between items or between tests. Psychometrika 10:1–19

Carroll JB (1993) Human cognitive abilities: A survey of factor analytic studies. Cambridge University Press, New York

Chang H-H, Ying Z (1996) A global information approach to computerized adaptive testing. Applied Psychological Measurement 20:213–230

Chib S, Greenberg E (1995) Understanding the Metropolis-Hastings algorithm. The American Statistician 49:327–335

Christoffersson A (1975) Factor analysis of dichotomized variables. Psychometrika 40:5–32

Davey TC, Ackerman TA, Reckase MD, Spray JA (1989) Interpreting score differences when item difficulty and discrimination are confounded. Paper presented at the meeting of the Psychometric Society, Los Angeles

Davey TC, Oshima TC (1994) Linking multidimensional calibrations. Paper presented at the annual meeting of the National Council on Measurement in Education, New Orleans

Deese J (1958) The psychology of learning (2nd edition). McGraw-Hill, New York

DeGroot MH (1970) Optimal statistical decisions. McGraw-Hill, New York

Dempster AP, Laird NM, Rubin DB (1977) Maximum likelihood from incomplete data via the EM algorithm (with discussion). Journal of the Royal Statistical Society Series B 39:1–38

Dorans NJ, Pommerich M, Holland PW (eds) (2007) Linking and aligning scores and scales. Springer, New York

Drasgow F, Parsons CK (1983) Applications of unidimensional item response theory to multidimensional data. Applied Psychological Measurement 7:189–199

Ebbinghaus H (1885) Uber das Gedachtnis: Untersuchungen zur experimentalen Psychologie. Duncker and Humbolt, Leipzig

Embretson SE (1991) A multidimensional latent trait model for measuring learning and change. Psychometrika 56:495–515

Fischer GH (1995a) Derivations of the Rasch model. In Fischer GH and Molenaar IW (eds) Rasch models: Foundations, recent developments and applications. Springer-Verlag, New York

Fischer GH (1995b) Linear logistic test models for change. In Fischer GH and Molenaar IW (eds) Rasch models: Foundations, recent developments and applications. Springer-Verlag, New York

Fischer GH, Molenaar IW (eds) (1995) Rasch models: Foundations, recent developments, and applications. Springer-Verlag, New York

Fisher RA (1925) Theory of statistical estimation. Proceedings of the Cambridge Philosophical Society 22:700–725

Fraser C (1998) NOHARM: A Fortran program for fitting unidimensional and multidimensional normal ogive models in latent trait theory. The University of New England, Center for Behavioral Studies, Armidale, Australia

Frederiksen N, Glaser R, Lesgold A, Shafto MG (eds) Diagnostic monitoring of skill and knowledge acquisition. Lawrence Erlbaum Associates, Hillsdale, NJ

Galton F (1870) Hereditary genius: An inquiry into its laws and consequences. D. Appleton, London

Gamerman D, Lopes HF (2006) Markov chain Monte Carlo: Stochastic simulation for Bayesian inference (2nd edition). Chapman & Hall, Boca Raton, FL

Geman S, Geman D (1984) Stochastic relaxation, Gibbs distributions, and the Bayesian restoration of images. IEEE Transactions on Pattern Analysis and Machine Intelligence 6:721–741

Gentle JE (1998) Numerical linear algebra for applications in statistics. Springer, New York

Gessaroli ME, De Champlain AF (1996) Using an approximate chi-square statistic to test the number of dimensions underlying the responses to a set of items. Journal of Educational Measurement 33:157–179

Glas CAW (1992) A Rasch model with a multivariate distribution of ability. In Wilson M (ed) Objective measurement: Theory into practice volume 1. Ablex, Norwood, NJ

Glas CAW, Vos HJ (2000) Adaptive mastery testing using a multidimensional IRT model and Bayesian sequential decision theory (Research Report 00-06). University of Twente, Enschede, The Netherlands

Gosz JK, Walker CM (2002) An empirical comparison of multidimensional item response theory data using TESTFACT and NOHARM. Paper presented at the annual meeting of the National Council for Measurement in Education, New Orleans

Gower JC, Dijksterhuis GB (2004) Procrustes problems. Oxford University Press, Oxford, England

Gulliksen H (1950) Theory of mental tests. Wiley, New York

Haberman SJ (1977) Log-linear models and frequency tables with small expected cell counts. Annals of Statistics 5:1148–1169

Haebara T (1980) Equating logistic ability scales by a weighted least squares method. Japanese Psychological Research 22:144–149

Haley DC (1952) Estimation of the dosage mortality relationship when the dose is subject to error (Technical Report No. 15). Stanford University Applied Mathematics and Statistics Laboratory, Stanford, CA

Hambleton R, Swaminathan H (1983) Item response theory: principles and applications. Kluwer, Boston

Harman HH (1976) Modern factor analysis (3rd edition revised). The University of Chicago Press, Chicago

Hastings WK (1970) Monte Carlo simulation methods using Markov chains and their applications. Biometrika 57:97–109

Healy AF, McNamara DS (1996) Verbal learning and memory: Does the modal model still work? In Spence JT, Darley JM, Foss DJ (eds) Annual Review of Psychology 47:143–172

Holland PW (2007) A framework and history for score linking. In Dorans NJ, Pommerich M, Holland PW (eds) Linking and aligning scores and scales. Springer, New York

Holzinger KJ, Harman HH (1941) Factor analysis: A synthesis of factorial methods. The University of Chicago Press, Chicago

Horn JL (1965) A rationale and test for the number of factors in factor analysis. Psychometrika 32:179–185

Horst P (1965) Factor analysis of data matrices. Holt, Rinehart & Winston, New York

Hulin CL, Drasgow F, Parsons CK (1983) Item response theory: application to psychological measurement. Dow Jones-Irwin, Homewood, IL

Jang EE, Roussos L (2007) An investigation into the dimensionality of TOEFL using conditional covariance-based nonparametric approach. Journal of Educational Measurement 44:1–21

Kallon AA (1916) Standards in silent reading. Boston Department of Educational Investigation and Measurement Bulletin No. 12, School Document 18. Boston

Kelderman H (1994) Objective measurement with multidimensional polytomous latent trait models. In Wilson M (ed) Objective measurement: Theory into practice, Vol. 2. Ablex, Norwood NJ

Kelderman H, Rijkes CPM (1994) Loglinear multidimensional IRT models for polytomously scored items. Psychometrika 59:149–176

Kendall MG, Stuart A (1961) The advanced theory of statistics. Hafner, New York

Kim HR (1994) New techniques for the dimensionality assessment of standardized test data. Unpublished doctoral dissertation, University of Illinois, Champaign-Urbana, IL

Kim J-P (2001) Proximity measures and cluster analyses in multidimensional item response theory. Unpublished doctoral dissertation, Michigan State University, East Lansing, MI

Kirisci L, Hsu T, Yu L (2001) Robustness of item parameter estimation programs to assumptions of unidimensionality and normality. Applied Psychological Measurement 25:146–162

Kolen MJ, Brennan RL (2004) Test equating, scaling, and linking: Methods and practices (2nd edition) Springer, New York

Kulback S (1968) Information theory and statistics (2nd edition). Dover, New York

Ledesma RD, Valero-Mora P (2007) Determining the number of factors to retain in EFA: an easy-to-use computer program for carrying out parallel analysis. Practical Assessment, Research & Evaluation 12:1–11

Lehmann EL, Casella G (1998) Theory of point estimation (2nd edition). Springer-Verlag, New York

Lee Y-H, Ip EH, Fuh C-D (2008) A strategy for controlling item exposure in multidimensional computerized adaptive testing. Educational and Psychological Measurement 68:215–232

Lord FM (1980) Applications of item response theory to practical testing problems. Lawrence Erlbaum Associates, Hillsdale, NJ

Lord FM, Novick MR (1968) Statistical theories of mental test scores. Addison-Wesley, Reading, MA

MacCorquidale K, Meehl PE (1948) On a distinction between hypothetical constructs and intervening variables. Psychological Review 55:95–107

Maris E (1995) Psychometric latent response models. Psychometrika 60:523–547

Masters GN (1982) A Rasch model for partial credit scoring. Psychometrika 47:149–174

Masters GN, Wright BD (1997) The partial credit model. In WJ van der Linden RK Hambleton (eds.) Handbook of modern item response theory. Springer, New York

Maydeu-Olivares A (2001) Multidimensional item response theory modeling of binary data: Large sample properties of NOHARM estimates. Journal of Educational and Behavioral Statistics 26:51–71

McCall WA (1922) How to measure in education. The Macmillan Company, New York

McDonald RP (1967) Nonlinear factor analysis. Psychometric Monograph 15

McDonald RP (1985) Factor analysis and related methods. Lawrence Erlbaum Associates, Hillsdale, NJ

McDonald RP (1997) Normal-ogive multidimensional model. In WJ van der Linden and RK Hambleton (eds) Handbook of modern item response theory. Springer, New York

McDonald RP (1999) Test theory: A unified treatment. Lawrence Erlbaum Associates, Mahwah, NJ

McKinley RL, Reckase MD (1982) The use of the general Rasch model with multidimensional item response data (Research Report ONR 82-1). American College Testing, Iowa City, IA

Metropolis N, Rosenbluth AW, Rosenbluth MN, Teller AH, Teller E (1953) Equations of state space calculations by fast computing machines. Journal of Chemical Physics 21:1087–1091

Miller MD, Linn RL (1988) Invariance of item characteristic functions with variations in instructional coverage. Journal of Educational Measurement 25:205–219

Miller TR (1991) Empirical estimation of standard errors of compensatory MIRT model parameters obtained from the NOHARM estimation program (Research Report ONR 91-2). American College Testing Program, Iowa City, IA

Miller TR, Hirsch TM (1992) Cluster analysis of angular data in applications of multidimensional item response theory. Applied Measurement in Education 5:193–211

Millman J, Greene J (1989) The specification and development of tests of achievement and ability. In Linn RL (ed) Educational measurement (3rd edition). American Council on Education and Macmillan, New York

Moulton MH (2004) One use of a non-unidimensional scaling (NOUS) model: Transferring information across dimensions and subscales. Educational Data Systems, Morgan Hill, CA

Mroch AA, Bolt DM (2006) A simulation comparison of parametric and nonparametric dimensionality detection procedures. Applied Measurement in Education 19:67–91

Mulaik SA (1972) A mathematical investigation of some multidimensional Rasch models for psychological tests. Paper presented at the annual meeting of the Psychometric Society, Princeton, NJ

Muraki E, Carlson JE (1993) Full-information factor analysis for polytomous item responses. Paper presented at the annual meeting of the American Educational Research Association, Atlanta

Muraki E, Englelhard G Jr (1985) Full-information item factor analysis: applications of EAP scores. Applied Psychological Measurement 9:417–430

Muthén B (1978) Contributions to factor analysis of dichotomous variables. Psychometrika 43:551–560

Oshima TC, Davey TC, Lee K (2000) Multidimensional linking: Four practical approaches. Journal of Educational Measurement 37:357–373

Osterland SJ (1990) Toward a uniform definition of a test item. Educational Research Quarterly 14:2–5

Owen RJ (1975) A Bayesian sequential procedure for quantal response in the context of adaptive mental testing. Journal of the American Statistical Association, 70:351–356

Parshall CG, Spray JA, Davey T (2002) Practical considerations in computer-based testing. Springer, New York

Patz RJ, Junker BW (1999) A straightforward approach to Markov chain Monte Carlo methods for item response models. Journal of Educational and Behavioral Statistics 24:146–178

Perie M, Grigg W, Donahue P (2005) The Nation's Report Card: Reading 2005 (NCES 2006-451). U.S. Department of Education, National Center for Education Statistics, U.S. Government Printing Office, Washington, DC

Rasch G (1960) Probabilistic models for some intelligence and attainment tests. Danmarks Paedagogiske Institut, Copenhagen

Rasch G (1962) On general laws and the meaning of measurement in psychology. Proceedings of the fourth Berkeley symposium on mathematical statistics and probability 4:321–334

Reckase MD (1972) Development and application of a multivariate logistic latent trait model. Unpublished doctoral dissertation, Syracuse University, Syracuse, NY

Reckase MD (1985) The difficulty of test items that measure more than one ability. Applied Psychological Measurement 9:401–412

Reckase MD, Ackerman TA, Carlson JE (1988) Building a unidimensional test using multidimensional items. Journal of Educational Measurement 25:193–204

Reckase MD, Davey TC, Ackerman TA (1989) Similarity of the multidimensional space defined by parallel forms of a mathematics test. Paper presented at the meeting of the American Educational Research Association, San Francisco

Reckase MD, Hirsch TM (1991) Interpretation of number-correct scores when the true numbers of dimensions assessed by a test is greater than two. Paper presented at the annual meeting of the National Council on Measurement in Education, Chicago

Reckase MD, McKinley RL (1991) The discriminating power of items that measure more than one dimension. Applied Psychological Measurement 15:361–373

Reckase MD, Stout W (1995) Conditions under which items that assess multiple abilities will be fit by unidimensional IRT models. Paper presented at the European meeting of the Psychometric Society, Leiden, The Netherlands

Reise SP, Waller NG, Comrey AL (2000) Factor analysis and scale revision. Psychological Assessment 12:287–297

Rijmen F, De Boeck P (2005) A relationship between a between-item multidimensional IRT model and the mixture Rasch model. Psychometrika 70:481–496

Roberts JS, Donoghue JR, Laughlin JE (2000) A general item response theory model for unfolding unidimensional polytomous responses. Applied Psychological Measurement 24:3–32

Rosenbaum PR (1984) Testing the conditional independence and monotonicity assumptions of item response theory. Psychometrika 49:425–435

Roussos LA, Ozbek OY (2006) Formulation of the DETECT population parameter and evaluation of DETECT estimation bias. Journal of Educational Measurement 43:215–243

Roussos LA, Stout WF, Marden JL (1998) Using new proximity measures with hierarchical cluster analysis to detect multidimensionality. Journal of Educational Measurement 35:1–30

Samejima F (1969) Estimation of latent ability using a response pattern of graded scores. Psychometric Monograph Supplement, 34 (Monograph No. 17)

Samejima F (1974) Normal ogive model on the continuous response level in the multidimensional space. Psychometrika 39:111–121

Samejima F, Livingston P (1979) Method of moments as the least squares solution for fitting a polynomial (Research Report 79-2). Univerrsity of Tennessee, Knoxville, TN

Sands WA, Waters BK, McBride JR (eds.) (1997) Computerized adaptive testing: from inquiry to operation. American Psychological Association, Washington, DC

Savalei V (2006) Logistic approximation to the normal: the KL rationale. Psychometrika 71: 763–767

Schilling S, Bock RD (2005) High-dimensional maximum marginal likelihood item factor analysis by adaptive quadrature. Psychometrika 70:533–555

Segall DO (1996) Multidimensional adaptive testing. Psychometrika 61:331–354

Sinharay S, Holland PW (2007) Is it necessary to make anchor tests mini-versions of the tests being equated or can some restrictions be relaxed? Journal of Educational Measurement 44:249–275

Sokal RR, Michener CD (1958) A statistical method for evaluating systematic relationships. University of Kansas Science Bulletin 38:1409–1438

Spiegelhalter D, Thomas A, Best N (2000) WinBUGS version 1.3 (Computer program). MRC Biostatistics Unit, Institute of Public Health, Cambridge, England

Spray JA, Davey TC, Reckase MD, Ackerman TA, Carlson JE (1990) Comparison of two logistic multidimensional item response theory models (Research Report ONR90-8). ACT, Inc., Iowa City, IA

Stern W (1914) The psychological methods of testing intelligence. Warwick & York, Baltimore

Stevens SS (1946) On the theory of scales of measurement. Science 103:677–680

Stevens SS (1951) Mathematics, measurement, and psychophysics. In SS Stevens (ed) Handbook of experimental psychology (pp. 1–49). Wiley, New York

Stigler SM (1986) The history of statistics: The measurement of uncertainty before 1900. Belknap Press, Cambridge, MA

Stocking LM, Lord FM (1983) Developing a common metric in item response theory. Applied Psychological Measurement 7:201–210

Stone CA, Yeh C-C (2006) Assessing the dimensionality and factor structure of multiple-choice exams: An empirical comparison of methods using the Multistate Bar Examination. Educational and Psychological Measurement 66:193–214

Stout W (1987) A nonparametric approach for assessing latent trait dimensionality. Psychometrika 52:589–617

Stout W, Douglas B, Junker B, Roussos L (1999) DIMTEST [Computer software]. The William Stout Institute for Measurement, Champaign, IL

Stout W, Froelich AG, Gao F (2001) Using resampling to produce and improved DIMTEST procedure. In Boomsma A, van Duijn MAJ, Snijders TAB (eds.) Essays on item response theory (pp. 357–375). Springer-Verlag, New York

Sympson JB (1978) A model for testing with multidimensional items. In Weiss DJ (ed) Proceedings of the 1977 Computerized Adaptive Testing Conference, University of Minnesota, Minneapolis

Tam SS (1992) A comparison of methods for adaptive estimation of a multidimensional trait. Ph.D. thesis, Columbia University

Tate R (2003) A comparison of selected empirical methods for assessing the structure of responses to test items. Applied Psychological Measurement 27:159–203

Thissen D, Wainer H (2001) Test scoring. Lawrence Erlbaum Associates, Mahwah, NJ

Thorndike EL (1904) An introduction to the theory of mental and social measurements. The Science Press, New York

Thurstone LL (1947) Multiple-factor analysis: A development and expansion of The Vectors of Mind. The University of Chicago Press, Chicago

Timm NH (1975) Multivariate analysis with applications in education and psychology. Brooks/Cole, Monterey, CA

van der Ark LA (2001) Relationships and properties of polytomous item response theory models. Applied Psychological Measurement 25:273–282

van der Linden WJ (2005) Linear models of optimal test design. Springer, New York

van der Linden WJ, Glas CAW (eds) (2000) Computerized adaptive testing: theory and practice. Kluwer Academic, Dordrecht, The Netherlands

van der Linden WJ, Hambleton RK (eds.) (1997) Handbook of modern item response theory. Springer, New York

Veldkamp BP, van der Linden WJ (2002) Multidimensional adaptive testing with constraints on test content. Psychometrika 67:575–588

Vernon P (1950) The structure of human abilities. Methuen, London

Verhelst ND, Verstralen HHFM (1997) Modeling sums of binary responses by the partial credit model (Measurement and Research Department Reports 97-7). Cito, Arnhem, The Netherlands

Volodin N, Adams RJ (2002) The estimation of polytomous item response models with many dimensions. Unpublished report, University of Melbourne, Victoria, Australia

Wainer DJ, Dorans DJ, Flaugher R, Green BF, Mislevy L, Steinberg L, Thissen D (1990) Computerized adaptive testing: A primer. Lawrence Erlbaum Associates, Hillsdale, NJ

Wang M (1985) Fitting a unidimensional model to multidimensional item response data: The effect of latent space misspecification on the application of IRT (Research Report MW: 6-24-85). University of Iowa, Iowa City, IA

Wang M (1986) Fitting a unidimensional model to multidimensional item response data. Paper presented at the Office of Naval Research Contractors Meeting, Gatlinburg, TN

Wang W-C, Chen P-H (2004) Implementation and measurement efficiency of multidimensional computerized adaptive testing. Applied Psychological Measurement 28:295–316

Wang W, Wilson M (2005) Exploring local item dependence using a random-effects facet model. Applied Psychological Measurement 29:296–318

Ward JH (1963) Hierarchical grouping to optimize an objective function. Journal of the American Statistical Association 58:236–244

Warm TA (1989) Weighted likelihood estimation of ability in item response theory. Psychometrika 54:427–450

Weiss DJ (1974) Strategies of adaptive ability measurement (Research Report 74-5). Psychometric Methods Program, University of Minnesota, Minneapolis

Whipple GM (1910) Manual of mental and physical tests. Warwick & York, Baltimore

Whitely SE (1980a) Measuring aptitude processes with mutlicomponent latent trait models (Technical Report No. NIE-80-5). University of Kansas, Lawrence, KS

Whitely SE (1980b) Multicomponent latent trait models for ability tests. Psychometrika 45: 479–494

Wilson M, Adams R (1995) Rasch models for item bundles. Psychometrika 60:181–198

Wu ML, Adams RJ, Wilson MR (1997) ConQuest: Generalized item response modeling software. ACER, Victoria, Australia

Yao L (2003) BMIRT: Bayesian multivariate item response theory. CTB/McGraw-Hill, Monterey, CA

Yao L, Schwarz R (2006) A multidimensional partial credit model with associated item and test statistics: An application to mixed-format tests. Applied Psychological Measurement 30: 469–492

Yen WM (1984) Effects of local dependence on the fit and equating performance of the three-parameter logistic model. Applied Psychological Measurement 8:125–145

Yoakum CS, Yerkes RM (1920) Army mental tests. Henry Holt, New York

Zhang JM, Stout W (1999a) Conditional covariance structure of generalized compensatory multidimensional items. Psychometrika 64:129–152

Zhang JM, Stout W (1999b) The theoretical DETECT index of dimensionality and its application to approximate simple structure. Psychometrika 64:213–249

Zimowski MF, Muraki E, Mislevy RJ, Bock RD (2003) BILOG-MG for Windows. Scientific Software International, Inc., Lincolnwood, IL

Index

I

J

K

L

M

Made in the USA
Monee, IL
13 September 2026

62976968R00201